Budapest 1938

Between Russia
and the West

Between Russia and the West

HUNGARY AND THE ILLUSIONS OF PEACEMAKING 1945–1947

STEPHEN D. KERTESZ

UNIVERSITY OF NOTRE DAME PRESS
NOTRE DAME   LONDON

Library of Congress Cataloging in Publication Data

Kertesz, Stephen Denis, 1904-
    Between Russia and the West.

    Includes bibliographical references and index.
    1. World War, 1939-1945—Hungary.   2. Paris Peace
Conference (1946)   3. World War, 1939-1945—Diplomatic
history.   4. World War, 1939-1945—Territorial questions
—Hungary.   5. Hungary—Foreign relations—1945-
    6. Kertesz, Stephen Denis, 1904-   I. Title.
D765.56.K44   1984   943.9'052   83-40594
ISBN 0-268-01079-X

To the Memory of Philip E. Mosely

Contents

Acknowledgments

Jean-Baptiste Duroselle, *Membre de l'Institut*, professor at the Sorbonne, made possible research in the archives of the Quai d'Orsay, under exceptionally favorable conditions. In the Diplomatic Branch of the National Archives in Washington, I enjoyed the thoughtful advice of Milton O. Gustafson and the assistance of his knowledgable and efficient staff. It is a pleasure to express my indebtedness to Robert H. Ferrell for his unfailing assistance throughout the changing dimensions of this writing. My foremost critic, John C. Campbell, participated in peace preparatory work of the Department of State and was a member of American delegations to postwar conferences. Both Ferrell and Campbell, close friends over three decades, have read the entire manuscript. Their examples have strengthened my respect for traditional American values, and their challenging criticism has stimulated my work.

George A. Brinkley, Robert F. Byrnes, Kenneth W. Thompson, and Leslie C. Tihany likewise read the manuscript. Theodore B. Ivanus, director of the International Documentation Center and head of the International Studies Library at the University of Notre Dame, has been most helpful in locating source materials and in verifying data and also in reading all chapters. Cyril E. Black, Stephen Borsody, Matthew A. Fitzsimons, John J. Kennedy, William Miscamble, Count Istvan Révay, Thomas J. Stritch, Aladár Szegedy-Maszák, and Francis S. Wagner each read passages of the manuscript or gave advice on specific questions. Mrs. Anne Marie de Samarjay-Papworth, my secretary in Budapest, Paris, and Rome, handled my confidential papers and has read some of the chapters.

In the last stage of this writing, it has been a great pleasure to work with my thoughtful press editor, Joseph Wilder. His impressive linguistic talent and his searching questions have been instrumental in final stylistic formulations. In doubtful cases his resourcefulness has always been forthcoming.

Mrs. Raeffa Miller, my secretary in the Institute for International Studies, took dictation and typed several versions of some of the chapters with patience and accuracy. Her help with manuscripts over many years has been invaluable. The personnel of the Word Processing Center of the University of Notre Dame, a group of wonderfully patient and experienced typists, Cheryl Reed, Margaret Jasiewicz and their colleagues handled the final version.

Heartfelt thanks for all this most kind assistance. I have been particularly grateful for critical comments and suggestions, and carefully considered them, but confess that in the end I followed my own counsel, sometimes perhaps erroneously. The text reflects thoughts and experiences through many years of involvement in affairs of Danubian Europe. To be sure, definitive evaluation of some of the events mentioned herein will not be possible until opening of the archives of the Soviet Union.

I dedicate this book to the memory of Philip E. Mosely, one of the finest human beings I have ever known. Although the Department of State did not participate in major policy decisions during the Second World War, Mosely, in his work in the Department and in the European Advisory Commission in London and in his advice to the highest American officials — foreseeing the impending tragedy of East Central Europe — tried to restrict and mitigate the catastrophic course of events.

Introduction

This book sets forth the vicissitudes of an ex-enemy state, Hungary, at the Paris Peace Conference in 1946 and analyzes the intricacies of preparations for peace in the shadow of the Swastika and the Red Star. Although inter-Allied strategic and political decisions had settled the fate of the Danubian countries well before the end of the war, this fact was not known, and the cognoscenti in Hungary discounted such rumors. It seemed incredible that after a victorious war the Western powers would allow simply a "changing of the guard," the installation of Soviet domination after German occupation. Hungarian emissaries established contacts with British and United States representatives in neutral countries in 1942–43, and the Western negotiators did not contradict the Hungarian assumption that British and American forces would reach Hungary and occupy the mid-Danubian basin.

Although in several chapters I discuss events in which I took a part, I did not intend to write a memoir. I describe events as I observed them as an actor or witness. In the process of research and writing, I sought to use official publications, memoirs, and archives, including my private papers. Because I participated in peace preparations in the Ministry for Foreign Affairs in 1943–44, headed the peace preparatory division after the war, and served as secretary-general of the Hungarian peace delegation in 1946, I have included my personal experiences as well. In these years Hungary's destiny was like a Greek tragedy. German occupation in early 1944 was followed by Soviet invasion later in the year. Most parts of the country became battlefields and for nearly two months Budapest was under constant siege.

In the first chapter a personal account helps to explain the abrupt transition from the Horthy regime to the postwar era — the chaotic conditions during the last stage of the Nazi occupation, the siege of Budapest, and the first phase of the Soviet occupation. In similar fashion, I relate from my vantage point the peace preparations in postwar Hungary and events at the Paris Conference, hoping to convey a direct and realistic sense of the many strange happenings during this period of seemingly whimsical changes. Chapter Two unfolds the domestic political transformations and the interplay of Soviet and Western diplomacy in postwar Hungary. These events influenced our preparations for peace. Chapters Three and Eight sum up Allied policies that led to the division of Europe and to postwar peacemaking. The rest of the chapters discuss Hungary's international political problems and the aftermath of peace negotiations.

Peace preparations in Hungary during and after the war assumed that the United States would play a major and probably decisive role at the peace table. This assumption seemed realistic because the United States was the only Great Power not affected by wartime destruction. Its industry and productive capacity was immensely strengthened during the hostilities, and its military power reached an unparalleled peak in the last stage of the war. It was not known in Budapest that by this time Danubian Europe had become the dark side of the moon for the Western allies. The Joint Chiefs of Staff had decided in the autumn of 1943 that the United States should take no responsibilities "in the area of the Balkans, including Austria." The political implications of this military ruling foreshadowed the future.

Another assumption during our peace preparations was that the convocation of a comprehensive peace conference would establish a new international order. This assumption seemed plausible in the context and perspective of European history. In modern times, after major wars, belligerent countries had negotiated at a peace conference to establish a generally recognized political and territorial order. The Congresses of Westphalia, Utrecht, and Vienna were milestones not only in the art of peacemaking but also in formulating diplomatic and juridical rules for a developing state system. After the Napoleonic wars, the settlement worked out by the Congress of Vienna secured general peace in Europe for a century. The informal cooperation of the continental Great Powers and the only world power, Great Britain — known as the Concert of Europe — solved international issues and isolated wars. Even major changes, such as the unification of Germany and Italy, were achieved through isolated wars. But this system began to deteriorate after the Congress of Berlin (1878), when the formation of the Triple Alliance and the Triple Entente brought about a rigid bipolar balance of power in Europe. The failure of diplomacy in 1914 was a major immediate cause of the outbreak of one of the most irrational wars in history, which in turn triggered a series of catastrophic events and fundamental transformations in international relations. The war demonstrated to the world the breakdown of solidarity among the European Great Powers and showed the weaknesses of Western civilization.

At the Paris Conference in 1919, the three great Western democracies — the United States, Britain, and France — formed the core of peacemakers; Italy and Japan participated in some of the deliberations. A momentous result of the war was the temporary eclipse of two European Great Powers, Germany and Russia, and the dissolution of Austria-Hungary. The Congress of Vienna could not serve as a model for peace in 1919 because the traditional state system of Europe was destroyed and world conditions were in a stage of rapid transformation. Social and technological changes had a large impact on diplomacy, and revolutionary events and ideologies became again factors in world politics. Talleyrand was an influential participant at the Congress of Vienna, but after the First World War, Germany and the other defeated countries were excluded from the peace negotiations. Russia, still torn by civil war, was not invited to attend the conference. Instead of creating a democratic federation in the Danubian gateway to Western Europe, the peacemakers replaced the Austro-Hungarian monarchy by small quarrelsome states.

Few serious conflicts of interest existed among the major victorious powers in 1919, and their visions about the future were compatible. Under President Woodrow Wilson's leadership they sought to replace the balance of power with a system of collective security built around a League of Nations. The Covenant of the League was incorporated in each peace treaty, and the treaties established the territorial status quo and juridical order the League was obligated to defend. Yet the League could not replace the Concert of Europe in power politics because resolutions were not effective for the maintenance of order and law.

As long as France was the dominant power and the guardian of the status quo in Europe, the new system seemed to work satisfactorily. But in the 1930s French power sharply declined, and the lack of political leadership in Britain and France increased disagreements between them and paralyzed their effectiveness in European politics.[1] There were no "international policemen" to maintain law and punish aggressors. Isolationist policies and neutrality legislation in the United States contributed to international conditions which made Europe a safe place for dictatorship and war. The safety valves of the traditional European system no longer existed, and the old order and society disintegrated.

Hitler's aggressions and declarations of war created a de facto alliance between the Western democracies and the Soviet Union. Stalin endorsed the Atlantic Charter and in his speeches praised the virtues of democracies, dissolved the Comintern, fought a "Great Patriotic War," and at Yalta accepted the Declaration on Liberated Europe. In Roosevelt's "Grand Design" for the postwar world, the USSR was one of the four policemen. Leaders of the United States, particularly Secretary of State Cordell Hull, assumed that wartime cooperation with Moscow would continue as a partnership in peace. This belief still prevailed when the Conference of San Francisco approved the Charter of the United Nations in June 1945 and at the Potsdam Conference. Unlike the Covenant of the League of Nations, the Charter was not part of a peace settlement. Peace treaties were not concluded with the major enemy states, Germany and Japan, and an internationally recognized status quo was not established. Major Western states signed a peace treaty with Japan only in 1951, and the Western and Communist countries later concluded patchwork agreements with the two Germanys, but this tortuous procedure was a poor substitute for a comprehensive peace settlement — the declared purpose of American foreign policy. In 1945 an unprecedented method of peacemaking began. Conclusion of peace treaties was restricted to the five less important ex-enemy states. The plan for a major peace conference was not abandoned explicitly but rather unwittingly with the acceptance of a gradual approach to the conclusion of peace.

At the Potsdam Conference of the Big Three in July-August 1945, the American delegation proposed and the conference accepted a Council of Foreign Ministers (CFM) of the five principal victors — the Soviet Union, United Kingdom, United States, France, and China. It was agreed that in drawing up treaties with the ex-enemy states each treaty should be drafted by the nations that signed the armistice with that particular enemy. This meant that Britain and the Soviet Union prepared the treaty for Finland. For the three Danubian countries it was Britain, the Soviet Union, and the United States. The French government accepted the invitation to participate in the Council of Foreign Ministers and emphasized that France was "interested in all important questions concerning Europe in any region of Europe." For the Italian settlement France was to be regarded as a signatory to the armistice, and so for Italy, France and the Big Three prepared the peace treaty. Here was the origin of the 4-3-2 formula of peacemaking. Western expectation was that the Council of Foreign Ministers at an initial meeting would consider these drafts ad decide controversial questions. Texts prepared by the council would be submitted to "the United Nations," and their recommendations would be considered when the council approved the final version of the five treaties.

Secretary of State James F. Byrnes noted in his memoirs that he thought at the time of the Potsdam Conference that a start should be made promptly, and he hoped experiences with the five minor peace treaties would make it easier to agree on a treaty for Germany. He supposed that after agreement on principles, the foreign ministers would appoint deputies to draft the detailed provisions. The peace treaties then "would be presented to all the United Nations for considerations and amendment." He contemplated that a similar course would be followed later for Japan. When the meaning of the reference to the United Nations was discussed at Potsdam, Stalin remarked that the inclusion of such a phrase in the document made no difference as "the three powers would represent the interest of all." Byrnes had assumed that "at the end of hostilities an era of peace would be so deeply desired by those nations that had fought the war in unity that the inevitable differences of opinion could be resolved without serious difficulty."[2] In this spirit Byrnes believed that the peace treaties could be prepared in a few months.

The gradual approach to peacemaking might have worked during the nineteenth century, the era of the Concert of Europe, and even after the First World War when the Great Powers had the same view of the world, and their aspirations and expectations were compatible. But the Western and Soviet visions of political and juridical order to be established by the peace settlement differed greatly. In the war against Napoleon, Russian troops had marched across Europe, and the Czar himself had arrived in Paris with his army. But at the subsequent Congress of Vienna, Russian ambitions had received satifaction with award of Polish territories, and the Russian army withdrew from other European countries. Although Western nations hoped in 1945 that the Soviets would imitate this precedent, Stalin had no such intention. In addition to the differences in political goals and interpretation of agreements, the compromise-inclined British and Americans were surprised by the Soviet code of conduct in negotiations.

The piecemeal approach to peace after the Second World War might have worked better, had the Big Three included in their design a treaty with Austria. The Moscow Declaration of 1943 had recognized that Austria was an occupied country to be liberated. A state treaty with Vienna should have preceded the conclusion of peace treaties or should have been concluded simultaneously with them. This procedure would have made possible the simultaneous evacuation of foreign troops from Italy and the Danubian countries. At the time of the Potsdam Conference the United States was in an over-whelming position of power. Stalin understood the meaning of power and could have been persuaded to accept an Austrian treaty. With rapid American demobilization after the close of hostilities, the power equation in Europe changed drastically. The United States proposed in February 1946 that the Austrian treaty be prepared along with the other treaties, and Byrnes submitted a treaty draft to the CFM in April "For the Reestablishment of an Independent and Democratic Austria." Molotov was unwilling to discuss it. Byrnes argued politely but did not insist, and the occasion was lost. When the CFM decided that Italian sovereignty should be restored on the conclusion of peace, and foreign troops withdrawn, Molotov reluctantly agreed to with-draw Soviet troops only from Bulgaria.

The expectation for a speedy conclusion of the five peace treaties proved to be an illusion. The first session of the CFM met in London in September 1945 and ended in three weeks without accomplish-ing its task. The council was unwilling to consider far-reaching Soviet aspirations in Japan, the Mediterranean, and the Balkans, and Molo-tov retaliated with procedural demands that the other participants could not accept. After this failure, the definitive pattern of peace-making was worked out in December 1945 at the Moscow meeting of the foreign ministers of the United States, Britain, and the Soviet Union. There the Big Three resolved that draft treaties prepared by the foreign ministers on the basis of the 4-3-2 formula should be sub-mitted to a conference consisting of the five members of the council and the sixteen other Allied nations that had fought in Europe with substantial contingents. The conference was to meet in Paris not later than May 1, 1946, to discuss the draft treaties, express opinions, and make recommendations. The Soviet government had opposed a peace conference with wider jurisdiction and would have preferred a peace settlement exclusively by the Big Three. After the conference rituals, the council was to establish the final text of the treaties and forward them to the other victorious and ex-enemy states.

At the insistence of the Western governments it was decided that adequate opportunity should be given to the ex-enemy states to discuss the treaties and present their views at the Paris Conference. France was particularly anxious to avoid even the appearance of dicta-tion, in view of its experiences with "dictated" peace treaties after the First World War.

The deputy foreign ministers began their deliberations in London in Januray 1946, and the Council of Foreign Ministers held two sessions in Paris, where the peace conference duly assembled at the end of July 1946 and concluded its deliberations in mid-October.

Preparations for peace in postwar Hungary were made difficult by the heritage of the past, the Soviet occupation and restrictions of the armistice agreement, and the lack of agreement among the coalition parties on peace aims. Within one generation Hungary found itself on the losing side in two cataclysmic world wars. After the First World War the Peace Treaty of Trianon had shifted large territories with three million ethnic Hungarians — almost one-third of the Hungarian nation — to neighboring states, and in the ensuing situation a revisionist policy hindered friendly relations with those countries. The two Vienna awards delivered by Germany and Italy in 1938 and 1940 returned to Hungary some of these territories from Czechoslovakia and Rumania; Hungarian troops occupied Sub-Carpathian Ruthenia in March 1939 and Yugoslav territories in April 1941, following the German aggression on Yugoslavia and the declaration of Croatian independence. The armistice agreement of January 20, 1945, then obligated Hungary to evacuate all Hungarian troops and officials within the frontiers existing on December 31, 1937.

Although Hungary as an ex-enemy state was not a partner at the peace negotiations, peace preparatory notes between July 1945 and May 1946 presented Hungarian views and proposals concerning the future of the Danubian nations. The notes were addressed to representatives of the three Great Powers in Budapest and subsequently were submitted to the Council of Foreign Ministers and the Paris Conference. The notes disapproved the antagonistic relations in Danubian Europe and emphasized the need of close economic and cultural cooperation and political reconciliation of neighboring nations and made specific proposals in these fields. These "peace aim" notes posed the general problems of Danubian Europe in constructive terms, advocating regional economic reorganization, freedom of navigation on the Danube and revival of international control over the river, deemphasis of narrow nationalism, "spiritualization" of frontiers, self-determination of peoples, and protection of national minorities.

But during the armistice period Hungarian sovereignty was subordinated to the Soviet-dominated Allied Control Commission (ACC). The Soviet envoy in Budapest, Georgi J. Pushkin, expressed dissatisfaction with the Hungarian proposals. In countries under Soviet occupation, Russian policy was not the reconciliation of nations but "divide and rule." When Philip E. Mosely, a member of the American delegation at the Paris Conference, later appraised the volumes published in 1947 by the Hungarian Foreign Ministry on peace preparations and the Conference of Paris, he concluded that

> The general impression left by the three volumes so far published is that the Hungarian government had prepared its case with care on the assumption that the issues would be treated on their merits by the Great Powers, all of them concerned primarily with promoting peace and stability in the Danubian region. In the procedural and substantive tussles of the Paris Conference this assumption proved illfounded. The struggle over the formal terms of the treaty was merely one aspect of a more general struggle to extend or confine Soviet power in Europe. In that struggle Hungary had little to hope for and much to fear.[3]

By the time the peace conference convened in Paris, the Council of Foreign Ministers had formulated most provisions of the peace treaties, and members of the council were obligated to support them at the conference table. Consider the result for Hungary in connection with its territorial claims on Rumania. Transylvania had been a major bone of contention during the war and in the armistice period. Despite Soviet encouragement given to postwar political leaders in Budapest concerning Hungary's territorial claim in Transylvania, at the London session of the CFM the Soviet delegation was unwilling to consider an American proposal even to study the possibility of a modest revision of the Hungarian-Rumanian boundary along ethnic lines. In view of the unyielding Soviet opposition, Secretary Byrnes, in a period of East-West concessions in May 1946, proposed in the CFM the reestablishment of the Trianon boundary between Hungary and Rumania.

The greatest immediate threat to Hungarian interests at the Paris Conference was a Czechoslovak proposal for the expulsion of 200,000 Hungarians from Czechoslovakia. Since the proposal was an amendment to the draft treaty accepted by the CFM, only a unanimous approval of the Big Three would have made possible its inclusion in the treaty. The United States opposed the punishment of an ethnic group on the basis of collective responsibility, and in the last stage of the debates Great Britain joined American opposition. The peace treaty, instead of the original amendment, obligated Hungary to enter into bilateral negotiations with Prague to solve the problem of Magyar inhabitants of Slovakia. This incident was one of the consequences of the Czechoslovak policy of expelling all non-Slavic inhabitants. In the spirit of Hitlerite legislation, Hungarians were deprived of their citizenship, of all political and elementary human rights, and they were persecuted by a series of administrative measures. The Hungarian government was forced to conclude a population exchange agreement with Czechoslovakia in February 1946. Through this exchange, as well as expulsions and persecution, over 90,000 Hungarians left Czechoslovakia for Hungary.

Peacemaking in 1945–47 was not much more than recasting the armistice agreements into peace treaties. This implied the recognition of an unprecedented division of the Old Continent, an iron curtain that still exists throughout Central Europe. Soviet troops remained in Hungary and Rumania to maintain the lines of communication with the Soviet zone in Austria. While geography played an important role in military decisions, it is true that Britain and the United States did not have vital economic or other interests in any East European or Danubian country, and this fact influenced their wartime and postwar policies. Yet the shift to Russia's Europe of a substantial part of the continent with over a hundred million people, affected their power position, greatly reducing the rimland necessary for the defense of the Western world.

The North Atlantic Treaty Organization and American troops in Europe later reestablished a military balance, which in more recent years has been perilously affected by new weapons systems and rapidly changing military technology. Despite this gloomy picture, as an optimist by nature I do not agree with doomsday predictions. I hope that the precarious military balance and the makeshift postwar arrangements will be replaced one day by a worldwide cooperative state system for the benefit of all mankind. Although human folly has few limits, it seems futile to contemplate the alternative to negotiated settlement on the basis of self-determination of peoples and respect for human rights and fundamental freedoms. For centuries war was considered diplomacy by other means. In our time, the military resolution of a major international conflict would almost inevitably result in the mutual suicide of the superpowers, atomic devastation of the northern hemisphere with far-reaching global side-effects and with benefit to no one.

Part I

HUNGARY'S PREDICAMENT

1

Between Scylla and Charybdis: 1944–1945

Prelude

On a spring day in 1934, I arrived in my government office in Buda to find a message from the National Scholarship Council: I should see that same morning a Mr. Kittredge from the Rockefeller Foundation, at the Hotel Astoria, to talk over my studies in the United States. I knew nothing about such plans and called the secretary of the council, who informed me that its chairman, Count Pál Teleki, had suggested some months earlier that a young Hungarian scholar with an international studies background in Western Europe should be given an opportunity to study in the United States. The council, having explored the matter with the Rockefeller Foundation and examined files of fellows who had studied in Western Europe, agreed that I should apply. I went to see Mr. Kittredge and gave him such references as Ake Hammarskjöld of the Permanent Court of International Justice at the Hague and names of a few professors at the Institut des Hautes Etudes Internationales at the Sorbonne where I had been awarded a diploma.

The following year I received a Rockefeller fellowship to study at Yale. Before I left I discussed my proposed studies and research with Teleki, who emphasized the increasing importance of the United States in international affairs and predicted that Washington would have a leading role in the reorganization of Europe at the next peace settlement. He recommended that besides my special studies, I should consider the major trends of United States foreign policy.

My wife Margaret and I left for New York from Le Havre aboard the S.S. Washington in early September 1935. As a Rockefeller fellow at Yale, attached to the Law School and the Graduate School, I soon realized that Yale offered an exceptional opportunity not only for my studies but to learn about American political and intellectual currents. My advisor in the Graduate School, Professor Nicholas Spykman, believed in the League of Nations and advocated full-fledged American participation in world affairs. In the Law School, I worked mainly with Professor Edwin M. Borchard, a trusted adviser of isolationist senators in Washington. At the time he was exchanging long letters with such senators as William E. Borah, Arthur H. Vandenberg, and Hiram Johnson, and shared his correspondence with me. Borchard and these senators were convinced that the collective security system of the League of Nations would lead to a generalization of all wars, contrary to the practice of traditional diplomacy, which sought to isolate wars. Instead of participation in any sort of collective security arrangement, Borchard and his political followers advocated American neutrality. This view was supported by a majority in Congress in the later 1930s and led to enactment of neutrality legislation to keep the United States out of any war.

The world press and even a huge headline in the New Haven Register related in early March 1936 that German troops were goosestepping into the Rhineland—a violation not only of the Treaty of Versailles but of the Locarno Treaty of 1925 to which Germany had freely adhered. Although remilitarization of the Rhineland changed the strategic situation in the heart of Europe, and strengthened immensely Germany's power in Eastern Europe, Hitler's move encountered no serious opposition. France, even if it had acted alone, could have crushed the German army, but French public opinion was influenced by pacifist ideas and the government was unwilling to mobilize six weeks before the general elections. Belgium and Britain were even less eager to participate in reprisals against Germany, and in the United States some isolationists suggested that the Germans were eliminating one of the injustices of the Versailles Treaty.

I visited several American centers of learning and was surprised to discover that prominent scholars in international relations were not aware of the political and military consequences of Germany's remilitarization of the Rhineland, believing that the collective security system of the League of Nations would block any further German expansion and secure peace. Professor Quincy Wright of the University of Chicago vigorously expressed this view to me. I concluded that the result of both "isolationist" and "internationalist" approaches in the United States might mean in practice less American participation in world politics. In my report to the Rockefeller Foundation, I noted this scholarly disregard of the realities of international life.

My fellowship happily was extended for another year, 1936–37, and I left American shores for England on the S.S. Manhattan to study the differences between American and British approaches in foreign policy. At Oxford, I was attached to All Souls and made contact with prominent scholars in other colleges as well. Intellectual life was lively and rewarding at Oxford, but British foreign policy in European affairs was not helpful and this was not entirely Britain's fault. There was no consensus on a European public order and so governments often turned to improvisation when they acted according to their real or fancied interests. The British government and people strongly condemned Nazi atrocities and abuses. Yet influential circles in Britain considered Hitler's rise to power as one of the German reactions to the inequalities institutionalized by the Versailles Treaty and to French punitive policy toward Germany. While there was some truth in these views, the assumption that concessions might facilitate Nazi Germany's return to the League of Nations and a more cooperative policy in Europe was alarm-

ing. A prize example of this approach was the Anglo-German Naval Agreement, concluded in June 1935. This instrument might have had a beneficial effect if France and Italy had been involved. But those states had not been informed of the negotiations, although the bilateral agreement was a revision of the Versailles Treaty. The resulting weakening of faith in British reliability both in France and Italy marked a further deterioration in the political atmosphere of Europe. A policy of concessions which could have stabilized Weimar's democracy in Germany only increased Hitler's appetite for conquest.

In the autumn of 1936 British society was disturbed by rumors about King Edward's relationship to Mrs. Wallis Warfield Simpson, the American divorcee. In the wake of that affair, the king's unprecedented abdication shocked the British public. Because of this preoccupation the troubles of Europe seemed remote. The winter fog over the English Channel blissfully "isolated" the nearby disorderly continent.

For the last few months of the second year of my fellowship I moved to Geneva where the League of Nations' cosmopolitan bureaucracy watched with trepidation the adverse turns of international affairs. Officials of the League and reporters had been impressed by the clever diplomatic performance of a new actor, Maxim Litvinov. After Hitler's seizure of power, the Kremlin had initiated a rapprochement with the Western democracies, and the USSR had been admitted to the League of Nations in September 1934. Litvinov skillfully used the catchphrases of Geneva and became a champion of collective security. His moderation and civility created confidence in Soviet behavior. Yet the League's ineffective sanctions against Italy during the invasion of Ethiopia demonstrated its powerlessness. The League's council, of course, had protested when Germany had violated its international obligations, but the Western powers allowed the Nazi regime to take what its democratic predecessor, the Weimar Republic, could not obtain. The tranquillité d'esprit of most Western politicians was not affected by Hitler's preparations for conquest. They found it comfortable not to take him seriously.

In the spring of 1937, I decided to visit some centers for international relations in Germany, and the Rockefeller Foundation, after some hesitation, approved my trip. The chairman of the League's committee that had prepared a revision of the Covenant of the League of Nations, Professor Maurice Bourquin, asked me to find out what modification of the Covenant would induce Germany to reenter the League. When I raised this question with well-informed people in Berlin their reaction was completely negative. Hitler would not permit application for membership in the League under any conditions, they said. At the convention of the Hansische Arbeitsgemeinschaft für Völkerrecht in Hamburg, I brought up Bourquin's initiative in conversation with an aristocrat on good terms with the Nazis, Professor Freiherr von Freytag-Loringhoven. He was interested and told me that nobody had suspected that the war in Ethiopia and the League sanctions against Italy would make possible the occupation of the Rhineland, adding that membership in the League might open doors and opportunities for Germany. He suggested a private meeting with Bourquin near Berlin on the estate of Rudolf Nadolny, a former German ambassador to the Soviet Union. I gave this message to Bourquin at Geneva, but did not inquire later if the meeting ever took place.

In Hamburg I participated in several social events at the convention of the Hansische Arbeitsgemeinschaft. During an after-dinner beer party the Stimmung and voices were rising and my companions had started to talk about the consequences of the First World War. I interjected casually that the peace settlement in Danubian Europe had been favorable to Germany because it replaced the Austro-Hungarian Monarchy, the second largest state in Europe, with quarreling small states that could not resist German expansion. Since my remark implied that Austria-Hungary could have resisted German pressure, my companions were shocked and retorted emphatically that no power on earth could resist Hitler's rejuvenated Germany. According to their perception, England was a declining power, the French had degenerated, inferior people lived in the East, and the Americans were interested only in business and did not have an army. They offered these explanations with aplomb. During the preceding dinner there had been conversation about Germany returning to pre-Christian heroic virtues and the religion of the ancient German tribes. These were strange Tischengespräche.

During the trip to Germany, I had met all sorts of people — enthusiastic Nazis as well as democrats frightened into cooperation. At the Kiel Institut für Weltwirtschaft, I visited a former Rockefeller fellow and had an informative conversation about conditions in Germany. When he accompanied me back to my hotel he often raised his hand, giving the "Heil Hitler" salute. He explained to me apologetically that he had had to do this during the past few months in order to keep his position.

After I left Germany, I visited friends at The Hague and in Paris. I was surprised when Ake Hammerskjöld suggested that the Germans did not have well-trained officials for international organizations and that this was the major reason they had left the League. He told me that a German member of the Permanent Court's secretariat was recalled because of a misunderstanding. These were benevolent interpretations, coming from a great European who was a gentle man. In France most Frenchmen thought that Hitler was a ridiculous clown and a despicable demagogue, and felt safe behind the Maginot Line. Few people took seriously the political program spelled out in Mein Kampf.

By the end of my fellowship I was greatly disturbed by the political disarray of the Western world. I thereupon discovered it in my own country. Upon return to Budapest, I was astonished by the greatly strengthened position of the political parties under Nazi influence. Agitation of the various Nazi groups made good use of Hungary's economic difficulties and of the defects of the obsolete social system. In foreign affairs Nazi propaganda emphasized the inability of the Western powers to bring about a viable system

*in the Danubian Valley and promised that Germany would correct the in-
justices of the Trianon Treaty.*

*In the countries I had visited, knowledgable people were certain that the
growing tensions in Europe and the Far East would culminate in some sort
of crisis in world affairs. While no one could foresee its exact nature or when
precisely it would occur, I was convinced that the interaction of aggressive
dictatorships with the passivity of democracies was bound to lead to a catastrophic conflict. Disregarding the gathering storm, I went ahead and produced a scholarly book on the international responsibility of the state. But
as it came to pass, the principles and rules of international law I discussed
in that volume were finally of no use to me nor anyone else in the lawless
years ahead.*

At the close of the Second World War, geography proved decisive in
the misfortune of Hungary, a country that had been in the inner circle of the German power sphere. From this came the basic problem
of Hungarian diplomacy—attempting to preserve Hungarian independence in an almost impossible situation. None of the other
Axis satellites was in so precarious a position. The peripheral location
of Italy, Finland, Rumania, and Bulgaria made possible their early
surrender, but events in Hungary turned out differently. Although
in the early stage of the European war Hungary was considered an unwilling satellite, with the German occupation in March 1944, the
country lost its independence and under a German-imposed Arrow
Cross regime, it became Nazi Germany's last satellite. As a junior
partner of the Axis, Hungary did not enjoy much sympathy in the
West. And she was positively disliked by the Russians; Foreign
Secretary Anthony Eden said to President Roosevelt that he "thought
Stalin would want to be pretty arbitrary about Hungary because the
Russians do not like the Hungarians, and that Stalin would be un-
willing to give them any favors at the Peace Table."[1]

The Arrow Cross government installed by the Germans in October
1944 was the Hungarian version of Nazism. In view of the impending
Soviet occupation, some Arrow Cross politicians announced that the
population of Hungary would be transferred to Germany for the
winter. People were supposed to return the next spring when the new
German secret weapons would definitely defeat the Russians. This
scheme for wholesale transfer of population proved impracticable,
both because of logistic impossibility and because of general resistance. But as a consequence of forced evacuation, several thousand
families, many young men, and most of the ranking government

officials left the country along with the retreating German troops and the remnants of the Hungarian army. When news spread about the lootings, rapes, and other atrocities of the invading Soviet army, the flight became more widespread.

The country was first ravaged by the Germans, then systematically looted by the Russians. The retreating Germans blew up many bridges and destroyed a substantial part of the transportation and communication system. The physical destruction, the vacuum of political power and the lack of administrative structure were extensive throughout Hungary.

The invading Soviet army found a ruined country without administration or political authority. The old adminstration was nonexistent or not recognized by the occupying army, and so the Russians, with the help of Moscow-trained Hungarian communist advisers, created a new political framework. Eastern Hungary was in Russian hands in the last months of 1944, but the Germans were not driven out of western Hungary until April 4, 1945. The Soviet army encircled Budapest on December 25, 1944, and the siege of Buda lasted until mid-February. In late 1944 and early 1945, at one time or another, most regions of Hungary were battlefields. In addition, the Nazis and their Arrow Cross henchmen, and later the Soviet authorities and their communist collaborators, liquidated selected groups of Hungarians.

How, then, would Hungarians survive such a catastrophe? The answer is that many of them did not. A world full of uncertainties first had developed in Hungary during the Nazi occupation. Mass deportations of Jews occured. Prominent people disappeared, temporarily or for good; it was not possible to clarify their fate. In this chaotic world the survival of individuals depended on chance. My personal experience in occupied Hungary may best convey the chaos and tragedy of that period.

A week before the German occupation of Hungary, my wife Margaret and I enjoyed a pleasant Sunday lunch at the house of Joseph Balogh, editor of *The Hungarian Quarterly*. He had close contacts with the Ministry for Foreign Affairs and we talked about Hungary's long-range perspectives and the dangerous alternatives in the immediate future. At that time battle-ready German divisions were concentrated along Hungary's western frontier. Although the German military threat of invasion seemed probable, we preferred to discuss mainly the possibility and modalities of institutionalized cooperation with neighboring countries after Armageddon. It was a beautiful spring day, full of sunshine, and Margaret and I decided after lunch to walk through the Andrássy Avenue to Buda. The streets were almost empty, the atmosphere was pleasant, tranquility dominated the city, and I remarked casually to Margaret that this was perhaps our last walk through peaceful Budapest. Despite catastrophic defeats of the Hungarian army in faraway Russian battlefields, life was unrealistically quiet in Hungary amidst a destructive world war fought in three continents and on several oceans. Hungary did not suffer bombardment because the American flying units in passing over Hungary were not fired upon or chased by Hungarian fighter planes. Their safe flights were facilitated by information about location of air defense. The Kállay government in September 1943 rejected the demand of the German High Command that it should be allowed to garrison western Hungary with five German flying units. This unique situation changed drastically under German occupation, during which our gracious host, Balogh, was deported. He never returned.

With the German occupation the position of most officials of the political division of the Foreign Ministry—where I worked in charge of peace preparations—became precarious. Leading officials were arrested and deported to Germany. The Gestapo arrested my immediate superiors, Aladár Szegedy-Maszák, head of the political division, and Andor Szentmiklóssy, deputy foreign minister. A few months later they were deported to the concentration camp of Dachau where Szentmiklóssy died. Szegedy-Maszák was liberated by the American army and was appointed Hungarian minister to the United States in December 1945.

In the midst of these events I withdrew into another agency of the Foreign Ministry which represented the Hungarian government before the Mixed Arbitral Tribunals and the Permanent Court of International Justice. By a bureaucratic miracle this agency had survived even in the war years, and because I had been attached to it off and on since 1931, my return did not create a sensation or bureaucratic problems. Under the cover of this inconspicuous office I continued the peace preparatory work with my most reliable collaborator.

Immediately after the German occupation I had decided to take out from my office all remaining documents concerning peace preparations, and since I did not know the measures taken by the Nazis to control the Foreign Ministry, I asked my brother, Emeric, a medical student, to accompany me. The ushers in the ministry greeted me as usual, and we reached my office without difficulty. I put all materials relevant to peace preparations in two large briefcases and gave them to my brother. I thought I might be arrested at the gate by police agents and wanted to detain them while my brother walked out with the briefcases. But nobody paid any attention when we left the ministry. Apparently the Germans trusted the newly appointed key government officials and had not installed supervisory agents at the gates.

At that time I was living alone in our apartment in Buda—my wife and two daughters had gone to the country because of the bombing of Budapest—and I received there some of my collaborators in the peace preparatory work, although I was cautious because our janitor was a vociferous Nazi sympathizer. (After the Soviet occupation he became a loyal supporter of the Communist party; changes from one totalitarian allegiance to another for strictly opportunistic reasons were not unusual.)

Each day I had a sort of routine. I turned on the radio in the morning, which announced when American bombers, coming from Italy, were approaching the capital. The radio usually indicated that planes were coming from the direction of southern Hungary. The watchwords announced on such occasions were "Bácska, Baja, Budapest." This meant that I had just time to take a quick bath, shave, and go over to my parents' house to have breakfast with them in their air-raid shelter during the bombardment, which lasted about a half hour. When the "all clear" signal came I went to my office. The Americans bombed mainly the industrial districts, which were on the outskirts of the city.

All the while a clandestine, uncertain world had developed in Hungary, and as we went along we had to take the hazards of existence on a day-to-day basis. The rules of clandestine activities and contacts with the underground were a new experience for me in the spring and summer of 1944, and I learned a few elementary precautions. Most of the time I met my confederates in the anti-Nazi resistance in parks and streets, seldom in private houses, and because I continued an official life I often used intermediaries. One of my contacts was a young English lady, Miss Gore-Symes, with whom I met twice a week to practice English conversation. On the side she cooperated with Charles Szladits, a lawyer and legal counsel of one of the major banks in Budapest, to shelter a group of British and Dutch officers who had escaped from German prisoner of war camps. A few of them lived for a while in the crypt of a Catholic church in Buda. These officers ran an efficient "factory" for false birth certificates, military passes, passports, and other identity cards. Szladits came to see me in this matter, and periodically I made some financial contributions for support of this clandestine group. Miss Gore-Symes remained my permanent contact with them. When the Soviet army occupied Budapest some of these officers reported to the Russians who interned them in the town of Hatvan. Some of them were not released, and disappeared mysteriously.

My assistance to the escaped officers had an interesting epilogue. In the autumn of 1945 a British major visited me in the Foreign Ministry. Thanking me for my support of the underground in Budapest, he handed me a certificate as "a token of gratitude for and appreciation of the help given to the Sailors, Soldiers and Airmen of the British Commonwealth of Nations, which enabled them to escape from, or evade capture by the enemy." The certificate was signed by Field Marshal H.R. Alexander, Supreme Commander, Mediterranean Theater. To my surprise the major wanted to reimburse me for the money given to assist the Commonwealth officers. I would not accept his offer and explained that we were not thinking of any sort of monetary compensation or reward.

All this came later. In the summer of 1944 Regent Miklós Horthy's position had strengthened somewhat. Since the Germans did not take over direct control of the major government agencies, some residual power remained in Horthy's hands even after the occupation in March 1944. Horthy dismissed the pro-Nazi prime minister, Döme Sztójay, and replaced him with General Géza Lakatos. The attempt to kill Hitler on July 20, 1944, had created confusion among German authorities in Hungary, momentarily increasing Horthy's freedom of action, and he was able to block the deportation of Jews from Budapest. Under the new government the Foreign Ministry had more freedom, and Deputy Foreign Minister Mihály Jungerth-Arnóthy asked me to continue the peace preparations in the Foreign Ministry and to use for this purpose the additional documents accumulated during the German occupation. It was ironic to read German requests for flour and other foodstuffs to feed the Jews deported to death camps.

At this juncture I turned down a diplomatic appointment in Switzerland. The deputy foreign minister informed me that the government intended to appoint me consul in Zurich where I could continue my work undisturbed by immediate events in Hungary. He pointed out that under the forthcoming Russian occupation the government agencies might be paralyzed, whereas in Switzerland I could make good use of material deposited at our Bern Legation. I declined the appointment for a variety of reasons. From a purely personal point of view I would have been comfortable to observe the apocalyptic events in Europe from a quiet post. But I felt that it would have been a cowardly action to run from danger and not share the fate of my countrymen. Moreover, contacts with the Western powers had convinced me of the slight value of backdoor diplomacy. If Hungary was to survive the holocaust there must be a government in the country, and it might be more useful to try to influence events while at home than to seek the good will of foreign powers. It seemed probable at the time that the Allied powers had made decisions according to their own well-considered interests; I had no illusion about our capacity to influence the course of events in the last phase of the war. Time and again since 1939, I had advocated the establishment of a government-in-exile. "The Hungarian nation should remain united" was the answer to such arguments. It became clear after the war that I was wrong. A government-in-exile could not have alleviated Hungary's fate under Soviet occupation. The Teleki government had made some preparatory steps in early 1940, when five million dollars in bank notes and securities were deposited in the United States for certain contingencies. Such plans were abandoned later.[2] But in the summer of 1944 burdened with our wartime status, we were decidedly late for this sort of action. At that time nobody suspected that the ultimate fate of Hungary would not depend upon our wartime attitude.

Jungerth-Arnóthy appreciated my reasons for declining the Zürich appointment, and we agreed upon a compromise, which, unfortunately, came to naught. I was to go to Switzerland as a diplomatic courier as soon as possible and spend two or three weeks there organizing and preparing the deposited material for publication and other uses. The Foreign Ministry asked for a German transit visa, which I received promptly, and I was scheduled to leave Hungary on October 16 with another official of the political division. Regent Horthy's armistice proclamation of October 15 intervened and made my departure impossible. The ill-prepared armistice attempt then failed, and German armored divisions concentrated on the outskirts of Budapest moved into the capital. Pro-Horthy military commanders were arrested, the Lakatos government deposed, and the Germans installed an Arrow Cross government under Ferenc Szálasi. Horthy was taken prisoner and deported with his family to Germany.

With the violent end of the Horthy regime, a chapter of Hungarian history came to a close; a new wave of mass arrests began, this time turning very personal indeed, for the Arrow Cross government's agents arrested me at the house of my parents. My wife and daughters had returned from the country, and a family dinner was interrupted by the intrusion of three gunmen, allegedly detectives, who arrested me after a thorough search. I learned later that four of my colleagues from the Foreign Ministry had shared my fate—Denis Nemestóthy,

Baron Maurice Czikann-Zichy, Álmos Papp and Ádám Koós. I was accused of having been in contact with the underground parties and of having taken part in preparation of the armistice negotiations—actions considered treasonous.

After my arrest our apartment, especially my library, was thoroughly searched in my presence, but fortunately I was able to avoid any focusing of attention on some compromising documents hidden among the files of a Hungarian case we had before the Permanent Court of International Justice. While three detectives discussed whether or not to go through this huge bundle of files, I called their attention to some more books and files in the next room and suggested that they should inspect everything carefully and divide their time accordingly. They began to swear but dropped the critical files and, confronted with a great mass of material, became confused. After seizing a few ridiculously irrelevant papers, they decided to return for a detailed search if deemed necessary by their superiors.

My first jail was a huge schoolroom in Rökk Szilárd street where about fifty people were sitting like statues on the floor with crossed legs. I learned later that most of them were suspected, or actual, Communists. In front of them sat a gendarme, playing carelessly with his tommy gun. When I was escorted into the room the gendarme explained that only his merciful heart kept him from shooting the whole collection of worthless dogs. Such were the mild epithets used in his endless harangues. The young gendarme was not, however, without a sense of humor. When he asked a Serbian partisan in the group to tell a story, the latter told an anti-Nazi joke, which caused a hilarious outburst. The gendarme laughed with the rest of us, and the Serbian was not punished.

In the crowd I discovered two colleagues from the political division of the Foreign Ministry, one of them nursing head wounds, the result of torture inflicted personally by the new chief of cabinet of the Arrow Cross foreign minister. We were not allowed to speak to each other. Anyone who moved or uttered a word to his neighbor was beaten or otherwise punished. Suddenly an air raid began, and we were ordered down into the basement—happily for us the gendarmes prized their own lives. While marching downstairs Nemestóthy managed to get next to me, whispered the accusations against us, and indicated the documents they were after. They knew, he said, of our contact with prominent members of the Smallholder party underground (the leading democratic party of Hungary). His words came as a great relief. Relatively speaking, these were minor matters. During subsequent interrogations it was a great help to know the goal of the enigmatic questions. I did not deny that I had contact with Smallholder politicians and that I had favored an armistice instead of the senseless destruction of Hungary, but I refused to confess that I possessed the documents they were looking for.

The detective inspector who led the interrogations was a short fellow with gray hair and sharp-looking cold eyes. He acted with the skill of a professional, and wanted to deliver something to his new masters. When I continued in my refusal, he suddenly punched me in the face, a blow meant to be a *captatio benevolentiae*, because he emphasized that his superiors had much stronger means to open the mouths of stubborn plotters and reminded me that I had a family against whom they could apply reprisals. His arrogance strengthened my determination not to reveal anything, whereupon he explained that he had to produce something for the foreign minister and suggested that I should compose a copy of the document drafted originally by myself. We compromised on that, and during the night I wrote a document that proposed armistice negotiations in a cautious way and omitted incriminating passages—or at least I thought so.

Next day the atmosphere changed. The detective inspector obligingly expressed his conviction that we were gentlemen and that he had always known it. We were conducted to another prison, a former private villa in the Swabian hills of Buda, and in the villa we were put into a small room with two policemen who were told by the detective inspector that they would be shot if they even let us speak to each other. As soon as he left the room the policemen locked the doors and asked us politely whether we would like to play cards. We did. Our guards were changed every six hours, and with one exception all of them treated us well. We slept on the floor and did not get food every day, although later our relatives were allowed to bring supplies. Interrogation continued under decent conditions. Margaret was permitted to visit me, and she brought in a suitcase containing badly needed underwear and shirts. A friend accompanied her, and they took the electric funicular from town to the top of the Swabian hills. Unexpectedly the funicular stopped at mid-course, and a gallant German officer helped the two ladies carry the suitcase to the gate of the elegant villa. We learned later that during their trip the explosives put under the Margaret bridge by the German army were blown up by mistake in rush-hour traffic, and the explosion had destroyed the electric cables as well. During Margaret's visit I was able to whisper instructions concerning what papers to destroy at home; she succeeded in getting rid of them with the help of my brother Emeric, to whom I was later to give supplementary instructions.

During the few days in the villa we met some strange people. For a short time two Arrow Cross leaders were imprisoned in our room. One of them was an old man, bleeding about the head and ears. He introduced himself as a professor and the national ideological educator of the Arrow Cross party. He contended that Szálasi was not sincerely pro-German and therefore had to be eliminated as a leader. Such doctrines were the cause of his arrest and injuries, but he refused to compromise. The other man, allegedly a candidate of the new regime for a diplomatic post abroad, had had a disagreement and fistfight with the new deputy foreign minister over some looted Jewish property, and landed in jail. His fantastic stories about his heroic past greatly amused us and provided some necessary comic relief. In our struggle for survival in the face of overwhelming tragedy, a sense of the absurd and a taste for gallows humor were indispensable for morale—a lesson quickly learned by the stubborn and ever-resourceful Hungarian population.

We were soon separated from the Arrow Cross dignitaries and transported to a sinister-looking military prison in the Margit Körút full of ranking army officers, government officials, and political leaders. All of the common criminals had been released from this prison to make room for this strange group. When we told the man who registered us in the "admission office" that we were innocent, he just waved his hand sadly and whispered: "In this prison everybody is accused of treason." We understood later that he was a fellow prisoner and a Serbian Orthodox priest from southern Hungary. Our barbers were alternately a Serbian partisan and a Ukrainian partisan who had been parachuted into Hungary. They visited us twice a week and brought news about the fate of our fellow prisoners and events of the outside world. They were surprisingly well informed and spoke fairly good Hungarian. During air raids we were not taken to shelters, but the Ukrainian partisan assured us that Soviet fliers had instructions not to bomb the neighborhood of our prison. Each evening a few prison guards visited the cells and counted the inmates. One evening they repeated the headcounts, and when they returned for the third time the count was made in English. We learned later that the numbers were not right, and the guards had asked a member of the Royal Air Force to make the recount. Almost every day we were escorted for a short walk in the prison yard, and during one of these promenades we managed to meet Colonel Julius Kádár, the former head of the counterintelligence section of the general staff. With expert knowledge he explained the factors involved in our case and concluded: "Boys, most probably all of us will be shot before long." His matter-of-fact prediction was something of a shock to us, but gradually we got used to the idea. Meanwhile the daily executions in the prison yard created a disheartening atmosphere.

Because Budapest at this time was threatened by encirclement, around November 20, 1944, we were suddenly put into buses and taken to western Hungary. One bus took the civilian prisoners, the other the army officers. On our bus we had a pro-Western former prime minister, Miklós Kállay, our neighbor in the prison, and because of his presence we were accompainied by SS guards, in addition to the Hungarian gendarmes and soldiers. During a stop we were able to exchange a few words with General Lajos Veress, commander in chief of the Second Hungarian Army. I asked him how, with a whole army under his command, the Germans had been able to arrest him. Veress replied that his own chief of staff had betrayed him to the Germans, who had sent a huge armored unit to escort him to Budapest. He posed the question as to whether we should attack our guards and disarm them. The futility of such a plan was obvious, for even if we had succeeded the problem remained of what to do and where to go; Hungary appeared in a state of dissolution, and it was difficult to see any goal that justified fighting against our countrymen.

Our destination was the concentration camp of Sopron-Kőhida, a well-known prison in western Hungary, near Austria. But our small group soon returned to Budapest, since our indictments had been prepared and the advance of the Red Army was temporarily stalled. After our departure the Bishop of Veszprém, József Mindszenty (later Cardinal Archbishop of Esztergom) and his entourage were brought to Sopron-Kőhida.

Upon our return to Budapest we found that a new category of political prisoners now filled the military jail—members of the anti-Arrow Cross committee of liberation under the leadership of the Smallholder Endre Bajcsy-Zsilinszky and military officers including General János Kiss had been arrested. The committee members were tortured for weeks, and their leaders later sentenced to death and executed. In comparison with this important plot of politicians and soldiers aiming at overthrow of the Arrow Cross government by force, our case became much less interesting—a fact that we welcomed. In the early period of our captivity the foreign minister had asked for daily reports about our hearings, but by the end of November we had become figures of the past, overshadowed by recent plots against the Arrow Cross regime. Nonetheless the atmosphere was menacing. Torture was commonly used by investigators in cases not yet before the military prosecutors. Besides electric instruments, there were various forms of sophisticated beatings. A few young army officers were arrested because they had wanted to dismantle the explosives from Danube bridges in Budapest. They could hardly walk, because first the soles of their feet were badly beaten, and then, with bleeding feet, they had to jump around in a room on one foot until they collapsed.

Isolation in prison is depressing, and links with the outside world are important; yet we could not have contact with anybody, except our lawyer. We planned to send a message to the papal nuncio or a neutral legation but did not succeed. Fortunately our case soon was in its last stage, and our military prosecutor observed legal formalities and showed understanding toward us. During interrogations he did everything but suggest the best lines for our defense. Still our position was not reassuring. The court-martial consisted of a single professional military judge and four Arrow Cross officers appointed by the Szálasi regime. Our fate depended upon many imponderables under martial law; death sentences could be and were rendered for almost anything. Our counsel sought to reassure us, suggesting that we would not get more than ten to fifteen years at hard labor, which was consolation of a sort. Our main problem was to survive the coming weeks; we did not think in terms of years.

In the winter of 1944–1945 the fury of the Hungarian Nazis as they sensed their doom was unrestrained. When being taken to hear our indictment I saw the corpse of a fellow prisoner, who had been tortured to death, carried by in the corridor. Just below our windows the rifles of the firing squad rattled day and night. At least sixteen prisoners were executed daily, many of them were simple peasants and workers who had deserted from the army. Not knowing when our turn might come, we prepared ourselves for the worst. It was reassuring to see the quiet and determined attitude of my fellow prisoners. In the face of death one discovers much strength in the soul. In this prison uncertainty was the only certainty about the future.

We witnessed many human tragedies. We understood through the grapevine that a former minister of defense, Louis Csatay, and his wife who was visiting him in the prison, had committed suicide. A shy-looking young newspaperman had made the return trip from Sopron-Kőhida with us. He had served in the army and was accused of having designed an anti-Szálasi poster. Experts could not identify his handwriting, but the son of his janitor testified against him, and he was court-martialed on the day we were transported from Budapest to Sopron-Kőhida. The sentence had not been handed down, and we discussed his case during our journey. None of us expected a fatal outcome. When we returned to Budapest he was put into the same prison room with us. Next morning he was escorted to a routine hearing. We never saw him again. A death sentence was imposed, and he was executed immediately.

On December 2, 1944, I stood with my colleagues before a court-martial, accused of treason. Although the court consisted of five "judges," only the president, as mentioned, was a professional judge, and it was my feeling that the president and the military prosecutor had tried to save us, but the decision would not be theirs. (I testified after the war in their defense when, in turn, their case was taken to court.) During our trial I stated in defense that Hungary had been a battlefield for many wars in past centuries, and that by our actions we had only tried to save the country from a repetition of this tragic fate. The court reprimanded me for this "foolhardy" statement. I pointed out that we knew, from a report of the Hungarian envoy to Germany, of Japanese mediation and German peace overtures, and we had proposed similar parleys. Before the trial our military prosecutor had encouraged me to emphasize this motive for our action.

Then, at long last, after a rough trial lasting five hours, the court-martial released us. We did not attribute this action to any particularly eloquent pleading. The decisive factor in our release probably was the proximity of the Soviet army, for the Arrow Cross officers were fearful of the approaching Russians. During our trial Budapest was almost encircled by the Soviet army, and on such days the Nazis were not anxious to have dead bodies in the prison's yard.

Following our release I went home for a few hours and then took refuge in a private hospital in Buda as a precautionary step, since a new arrest was possible at any time. Nemestóthy joined me in the same hospital room. We acted as strangers and seldom spoke to each other. The third man in the room was a dying Arrow Cross party member. Only the director of the hospital knew our identity and he was most helpful. I feigned colitis and periodically received hypodermic injections, which caused high fever. A few days later our lawyer visited us and explained that the Nazis were again searching for us, with more serious charges: we were accused as representatives of the Hungarian diplomats abroad who had denounced the new Hungarian regime, and they had already been sentenced to death *in absentia*. A friend visited me from the Foreign Ministry and offered false identity documents. I refused to accept them because the false documents could have become channels to find me. In our precarious situation I preferred to rely on my own wits.

On the afternoon of December 24 the hospital arranged a Christmas party for the staff and those patients who were not confined to bed. While a young doctor in a solemn Christmas speech vehemently denounced the Russians and Communists, I wondered about his future. Fighting had intensified in our neighborhood, and the Russian conquest seemed only a matter of hours. Several months later I received a summons to testify in the case of the hospital director, Gábor Perémy, who had sheltered us during the last stage of Nazi domination. All administrators were investigated after the liquidation of the Arrow Cross regime, and I was glad to take a stand on behalf of our courageous protector. I used the occasion to inquire about the fate of the young anti-Communist doctor, our preacher on Christmas Eve, and to my surprise I was told that he became the all-powerful spokesman for the Communist party in the hospital. As noted above, this was not unusual; after the Soviet occupation many Nazis switched with lightning speed to the Communist camp.

On Christmas Day the Soviet troops reached the hospital's garden and a battle began nearby. As a safety measure we were ordered to go down to the basement. I debated with Nemestóthy what to do. We wanted to remain in the hospital because it seemed that the Soviet army would occupy the city in a few days and peace would return. It seemed to us that it would be better to get it over with as soon as possible. But the fight continued around the hospital, and the odor in the basement turned from bad to worse, so we decided to escape through the hospital yard. Amidst whistling bullets we succeeded in reaching a quiet street and made our way home. This was a narrow escape in more than one sense. Shortly after our departure, Soviet troops occupied the hospital, arrested all able-bodied men, and shipped them as war prisoners to Russia. Many of them perished.

The Siege and Soviet Occupation

The siege of Buda lasted seven weeks, much longer than anybody expected, and I spent the long ordeal with my family in the basement of our apartment house. More than a hundred persons were crowded into the small basement, which was transformed into a shelter. Conditions were precarious; there was no running water, gas, or electricity. The house was about 800 feet from the Russian lines, so we lived in the midst of the fighting. Human nature is elastic, and after the first few days of the siege nobody paid much attention when the building was hit by mortar shells or bullets. The apartment house was struck twice by thousand-pound Russian bombs. They pierced three or four floors, but neither bomb exploded. Other huge bombs exploded about twenty feet from the house, and on these frightful occasions the earth shook, and the building moved like a ship on a stormy sea. Each time we thought it meant the end of our suffering. My twelve- and six-year-old daughters were frightened on such occasions, and I jokingly told them "don't stamp, don't stamp, you make terrible noise." They laughed and the tension lessened. Gradually they got used to battlefield noises and took in stride the adversities as the days went by and our predicament became more gruesome and precarious.

Several times a day during the siege I had to climb upstairs to our apartment on the third floor to get articles needed for our daily existence. One of my duties was to prepare candles, which offered at least some light in the darkness of the shelter. Remembering the adventures of Robinson Crusoe, I used shoelaces as wicks and collected all the fat and oil I could find. The wind, snow, and bullets whistled through the apartments, long since without windowpanes. The apartment house was a ghostly castle, inhabited by a few scarcely living shadows. Because no one had prepared for a long siege, food was soon exhausted. Old people, incapable of enduring the hardship, died, and it was difficult to dig their graves in the deeply frozen courtyard. Yet the frost was not without its uses, for it prevented the epidemics that surely would have followed otherwise, when elementary hygienic rules could not be observed. A primitive latrine was constructed in the snowcovered backyard.

People were starving all over the city. When horses were killed in the streets, news spread quickly, and the population of neighboring blocks assailed the frozen bodies with all kinds of knives and axes. We had horse meat twice—a delicacy compared to our usual diet of beans, potatoes, and occasionally, sauerkraut. Even in the early stage of the siege it was difficult to obtain bread. There were impossibly long lines before bakeries. In the early days of the siege, such shopping expeditions were still feasible. It was a fortunate coincidence that our cook was pregnant, and thus she had priority and was not obligated to stand in the bakery line. As weeks went by, supplies ran out, and bakeries and other shops closed. In any case it was risky to leave the shelter. Besides the bombardment, bullets whistled through the area. Yet human inventiveness was a helpful force even under these trying conditions. All sorts of barters took place. My wife had special baby cream, for which she obtained a few pounds of potatoes. I was surprised when in early February 1945 the owner of a small, nearby restaurant offered to sell me sauerkraut, a commodity more valuable than gold during the last stages of the siege. I told her that I was not sure about my own survival, so I could not guarantee her the payments she asked for after the siege. She explained that she did not want to keep any supplies because the Russians would seize them when they moved in. She would rather give food to me and ask for a price necessary for buying the same amount of sauerkraut when normal conditions returned. This seemed good thinking. I gladly accepted her proposal. Both of us survived, and some months after the siege, I paid her a more than satisfactory price.

At least once a day I had to go to an empty lot across the street to fetch water from an improvised well. One never knew whether he would return from such an expedition, since there was fighting in the area. We often found dead or wounded people around the well.

During this dismal era we lived on hope, and—alas—we almost lost even that. We knew the Russian occupation was inevitable, and we were waiting in hope that it would bring an end to the Nazi terror and senseless destruction. Even during the last days of the siege, military vehicles with huge loudspeakers spread the news about approaching German army units with miracle weapons that would annihilate instantaneously the Russian army. A few Arrow Cross sympathizers in our midst received the news with great joy. That, of course, was not the sort of hope most people had.

The blatant Nazi propaganda had so often turned out to be untrue that many people did not want to believe the widely publicized stories about Russian atrocities. We had been through so much. During the first days after the siege it was difficult to walk on the streets covered by deep snow and snowdrifts. Here and there hands and feet of dead bodies emerged from the snow, a reminder of the seven-week drama of the siege of Buda. Unfortunately, this time the Nazis told a great amount of truth about what the Soviet occupation would be like. It was far worse than most people anticipated. The siege was followed by wholesale looting, robbery, and rape committed by the "liberators." The frightened population regarded the first misdeeds of the invading Russians as a cruel consequence of the long and bloody fighting. But systematic looting continued for several months. After darkness nobody dared to walk on the streets and the gates were barricaded. People became desperate, but they were helpless, for there was no remedy or protection against Russian action. In the midst of these outrages it was good to see occasional signs of human solidarity. Some Russian soldiers gave bread and candy to starving children, and I heard about cases when army officers restrained abuses.

During the occupation Soviet troops rapidly stripped entire factories, without the slightest expert knowledge. Disassembled machinery was loaded on railroad cars and taken to the Soviet Union as war booty. Much of it remained to rust on sidings; few of the disassembled factories could be reconstructed. This senseless vandalism was a loss to Hungary and a sheer waste for the Soviet Union. Later the Foreign Ministry submitted to the Soviet mission in Budapest a list of disassembled factories transported to the Soviet Union and asked that their estimated value be counted in the reparation payments. The request was rejected. Rational discussion of such matters was not possible with Soviet military or diplomatic representatives or with the Moscow-educated Hungarian Communists who automatically accepted the Soviet point of view and supported Soviet denials and claims. The Communist leader, Mátyás Rákosi, denied later that the Russians transported disassembled factories to the Soviet Union, although the Foreign Ministry referred to these actions in several notes addressed to Marshall Klementy Voroshilov, chairman of the Allied Control Commission.

Soviet patrols asked for personal papers on the streets. At first, on such occasions, the soldiers respected documents, although they could not read our alphabet. For a few days I used a diplomatic card received three years earlier from the Rumanian Foreign Ministry in Bucharest. Then I met a Russian-speaking colleague from the Foreign Ministry who owned a typewriter with Cyrillic letters, and he was able to prepare identity cards in Russian that stated that so-and-so is a member of the Hungarian Foreign Ministry and is in charge of some important duties. Another colleague found a seal in the ruins of the Foreign Ministry, and these documents in Russian were properly sealed and looked almost authentic. In most cases such documents were helpful. In other instances they were torn up and thrown away by Russian patrols. I had experiences with both alternatives. Chance and composure were the important factors those days.

During a walk in Buda I saw many soldiers of a Mongolian type. This encounter, and the abusive excesses of the Soviet forces, reminded me that Gengis Khan's hordes had wrought havoc in Hungary during the thirteenth century, and I wondered how we could survive now and save our country from a similar fate. Were we facing a situation comparable to the earlier Tartar and Turkish invasions, or a more sophisticated exploitation? Would the Soviets impose a Communist regime? Would our country survive as an independent state? These were troublesome thoughts and questions without answers.

My first direct contact and "negotiation" with the Russians occured in a rather peculiar way. One day a Russian captain came to my home with an interpreter and courteously explained that his superiors knew about my resistance to the Nazis and would like to talk over with me the problems of Russian-Hungarian cooperation. I had to spend the following two days at Russian headquarters, where the officers were exclusively concerned with names and whereabouts of Nazi spies and collaborators. I vainly explained that I worked in the political division of the Foreign Ministry, in charge of preparation of the Hungarian case for the peace conference, and knew nothing about spies. Having first been in prison and for the last few months in a shelter, I could have no knowledge about the behavior and whereabouts of the suspected persons. The Russians were convinced I knew much more and was reluctant to tell it. The second day their attitude became threatening, and finally they handed me a register from the cultural section of the Foreign Ministry, containing a list of students who had received scholarships in foreign countries. I was supposed to disclose the spying assignments of these students. I tried to explain that the students had gone abroad to make special studies in such fields as chemistry or modern languages. By this time my interrogators had grown angry and excitedly told me that nobody could go abroad without a spying assignment and that I should cease talking nonsense. At that moment I had the same feeling I had experienced with the Nazi interrogators, who could not believe the truth but were pleased and impressed by fantastic stories. So I explained that these fellows might, after all, have been spies, but if so their assignment had been given by the Ministry of Defense, and the Foreign Ministry knew nothing about it. This devious explanation partly satisfied the single-minded Russians, and I got away with a promise that I would try to find out the names and whereabouts of the spies and collaborators. Fortunately this Russian headquarters moved away, and I was not molested by them again.

A few days later our apartment house received a summons from the Russian military police that all men of military age — eighteen to fifty years — should appear the next day at 6:00 A.M. with their personal documents. At headquarters they would get identity cards, which would assure them of free movement in town. The reason for the early hour was to enable everybody to get to his job on time. According to the Russians the procedure would not take more than five minutes. The whole thing seemed strange and aroused my suspicion. I decided not to go.

In the morning I left the house with the other men and asked them to tell the Russians that I had to see the Soviet commandant in Pest that morning and therefore would have to present my documents another time. Actually I went to see friends living on the banks of the Danube. There I met two girls who were rowing champions. The day before they had found a derelict light boat on the Danube and hidden it in their own apartment. Although crossing the river was strictly forbidden by the Russians the girls offered to take me to Pest in the boat, along with two other persons, Count Béla Bethlen from Transylvania and Francis Durugy from the Foreign Ministry. This was the only way to cross the river, since all bridges had been blown up by the retreating Germans. At this time of the year the crossing was doubly hazardous because of the floating ice. We lifted the boat to our shoulders and headed for the river, but as we approached the bank we noticed four Russian soldiers, apparently under the command of a civilian.

The latter shouted at me in a fluent but hardly understandable Hungarian: "Who are you?"

"I am an official of the Hungarian Foreign Ministry and was asked by the Soviet commandant in Pest to go to see him," I replied. "These girls will take me over to the other side of the river."

The stranger snarled at me "Where is the Hungarian Foreign Ministry? Where is such a country as Hungary? All these are of the past. A new world is here, don't you know this?"

"Of course I know very well that a new and better world will be established after the ordeals of war," I answered. "The Atlantic Charter and the Yalta Declaration on Liberated Europe, signed by Stalin, Roosevelt, and Churchill, are a guarantee of that." (After the siege the Declaration on Liberated Europe had been posted in Hungarian all over Budapest.)

We continued our strange conversation in this vein, surrounded by the ruins of a ghost city. In the meantime my companions had disappeared into their house with the boat, and when the Russians began to look for them I gave wrong directions and returned to my friends' house. We waited for about an hour until everything seemed clear and then tried the crossing again. This time no Russians were in sight. Now we would see whether a boat built for three lightly clad sportsmen could carry five persons in heavy winter clothes. As we stepped in, the boat settled lower and lower, until the icy water reached within inches of the gunwales. But the boat did not sink, and slowly and precariously we made our way across the Danube to Pest on the far shore.

The building of the Foreign Ministry in Buda had been destroyed, and a new office established in Pest—where, I did not know, but finally in an old apartment building without doors or windowpanes I found it and met a few colleagues who told me about a new national government at Debrecen, the principal town in northeastern Hungary. I was amazed to hear the following message from the new foreign minister, János Gyöngyösi: "The officials of the Foreign Ministry should not go to Buda [the part of town where I lived] because they might be deported by the Russians and in this case the Hungarian authorities could not help at all." My originally skeptical outlook changed to deep suspicion. I understood that experiences with the Russians in Pest were the same as in Buda, if not worse. Popular feeling at this time expressed equal contempt for Hitler and Stalin: scrawled in huge letters on the walls of the city were such slogans as: "Hitler is brown; Stalin is red; both are bastards to us."

On my return later in the day I had to wait two hours in a snow-storm on the bank of the Danube; because of Russian patrols my girl friends could not risk the crossing at the agreed time. When I finally arrived home in Buda in the evening, half-frozen and exhausted, I learned that none of those men who had gone to Russian head-quarters in the morning for the five-minute interview had returned. We later found out that they had had to march first to a concen-tration camp installed in Gödöllő in the gymnasium (high school) founded and run by the Order of Premontre, and three or four months later those men who survived the starvation ration and other hardships in the camp had been sent as prisoners of war to the Soviet Union. Some of them came home several years later.

That evening after the excursion to Pest I had a high fever, and next morning my wife, accompanied by my father, went to the Rus-sian military police to explain that I was ill and could not submit my documents for a couple of days.

"It does not matter, the MP will go to get him anyhow," was the brusque answer.

After this incident I decided to flee. I did not know that the Rus-sians were not like the Germans, that their method of operation was vastly different and unpredictable. On the street where I lived they made no attempt to get the men who had not gone to headquarters. Whereas we were accustomed to the uniformly enforced German system, Russian procedure was a whimsically changing pattern. Even when Soviet troops were marching through the city, we were not sure whether they were coming or going. Unenlightened, I went to the house of a Russian-speaking friend who made arrangements to cross the Danube again by boat the next morning. The same evening, however, three Russian soldiers came to the house and told my friend he must go with them the next day as a translator. My friend gave me a huge Red Cross badge and introduced me as the president of the Red Cross in Buda. He explained to the Russians that I had promised to go to Pest to get milk for the children in Buda, and that he must go with me in the morning. The Russians replied cheerfully that all of us would go together in a truck, over a Russian military bridge built outside the city. We made an appointment for 9:00 A.M.

Next morning the Russians were not to be found. We searched for them and at last found them — dead drunk. It took at least an hour before we succeeded in getting them into the truck. Finally, though the driver was still intoxicated, we miraculously arrived at Pest.

It was dangerous even to walk in the city, for the Russians continued to seize men on the street, and I felt ill and found it necessary to look for an accommodation to take a rest. By chance I went to see a friend who invited me to stay with him in a household typical of those days. The host could hardly move; he had been shot in the left foot by the Germans while escaping through their lines. His brother-in-law, a very young man, had been shot in the lung; the boy had gone to the garden to fetch some fresh snow, used instead of water during the siege, and German SS troops in the next house shot him simply for sport. A doctor living in the house took care of both of them. I had a high fever, and the doctor discovered that I had pneumonia, but fortunately he was able to procure sulfa medication — a rarity in those days. I stayed in bed for ten days, in rather serious condition.

There followed an unusual odyssey. While still convalescing I managed to obtain from the only government office in Pest the necessary official papers and recommendations to get me to Debrecen. I realized later that these papers were of no great value since the Soviet army did not respect documents issued by Hungarian authorities. Trucks were operated by the communist party, and the drivers took no interest in official papers. They were willing to take passengers, but only for a huge tip, which I was not able to afford. Three times a week there was an overcrowded train to Debrecen. By train the journey of about 120 miles took at that time from two to five days. It was necessary to change trains at least twice, and on these occasions the passengers were often taken by the Russians and put to work for a couple of days or seized as prisoners of war and taken to the Soviet Union.

The fate of civilians kidnapped as war prisoners depended on chance. When shipped by the trainload to Russia, some prisoners in desperation jumped out of the moving train or otherwise escaped. Sometimes goodhearted soldiers released Russian-speaking prisoners who described the agonies of their families. But the convoys had to hand over to the authorities at their destination a certain number of prisoners, so to make up for the losses the guards occasionally encircled railroad stations and picked up the necessary number of persons to replace the missing men. The train then continued on the journey to the USSR. It was merely accidental whether one was kidnapped as war prisoner. Sometimes Jews returning from Nazi concentration camps were intercepted and rerouted to Russia. A young man living in the neighborhood of a Budapest railroad station left his home to buy matches, and four months later his family received the first news of him from Archangel.

Such prospects were unappealing, but the situation in Pest was intolerable, and I had to risk the journey to Debrecen. Personal safety did not exist, and I was in bad shape after the pneumonia. I had lived for months chiefly on beans and potatoes and was very weak. In Debrecen more food was available, and I hoped to recover strength and be able to send food to my family. Together with a colleague from the Foreign Ministry, I succeeded in getting on a train. The colleague spoke Russian, and at that time such ability was a great advantage. Of course the train consisted only of freight cars. Everybody had to stand, and people were pressed together like sardines. The warmth of the human bodies made up for the lack of heat. For two days we traveled under these conditions, but after some narrow escapes from being taken prisoner of war, we reached Debrecen. I had started the journey weak from pneumonia and arrived emaciated and exhausted.

Meanwhile, a Russian-speaking friend proved a great help to my family in Budapest. Before leaving home I had given my wife my Omega wristwatch in hope that she might barter it for some basic foodstuffs. The Russian soldiers had an obsession with watches, and after the first wave of looting and confiscating, some of them specialized in valuable watches. I had saved this Omega by walking out of our dark shelter when the first Russian patrol demanded that all men deposit their watches in a weatherbeaten army cap. (On the street a wristwatch could be saved by hanging it on a long string in one's trousers.) My friend eventually succeeded in finding an Omega-collecting soldier who gave to my family about 100 pounds of fine white flour for my watch. The flour was a lifesaver, an almost un-believeable treasure in those days.

In Debrecen I got in touch with the new foreign minister, Gyöngyösi, and told him about the peace preparatory work done under the old regime. In the course of our conversation I reported that the bulk of the material had been deposited with the Hungarian legation in Bern, while a smaller portion was hidden in Buda. The foreign minister showed little interest in the matter. His lack of in-terest in all probability was due to mistrust of individuals who had served under the old regime. To some extent his apathy may have stemmed from the realization that to continue peace preparatory work in the face of the Soviet occupation was futile.

I did not make further efforts to see the country's new leaders, but was glad to receive my salary for the past five months and did my best to regain strength and send food to my family. In April 1945, I re-turned to Budapest, this time traveling under decent conditions on a special government train that took officials back to the capital. I did not begin to go regularly to the Foreign Ministry in Budapest until the end of May when I had to assume new responsibilities.

2

Postwar Hungary

Domestic Political Changes

Hungary's transformation into a republic occurred under unusual circumstances. With the German occupation in March 1944, the country lost its independence, and drastic changes occurred in domestic politics. The new government dissolved the labor unions and the opposition parties, like the Smallholders and Social Democrats. These parties continued political activities underground, and together with the illegal Communist and Peasant parties, formed the National Independence Front which became the structure of postwar politics in Hungary. The Citizen Democratic party and the Christian Democratic People's party were also admitted to the Independence Front, but the latter party was not allowed to play a political role.

In the autumn of 1944, the Red Army occupied eastern Hungary, and under the leadership of Mátyás Rákosi a group of Hungarian Communists arrived who had emigrated to Moscow after the failure of the Béla Kun regime in 1919. Members of this group, the so-called Muscovites, moving around in army cars in Soviet-occupied territories, picked up available leaders of the underground parties and took them to Debrecen. This group of hand-picked politicians convoked a Provisional National Assembly. In the larger villages and towns the quickly formed National Committees organized meetings which elected representatives by acclamation. The Provisional National Assembly consisted of 230 deputies, of whom 72 were Communists, 57 Smallholders, 35 Social Democrats, and 12 members of the Peasant party. The other deputies were without party affiliation or belonged to insignificant small parties. When the Germans were driven out of Hungary, and the government could move to Budapest in April 1945, the number of deputies in the Provisional National Assembly increased to 495. With support of the Social Democratic and trade union representatives the Communists had an absolute majority.

At the first session of the Assembly, on December 21, 1944, a leading Muscovite Communist, Ernő Gerő, emphasized that "the policy of the Communist Party is a Hungarian, democratic, and national policy." The next day the Assembly elected a provisional national government and authorized the new government to conclude an armistice with the Allied powers. The Muscovite Communists did their best to gain approval of the Hungarian public. The composition of the cabinet was an example. The Smallholders, Social Democrats, and the Communists each had two portfolios and the Peasant party one. Besides the seven party men, there were five non-party men in the cabinet. The prime minister, General Béla Dálnoki Miklós, was commander of the First Hungarian Army, and he went over to the Russians after Horthy's armistice proclamation on October 15, 1944. So did the minister of defense, General János Vörös. There was even a count in the cabinet, Géza Teleki, the son of the popular late prime minister, Pál Teleki, and a general of gendarmerie, Gábor Faraghó. A fifth non-party appointee, Erik Molnár, turned out to be a member of the Communist party. The apparent balance in the cabinet between the parties was offset by the fact that the Communists seized the effective power positions.

In the early postwar period the minuscule Communist party under Muscovite leadership advocated a coalition government, praised the principles of democracy, and preached the necessity of collaborating with the Catholic church. The Muscovites publicly extolled the bourgeois and peasant leaders of the coalition as progressive and reliable democrats who were entitled to share the leadership of the country.

The first important legislative act of the new regime was a radical agrarian reform, promulgated in March 1945 under the dictation of Marshal Klementy Voroshilov, chairman of the Allied Control Commission (ACC). An agrarian reform was long-overdue in Hungary, but this decree enacted many provisions with exclusively political objectives. The reform had two major goals: one was liquidation of the old landowner class, the other to win support of the landless peasantry and control over the whole agrarian population. Too-small allotments and the structure of the decree were designed to prove that private property cannot effectively operate in modern agriculture. The execution of the agrarian reform often went far beyond the provisions of the law. Excesses were facilitated by the Communist seizure of the police and the municipal administration. The minister of interior controlled domestic security, and this powerful portfolio was given to Ferenc Erdei, ostensibly a member of the Peasant party but actually owing allegiance to the Communists. Under his cloak and protection the Communists continued to organize the police all over the country. The political police became practically a branch of the Communist party and were supervised by the Soviet secret police.

The power of the police increased by the establishment of the People's Courts. This was one of the first institutions introduced in all countries under Soviet occupation. The activities of these courts contributed considerably to the creation of an atmosphere of fear, intimidation, and insecurity. The People's Courts were organized by decree in January 1945, at all the seats of courts of justice. Members were selected from a list prepared by the political parties which belonged to the National Independence Front. Later a decree authorized the Trade Union Council to appoint a member. Originally the People's Courts had arisen to judge war criminals, but later the various "conspiracy" and "sabotage" trials were staged before these packed courts. The police played an important role in preparation of these trials.

Communist seizure of municipal administration occurred at the outset of Soviet occupation through organization of National Committees in villages, towns, and counties. In theory, member parties of the National Independence Front and the trade unions were represented in these new administrative bodies. But in reality the committees were established almost everywhere by Communist emissaries who selected from all parties docile fellow travelers as members. From the very beginning of the new regime, the Communist-dominated National Committees handled all public affairs and the administration on the municipal level. The situation was particularly anomalous in the villages where the Communist party did not previously exist, the Social Democratic party had but a few members, if any, and the Peasant party just had begun to organize itself. The trade union membership meant everywhere the doubling of Communist representation. The population soon realized that through the National Committees they were being ruled by a new oligarchy of incompetent persons who were unknown or of dubious reputation. Since the peasants had bitterly complained, municipal elections were repeatedly promised but actually never held, except in Budapest.

The Communists were convinced that the working class districts of the capital would assure a sweeping victory of the united Communist-Socialist ticket. For this reason it was part of Communist tactics to have the Budapest municipal elections on October 7, 1945, a month before the general elections. But the outcome of elections was a shocking disappointment to the Communist brain trust, for the

Smallholders obtained an absolute majority of the votes in Budapest. Feverish Communist and Soviet activities followed the defeat. They proposed a single electoral ticket for the general elections; Voroshilov himself intervened and offered 47.5 percent, of the single electoral list to the Smallholders, who refused. The embittered Socialists also insisted on separate electoral lists because they attributed their defeat in Budapest to the anti-Communist feeling of the population. Instead of a single block ticket, the four parties agreed to continue the coalition government whatever the result of the elections might be. It was a surprise to the Communists and the Soviets that at the general elections held on November 4, 1945, the Communists polled only 17 percent, and the Smallholders 57 percent. Seats in Parliament were divided as follows: Smallholders, 245; Communists, 70; Socialists, 69; Peasant party, 21; Civic Democratic party, 2. Only political parties authorized by the ACC could participate in the elections.

Defeat of the Communists and the victory of the Smallholder party in the Budapest municipal elections and at the general elections caused a short-lived optimism in the country and abroad. Western newspapers published editorials on these elections and saw an indication "that even in the areas beyond Anglo-American control . . . the peoples of Europe can be given a chance to choose their own officials honestly and openly."[1]

After the elections Voroshilov was quick to point out to the Smallholder leaders that "the Soviet Union wished to base its friendship with Hungary on its relations with the Smallholders party."[2] The Smallholders were greatly pleased by this statement, and they visualized a new era of constructive Hungarian-Soviet cooperation. The Communists were flabbergasted because this defeat proved that they had not gained overwhelming support from the agrarian proletariat which had been their greatest hope. As a whole, however, the political situation was favorable for them. The coalition parties agreed that the minister of interior should be a member of the Smallholder party, but Voroshilov had vetoed the arrangement, and this important portfolio was given to the Communist party. The Smallholders obtained an imposing number of seats in the cabinet, but not the real power positions and had no majority. The prime minister, Zoltán Tildy, one minister of state, seven other members of the cabinet, the Speaker of the National Assembly, and later the president of the republic — all were Smallholders. The Communist and the Socialist parties each obtained three portfolios and the Peasant party one. The Communist and Socialist parties each had a deputy premiership.

The Smallholder electoral victory did not change the power of the Communists. They enjoyed the all-out support of the Soviets. An agreement of collaboration concluded with the Socialists in October 1944 provided for the merging of the two parties after the war. The same agreement provided for the immediate unification of the workers through the trade unions. When Charles Payer, the old leader of the Socialist party, was deported by the Germans, Árpád Szakasits assumed leadership. He was eager to accept Communist suggestions when he reorganized the party after the war. Left-wing Socialists were put into key positions, and the moderate Socialists were declared rightist deviationists and traitors of the unity of workers.

Under these conditions Communists obtained an absolute majority in all agencies established by the coalition parties. The delegates of the trade unions and of the Social Democratic party supported invariably the Communist position. Since the Peasant party was infiltrated by Communists, the Smallholder representative usually remained isolated. Russians and Communists controlled all mass media of communication, like radio, movies, and newspapers. First the Russians, later the Communists, allocated all newsprint. Publication of newspapers was authorized through a licensing system. At the outset only the Communist and Socialist parties, and later only political parties belonging to the coalition, could publish newspapers. Even so, Communists exercised strict control over all publications through the allocation of newsprint.

The first legislative act of the National Assembly declared Hungary a republic on January 31, 1946, and provisions of the new constitution corresponded to western standards of parliamentary democracies. Zoltán Tildy was elected president of the republic, and he appointed Ferenc Nagy, another leading Smallholder, as prime minister. Yet the freedoms guaranteed by the constitution became questionable when shortly afterward a law was promulgated to protect the democratic order of the republic. This law declared as criminal any statements which could be interpreted as contemptuous of the democratic state order or as harmful to the international prestige of the republic, whether the statements were true or false. And as the democratic order of the state gradually became identified with Communist tenets, this law began to be used against anyone who criticized Communist activities.

At the same time, the Communists, together with the Socialist and Peasant parties and the Trade Union Council, established a left-wing bloc and addressed ultimata to the Smallholders in the name of the progressive Hungarian people. Politicians opposing the leftist demands were denounced as "Fascists" and "enemies of the people." Communist-organized mass meetings, synchronized with Soviet political and economic demands, pressed the government toward a leftist policy.

The Smallholder party was maneuvered into a self-liquidating process which began in March 1946, with the expulsion of twenty-one deputies, attacked by the Communists as "reactionaries." This was a compromise measure, since the Communists had originally demanded the expulsion of eighty deputies. Simultaneous with Communist actions, strong Soviet pressure was exerted on the Hungarian government. In the coming months this action was followed by the adoption of various Soviet and Communist-dictated political and economic measures. But the Smallholders still kept parliamentary majority. The ousted Smallholder deputies remained members of parliament and certainly did not strengthen Communist voting power. Under the leadership of Dezső Sulyok, they formed a new opposition party which was later authorized by the ACC as the "Hungarian Freedom Party."

Subsequently the Smallholders took a stand against Communist abuses. Under the leadership of Béla Kovács, the secretary general of the Smallholder party, they launched a counteroffensive and, in June 1946, handed the Communist party a list enumerating their political demands. The most important among them were: proportional representation in the administration in general and in the political police in particular; municipal elections in the fall of 1946; abolition of the People's Courts and reestablishment of the jury system; abolition of the internments; and passage of an act by the Assembly concerning the trade unions and another act for representation of peasant interests.

In the course of interparty negotiations the Communists accepted, in principle, some of the Smallholders demands, such as their demand for municipal elections and a more adequate proportional representation in the administration and in the political police, upon condition that the Smallholders first liquidate all "reactionary" elements in their party. The Communists wanted to determine who was "reactionary" according to their doctrine and then compel the Smallholders to exclude them from political life. The practical result of the negotiations was the gradual release of a substantial number of persons from the internment camps and the reinstatement of a few dismissed civil servants. In speeches and articles, Smallholder leaders challenged the Communist party and advocated the fulfillment of the Smallholder demands. The Communists reacted violently.

Despite all the ominous signs, a strange optimism prevailed in the coalition parties. Some politicians believed that the Communist defeat in the free elections created for Hungary an exceptional position in Russian-occupied Europe. This seemed almost a miracle, and many people hoped that after the conclusion of peace and evacuation of Soviet forces, developments along genuine democratic lines would follow. It was an important fact that the non-Communist parties in the coalition were progressive on social, economic, and cultural questions, and the Communists adapted their tactics accordingly to the general mood of the country.[3] The coalition parties, during the Horthy regime, were all in opposition, and they cooperated to some extent with the Communists during the German occupation. As throughout Nazi-oppressed Europe, so in Hungary the common fight against the Nazi foe developed into a marriage of convenience, if not into a sort of camaraderie between the Communist and non-Communist politicians. The mere fact that Hungary survived a disastrous war seemed a promise for a better future, and the leading politicians of the new regime were determined to make the most of a desperate situation. This task called for courage and an optimistic outlook, especially in regard to the possibilities of cooperation with the Russians and Communists. Western representatives in 1943–1944, gave encouraging advice to Hungarians as to the possibility of such cooperation. In the postwar period there were no alternatives. Above all there was a great common task before the parties: the rebuilding and rehabilitation of the devastated country. In that respect the Communists displayed zeal and energy. They controlled the industrial work force through trade unions and factory committees. Rákosi told H.F.A. Schoenfeld, American minister to Hungary, that "strikes for the improvement of working conditions or higher wages were not permissible in Hungary; they were a luxury which only the American economy could afford."[4]

Non-Communist leaders "thought it natural that the Communist Party should be more radical than other parties, but expected it would work shoulder to shoulder with the others in reviving the country."[5] Largely because of apparent Communist moderation during the prelude of the postwar Hungarian drama, the opinion of some foreign observers was even more optimistic. For instance, Oscar Jaszi, an American professor, who in 1918 was a member of Mihály Károlyi's cabinet, rejected the suggestion that "what is taking place in Hungary is simply a repetition of what has occurred in the Baltic states, in Bulgaria, Rumania, and Yugoslavia."[6] He characterized the Hungarian situation in the following manner:

> The old demagogy of the first Bolshevik revolution was completely absent; Communism had become respectable and gentlemenly. Even the criticism of certain Governmental measures by the Roman Catholic hierarchy was listened to with respect, and when Archbishop Mindszenty attacked the expropriation of the estates as a "product of hatred," the rejoinder was moderate and tactful. Though the large ecclesiastical estates were dismembered like the others, liberal grants-in-aid were provided for the maintenance of the lower clergy, the Churches and parochial buildings. Generally speaking, there is not much talk about Communism in Hungary today; the leitmotiv is democracy with intensely patriotic overtones.[7]

It took some time to realize that this optimistic view was not justified. It became clear that in decisive questions the Muscovites did nothing but carry out the orders of the Russians, and that the Communist party was, in reality, a disguised branch of the Soviet administration represented in Hungary outwardly by the Soviet army, Soviet officials, and the ACC. In addition to Soviet support, the Muscovites had two other advantages. One was a concrete program — the Leninist-Stalinist blueprint of conquest applied to the Hungarian situation. The other was the disregard of moral and political ethics in carrying out their plans. The Muscovites did not feel any obligation to keep promises but were outraged if others did not abide strictly by agreements or act according to expectations. They were proud of the political "know-how" learnt in the Soviet Union, but these methods would not have worked without Soviet intervention and the presence of the Red Army. In all phases of Hungarian politics, energetic Soviet actions helped Communist initiatives. If the Hungarian government was not responsive to Communist suggestions, there quickly followed threats, ultimata, and the use of sheer force. The methods by which Hungary's political structure was manipulated and transformed were repeatedly admitted and proudly praised by leading Communists. Joseph Révai pointed out retrospectively:

> We were a minority in Parliament and in the government, but at the same time we represented the leading force. We had decisive control over the police forces. Our force, the force of our Party and working class, was multiplied by the fact that the Soviet Union and the Soviet army were always there to support us with their assistance.[8]

Rákosi said more explicitly that it was "the imperishable merit and the support of the Soviet Union that tipped the scales" and helped to establish the Hungarian People's Democracy. He pointed out that the presence of the Soviet army in Hungary precluded any attempt at armed rebellion, and protected the country "from imperialistic intervention."

Notwithstanding many difficulties and odds, political life in postwar Hungary was rich in potential democratic leadership. A correspondent of the London *Times* noted (October 16, 1946) that a visitor in Hungary "will be surprised by the vigorous intellectual activity displayed both in print and in conversation. In comparison with the mental sterility and haunting fear prevalent in the Balkans, Hungary seems an oasis of culture and liberty."

The great issues were settled by external and not by internal forces. Hungarian democracy would have developed on sound lines and would have restricted Communist influence to due proportions—if a free political evolution could have taken place. The decisive factors in Hungary were not the shrewd Communist leaders but the occupying Soviet army, Soviet domination in the Allied Control Commission, the proximity of the Soviet Union, and the lack of Western assertiveness.

Armistice and Soviet Policy

The armistice agreement contained military, political, economic, and financial obligations, and reduced Hungarian sovereignty to a minimum. It established an Allied Control Commission; its chairman was Marshal Klementy Voroshilov whose political adviser was Georgij Pushkin, a diplomat. Hungarian authorities were to carry out the orders and instructions issued by the Soviet High Command or the ACC. Voroshilov, commander of the Soviet army in Hungary, or his deputy acted in the name of both. The ACC had American and British sections as well, but for all practical purposes it was run exclusively by the Soviets; they freely intervened in Hungary's domestic and foreign affairs. In the entire armistice period the Soviet technique in Hungary was to act in the name of the three major Allies while keeping Britain and the United States from meaningful participation. Article 18 of the armistice agreement stated:

> For the whole period of the armistice there will be established in Hungary an Allied Control Commission which will regulate and

supervise the execution of the armistice terms under the chairmanship of the representative of the Allied (Soviet) High Command and with the participation of representatives of the United Kingdom and the United States.

During the period between the coming into force of the armistice and the conclusion of hostilities against Germany, the Allied Control Commission will be under the general direction of the Allied (Soviet) High Command.

While Article 18 of the Bulgarian and Hungarian armistice agreements provided for Soviet chairmanship until the conclusion of hostilities against Germany, the earlier-concluded Rumanian armistice provided for Soviet control until the conclusion of peace and did not mention explicitly British and American participation.

At the outset, the American military mission believed that the provision for their participation in the execution of the armistice terms meant taking part in the work of the ACC. Colonel Dallas S. Townsend, the deputy commander of the American military mission in Budapest, prepared an elaborate plan for the operation of the ACC. As he described it to me in a letter of May 1955 (at that time he was assistant attorney general), the first and perhaps most important feature of this plan was

> the establishment of a Secretariat, which would have the function, and be charged with the duty, *inter alia*, of receiving and translating all incoming and outgoing communications, furnishing copies to each Mission; and of authenticating and formalizing documents, maintaining liaison with other Missions not directly represented in the ACC, such as the French and the Czech, and so on. Upon the submission of our plan Marshall Voroshilov commented that the Agreement said nothing about a Secretariat, a comment which had the merit of brevity, if not of profundity, and that was the beginning and the end of our plan . . .

After rejection of this plan the American military mission asked for copies of all communications the ACC received from the provisional government, and Townsend noted in his letter:

> We were informed there were no communications from the Provisional Government to the ACC. Of course this was absurd. Moreover, from our own Intelligence sources we received copies of notes from the Provisional Government to the Commission. On one occasion we had a copy of a note that had been submitted by the Hungarians to the Russians and had been returned with marginal notations by the very Soviet officer who told me there was no such note. Of course I did not

tell him that I had a copy of it; that would only have led to trouble and would have accomplished nothing except perhaps the tracking down and execution of my informant.

In view of the end of hostilities against Germany, the Potsdam Conference agreed on a greater participation of the British and American missions in the work of the ACC in the three Danubian countries, but in reality only cosmetic changes took place. Control commissions remained under Russian domination throughout their existence. For example, General V.P. Sviridov, deputy chairman of the ACC in Hungary, without consulting or informing the American and British representatives, dissolved certain Catholic youth organizations in June–July 1946, and he recommended dismissal of some government officials. Instructions were issued by the Soviet High Command regarding the size and organization of the Hungarian army, without consulting Western representatives. The chairman of the ACC refused the American members permission to visit Hungarian army units and free movement in the country. In short, the Soviet chairman consistently acted unilaterally in the name of the ACC, without consultation with, or notice to, the American and British representatives. Even a semblance of effective participation in the work of the ACC was denied to them. Sometimes the Soviet chairman simply stated that the matter was not within the jurisdiction of the ACC and must be referred to Moscow.

The argument that in this exclusion of the Western Allies from the business of the ACC in Hungary, Rumania, and Bulgaria, the Soviets followed the precedent set in Italy, is not without foundation.[9] In Italy, the Soviets had membership only on an advisory council, which in fact did little. It was a joint Anglo-American agency, and the Soviets resented their exclusion. Legalistically the arrangements were comparable: one side ran the show and the other merely observed, although the institutions were not quite parallel. But in substance the role of the ACC was entirely different in Italy than in the Danubian states. The Western powers did not abuse the provisions of the armistice agreement. Italy had no reason to complain about the behavior of her liberators. She was not looted or otherwise abused by the Anglo-Americans but was in fact greatly assisted in her rehabilitation. As early as January 1945, the political section of the ACC in Italy was abolished, and in the following two years the remaining sections of the commission fulfilled only an advisory function. While the Allied powers did not restrict the activities of the Communist party in Italy, the ACC in the Danubian states brought ruthless pressure on the governments and, closely cooperating with the local Communist parties, engineered the political transformation of these countries.

The political advisers to the ACC were not accredited to the Hungarian government. An American representative with the personal rank of minister, H. F. Arthur Schoenfeld, arrived in Budapest in May 1945. He functioned as the representative in Hungary for the general protection of American interests in addition to, and separate from, the ACC. He maintained informal contacts with the provisional Hungarian authorities.

At the first meeting of the Council of Foreign Ministers, in September 1945, Secretary Byrnes declared that the United States would not sign treaties with the unrepresentative governments of Rumania and Bulgaria, but was ready to recognize the government of Hungary on receipt of a pledge of free elections. This move clearly aimed at strengthening non-Communist elements in the Hungarian coalition. Molotov countered by immediate and unconditional recognition of the Hungarian government. Thus the American and Soviet missions were changed to legations, and the American and Soviet diplomatic representatives to the ACC presented their credentials to the Hungarian government as plenipotentiary ministers. Britain was not willing to reestablish regular diplomatic relations with Hungary — a country still technically at war with the Allied powers — and appointed as British political representative to Hungary the British political adviser to the ACC, Alvary D. F. Gascoigne.

Renewal of diplomatic relations with Hungary did not strengthen the position of the British and American representatives in the ACC. In the course of the execution of the armistice agreement the Russians committed many abuses, notably in enforcing their interpretation of "democracy" and "fascism." They had a wide choice of means in exerting pressure on Hungarian authorities. Personal liberty, as well as the daily bread of the population, and most of the necessities of life, depended on them.

One of the terrifying actions of the Red Army was the deportation of civilians. First, it was supposed that the largest number of civilians were taken as prisoners of war after the siege of Budapest. But later requests pouring in by the thousands into the Foreign Ministry from most parts of Hungary made it evident that the same practice was followed all over the country. This procedure was particularly cruel in east Hungary, where, in communities inhabited by people of German origin, the entire adult population of many villages, men and women alike, were taken into the Soviet Union. In other parts of the

country Soviet military practice usually disregarded political affiliation, social position, or ethnic origin of captured people. They simply
needed a certain number of prisoners, and anybody was good enough
to fill the quota.

Deportation of politicians and other public figures happened without publicity or accusation of any sort. They were simply rounded up.
This procedure of elimination was a warning to all persons in public
life. Among those who suffered this fate was Count István Bethlen,
prime minister of Hungary between 1921 and 1931. He denounced
Nazi ideas and anti-Jewish laws and in the Crown Council advocated
armistice negotiations with the Soviet Union. A strongly anti-Nazi
publicist, Iván Lajos, was taken by the Germans to Mauthausen.
Upon his return after the war he was one of the advocates of cooperation of the Danubian peoples. One day he informed me, enthusiastically, that he had discussed the various possibilities of Danubian
cooperation with a Soviet captain who showed much interest. Shortly
thereafter he disappeared. This too was the fate of Raoul Wallenberg,
the courageous Swedish diplomat who saved thousands of lives during the deportations of Jews from Hungary. The Russians abducted
him while attempting to return to Sweden.

The mass deportation of civilians and selected politicians was but
one of the initial means to frighten the population into conformity
with Soviet wishes. At first it was difficult to understand the apparently senseless Soviet behavior, which seemed harmful even to the
Communist cause. After a while, it became obvious that behind
these actions there had been an over-all plan. Abuses and atrocities
were carried out to frighten the population and to weaken its moral
and economic resistance. The Soviets did not care for popularity.
They wanted servile submission; they preferred to be feared rather
than loved. The abuses of the Red Army made the Russians and
Communists unpopular but at the same time created a feeling of
helplessness in all social classes. The creation of an atmosphere of
fear and absolute personal insecurity was a necessary precondition
for subsequent Soviet political actions supporting the Hungarian
Communists.

One of the tasks of the newly organized Foreign Ministry was intervention with the Soviet authorities on behalf of civilians taken as
war prisoners. This action began in Debrecen as early as March 1945
as part of the activities of the political division of the Foreign
Ministry. A few weeks later when the ministry moved to Budapest,
it became necessary to organize a special division for the prisoner of
war cases. This division dealt mainly with requests for intervention

from the relatives of deported civilians. In a few weeks tens of thousands of cases were registered in the files of the ministry. In such cases routine iterventions were made with the Soviet authorities. They paid no attention to them.

Because of the practical exclusion of the British and Americans from the business of the ACC, the Hungarians had no forum whatever to deal with Soviet violations and abuses of the armistice agreement. Hungarian sovereignty was reduced to a minimum. The diplomatic representatives of neutral powers were expelled at the outset of Soviet occupation. The country was isolated. The government could not renew diplomatic relations without permission of the ACC. This permission was in some cases delayed, in others refused. Usually the ACC did not even acknowledge these or any other notes. All travels abroad needed Soviet permission. Although Gyöngyösi followed a policy of strict cooperation with the Soviet Union, the ACC seldom used the Foreign Ministry as a channel of communication with Hungarian authorities but intervened directly with various government agencies. The Foreign Ministry was informed later—if at all—through the Hungarian authorities of various Soviet demands and interventions. This practice made an integrated Hungarian policy toward the ACC and Red Army impossible. If the Foreign Ministry gave an unsatisfactory answer to a certain demand, they simply addressed the same demand to the prime minister or another government agency.

Soviet Economic Stranglehold

It would be impossible to appraise Hungary's enormous difficulties in the armistice period without considering what the Soviet occupation was doing to Hungary's economy. Without such understanding it would be difficult to comprehend why political and diplomatic questions were settled as they were. One of the fundamental problems in the armistice period was the fact that the Soviets were exploiting Hungary. At the same time the government's pressing task was to provide for the physical survival of the people. This situation gave the Soviets effective means for applying pressure.

The Soviets took the old principle of *la guerre doit nourrir la guerre* seriously, and the Red Army lived off the land. Besides carrying the legal burden of the armistice obligations, Hungary suffered through illegal seizures and large-scale looting. The Red Army seized a substantial part of Hungary's livestock, food supplies, means of transportation, currency, and industrial equipment. Safe-deposit boxes were forced open and their contents removed. Private homes, public warehouses, stores, government agencies, and banks were looted in the same way. Nor were the legations of neutral powers spared. The armistice agreement authorized the Red Army to issue currency to be redeemed by the Hungarian government, and the Soviet High Command was entitled to demand payments from the Hungarian government to cover the expenses of the occupation. The government had no money or any other means of meeting these and other financial obligations, including the expenditures of the ACC. Bank notes seized in financial institutions were given as a loan to the Hungarian government.

Desperate economic conditions notwithstanding, Hungary in 1945 had to begin reparation deliveries. The armistice agreement obliged the country over a period of six years to deliver commodities worth $200 million to the Soviet Union and $100 million to Yugoslavia and Czechoslovakia. The economic agreement between the USSR and the provisional Hungarian government pertained to the fulfillment of this obligation. This agreement, signed in June 1945 under Soviet threats, provided for deliveries of industrial equipment, vessels, grain, livestock, and other articles, to be made in equal installments annually during the period from January 20, 1945 through January 20, 1951. The Soviet dictated bilateral agreement defined the prices of the commodities and the conditions of delivery in such a way that it doubled and in some cases tripled the original amount of reparations. There was a five percent monthly penalty for delayed deliveries.

At the Paris Conference Molotov submitted an amendment which extended the delivery time from six years to eight years, as Stalin promised to the Hungarian government delegation in April 1946. But an American proposal for the reduction of the reparation to be paid by Hungary from $300 million to $200 million was rejected at the Paris Conference.[10]

The cost of the ACC and the occupation, added to the reparation burden, totaled some 60 percent of the state expenditure during the last four months of 1945 and amounted to almost 40 percent of the total expenditures during the first half of 1946. The Soviets received large deliveries of manufactured goods; they paid nothing for them, but the workmen who produced the goods and the supplies of raw materials had to be paid. Skyrocketing wages fomented inflation.

In the postwar months it was impossible to proceed with the assessment and collection of taxes. Enterprises and most private persons were looted and many factories dismantled; consequently, economic activity was slow to revive. Securing the necessary money for public administration, rehabilitation of factories, occupation costs, and reparation deliveries was mainly a problem of printing bank notes. As a result, Hungary experienced a record inflation which completely disintegrated its economic system. People bartered their belongings for subsistence. Stabilization was carried out with the help of the gold reserves of the Hungarian National Bank, returned to the Hungarian government by the American authorities. This gold reserve, taken into Germany by officials of the Hungarian National Bank in late 1944, rendered a great service to the country. Had it remained in Hungary, the Red Army would have seized it as war booty, according to its consistent practice. On August 1, 1946, the forint replaced the pengő as the new monetary unit. One forint was equivalent to 400,000 quadrillion pengős (30 zeros).

Under Soviet pressure Hungary was compelled to conclude an economic cooperation agreement with the USSR for five years.[11] Despite catastrophic economic conditions, the ACC and the Soviet government refused to consider reiterated American proposals aiming at inter-Allied assistance for Hungary. Moscow claimed that the working out of such a plan belonged exclusively to competence of the Hungarian government.[12]

The Soviet interpretation of the Potsdam Agreement opened further possibilities for the conquest of the Hungarian economy. The Potsdam Conference granted to the Soviet Union the undefined category of "German assets" in Hungary as reparations, and the Soviets considered as German assets all properties and rights seized by the Germans during the occupation; they claimed that they had acquired only the net assets and credits, without any debts or liabilities whatsoever. All liabilities were left to the non-Soviet part-owners and creditors. Moscow demanded from Hungary $240 million as equivalent to certain German claims in Hungary, whereas the much larger German debts to Hungary were considered null and void. After protracted negotiations the Soviets settled this part of their Potsdam claims for a lump sum of $45 million, together with certain concessions and privileges for Soviet-controlled enterprises in Hungary.

The combination of the Potsdam Agreement and the economic cooperation agreement assured a practically free hand to Russia in the Hungarian economy. Under these circumstances Hungary agreed to establish joint companies, with theoretically equal Soviet-Hungarian participation but actually under Soviet control. The manager in charge of the operation of each company invariably was a Soviet citizen. The Hungarian chairman was a mere front. Through these joint companies the Soviet Union controlled Hungarian aviation, river transportation, crude oil and petroleum-refining industries, the bauxite industry, and other connected industries and enterprises. In addition to the joint stock corporations, exclusively or overwhelmingly Soviet-owned enterprises were created with the help of the former German interests in the various industrial, commercial, and financial companies.[13]

In addition to such various devices, the shrewd use of Hungarian-Soviet trade agreements diverted Hungarian goods from their usual markets and made commerce difficult with the West. Through the trade agreements Moscow arbitrarily determined the prices of both raw materials and finished products. Thus, during the armistice period the Hungarian economy was prepared for further integration with the USSR.

Diplomatic Interaction of East and West

Contacts between Russians and the Americans and British in Hungary were only a small segment of their larger relationships. When representatives of the United States and Britain arrived in Hungary, they clearly based their policy on Allied unity and avoided taking a stand on any delicate political issue which might have antagonized the Soviets. Western policy was influenced by the military and political situation. At that time the English-speaking powers were still fighting the war, with the Soviets as allies, and were building, together with them, a new security organization on which the Western hopes for future peace and cooperation were based. Soviet military intervention against Japan was considered necessary. The Western powers were trying to work out ways of dealing with the liberated areas which would respect the rights of the poeples of these areas and also preserve the unity of the great powers. A few British and American statesmen and diplomats were skeptical during the whole period. Nevertheless, the leaders of American and British foreign policy decided that under the circumstances the attempt had to be made.

At the outset American and British goodwill toward Hungary was displayed mainly in the form of advice and friendly gestures, but there also were the humanitarian gifts badly needed in the impoverished country. One of the first American moves was a considerable gift of medicine to the Hungarian Red Cross. Later the United States granted loans totaling $30,000,000 for the purchase of surplus property.[14] UNRRA relief supplies were sent to Hungary at a value of over four million dollars.

Secretary Byrnes noted in his memoirs that his action at the Moscow Conference in December 1945 still stemmed from the hope that "the Soviet Union and the United States had a common purpose."[15] But Soviet reluctance to evacuate northern Iran, and Stalin's emphasis on rearmament in his speech on February 9, 1946, brought about in Washington a firmer attitude toward Moscow. When Soviet bad faith became altogether too conspicuous, American policy slowly underwent a change, and the American protests increased in number, became stronger in tone, and embraced a variety of political and economic problems. Schoenfeld's reports to Washington and the State Deparment's instructions to him in 1945–47,[16] reflected a more assertive American attitude as time went on.

British and American interest in Hungary was significant since it was the only Soviet-occupied country in which free elections took place and a coalition government survived. The Western powers welcomed the natural inclination of the Smallholder politicians to cooperate with the Western democracies and, in some cases, encouraged them to resist Communist demands and disregard the ruling of the ACC and Soviet policy. Requests for an official Hungarian memorandum on the country's economic plight and for landing rights of American aircraft in Hungary were cases in point.

The British and American missions consulted Hungarian economists and, in some instances, received privately copies of Hungarian memoranda addressed to the ACC on the country's economic conditions. Arthur Kárász, president of the Hungarian National Bank prepared a confidential memorandum to the British and American missions on the magnitude of the reparations burden and other factors which disintegrated the economy.[17] As a result the Western powers possessed the data proving Hungary's catastrophic economic situation, and the American notes which proposed tripartite examination of Hungary's economy used realistic figures, but the Soviets denied their accuracy. Washington and London assumed that they could argue more forcefully in Moscow if the Hungarian government would send them an official note on the country's economic conditions. When I visited the British representative, Gascoigne, in early 1946, he emphasized the importance of a direct communication from the Hungarian government to Britain on the country's economic plight and asked to express to the foreign minister their desire for an official note. I informed Gyöngyösi and returned to Gascoigne with his answer, suggesting that the annulment of the pertinent ACC ruling—

which banned such communication[18] — should precede the Hungarian note. When I gave this negative message to Gascoigne, he almost lost his temper.

The American legation in Budapest requested similar information, and in June 1946, Acting Secretary of State Dean Acheson brought up the question to Prime Minister Nagy and complained that information had not been furnished on Hungary's economic conditions. Nagy replied that the Hungarian government was precluded to give such information by regulations issued by the ACC. The Americans promised to approach the ACC again in this matter.

The British and Americans might have scored a diplomatic point in Moscow with a Hungarian note, but the Soviets would have continued to deny the facts and would have retaliated in Hungary for violation of ACC rules. In such cases Western intervention with the ACC proved ineffective, and Western diplomatic steps in Moscow would not have changed the Kremlin's policy.

The case of landing rights for American aircraft in Hungary was a more complicated affair. In February 1946 I was asked to go over to the American legation, where I met a group of diplomats, including Francis Deak, the American civil air attaché for Central Europe. He came from his headquarters in Bern, Switzerland and explained that the United States would like to obtain landing rights in Hungary for Pan American planes flying from Vienna through Budapest and Belgrade to the Middle East. He asked me to inform the foreign minister and, in case of favorable reaction, they would be interested in the size and facilities of the airports near Budapest.

Gyöngyösi and other cabinet members, including Gerö, the minister of commerce and transportation, welcomed the idea of Hungary's participation in international air traffic. The American legation dispatched a note to the Foreign Ministry requesting landing rights. A Hungarian reply informed Schoenfeld that the government was prepared to consider favorably the landing rights for American aircraft and would be willing to begin technical negotiations, but during the armistice period was in no position to grant air traffic rights.

In early March, Deak visited Prime Minister Nagy who pointed out that the request for landing rights was the first indication of affirmative American interest in Hungary. He claimed that current negotiations with the Soviets for a civil aviation agreement would have taken a different course if the American proposal had been received sooner. Nagy stated that he and most members of his cabinet "will do everything in their power to render passage of designated United States air carrier through Hungary possible."[19]

Meanwhile the Hungarian-Soviet negotiations led to the conclusion of a civil aviation agreement on March 29. An American note to the Hungarian government pointed out that the agreement provided for the establishment of a jointly owned Hungarian-Soviet civil air transport company to participate in domestic international air traffic, and a protocol signed on the same day granted landing and operational rights on and over Hungarian territory to the civil air fleet of the Soviet Union without reciprocity. The American note remarked that the civil aviation agreement with the Soviet Union showed that the armistice regime did "not preclude the making of interim commercial agreements between Hungary and the governments represented on the ACC for Hungary."[20]

Since all airfields in Hungary were in Soviet hands, Gyöngyösi informed Pushkin of the American request and the positive Hungarian reaction. The Soviet envoy blew his top, saying that the Americans have military purpose in mind with flights over Hungary, and vetoed any favorable Hungarian decision. The foreign minister instructed me to visit Schoenfeld to explain our predicament, and the American envoy reported to Washington my communication as follows:

> Kertesz of FOROFF told me today FORMIN desired me to know privately and unofficially that Russians are taking very stiff opposition line re operational landing rights for American aircraft. Pushkin argues that inasmuch as it is unthinkable that Soviet aircraft would be granted such rights in American Zone in Germany or in Italy and since Russian aircraft have allegedly been shot down in American Zone, Soviet Government is not willing to permit aircraft to fly (presumably without Russian clearance in each case) in any zone under Soviet control. Pushkin reportedly added that American aircraft would not be permitted to fly operationally in areas such as Hungary within five hours flying time of Moscow.

Exchange of notes about landing rights continued between the American legation and the Foreign Ministry.[21] Schoenfeld, in his report of June 6, suggested that during the visit of the Hungarian government delegation in Washington, the State Department emphasize American disappointment because of "denial of landing rights for American aircraft while we have refrained from pressing claims affecting American property and Hungarian obligations with reference thereto." Consequently, Acheson brought up the question to the Hungarian government delegation in June 1946[22] and the debate about landing rights continued. In this controversy the American negotiators assumed as a matter of course that the Soviet evacuation of Hungary was only a question of time.

An aspect of Anglo-American policy in 1946 was to blame the Hungarian government for concessions made under Soviet-supported Communist pressure and to encourage Hungarians to resist. Ambassador Harriman's report from London on May 3, 1946, reminded that

> late in March United States and British Governments instructed their representatives in Budapest that, if their opinions were sought, they might inform members of Hungarian Government that view of our two governments is that policy of maintaining coalition at all costs was of questionable wisdom and that continued concessions to a minority group would only end in the negation of people's mandate expressed at recent elections.

In the same report Harriman noted that the British are not in a position to offer to Prime Minister Nagy concrete assistance but are "in favor of doing anything possible to show interest in a real democratic regime and to encourage Smallholders to stand up to Communist minority."[23] In line with this policy Gascoigne pointed out time and again the shortcomings of Hungarian democracy, such as the lack of freedom of speech and guarantees of personal liberties and the abuses of the political police. Such preaching by the British representative to Smallholder leaders was not helpful because the Hungarian authorities had no power to improve the conditions he deplored. It was like condemning rape to people who were actual or potential victims of rape.

The Smallholders were not afraid to stand up to the Communist party, but they had experiences with the Soviets who supported the Communists to the hilt and orchestrated their moves. Western diplomats understood intellectually Hungary's predicament, but because of their own frustrations they were inclined to put more blame on the leaders of the majority party than was justified. It was one thing to evaluate from the shelter of a diplomatic mission the Soviet and Communist abuses and the weaknesses of the Smallholder party and quite another to face the Soviet music not only as individuals but as the representatives of a downtrodden people. Schoenfeld was pessimistic in the autumn of 1945 about the possibility of free elections in Hungary. After the electoral defeat of Communists and victory of Smallholders, he overlooked the fact that in Soviet-ruled Hungary the parliamentary majority did not mean an increase of actual power. He and Gascoigne encouraged the Smallholder leaders to stand up and be counted but could not give effective assistance in crisis.

Not only foreign diplomats entertained unrealistic expectations. Some Hungarians, including myself, disagreed with the policy of concessions and suggested that the majority party must draw the line and reject further demands. Although this was not done, and Rákosi's "salami tactic" was slicing the majority party, retrospectively I believe that there was an instinctive shrewdness in the compliant policy of the Smallholder leaders. *Qui habet tempus, habet vitam.* They played for time in the hope that after the conclusion of peace Hungary would regain its sovereignty, the majority in parliament prevail, and true democracy develop. In case of an all-out Smallholder resistance to Soviet-supported Communist demands in 1946, a coup might have taken place much earlier than it did. Western verbal encouragement could not balance the Soviet military and political advantages which constituted the muscle of the Communist party.

The situation was complicated by misunderstandings about the meaning of the Yalta Declaration on Liberated Europe, publicized in Hungary after the Soviet occupation. Many Hungarians were convinced that the three major powers made a pledge to them for free elections and a government responsive to the will of the people. In reality the Yalta Agreement was a diplomatic instrument and a policy declaration by the Big Three. Britain and the United States did not violate the pledge, and although they protested Soviet violations, they did not contemplate further steps. The average Hungarian, however, did not think in terms of legal niceties and diplomatic formulas and assumed that the Western powers were obligated to carry out the pledge even against Soviet opposition. Some people speculated that the British and Americans eventually would vote down the USSR in the ACC. The picture was further confused because the Soviet chairman of the ACC acted in the name of the British and Americans as well.

One of the public figures who overrated British and American power in Hungary was József Cardinal Mindszenty, Archbishop of Esztergom and Primate of Hungary. I briefed him regularly about the persecution of Hungarians in Slovakia, part of which used to belong to his archdiocese. In turn he informed me of the steps he took or contemplated to take through ecclesiastical channels on behalf of the persecuted people. In view of his antagonistic relations with the government, the foreign minister suggested that I meet the cardinal secretly. I did not follow his advice; there were no secrets in postwar Hungary. The political police would have known of a "secret" meeting within hours. When I visited the cardinal in Esztergom, I did it as publicly as possible: I took one of the Foreign Ministry's automobiles, flying Hungarian colors, and a driver—probably a police agent.[24] As I have known Mindszenty since the early 1920's, he talked

freely with me and on one occasion told me he had sent memoranda
and letters to the British and American missions and asked me to
ascertain if they had received them. I did so and found the British
and Americans perplexed; they did not know what to do with the cardinal's requests. Eventually, the American minister Schoenfeld replied on December 27, 1946, and stated:

> It is noted that your letters of December 12 and December 18
> touching on internal political problems of Hungary, requested the
> assistance of the United States Government in altering certain condi-
> tions which your Eminence deplores. In this connection you are of
> course aware of my Government's long standing policy of non-
> interference in the internal affairs of other nations. This policy has
> proven over a long period of time and through many trying situations
> the best guarantee of spontaneous, vigorous and genuine democratic
> development. It will be clear to Your Eminence that it necessarily
> precludes action by this Legation which could properly be construed
> as interference in Hungarian domestic affairs or which lies outside the
> normal functions of diplomatic missions.[25]

Mindszenty was not the only one who misunderstood the role of
the Western powers in Hungary. Since the United States was the
strongest world power at the close of hostilities, some Hungarians were
convinced that American strength would prevail diplomatically along
the Danube sooner or later. In this spirit, some politicians thought it
appropriate to ask for American support in connection with the rights
pledged at Yalta. On these occasions the American attitude was most
reserved. As Schoenfeld put it, Western representatives

> were frequently sounded out as to how much help they would provide
> to the non-Communist political groups. When our invariable reply
> was that American diplomatic practice excluded the possibility of such
> interference in the internal political affairs of foreign countries, there
> was bewilderment at what seemed so unrealistic an attitude compared
> with that of the Russians.

Western diplomats, of course, were aware of Soviet violations of
solemn agreements which affected the domestic affairs of Hungary,
and the Western governments lodged protests in important cases.
The United States invoked in notes addressed to Moscow the joint
responsibility of the three victorious powers established by the Yalta
Agreement and reaffirmed by the Potsdam Conference. Although
the futility of diplomacy by protest notes was clear, London and Washington did not plan any other action. Under these circumstances
Schoenfeld's invocation of the doctrine of non-interference in domes-

tic affairs served as an appropriate diplomatic formula to camouflage the impotence of the Western powers in Russia's Europe. It was a curious coincidence that the Soviet government used a similar argument when it refused to participate in the tripartite undertaking in Hungary proposed by the United States on the basis of the Yalta Agreement. Thus, both East and West in the Aesopian language of diplomacy emphasized the sovereignty of powerless Hungary, though the reasons and purposes of such verbalizations were quite different. The wartime strategy and policy of the Allied powers determined the fate of Danubian Europe. The will of the Hungarian people expressed at free elections in the autumn of 1945 could not change the inexorable course of events.

3

The Great Powers: 1939–1945

The democratic states were quite unprepared for the Second World War when that great conflict began in 1939, and they struggled for years thereafter to bring their military forces up to a level of readiness sufficient for victory. After Pearl Harbor, the concern of President Franklin D. Roosevelt was to mobilize the country's economy, to build ships, and to train a huge army for battle in the Pacific and in Europe. Meanwhile it was necessary to support Britain and Russia through Lend-Lease and to foster their fighting spirit, for the loss of either country from the Allied coalition would have postponed victory into an uncertain future. At the outset of Nazi Germany's campaign in Russia, in the summer of 1941, most of the general staffs in Europe and the leading American generals, estimated that the Soviet army would collapse in a matter of weeks or months. It was imperative to promise aid to Russia and to give as much immediately as was possible; this fact became even more obvious after the sudden Japanese attack upon the Pacific Fleet, followed within days by German and Italian declarations of war upon the United States. American entrance into the war automatically created a de facto alliance between the United States and the Soviet Union.

The goal of the Big Three was to defeat the Axis powers and destroy the Nazi and Fascist political systems. Otherwise, their aspirations and expectations for the postwar era were quite different, if not contradictory. Prime Minister Winston S. Churchill desired to preserve the British Empire, to keep open the world's sea lanes for the British navy, and to maintain a balance of power in Europe so as to limit Soviet expansion. These were reasons for his Mediterranean strategy, for British diplomatic support given to France to regain Great Power status, and for eventual British opposition to dismemberment of Germany. Premier Joseph V. Stalin was not bashful about expressing territorial goals in Europe and the Far East, in accord with centuries-old Russian expansionist policy. The United States wanted to defeat the enemy as rapidly as possible and bring back the American forces from foreign lands. Unlike the European Great Powers, the United States did not have a tradition of continuous participation in world affairs. The American hope was that in the postwar era the victorious Allied powers would cooperate in a world organization for the benefit of mankind.

While Britain and the Soviet Union followed traditional foreign policy practices during the war, such was not the case in the United States. Roosevelt was his own secretary of state, and he often made important decisions without consulting or even informing the Department of State. Although the president appreciated Secretary of State Cordell Hull's authority, especially with the Senate, he preferred to discuss foreign policy questions with Undersecretary of State Sumner Welles, who resigned in August 1943. According to Welles, Roosevelt harbored a "deep-rooted prejudice against the members of the American Foreign Service and against the permanent officials of the Department of State."[1] At the Cairo conference with Chiang Kai-shek and at Yalta, the president had no expert on Far Eastern affairs at his side, and American diplomats trained in the 1920s to deal with Russian affairs did not participate in formulation of foreign policy toward the USSR. Roosevelt's far-reaching decision was that military considerations should prevail during the period of hostilities and that political and territorial questions should be postponed to the peace conference. It is true that without military victory political ideas usually do not prevail, no matter how wise, but Roosevelt's approach gave the military a role for which their training did not prepare them. During the last stage of the war spectacular Western military successes were not used for political purposes. When the British insisted that the Western armies occupy Berlin and later Prague, American military leaders refused to hazard American lives purely to gain political advantage. General Omar Bradley commented in his memoirs: "As soldiers we looked naively on this British inclination to complicate the war with political foresight and nonmilitary objectives."[2] The American military leaders' way of thinking disregarded the fact that before the atomic age war was considered to be an extension of diplomacy by other means.

Karl von Clausewitz, a century and more earlier, had expressed a generally accepted view on wartime decisions, namely, that "The art of war in its highest point of view is policy, but of course a policy that fights battles instead of writing notes." He added that "in spite of the great diversity and development of the present system of war, the main outlines of a war have always been determined by the cabinet; that is, by a purely political and not a military organ."[3] This consideration was not followed in the United States. Declarations of principles, such as the Four Freedoms and the Atlantic Charter, fostered hope in Europe, but declarations were no substitute for concrete political objectives. Roosevelt did not have plans for postwar Europe and the Far East. George F. Kennan in a letter to Charles E. Bohlen during the Yalta Conference pointed out one of the consequences of the lack of American policy for Central and Eastern Europe: "we have consistently refused to make clear what our interests and our wishes were . . . We have refused to name any limit for Russian expansion and Russian responsibilities, thereby confusing the Russians and causing them constantly to wonder whether they are asking too little or whether it was some kind of a trap."[4]

William C. Bullitt, a former ambassador to the USSR and to France, submitted a memorandum to Roosevelt in August 1943 in which he suggested obtaining Stalin's pledge for a renunciation of conquest in Europe and recommended a military advance from the south through Eastern and Central Europe: "We must also make clear our position toward the whole problem of Europe," he said. "No one in Europe has the slightest idea what our program is. This is natural since we have no program. Stalin has a clear program and a vast organization working day and night to carry it out. We cannot beat something with nothing."[5]

The Department of State had sought to prepare for peace, long before the end of the war, and actually began to plan for events in 1939. In the following year, a department memorandum explored the "consequences to the U.S. of a possible German victory." Later peace preparation took on a more optimistic tone. There seemed three categories of postwar problems—establishment of an international organization, economic and financial policy, and plans for an eventual peace conference.[6] Peace preparatory work was successful in establishing the United Nations and in economic and financial matters. The International Monetary Fund and the World Bank created by the Bretton Woods agreements in 1944 secured monetary stability and economic growth, and increased trade in the industrialized world and they helped the developing nations. Policy papers also were prepared for a peace conference that never met. Officials who prepared position papers for the peace negotiations assumed that the United States would possess overwhelming military and economic power at the close of hostilities and that the peace-making would be influenced by the Four Freedoms and the Atlantic Charter.

But the State Department did not participate in high-level decisions during the war and could not influence the course of events. By and large it was restricted to routine diplomatic activities. Ambassador Bohlen testified some years later before the Senate Committee on Foreign Relations that the State Department had no representatives who ever sat with the Joint Chiefs of Staff or the president. "In that sense, the war was run very much from the point of view of the military considerations." Bohlen explained that while he was an assistant to Secretary of State Edward R. Stettinius, Jr., one of his duties was to serve as liaison officer with the White House. He was appointed to this position at the end of 1944 because Roosevelt's confidant, Harry Hopkins, had come to realize that "it was a very dangerous thing for our purposes to have the Department of State so completely out of the picture."[7]

A grand design for Western strategy had been worked out by Churchill during a voyage to Washington on the *Duke of York* in December 1941. His plan for the forthcoming year suggested an Anglo-American occupation of the coast of Africa and the Levant, from Dakar to the Turkish frontier. A series of meetings in the White House at this time, known as the Arcadia Conference, established a Combined Chiefs of Staff Committee, but there was no comparable Anglo-American committee for political affairs. It was agreed that Germany was the primary enemy and its defeat the key to victory. While in Washington, Churchill signed the United Nations Declaration together with representatives of twenty-five nations.[8]

As for Stalin's policy during the war, it was not quite, as Churchill suggested, a riddle wrapped in a mystery inside an enigma. When Foreign Secretary Anthony Eden visited Moscow in December 1941, despite the precarious military situation, Stalin demanded immediate recognition of the Soviet Union's western boundaries prior to the German attack of June 1941. This meant incorporation into the USSR of a part of Finland, the Baltic states, eastern Poland, Bessarabia, and part of Bucovina. Stalin proposed other territorial changes in Eastern and Central Europe and was prepared in return to support acquisition of bases by Britain in Western European countries.[9] Although the United States and Britain rejected the Soviet demands, Churchill, three months later, proved willing to accept territorial provisions in the Anglo-Soviet Pact of mutual assistance.[10] Washington did lodge a protest; the American ambassador in London, John B. Winant, met Foreign Minister Vyacheslav Molotov and explained that according to the American position all territorial questions must be settled by the peace conference. An Anglo-Soviet alliance treaty hence was signed in London (May 1942) with omission of territorial clauses.

In military strategy Stalin's demand for a second front in France coincided with the desires of the American military leaders who, from the beginning, advocated a massive invasion of Europe across the English Channel because it was the shortest route to Berlin. General Marshall and his colleagues at an Anglo-American military conference (July 26, 1942) proposed the occupation of Cherbourg in the autumn of 1942, a preliminary move to a general attack in 1943. The British argued that there was no hope of Anglo-American forces still being in Cherbourg by the next spring. The American Chiefs of Staff reported back to the White House, and Roosevelt instructed them to agree to some operation that would involve American forces in action against the enemy that year. The conferees decided on an invasion of French Northwest Africa, which had been part of Churchill's grand design.[11]

In the African theater General Bernard L. Montgomery defeated General Erwin Rommel's forces at El Alamein in early November 1942, and a few days later an Anglo-American landing at Casablanca, Oran, and Algiers succeeded, despite some French military resistance and political complications. Churchill and Roosevelt met in conference near Casablanca in January 1943 and decided to exploit the success in Africa by invading Sicily, securing the line of communication in the Mediterranean, and intensifying pressure on Italy in expectation of an early Italian surrender. Roosevelt announced the much debated "unconditional surrender" principle, to the joy of the Nazi propaganda minister, Joseph Goebbels. This principle weakened the possibility of an uprising against Hitler, although it informed the world of American and British determination to fight until destruction of the enemy and thus assured the Russians that the United States and Britain would not conclude a separate peace.

The misfortunes of war in North Africa nonetheless deranged the timetable for victory in Europe. Hitler sent about 200,000 troops into Tunis, and the American and British armies were involved in a much longer campaign than Churchill anticipated. He remained convinced that crossing the Channel in 1943 would have led to "a bloody defeat of the first magnitude, with measureless reactions upon the result of the war," and considered postponement of a landing in France a blessing in disguise.[12]

The Americans continued to champion a massive landing in France, as soon as possible, and advocated early withdrawal of substantial forces from the Mediterranean. Churchill's insistence on a southern invasion of Europe produced an adverse reaction in American military circles, and the American Chiefs of Staff ruled in the autumn of 1943 that the United States should take no responsibilities "in the areas of the Balkans including Austria." This political ruling by the military foreshadowed the fate of Danubian Europe. One of the consequences of this decision was the opposition of the Chiefs of Staff to American involvement in Austrian affairs. Ambassador Winant had to persuade President Roosevelt in June and December 1944, respectively, of the importance of American participation in the Allied Control Council in Vienna and in the administration of a zone in Austria.[13]

A major purpose of Mediterranean strategy was the separation of Italy from Germany, and with the invasion of Sicily on June 10, 1943, and Mussolini's dismissal a fornight later, the stage was set for this policy. Although the Allies expected Italy's surrender, they had no military and political plans for so favorable a turn. Eisenhower's political adviser, Ambassador Robert D. Murphy, noted later that the British were hoping that quick success in Sicily and a Fascist collapse would "induce the Americans to assign men and supplies for an accelerated drive into Italy and the Balkans." He added: "Although I knew nothing of the military aspects of the British proposal, I did recommend the political advantages which might result if our forces could gain northern Italy and conceivably Budapest."[14]

The actors in the Italian drama indulged in a vast illusion. A document prepared by an Allied committee in London assumed that an Italian government could capitulate without German interference. At the time of Mussolini's dismissal there were only scattered German forces in Italy, and the Germans planned to defend a line north of Pisa and Rimini. If the Allies had deployed troops around Rome, the disgruntled Italian army could have changed sides. Because of misunderstandings between the Italians and the Allies, an armistice was signed only on September 3 and proclaimed five days later. Application of unconditional surrender to Italy was a great disappointment in Rome, for the Italians had wanted to change sides by becoming full-fledged members of the Western Alliance. While Prime Minister Marshal Pietro Badoglio was secretly bargaining for favorable armistice terms, the Germans sent nineteen divisions to Italy.[15]

The Anglo-American armistice with Italy incidentally provoked Stalin's wrath, and he complained in a letter to Roosevelt and Churchill that the Soviet government had not been kept informed. He said bluntly:

> To date it has been like this: the U.S.A. and Britain reach agreement between themselves while the U.S.S.R. is informed of the agree-

ment between the two Powers as a third party looking passively on. I must say that this situation cannot be tolerated any longer.[16]

Stalin proposed a tripartite military-political commission "for consideration of problems related to negotiations with various governments falling away from Germany," but later he was satisfied with establishment of the European Advisory Commission. He received a message from Roosevelt and Churchill on August 26 that indicated their objectives as "elimination of Italy from the Axis alliance and the occupation of Italy, as well as Corsica and Sardinia, as bases of operation against Germany."

All the while there were important developments on the vast eastern front where the Soviets faced more than two hundred German divisions. Delay in the promised second front in France, and the heroic fight of the Soviet army created a diplomatic atmosphere advantageous to Stalin. The turning point in Soviet politics came with the victory at Stalingrad in early 1943, and a few months later with the battle of Kursk, when Stalin realized that Nazi Germany would be defeated, for him the English-speaking powers thereupon became the potential enemy. Western political leaders congratulated Stalin, at first not recognizing the full implications of the new situation. When the political dimensions were realized, they faced poor alternatives.[17]

Moscow changed policy after Stalingrad to exploit the new military and political advantages. Military victory greatly increased Russian self-assurance, which manifested itself in diplomatic action. Stalin used the Katyn affair for severance of diplomatic relations with the Polish government-in-exile in London (April 29, 1943),[18] and Soviet policy was forcefully expressed during the Moscow Conference of Foreign Ministers (October 18–November 1, 1943) and, four weeks later, at the Teheran Conference.

Tripartite conferences began with a Moscow meeting of the foreign ministers: Secretary of State Hull, Foreign Secretary Eden, and Foreign Minister Molotov.[19] Unlike the unstructured Teheran and Yalta conferences, the three delegations proposed carefully prepared agenda. Stalin and Molotov were reassured about the imminence of an Anglo-American landing in France in May 1944. Since a major United States objective was the establishment of a United Nations organization before the end of the war, to continue Allied unity, it was a great satisfaction to Secretary Hull that the Russians accepted the American plan for general security, although they inserted some modifications to serve their interests.

Eden submitted a proposal on "Joint Responsibility for Europe" which would have made possible the establishment of a federation or union of states in East and Central Europe. Molotov read a statement on the future of Poland and the Danubian and Balkan countries, criticizing schemes for federation, and stated that the Soviet government regarded encouragement of such schemes as premature and even harmful not only to small countries but to European stability. Molotov claimed that Eden's plan reminded the Soviet people of the *cordon sanitaire* directed in the past against the Soviet Union. He denied that the Soviet government would be interested in separate spheres of influence and guaranteed that there was no disposition on the part of the Soviet government to divide Europe into such zones. After short comments by Hull and Eden, Molotov said he understood that his suggestion had met no objection, and so Eden's proposal was buried.[20]

The future policy of the Soviet Union manifested itself at the Moscow Conference in many ways. Molotov declared that Russia wanted an independent Poland, provided the future Polish government was "friendly to the Soviet Union," which meant a Communist-dominated government. The declaration on Italy stated that the Italian government "should be made more democratic by the introduction of representatives of those sections of the Italian people who have always opposed Fascism." This formulation became a model for Soviet-sponsored regimes in Eastern Europe. The anti-Fascist coalition government in Italy showed how Communists might enter governments of liberated countries, even in Western Europe. Abandoning a long-standing British policy, Eden agreed to the prompt conclusion of an alliance between the Soviet Union and Czechoslovakia and to President Eduard Beneš's impending visit to the Soviet capital. A few weeks later Beneš signed a treaty of mutual assistance in Moscow.[21] With this alliance the Polish-Czechoslovak treaty of November 1942 lost its political value. This treaty intended to establish a federation in Eastern Europe.

In the Declaration on Austria the three governments agreed "that Austria, the first free country to fall a victim to Hitlerite aggression, shall be liberated from German domination." Since the Soviet Union did not participate in the Italian Armistice, the conference established an Advisory Council for matters relating to Italy, to be composed of representatives of the Big Three and the French Committee on National Liberation. Provision was made for the addition of representatives of Greece and Yugoslavia. In reality the council had little power.

The conference decided to establish in London a tripartite European Advisory Commission (EAC) "for ensuring the closest cooperation between the three Governments in the examination of European questions arising as the war develops." The EAC's task was to study such questions and make joint recommendations to the three governments.[22]

On November 1 the three participants issued declarations on Austria, Italy, and on German atrocities. A Four-Power Declaration on General Security, including China as a signatory, meant acceptance of the principle of a world organization. For Secretary Hull the establishment of the new world organization seemed a cure-all for international issues, and he made this point enthusiastically in an address before Congress on November 18, 1943:

> As the provisions of the four-nation declaration are carried into effect there will no longer be need for spheres of influence, for alliances, for balance of power . . . through which, in the unhappy past the nations strove to safeguard their security or to promote their interests.

In this middle period of the war, and with these remarkable agreements at the Moscow Conference of Foreign Ministers, it is clear that relations between the Western Allies and the Soviet Union were beginning to fall into a pattern in which momentary and anticipated difficulties of a political nature were adjourned until a future peace conference. Meanwhile the Western Allies hoped the Soviet Union would conduct itself as other nation-states and behave itself. Lend-Lease shipments to Russia increased. Fire power of the Soviet Army was mainly home produced, but nearly half a million American, British, and Canadian trucks and other vehicles greatly increased the mobility of the Soviet army, making possible the advance of the Russians into Danubian and Central Europe in 1944–45.[23] According to a presidential directive of March 7, 1942, material promised to the USSR enjoyed preferential treatment over requirements of other Allies, and even over those of the United States. Major General John R. Deane, the American Lend-Lease representative in Moscow, later suggested that "this was one of the most important decisions of the war . . . it was the beginning of a policy of appeasement of Russia.[24] Deane's realistic recommendations failed to influence the overgenerous Lend-Lease program. Whenever Deane rejected a Soviet request in Moscow, the Russians usually obtained in Washington whatever they wanted. During a period when Russia needed American help, Deane experienced in Moscow suspicious, unresponsive, and frequently offensive behavior. All the while the Soviets used their purchasing commission in the United States, with more than a thousand employees, for extensive industrial espionage.[25]

The British and Americans were, of course, preoccupied by the possibility of a Soviet collapse and separate peace with Germany, and there is evidence that Soviet and German contacts occurred in late 1942 and in the first half of 1943, although details are still in the dark. Molotov in June 1943 reportedly traveled two hundred miles into German-occupied territory to explore the possibilities of a separate peace with Germany. Stalin was deeply suspicious about the delayed Anglo-American landing in France and may have thought it appropriate to negotiate simultaneously with Germany and the Western Allies.[26]

This, then, was the complex political situation in which the first Big Three conference was held at Teheran in November–December 1943. Roosevelt was sensitive to the need to be cautious with the Soviet Union and decided to make it plain to Stalin that the Americans were not "ganging up" with the British against Russia. (The Teheran Conference was preceded, actually, by a meeting of the Americans and the British with Generalissimo Chiang Kai-shek in Cairo in which the conferees discussed Far Eastern problems.) To this end, the conference was characterized by Roosevelt's endeavors to establish close personal relations with Stalin. On Stalin's invitation he moved into the compound of the Soviet embassy, and the two men had their first meeting without Churchill. Roosevelt went out of his way to please Stalin in condemnation of France and, according to Bohlen, some of his statements showed a remarkable ignorance about the Soviet Union.[27]

Procedure at Teheran was similarly unorthodox. No provision had been agreed upon for taking minutes of the conference proceedings. Each nation took its own minutes. Bohlen translated and took notes and dictated them in odd hours to four American soldiers with stenographic skill.[28] Joint records would have made the statements and decisions clear. When the State Department years later published a documentary volume on the Teheran Conference, the Soviet Foreign Ministry charged that the American record falsified history, and it released its own minutes of the conference.[29] The Western allies may have thought that free-wheeling discussions would be conducive to agreement, and Stalin welcomed this approach that gave opportunity for maneuver and revealed disagreement between the British and Americans. Teheran was possibly the last occasion when the Western powers could have initiated a meaningful discussion for reorganization of Europe after the German defeat. But the president, in his opening statement, emphasized that the "members of the new family" were gathered at Teheran "for one purpose, for the purpose of winning the war as soon as possible." At the conference Roosevelt brought up the possibility of a northeastward drive from the Adriatic into Rumania to effect a junction of Anglo-American troops with the Red Army advancing from Odessa. The proposal disturbed Harry Hopkins and was not supported by the United States Chiefs of Staff.[30] Churchill agreed with Roosevelt's suggestion. But Stalin explained that it would be unwise to scatter forces in the Eastern Mediterranean and suggested that from Italy the maximum number of troops should be sent to southern France to provide a diversionary operation two months before the invasion of northern France. General Marshall and Admiral Ernest J. King agreed with Stalin but suggested that D-Day should be the same for both operations in France, and the conference endorsed their proposal.

Stalin politely accepted Roosevelt's ideas as to a postwar security organization consisting of an Assembly, an Executive Committee, and a third organ described by Roosevelt as "the four policemen"— the U.S.A., U.K., USSR, and China—whose combined forces would check aggression throughout the world. Nobody brought up the possibility that an aggressor might be one of the four policemen.

The Polish question was not extensively discussed at Teheran, but Poland's postwar boundaries were practically arranged and this meant a partial abandonment of the American policy that all territorial questions should be settled at the peace conference. In a private meeting Roosevelt told Stalin there were some six to seven million Americans of Polish extraction; he did not wish to lose their votes during the forthcoming presidential election and for this reason could not take any position on Polish affairs, although he personally agreed with Stalin's view that Poland's frontiers should move to the west. At the formal session Roosevelt did not participate in the Polish discussion of Churchill and Stalin who, in vague terms, agreed on the future borders of Poland.[31]

Plans for dismemberment of Germany were discussed at Teheran but nothing was agreed, and it was decided that the subject would be considered by the EAC in London. On this occasion Stalin said he was "against the idea of confederation as artificial and one that would not last in that area, and in addition would provide opportunity for the German elements to control. Austria, for example, had existed as an independent state and should again. Hungary, Rumania, and Bulgaria likewise."[32]

It was typical that the State Department was not informed of the negotiations and decisions at Teheran. Secretary Hull, who had not been present, complained to William C. Bullitt in March 1944 that "he still did not know what happened at Teheran and that he had no knowledge whatsoever of the constant stream of communications that was being exchanged between the President and Churchill and Stalin." Hull added that he had never known Roosevelt to be so aloof, and he thought "this might be due to the fact that the President was complaining of constant headaches."[33]

Between Teheran and Yalta decisive military action took place; the landings in Normandy on June 6, 1944 were a sweeping success. By the end of the autumn, massive Anglo-American forces were at the German frontier. The landing in southern France was something else and proved, in the event, to be unnecessary. General Henry Maitland Wilson, the Supreme Commander in the Mediterranean, had foreseen as far back as March 1944 that logistical problems would delay the landing in southern France and had reported that the best course was "to abandon any attack on the Riviera and concentrate on Italy."[34] Occupation of the Istrian peninsula would have allowed a push through the Ljubljana Gap toward Vienna, and invading Western troops could have attacked German forces from the flank and moved in the direction of Hungary. This British proposal was rejected by the president and General Eisenhower in June 1944, Roosevelt referring to the strategy accepted at Teheran, and Eisenhower considering the second landing important for his campaign. Landing at the Riviera took place only in mid-August when Eisenhower's troops already controlled extensive ground in Normandy; and in retrospect it is clear that the second landing had little military importance. Roosevelt and Churchill in their message to Stalin on September 19 mentioned that in the event of a rout of German forces in Italy, Allied military operations should be possible toward the Ljubljana Gap.[35] But the German army retreated in orderly fashion, and the Allied offensive in the direction of Vienna did not take place.

Seeing the advance of Soviet troops in Rumania and the drift of Western strategy, Churchill tried to secure some British influence in the Balkans, primarily in Greece, by negotiating with Stalin and offering him controlling influence in Rumania. Secretary Hull opposed the arrangement, but during his absence from Washington (the secretary was increasingly ill and was to resign in November 1944) President Roosevelt accepted in July the Churchill-Stalin arrangement for a three-month trial period. In June Churchill proposed to Stalin that Bulgaria should be in the Soviet sphere and Yugoslavia in the British. However, the validity of the three months' arrangement was doubtful.

Meanwhile events were moving rapidly. On August 23, 1944, King Michael of Rumania surrendered to the Russians, appointed a new government of national unity, and promptly declared war on Germany. The armistice agreement with Rumania (September 12) gave full power to the Soviet High Command in the Allied Control Commission, until the conclusion of peace. Moscow declared war on Bulgaria in early September without notifying London and Washington, while the British and Americans were negotiating an armistice with the Bulgarian government in Egypt. The Soviet army then occupied Bulgaria without firing a shot, and the armistice negotiations were transferred to Moscow.

Under the circumstances Churchill decided to negotiate directly with Stalin; Roosevelt, in a message to Churchill and Stalin, expressed reservations concerning their bilateral meeting. He said that in the global war there was no question in which the United States was not interested and notified them that he considered their meeting as preliminary to a conference of the Big Three. The prime minister and Eden arrived in Moscow on October 9 and began negotiations with Stalin the same day. After a discussion on Poland they turned to the affairs of the Balkan peninsula, and Churchill expressed in percentages the relative influence that Britain and Russia should have in specified countries. Churchill proposed 90 percent British influence in Greece and 90 percent Russian influence in Rumania; in Hungary and Yugoslavia 50–50 percent influence; and in Bulgaria 75 percent influence for Russia. It appeared in Churchill's dramatic narrative that Stalin accepted these percentage figures.[36] Yet Foreign Office records released in 1973 showed that Stalin recognized overwhelming British influence in Italy and Greece but claimed in the case of Bulgaria the same 90 percent influence as in Rumania. Eventually they agreed that Eden and Molotov work out an agreement.

The Eden-Molotov meeting was complicated by the Bulgarian armistice negotiations and Soviet proposals to change the percentages in these countries, and concessions were combined with power in the Allied Control Commission. Eventually Molotov offered a compromise of an 80–20 percentage division in Bulgaria and Hungary and a 50–50 percentage in Yugoslavia, and he proposed to insert a provision in Article 18 of the Bulgarian armistice that until the conclusion of hostilities against Germany in the ACC the Soviet High

Command execute the armistice terms with the participation of representatives of the United Kingdom and the United States.[37] The British were satisfied with the compromise. Eden noted on October 11 that "We obtained what we wanted on almost all points. I should say 90 percent overall. In particular they will summon Bulgars out of Greece and Yugoslavia tonight."[38] This last point was most important because the British were afraid that the Soviet army might march to Greece and eventually to Istanbul.

During this period the West also suffered a defeat when Britain and the United States could not support the Polish uprising in Warsaw, for on this occasion Stalin showed his hand; the Soviet army stopped at the gates of the city for political-military reasons, and when Western Allied planes sought to take supplies to the Poles, Stalin refused to allow them to land and refuel at Soviet airfields. The Poles fought under desperate conditions from August 1 to October 2, 1944.[39]

All this was a prescription for disaster in Eastern Europe. Developments in the autumn of 1944 made clear what was in store for Poland and the Danubian countries. Stalin's position in inter-Allied relations strengthened when Hitler began his initially successful offensive in the Ardennes (Battle of the Bulge, December 16, 1944) and the Western Allies asked for a Russian offensive to divert German pressure from the West. Churchill addressed a special message to Stalin on January 6, 1945, who replied favorably the next day, and the Soviet army occupied Warsaw on January 17.[40]

Since the military decisions made at Teheran had been carried out to the letter, the Allied forces remaining in Italy and the eastern Mediterranean were not strong enough for decisive military actions. Therefore the Soviets could safely suggest a landing on the Balkans in early 1945. When Stalin proposed to Churchill at Yalta that British and Soviet troops meet at Vienna, Churchill said nothing. Both men knew there were no British troops available for such an undertaking.

The Yalta Conference (February 4–11, 1945) was preceded by a high-level Anglo-American meeting at Malta (January 31–February 2).[41] The Combined Chiefs of Staff were in session for several days, and Churchill and Eden exchanged views with the new secretary of state, Stettinius, and with Ambassador Harriman. On the last day of the conference Roosevelt steamed into Valetta harbor aboard the heavy cruiser U.S.S. *Quincy*, met the military leaders and entertained Churchill, Eden, and Stettinius for luncheon and dinner, and talked informally of political issues to raise at Yalta; that same night transport planes took the two delegations, seven hundred persons, to the airfield of Saki in the Crimea. The British and American delegations left Malta without having agreed on policy or tactics for confrontation with the Soviets.

When the Big Three met at Yalta Soviet troops were sweeping through Poland, had reached the Oder, and occupied most of Hungary. Possession of key territories created a favorable negotiating position for Stalin. The State Department had prepared a Declaration on Liberated Europe which promised democratic governments established through free elections. The declaration at first had been combined with a proposal for a four-power Emergency High Commission for Liberated Europe that was to supervise the application of the declaration. But Roosevelt decided to present only the declaration, which the Russians accepted after a short discussion.[42] Correct application of its principles might have made possible democratic institutions in East European countries.

In the case of Poland and Yugoslavia, East and West at Yalta backed rival governments, and so it was decided that the Communist-dominated provisional government of Poland should be reorganized "on a broader democratic basis with the inclusion of democratic leaders from Poland itself and from Poles abroad." A similar recommendation was made in the case of Yugoslavia. The Curzon line was slightly changed in favor of Poland and recognized as the Soviet-Polish border. The conference also recognized that Poland must receive substantial accession of territory in the north and west and that the final delimitation of the western frontier of Poland should "await the Peace Conference."

Zones of occupation in Germany were approved. These zones, including Berlin's anomalous position, were not results of shrewd Soviet diplomacy; they were proposed by a British cabinet committee in 1943, approved later by the United States and the European Advisory Commission, and accepted by the Russians at Yalta. Churchill noted that in 1943 "a common opinion about Russia was that she would not continue the war once she had regained her frontiers, and that when the time came the Western Allies might well have to try to persuade her not to relax her efforts.[43]

Thanks to Churchill's efforts, and Roosevelt's change of mind, Stalin reluctantly accepted France as one of the occupying powers in Germany and Austria and as a member of the Allied Control Council in both countries, but the French zones were carved out from the zones assigned to Britain and the United States.[44]

To make sure of a timely Russian intervention against Japan, Roosevelt negotiated with Stalin a secret agreement in which the

United States promised to support territorial concessions to Russia in the Far East. On the last day of the conference Churchill was informed of the agreement, and he signed it grudgingly.

By February 1945 events had demonstrated that—contrary to the original American policy—settlement of fundamental issues was not postponed to a peace conference. Decisions at the Moscow, Teheran, and Yalta Conferences, armistice agreements, and military occupations shaped postwar Europe.

In dealing with the Soviet Union, a multinational imperialistic Great Power, a country that respected military power more than the principles advocated by the West, one has to recognize that fatal misunderstandings had affected Western policies throughout the war. It is part of human affairs that the American, British, and Russian historical background influenced the result. So did Roosevelt, Churchill, and Stalin and their respective states of health. In summit conferences clear agreements were made in military matters, but important political questions remained in limbo. Usually the Soviets gained immediate advantages and made empty gestures accepting vague principles. Since there were no Anglo-American joint policies, Stalin had a field day at tripartite meetings. Eden considered him a superb negotiator and noted: "He never wasted a word. He never stormed, he seldom was even irritated."[45]

Relations between the Big Three and their tactics at summit meetings influenced policies. The fact that on some occasions Roosevelt and Churchill competed separately for Stalin's cooperation had not been helpful for Western interests. The president was fond of Churchill, and after September 1939, they exchanged more than 1,700 letters, telegrams, and other messages and participated in eight bilateral meetings, in addition to the Teheran and Yalta conferences with Stalin and conferences at Cairo with Generalissimo Chiang Kaishek and the president of Turkey, Inönü.[46] Yet Roosevelt considered the leader of the British Empire as a representative of a bygone world of nineteenth-century colonial imperialism and was convinced that the United States and Russia must get along in the postwar world. At Teheran he thought that Churchill and Stalin were competing for influence in the Balkans and told his son Elliott that he saw "no reason for putting the lives of American soldiers in jeopardy in order to protect real or fancied British interest on the European continent."[47] Both Roosevelt and Churchill were convinced that each could get more from Stalin through direct personal contact than through tripartite negotiation.

With President Roosevelt's sudden death, Harry S. Truman assumed the nation's highest office with a broad historical background and sound political instinct but next to no knowledge of the Roosevelt-Churchill-Stalin meetings, inter-Allied agreements, and other wartime decisions. He was not involved in White House discussions on foreign policy and was not even informed of such an undertaking as the Manhattan Project. It was a failure of the Roosevelt administration that the vice-president did not receive systematic briefing. The time span of less than three months between inauguration day and Roosevelt's death is an explanation but not an excuse of this omission. On April 12, 1945, the day Truman became president, he noted in his diary, "I knew the President had a great many meetings with Churchill and Stalin. I was not familiar with any of these things and it was really something to think about but I decided the best thing to do was to go home and get as much rest as possible and face the music."[48] Lack of political purpose during the war was followed by Western passivity during the immediate postwar period. President Truman continued policies established by the Roosevelt administration, despite changed circumstances, and the American military leaders in Europe were impressed by the Russians. A few days before the Potsdam Conference General Lucius D. Clay, second in command to Eisenhower for German affairs, told Bohlen that "the key to getting along with the Soviets was that you had to give trust to get trust."[49]

The sudden demobilization of the American army in 1945–46 changed drastically the power equation. There was an almost irresistible popular desire to bring the boys home and return to normalcy. General Marshall had to carry out this policy, and his predicament was truly pathetic. In the early autumn of 1945 he asked the journalist Marquis Childs to see him, and Childs noted the conversation:

Disbanding the 7 million Americans under arms with reckless haste meant abandoning vast military stores, he said. Supplies worth billions were being bulldozed under the earth or dumped into the sea. What I am to do? he asked. This is an advertisement to the world that we are giving up our positions of strength everywhere.[50]

Marshall commented later on the result of demobilization and told an audience at the Pentagon that when as secretary of state he attended the Moscow Conference of Foreign Ministers in March 1947 he was urged constantly by radio messages to give the Russians hell.

At that time, my facilities for giving them hell—and I am a soldier and know something about the ability to give hell—was 1 and ⅓ divisions over the entire United States. This is quite a proposition when you deal with somebody with over 260 and you have 1 and ⅓. We had nothing in Alaska. We did not have enough to defend the air strip at Fairbanks. . .[51]

A distinguished diplomatic historian, Raymond J. Sontag, pointed out some years ago that during the months between the Second Quebec Conference of September 1944 and the Potsdam Conference of July–August 1945 the United States attained a peak of strength unparalleled in American history. During the same period "the decisions were made which were to place our country, and the Free World, in a mortal peril which continues to this day." Then Sontag developed his thesis that "despite clear evidence of Soviet bad faith and Soviet ambitions . . . and despite the warnings of the Acting Secretary of State [Joseph Grew] and our Ambassador to the U.S.S.R. [Averell Harriman], the positions of strength were abandoned, and the western world placed in mortal peril: Why?"[52]

To this question historians have given a variety of inconclusive answers. There might be truth in the allegations that Roosevelt's increasing illness in 1944–45[53] and wrong military estimates concerning Japan's military capabilities and intentions[54] played a role at Yalta. But the Yalta Agreements, and especially the unassertive Western policy in 1945, cannot be explained by such factors. Roosevelt's health could have made the difference in decisions of lesser importance, but Yalta as a whole was the logical result of the wartime policy of the Western powers, their military weakness at the outset, and neglect of postwar problems in wartime diplomacy and at summit meetings. As John J. McCloy, a prominent member of the American establishment, put it: "We concentrated so heavily on the actual conduct of the war that we overlooked the need for political thinking."[55] Whether this or that was decided at Yalta or elsewhere in the closing period of the war was of little consequence in view of the absence of Anglo-American determination to reestablish a reasonable European system and check Soviet expansion. Disbanding the American army was unavoidable for domestic reasons, but in an unsettled world it symbolized a lack of political will in the international arena, giving the green light to Stalin in Eastern and Danubian Europe. Whatever the explanation, the new status quo in Europe greatly reduced the rimland necessary for defense of the Western world and shifted one hundred million people into the zone of Soviet domination.

Part II

PREPARATION FOR PEACE
ON THE
DARK SIDE OF THE MOON

4

Challenging the Inevitable

Wartime Endeavors

Preparations of defeated countries for a peace settlement are never easy. They were particularly difficult for countries occupied successively by the German and the Soviet armies. For people living in a free country it is difficult to appreciate the nature and intricacies of problems for which such countries had to find expedient solutions. Preparations for peace in Washington and London took a normal course and have been discussed in memoirs and scholarly works. Government documents are available and the national archives in Washington and London are accessible. In countries living in the shadow of the Swastika and the Red Star peace preparations were more complicated, of a different nature, and sometimes risky. Stamina was as important as vision and knowledge. Backdoor diplomacy often was a murky business, and some participants in this endeavor did not survive. In view of Hungary's peculiar position during the Second World War, policies often could not be discussed openly or spelled out in writing. In the Foreign Ministry a large number of confidential documents had been destroyed on the eve of the German occupation of Hungary in March 1944. During this period, beginning with the Moscow and Teheran Conferences in 1943, political and strategic inter-Allied decisions settled the fate of East Central Europe. From this time on, the area became the "dark side of the moon" for the Western Allies.

In Hungary, Prime Minister Miklós Kállay (March 1942–March 1944) sought to extricate Hungary from German domination, and although he received practically carte blanche from Regent Horthy for a reorientation of foreign policy, he found that extremely cautious steps were necessary; Hungary was in the middle of the German power sphere, and Hitler's hostile feelings toward Hungary were well known. The general political situation was muddled. The Hungarian army could not have cooperated with the Allied forces as long as it was not within negotiable distance, even if the leading generals were pro-Western. If Kállay in 1942 had attempted to disassociate Hungary from Germany, he would have brought a prompt occupation of the country, the avoidance of which was the major purpose of Hungarian foreign policy. To create a more reliable administration he had to make changes in key positions slowly. In the early period of his office Kállay emphasized Hungary's common cause with Germany, and this dissimulation encouraged the pro-Axis sympathies of many Hungarians, especially army officers. Kállay's political predicament thus produced a vicious circle in domestic affairs.

While the Hungarian government formally maintained unchanged relations with the Axis, contacts with American and British diplomatic representatives had begun in Stockholm, Istanbul, Lisbon, and Switzerland in 1942–43. This was the beginning of backdoor diplomacy. Exponents of Hungary's pro-Allied foreign policy had to be watchful; the cabinet and the civil service had pro-Nazi members. In his effort to reach an understanding with the Allies, Kállay placed absolute faith in only two members of his government, his minister of the interior, Ferenc Keresztes-Fischer, and his deputy in the foreign Ministry, Jenö Ghyczy. To Ghyczy he had turned over the portfolio of that ministry in July 1943.

The Ghyczy administration of the Foreign Ministry was inaugurated by the reshuffling of staff and of diplomatic representatives abroad, replacing pro-German officials with reliable ones. The most influential new high officials were Andor Szentmiklóssy and Aladár Szegedy-Maszák; the former took Ghyczy's place as deputy foreign minister, while Szegedy-Maszák became head of the political division.

Kállay's policy of moving cautiously toward the Allies was made easier by the turn of international events. General Montgomery's victory at El Alamein and an Anglo-American landing in North Africa in November 1942 were hopeful signs of an assertive Western strategy in the Mediterranean. The demoralized retreat of the Germans in the second winter of the Russian venture foreshadowed Germany's defeat, and the Voronezh disaster suffered by the Hungarian army (January 1943) caused widespread discontent; here was a calamitous defeat that reduced Hungarian military assistance to Germany to a badly equipped token force. Anti-Nazi politicians became more vocal, and Kállay had no reluctance in stating at a meeting of the foreign affairs committee of parliament that Hungary's interest in the war did not go beyond the Russian campaign. Still, much caution was needed. In a statement before parliament about the future peace negotiations, he named his minister of public instruction, Bálint Hóman, a staunch pro-German, head of a prospective peace delegation. In the meantime the real preparations for peace were made secretly under the leadership of the political division of the Foreign Ministry. I was in charge of peace preparatory work in this division. Szegedy-Maszák outlined in a memorandum the task of peace preparations in November 1942, followed by a more detailed document a few weeks later. Kállay appointed a small group of elder statesmen who approved the proposals. In the course of peace preparations I negotiated with government agencies, research institutions, and selected experts and publicists who received assignments without being informed of the scope and ultimate purpose of their endeavors.

By the end of 1943, Szentmiklóssy expressed to me his satisfaction with the progress of the peace preparatory work and told me Hungary might be occupied first by the Germans, then by the Russians, and it was uncertain who in our group would survive. He instructed me to send a copy of all peace preparatory documents to our legation in Switzerland, and these papers were promptly deposited in Bern. As soon as the Germans occupied Budapest the Gestapo arrested Szentmiklóssy, and a few months later he died in the concentration camp of Dachau.

Our peace preparations assumed that at the close of hostilities a major conference would settle the affairs of Europe under leadership of the United States, the only great power not affected by wartime destruction and immensely strengthened during the hostilities. In view of the failure of the small-state system that replaced the Habsburg Empire, we envisaged a cooperative democratic state system in Danubian Europe, if possible, a union or federation. Besides my official functions I discussed pertinent questions with a group of specialists and politicians with whom I met in coffee houses or residences. Plans were made for a democratic reorganization of Hungary's domestic political life, and it was taken for granted that in the last stage of the war the Danubian region would be occupied by British and American forces. The assumption that British and American troops would reach Hungary's frontiers was not contradicted by Western negotiators, although some of them advised the Hungarians to approach Moscow also. In Budapest nobody was aware of the inter-Allied decisions at the Moscow and Teheran conferences that decisively influenced the fate of East Central Europe.

Hungary's wartime endeavors for an armistice — and the related complex domestic and international problems—are outside the scope of this writing, but a glance at our first contact with an American emissary at Geneva will perhaps characterize the atmosphere of these encounters and illustrate Hungary's poor alternatives. As a diplomatic courier I took instructions to Geneva to Baron György Bakách-Bessenyey, who at that time was Hungarian envoy to the Vichy government and designated envoy to Switzerland to conduct negotiations primarily with an American emissary. My trip reflected conditions of the times. I left Budapest on the best available train and arrived in the evening at Vienna. Representatives of the Hungarian general consulate were waiting at the station and took my tri-lingual (Hungarian, French, German) courier passport to the station military commander's office, where an overworked sergeant saw the German version and apparently thought I was a German Courier and assigned a special compartment for me and my companion, a young girl who traveled with me to join relatives at our legation in Bern. This was a lucky break because the train was full—people were packed in the corridors like sardines. The windows were used as doors for people could not move in or out. Our privileged position changed when the commander of the train asked politely that three German army officers returning from Balkan duties be permitted to have seats in the compartment; of course I gave permission, but after formal introductions I did not want to talk too much. While simulating sleep during most of the night, I overheard their complaints about the desperate situation in the Balkans and Germany's deteriorating military position. During a stopover in Munich I noticed the empty shops and the subdued mood of the population. No one was singing the song so popular after the fall of France in 1940, *Wir fahren nach England* (We are traveling to England). The contrast between conditions in Germany and peaceful, clean, and prosperous Switzerland was almost unbelievable.

By this time the Allied powers had pressed the Hungarian government to withdraw its troops from Russia, and at the same time Hitler was urging Hungary to participate in occupation of the Balkan peninsula. The instruction I took contained Regent Horthy's idea for acceptance of the demands of both Hitler and the Western powers. Hungarian troops would be withdrawn from Russia and take part in occupation of certain Croatian territories, possibly reaching out to the sea, a move that could have resulted in contact with Allied forces. Like most Hungarian statesmen and some generals, Horthy supposed that an Allied landing in the Balkans was imminent. On August 28, 1943, Bessenyey explained Horthy's idea to the American negotiator,

Royal Tyler, who had spent several years in Hungary in the 1920s as a commissioner of the League of Nations reconstruction loan. Tyler emphatically opposed the proposal. His advice was that Hungary should withdraw all troops from Russia, not take part in occupation of the Balkans, and turn against the Germans as soon as Italy's surrender was announced. Otherwise the Hungarians would share the terrible punishment to be imposed on the German people. He suggested that for Hungary the last moment for jumping out without harm would come with the Italian armistice.[1]

During my stay in Geneva, I met several people in touch with the Western Allies and the exile governments in London and discussed the world situation with them, including the expected fate of Hungary. One of the best-informed persons I had known for years, Maurice Bourquin, a Belgian professor at the Graduate Institute of International Relations in Geneva, who told me that Stalin was no maniac like Hitler, that he was too shrewd a Georgian peasant to be misled into an expansionist policy fraught with danger. The almost certain Russian occupation of Hungary would be temporary. Hungary would be allowed to work out an independent political existence after the conclusion of peace. That did not mean that Soviet Russia would tolerate an anti-Bolshevist regime in Hungary of the Horthy type. No doubt it would be necessary to reform Hungary's antiquated social and political system and carry out a radical land reform in cooperation with such progressive parties as the Smallholders, the Democratic party, and the Social Democrats, supported in a coalition by the Communist party.

Since Bourquin had regular contacts with the Belgian government in London, I was impressed by his explanations and relayed them to Bessenyey. I also mentioned the possibly dubious value of our parley with the Americans in case of a Russian occupation of Hungary. Instead of arguing, Bessenyey simply referred me to the map of Europe in our Geneva consulate general. He pointed to the Danube valley with the remark that the Western powers could not afford Russian domination of this geographically important area, the gateway to Western Europe, because it would be more dangerous to their safety than German influence in the area. With these words he expressed the conviction of leading Hungarian officials. I had the same experience in Budapest when I reported this information predicting a Russian occupation of Hungary; the reaction was exactly like that of Bessenyey. Bessenyey's report about the Geneva parleys would have badly compromised both the Kállay government and Regent Horthy if it had fallen into the hands of the Germans. Since the Nazis were not discriminating in their choice of means, I put several small bottles of benzine and some inflammable material into my pouch containing the reports to facilitate their quick destruction should the Nazis try to acquire them during my two days transit through Germany. At night I slept with the pouch under my head, and a cigarette lighter was always at hand.

When news came of the Italian armistice of September 8, 1943, the political division of the Foreign Ministry set about drafting an announcement that the Tripartite Pact had ceased to be valid after the collapse of Italy and that Hungary had regained independence. But Kállay and Ghyczy thought it premature to expose the country to such a test in absence of the most elementary military and technical means necessary for a change of front. To proclaim the end of the Tripartite Pact would have provoked immediate German occupation, followed by extermination of all anti-Nazi elements, installation of a puppet government, and mobilization of all Hungarian resources and manpower.

Ghyczy reviewed Hungary's foreign political situation in the Council of Ministers on September 14, and the council decided to ask Germany for repatriation of Hungarian troops from Russia while opposing Hungary's participation in the occupation of the Balkans, recurring themes in Hungarian-German relations. Hitler did not permit repatriation of Hungarian troops, mainly for political reasons, but did not insist on Hungarian participation in occupation of the Balkan peninsula.

Contacts with British representatives were established mainly in Stockholm, Lisbon, and Istanbul. By the end of February 1944, the Hungarian government proposed to negotiate with Moscow directly or with British mediation about capitulation of Hungarian divisions on the Soviet front. Although Eden suggested to Moscow Soviet-Hungarian negotiations in the presence of a British representative, the German occupation of Hungary on March 19, 1944, made impossible the realization of this plan.[2]

Negotiations with American representatives continued mainly in Switzerland and Lisbon and eventually three American soldiers, called Mission Sparrow, were parachuted into Hungary on March 15, 1944.[3] The mission had no follow-up because the German army occupied Hungary four days later.

In view of the Allied strategy determined at Teheran, Anglo-American forces never reached Hungary, and the Horthy regime's only chance for an armistice came in September–October 1944. Horthy's representatives signed the preliminary armistice agreement in

Moscow on October 11, and his armistice proclamation was read on the Budapest radio on October 15. This poorly prepared attempt failed. German armored divisions were in readiness and promptly occupied the capital, the pro-Horthy military commanders were arrested, and Horthy's armistice proclamation countermanded within hours. Horthy was deported to Germany, and the Germans put in power an Arrow Cross government under Ferenc Szálasi.

A New Beginning

While Szálasi's government introduced a regime of terror and continued to fight a lost war under German command, in Debrecen the Soviet-sponsored provisional national government began to function. Foreign politics had to start from scratch, and the Foreign Ministry was organized anew. Foreign Minister János Gyöngyösi, an old member of the Smallholder party, signed the armistice agreement in Moscow on January 20, 1945. He was convinced that postwar Hungary had to win the confidence of the Soviet Union and its Western Allies, and then things might turn for the better. He hoped that the Soviet Union would become a huge market for Hungarian products, making possible the much needed expansion of Hungarian industry and broadening opportunities for the surplus agrarian population.

At the outset Gyöngyösi showed little interest in diplomacy in general or in preparation for the peace conference in particular. He believed that he could take care of such problems with the assistance of a few secretaries. But he changed his views within a short time. When the Foreign Ministry moved to Budapest in April 1945, he realized the impossibility of initiating any serious activity in foreign affairs without knowledgeable advisers and specialists. The newly appointed officials of the Foreign Ministry belonged to political parties of the National Independence Front, and few of them had experience in foreign affairs. The foreign minister had to rely increasingly on officials of the Horthy regime. His initial suspicion was reduced because most of these officials were active anti-Nazis and went through the political screening procedure with flying colors.

At the end of May 1945 the foreign minister asked me to organize and supervise a new division of the ministry, the function of which would be to prepare the Hungarian case for the peace conference. I undertook the work of preparation for peace in a devastated and occupied country under the most difficult political and technical circumstances. The Foreign Ministry began its work in one of the stripped

apartment houses of Budapest in which the peace treaty division occupied three rooms. The former building of the ministry and most
of its contents had been destroyed during the siege so it was necessary
to begin without files and documents. For a while office equipment
was not available, and even desks and chairs presented a problem,
not to mention such items as typewriters. There was no transportation, and undernourished officials had to walk several miles from
their homes. As late as autumn 1945, officials on their way home in
the evening were occasionally robbed by Soviet soldiers. Fuel was
scarce. During the winter of 1945–46 many civil servants worked in
offices without window panes and without heat. To add to their
hardship, their insufficient salaries made it necessary to fight inflation for their own physical survival. Jewels and other personal belongings were sold or bartered for food.

However serious the technical and personal difficulties, they appeared insubstantial in view of the general conditions resulting from
the Soviet occupation, the armistice agreement, and domination of
politics by the Communist party. Postwar Hungary was not a sovereign state; foreign affairs were under the control of the Russian-
dominated ACC. Civil administration was gradually reorganized by
the political parties, and this not only opened the way to many incompetent appointees but allowed Communists key positions. The
Foreign Ministry was headed by a Smallholder, and the Communists
secured important positions under the system of the coalition government. In every important division of the Foreign Ministry there was
a Communist who reported to the party. The chief of cabinet of the
minister, as well as the deputy head and later the head of the political
division, were Communists. Through these key men the Communist
party knew everything that happened in foreign affairs, and Soviet
authorities were consulted about all issues of importance. They could
intervene at an appropriate time and exert decisive influence. The
system of controls was even further developed, for the NKVD and
later the Hungarian political police summoned some non-Communist
officials of the Foreign Ministry and forced them to report regularly
on affairs and personnel. As soon as Hungary renewed diplomatic
relations with foreign countries, many officials who had served under
the Horthy regime were sent abroad; this development as well opened
new fields of opportunity for the Communists and decreased the
number of competent officials in Budapest.

When I began the peace preparative work anew, my first question
to the foreign minister was, "What are the peace aims of the government?" I asked this question repeatedly in the following months, but

never received an explicit answer. Gyöngyösi only explained those political difficulties of the coalition regime that hindered an agreement on our peace aims. Under such circumstances I concentrated on searching for and collecting materials and data and prepared a variety of alternative proposals. On the one hand, the wartime era of cautious doubletalk ceased—at least to the extent that we were able to obtain technical cooperation from all government agencies, without false excuses. On the other hand, we had to face new difficulties of greater magnitude.

In June 1945, I organized the peace treaty division in the Foreign Ministry and established an interdepartmental committee which held weekly meetings in the Hungarian National Bank building. The meetings were under my chairmanship until April 1946, with participation of the National Bank, the ministries, certain scholarly institutions, and experts in various fields. For important problems subcommittees were appointed, and they reported to the general committee. The object of this work was a detailed investigation that embraced the economic, cultural, and financial development of Hungary from 1919 until the end of the Second World War. We examined the existing conditions and drew conclusions concerning the needs of Hungary. Committee members included the country's foremost experts in many fields. Eventually over a hundred officials and scholars participated in the peace preparatory work. I openly stated that I needed specialists and would not want to have political appointees on the committee, and for a time it was possible to maintain this policy. I did not object to party membership but found it impossible to do constructive work with delegates whose only merit was membership in a party. Despite the nonpolitical character of this committee, some experts were timid and reluctant to express frankly their opinions. Some participants also had little understanding for political reality. At the first plenary meeting I gave general instructions concerning the nature of our work and schedules and suggested they ask questions. The first question was utterly unrealistic. I was asked about the size of the territorial aggrandizement Hungary might expect at the peace table because the ministries should plan projections for the future on this basis. Such people did not realize that we had to prepare for peace after a disastrously lost war and were still living under foreign occupation and control. During the armistice period the independence of Hungary was a fiction.

Besides the interdepartmental committee, several specialized committees and agencies participated in peace preparations. The Pál Teleki Institute for Political Science under the leadership of Count

István Révay prepared the material for territorial and nationality questions. An ad hoc committee supervised the financial and economic findings of the interdepartmental committee. This latter group consisted of the foremost economic experts in Hungary.[4] Besides its supervisory work it considered plans for the establishment of a Danubian federation. I invited this committee to hold weekly meetings over a period of about three months, and appreciated the lively debates therein. Some members favored a federation with Austria and Czechoslovakia, others with Rumania and Yugoslavia, and we pondered the advantages and disadvantages of larger units. We discussed about eleven variations. Our economic experts considered the possible effect of various federations or confederations on the Hungarian industry, agriculture, and trade. Then we examined the political consequences of particular unions, but we were never in a position to use the valuable material collected on this subject. The final committee report proposed that the government reveal Hungary's economic plight at the peace conference and ask for substantial reduction of reparation payments and inclusion of properties confiscated and removed by the Soviet army in any such payments. The foreign minister considered some of these proposals so unrealistic under the political conditions of the country that he did not even attempt to present them to the council of ministers.

Eventually the personnel associated with peace preparations consisted of several hundred officials and experts, and therefore their efforts required a high degree of coordination. After nearly a year of work and consultation, each ministry summed up its findings in a final report based on preparatory memoranda discussed at the weekly meetings. But in early 1946 the Communist party discovered the implications of this work and delayed its conclusion in certain ministries. Thereafter Communist delegates appeared in the general committee and sabotaged its work.

The disagreement among the coalition parties concerning peace aims remained the most difficult domestic problem throughout the peace preparatory period. Extreme differences made it impossible to find principles acceptable to all parties. Although the government avoided a stand in the matter, I had to look for some expedient in order to proceed in the muddled political situation. As soon as I began my work I attempted to get around the lack of governmental aims by asking for an advisory delegate for political problems from each coalition party. The delegates were appointed, and we pledged our mutual good will and readiness for cooperation. I stated that I would always be glad to give any information to the coalition parties but, for my own enlightenment, asked for their stand with regard to peace aims. For several months I did not receive any proposal from the parties, and I interpreted this passive attitude to mean that I could proceed with the preparatory work without further ado. My position was made easier, though this did not change the political difficulties.

Besides lack of positive peace aims, a further obstacle arose from the fact that left-wing representatives in the coalition government considered the members of the war governments, including that of Kállay (which initiated negotiations with Britain and the United States), as war criminals. Rákosi ironically remarked to me, "Mr. Envoy, you may soon greet your former boss, Kállay, here in Budapest, when he will stand before the People's Court." The foreign minister warned me at the outset that the coalition parties would strongly protest all arguments tending to exonerate the former governments and political leaders. This punitive attitude toward the past was not entirely of Hungarian origin. In the postwar period the Horthy regime was unpopular in both East and West. In the eyes of the victorious powers Hungary was a junior partner of the Axis and, with its revisionist claims, one of the chief troublemakers in European politics. Few people gave a second thought to the cause of Hungarian revisionism, the fact that after the First World War over three million Hungarians, almost one third of the Magyar people, were forced to become citizens of foreign countries without plebiscite or any popular consultation. Hungary's reluctant participation in the Second World War and endeavors toward an early armistice were not considered. Unlike other Axis satellites, Hungary did not change sides effectively during the hostilities, and the fact that some Hungarian troops fought with the Germans until the last became a special reproach to Hungary. It changed the image of the unwilling satellite to that of Hitler's last satellite.

The new Hungarian regime under the orders of the ACC had to carry out the policy of the victorious nations in punishing some members of former governments and leading politicians of the Arrow Cross and other pro-Nazi parties. As things stood it would have been difficult to adopt a different attitude. These actions were not within the exclusive jurisdiction of the Hungarian government. The armistice agreement compelled Hungary to "cooperate in the apprehension and trial, . . of persons accused of war crimes," and the Russians were greatly dissatisfied with the "lax" Hungarian attitude in the matter. The ACC under Soviet chairmanship gave the Russians a legal channel for intervention. The notion of "war criminals" was interpreted broadly at Nuremberg and elsewhere. At the close of hostilities legal and moral principles, let alone political wisdom, were not the most important sources of inspiration throughout Europe.

Even under such political conditions it was necessary to find ways to tell as much of the truth as possible. In view of the imposed limitations, the only alternative was to explain that a majority of the Hungarian people resisted nazism and that even the "reactionary pro-German" governments resisted under pressure of popular feeling. On December 28, 1945, in a memorandum addressed to Prime Minister Tildy, I summarized my views concerning the extent of war responsibility:

> My opinion concerning our responsibility for the war is that we have to present every possible argument which is apt to reduce such charges or at least explain reasons for our conduct during the war. Since the personality of the state remains the same in international relations, irrespective of a change of regimes, our international responsibility is not affected by internal changes. Therefore, we should not assume responsibility for the Hungarian nation above that which is absolutely necessary. To do so would be contrary to the best interests of the people.[5]

Even for the Communists it was difficult to reject this reasoning openly. Although the left-wing elements of the coalition disliked and criticized such arguments, they did not veto them. Thus it was possible to develop these ideas in pamphlets and books. The aim of such publications was to show by specific examples that even during the period of alliance between the German and Hungarian governments the mass of the Hungarian people opposed Nazi ideas and policies. The pamphlets and books moreover contained data concerning the fate of Allied war prisoners and political refugees in Hungary. They dealt with information concerning the Jewish problem, sabotage and resistance to Germany, economic help given to territories under German occupation, and explained some results of democratization of the country.[6]

Besides political difficulties there were many obstacles that disturbed the peace preparatory work, and a good illustration is the Soviet interpretation of the armistice agreement concerning destruction of Fascist literature. In fulfilling the terms of the armistice agreement, the Hungarian government appointed a commission to establish a list of Fascist books. Dominated by Communists, the commission determined the Fascist character of the publications according to Soviet wishes. All individuals, libraries, and public institutions were obliged to surrender all books on the list for destruction. Only two libraries were exempt, to preserve Fascist literature in closed rooms for use of authorized persons. Since the Foreign Ministry and other government agencies did not receive exemption, I attempted to persuade the Communists that it was practically impossible to explain Nazi expansionism or fifth column activity in Hungary if the relevant Nazi literature was not available. My explanations were not accepted, and all alleged Fascist books in the Foreign Ministry or belonging to the scholarly institutions associated with us were destroyed.

The Soviet commission controlling the destruction of Fascist books gave only limited consideration to the list established by the Hungarian commission. In some libraries, they declared as Fascist, and thus destroyed, German economic and statistical periodicals dating from the last decades of the nineteenth century. In the catalogue of the Library of the National Museum the Soviet Commission was looking for the word "Horthy" and asked for all the books catalogued under similar headings. Thus they destroyed all books on "horticulture," some published in the seventeenth century, claiming that such works spread Horthy propaganda. In this case the minister of religion and public instruction, Géza Teleki, personally intervened, albeit without result. Intervention in such cases was considered pro-Fascist not only by Soviet authorities but by Hungarian Communist leaders who were anxious to carry out promptly all Soviet orders and satisfy the wishes of Soviet authorities.

In addition to the official peace preparations, a group of scholars worked in secrecy under the leadership of Géza Teleki, after his resignation from the cabinet. This private group produced two mimeographed volumes with four annexes under the title, "The Hungarian Nation's Proposals and Basic Principles in Regard to the Peace Treaty." This substantial work discussed the general problems of Central Europe and Hungary's special problems with Rumania, Czechoslovakia, and Yugoslavia, and proposed solutions according to the traditions inherited from Pál Teleki. The presentation disregarded the restrictions of the coalition government and the political conditions of postwar Hungary. Through confidential channels the volumes were sent to Western political leaders, diplomats, and scholars, and deposited in some large libraries.

In the long course of history this work might be useful, but in the context of peacemaking in 1945–46 it had no effect. Scholarly arguments and suggestions emanating from an ex-enemy country could not penetrate the frame of peace negotiations established at Potsdam and at the Moscow conference in December 1945. My private contacts with Teleki were not unobserved, and in early 1947 the political police interrogated the personnel of the Pál Teleki Institute of Political Science concerning my relations with Teleki during the peace preparatory period.

Proposals for the Peace Settlement

Some politicians, particularly in the right wing of the Smallholder party, emphasized the necessity of foreign propaganda in view of the coming peace conference. They did not realize that as long as the coalition parties did not agree on peace aims, there was not much to publicize. It was obvious that the Hungarian government could not freely inform foreign countries about our fundamental troubles and especially our difficulties with the Soviet authorities. In view of Hungary's diplomatic isolation, and especially because of the meager finances at the disposal of the Foreign Ministry, any propaganda could have boomeranged. The wartime solidarity between the Soviet Union and the Western powers had its full effect on Danubian Europe. The Western Allies made it understood that they were not disposed to antagonize the Soviet Union on Hungary's account. Furthermore, Moscow could prevent all official Hungarian activities in foreign countries through the ACC.

To circumvent the difficulties and break down our isolated position, I began to draft peace preparatory notes, but the problem was how to use them. In the course of this procedure the difficult questions were: To whom could the notes be addressed? What could be said? How far could we go without arousing the Soviet Communist wrath? The alternatives were poor. One of them was siding completely with the Soviet Union in the hope that Moscow would give substantial support for Hungary, or at least the burdens of the Soviet occupation would be alleviated. This policy was proposed by the Communist party, the left wing of the Social Democratic party, and the fellow travelers in the National Peasant party. I listened to their arguments many times. They explained that a pro-Soviet foreign policy would assure Hungary's survival and adaptation to the new power constellation in Europe, and would receive Soviet good will and support. Time and again Rákosi pointed out that Hungary should imitate Petru Groza's democratic government in Rumania. I may add that in the early stage of Soviet occupation, there was a sincere desire in all coalition parties to get along with the Russians, if not for other reasons, then because of national survival. The German occupation and atrocities committed by the Nazis and the Arrow Cross regime automatically generated sympathy for the Russians.

At the close of hostilities no other Great Power existed in continental Europe. Britain was weak and showed little interest in Hungary's fate before and during the war; and afterwards the British were busy rehabilitating their country. The United States as the strongest world power was the ultimate hope of many Hungarians, but the attitude of the American minister in Budapest, Arthur Schoenfeld, made it clear that Washington might give some economic aid but was not thinking of supporting the Hungarians politically. Before his departure to Budapest, Schoenfeld received the instructions that the United States "would not, of course, take position of supporting Hungary against the Soviet Union . . . The United States government recognizes that the Soviet Union's interest in Hungary is more direct than ours."[7] We did not know about these instructions, but the inaction of the American and British diplomats in Budapest demonstrated *ad oculos* on many occasions the policy of Washington and London.

Although support was not coming from Western quarters, cooperation proved to be difficult with the Russians. They expected unconditional submission. Though I listened attentively to politicians who advocated exclusively Soviet orientation, my problem remained that I had not seen any Soviet willingness to support Hungarian claims no matter what we did. It became obvious that Moscow was following a punitive policy, although we did not know at that time that during the war Stalin expressed several times his dislike of Hungarians. According to a memorandum by Under Secretary of State Sumner Welles (March 16, 1943)

> Mr. Eden said that he had encountered upon his last visit to Moscow great antagonism towards Hungary. I asked Mr. Eden if he could tell me specifically what Stalin might have stated with regard to Hungary and Mr. Eden replied that he thought all that was said was that Stalin demanded that "Hungary be punished." Lord Halifax suggested that this might mean that Hungary would be obliged to make territorial concessions to the future Rumania. Mr. Eden said that he thought it was likely.[8]

It was a puzzling question how the Hungarian government could inform the victorious Great Powers about our peace proposals. Having lost our independence with the German occupation in March 1944, we knew little of inter-Allied decisions that shaped the postwar world; we had received only scattered news from abroad. After the

Soviet occupation, Hungary became even more isolated because the representatives of neutral powers were expelled, Hungarian officials could not leave the country without a Soviet exit permit, and we could not renew diplomatic relations without approval of the ACC.

It was necessary to break through our isolation, and I drafted a few memoranda and diplomatic notes about our urgent problems and proposals for the peace settlement. I presented some procedural alternatives to Gyöngyösi for dispatching notes to the victorious Great Powers, and he decided to address the first peace preparatory note only to the Soviet government. He did not wish to assume full responsibility for the content of the draft I presented to him and submitted it to the cabinet. The Council of Ministers toned down the note, to be signed by the prime minister, General Béla Miklós, who was in turn to present it personally to Marshal Voroshilov. Several days later the foreign minister by chance discovered that the prime minister had signed but not delivered the note dated on July 4, 1945. In those times, presentation of complaints to the Russians was not an enviable task, apt to result in unpleasant repercussions. Finally the foreign minister took courage and handed the note to Pushkin.[9]

This note contained propositions dealing with economic difficulties of the country, the persecution of Hungarians in Czechoslovakia, and the new territorial settlement to be established by the peace treaty. Among other things, the note complained that the industry of the country was disrupted because the Soviet army had confiscated raw materials, machine tools, and manufactured products. The note requested that these materials either be restored or that they be regarded as reparation deliveries, because under international law they could not be considered war booty.[10] Moreover, it proposed that confiscatory actions by the Soviet army should be categorically forbidden in the future.[11] The second part of the note described the drastic anti-Hungarian measures in Czechoslovakia, comparing them with Nazi methods. It asked for Soviet intervention to halt these discriminatory measures and persecutions. Concerning the new territorial settlement, the note proposed the adoption of the principle of nationality and plebiscites. The Soviet government did not even acknowledge receipt of this note.

The overbearing Soviet attitude and passivity of the Western powers generated a feeling of helplessness, and it was difficult for Hungarians to see any light at the end of the tunnel. Disorder and lawlessness in East Central Europe demonstrated that the centuries-old international system had come to an end. Despite, or rather because of, these desperate conditions, the only honorable policy was to make proposals for creation of a better world in Danubian Europe through institutionalized cooperation. At the same time we had to take a stand for the interests of the Hungarian people within and outside the boundaries of Hungary. Naturally the defense of the Hungarian minorities in the neighboring states was very difficult under the existing conditions, especially in Czechoslovakia. Realizing the ineffectiveness of our interventions with the ACC or the Soviet government and the complications caused by discussions in the Council of Ministers, I proposed to the foreign minister not to submit the peace preparatory notes to the cabinet but to deliver them directly to the representatives of the three major powers in Budapest, and afterward to send a copy to the coalition parties. As a result of the lesson learned from the first peace preparatory note addressed to the Soviet government, the foreign minister accepted this plan. He knew that he had to assume political responsibility for this procedure, which violated the rules of the ACC and the coalition government at the same time, and was willing to face the music later. Consequently the Communists, confronted with a fait accompli, could cause trouble only after our notes had been delivered.

The Hungarian peace aims were presented for the first time to the representatives of the three major powers in a note of August 14, 1945,[12] a note advocating close economic cooperation among the Danubian nations and an increased industrialization of Hungary to be carried out in the course of economic reconstruction of the Danubian region. It proposed international cultural commissions for the advancement of friendly cooperation among the Danubian peoples:

> The Hungarian Government thinks it desirable to set up international cultural commissions within the framework of the new world organizations—or at least limited to South-Eastern Europe—which would undertake to investigate in a friendly spirit those biased statements and harmful tendencies appearing in the press, school books and political publications, which are liable to hamper international cooperation and good neighbourliness.
>
> This commission could achieve positive constructive work by the promulgation of those tenets which would create a friendly atmosphere between the Danubian peoples. These principles could then be popularized by the different countries in their press, school books, and radio.[13]

As for territorial settlement at the peace conference, the Hungarian government suggested that if boundaries lost their significance, the ideal state of affairs would appear. Failing this, the cause of international cooperation would be best served if the boundaries were determined in conformity with the freely expressed wishes of the populations:

> The most effective measure to counteract national antagonism, which is still rampant in countries corrupted by Fascist doctrines and constantly stirred by chauvinist elements, would be the delimination of boundaries according to the freely expressed wish of the population and to the principles of nationality wherever the nationalities live on contiguous territories . . .
>
> The Hungarian Government is well aware of the fact that a settlement according to the principles of nationality is not sufficient in itself to solve economic problems. The economic problems of South-Eastern Europe cannot be eliminated by adjusting the boundaries one way or another but by extensive economic cooperation. On the other hand if the boundaries are delineated in conformity with the wishes of the population concerned, this would bring about the political stability necessary to economic cooperation.

Since the Hungarian government realized that ethnic minorities would remain outside the mother country, however the borders might be drawn, the note emphasized the necessity of providing for institutional protection of national minorities under the aegis of the United Nations.

Although ideas concerning political integration of the Danubian nations were hidden between the lines, the Communist party objected to the general principles expressed in the note. Rákosi declared that proposals for full-fledged cooperation of the Danubian nations were premature. These countries, he argued, must become truly democratic, and afterwards they would cooperate automatically. Coincident with Communist objections, Pushkin presented strong Soviet criticisms. The Western powers did not react at all.

In this situation the Hungarian political peace aims could not be developed in further detail, and I decided to prepare notes dealing with seemingly technical problems to which the Communists could not easily object. These were regulation of problems connected with citizenship, Hungarian water routes giving access to the sea, and improvements of hydrographic problems and development of water power in the Carpathian basin.

A note of October 31, 1945,[14] dealing with the citizenship question, explained that as a consequence of the Trianon Treaty, thousands of inhabitants of prewar Hungary, who had never left the country, had been deprived of their Hungarian citizenship without opportunity of acquiring citizenship in any of the successor states. The origin of this situation was the complicated and frequently contradictory provisions of the Treaty of Trianon, which enabled certain states to deny citizenship to members of an undesirable minority. These people were left in the neighboring countries without the enjoyment of the rights connected with citizenship, and greatly handicapped in their economic and other activities. In reference to this situation, the note proposed measures to be incorporated into the peace treaty in order to prevent such an anomaly.

A note dated November 12, 1945,[15] dealt primarily with an elaboration of landlocked Hungary's problem concerning free access to the sea. It proposed numerous improvements in the Danubian Convention of 1921, and the second part of the note was devoted to the Carpathian Basin waterways and suggested solutions that would have resulted in a development similar to the Tennessee Valley Authority. This note insisted on the maintenance of the international character of the Danube. It urged revival and strengthening of international control over the river, with continued participation of nonriparian states in an effectively functioning commission, and advocated freedom of navigation in the Danubian Valley. This aspect of the note later was referred to by Cavendish W. Cannon, head of the American delegation at the 1948 Danubian Conference in Belgrade, in the following statement:

> It is interesting to note that the postwar government of Hungary on November 12, 1945, addressed a note to the United States, British, and Soviet Governments, giving its views on the Danube question. It called attention to the great importance to Hungary of a regime which guarantees full freedom of navigation. It suggested that the prewar system of international navigation be reconstituted with provisions for changes required by new conditions. The Hungarian Government did not envisage elimination of nonriparian representation, for it suggested consolidation into one Commission of the Danube. Both Commissions, as the Conference is aware, had nonriparian representation. There have been changes since 1945 but we believe the long-term economic interests of Hungary remain the same.[16]

Such, then, were some of the efforts aimed at lasting peace and constructive cooperation with neighbors. Surely the task was difficult and full of frustrations. To some of us it was beginning to appear an almost hopeless undertaking.

Deadlock and New Efforts

In the second half of 1945, Soviet pressure for the expulsion of all Germans from Hungary and the persecution of Hungarians in Czechoslovakia and Rumania became acute. These issues were administratively outside the peace preparatory division and belonged within the jurisdiction of the political division of the Foreign Ministry. I was not always informed of the steps taken, but intervened whenever I could relate these issues to peace preparations.

Defeat of the Communists and victory of the Smallholder party in the Budapest municipal elections in October and at the general elections in November 1945, caused a short-lived optimism even in foreign affairs, although the new coalition government created under the premiership of Zoltán Tildy (November 15, 1945) proved no stronger than the Miklós government. Despite a Smallholder majority in parliament, the all-powerful Ministry of Interior remained in Communist hands.

Soviet engineered consolidation of the Communist-dominated puppet governments in Rumania and Bulgaria, in violation of the Yalta Declaration on Liberated Europe, presaged a gloomy future for the new Hungarian regime. Soviet malevolence was especially evident in connection with Soviet endorsement of persecution of Hungarians in Czechoslovakia, Soviet abuses violating the armistice agreement, and in general the extreme exploitation that characterized the Soviet Union's treatment of the Hungarian economy. Of course it had been clear that Russian influence would increase after the war and that under the new political balance in Europe, Hungary's political, social, and economic structure would undergo important changes. Russian abuses, methods, and general intolerance nevertheless caused bewilderment and consternation.

Despite all the difficulties, the preparations for the peace conference and a stand for the interest of the Hungarian people appeared to be both a political necessity and an elementary duty. Continuation of the peace preparatory work, however, became almost impossible because the new government—despite some consolidation of Hungary's internal and international affairs—could not decide on peace aims. The government did not take a stand on any fundamental question of foreign affairs. Despite my repeated proposals, it did not designate delegates and experts for the peace conference. It was an anomalous situation that while the Hungarian peace aims were expressed to the major victorious powers in our note of August 14,

1945, the very same principles were not endorsed explicitly by the government and could not be debated by the coalition parties. The Communist party and the left-wing of the Socialist party criticized the principles and proposals expressed in this note. In answer to my pressing inquiries, the foreign minister informed me that disagreement on peace aims might easily blow up the coalition, and that such a situation might open the door for developments similar to those in Rumania and Bulgaria. And so, *Maul halten und weiter dienen* (to shut up and do our duty) was necessary in the hope of a better future.

Another difficulty was that the Foreign Ministry remained at the mercy of party politics. When I criticized this situation, the foreign minister in turn complained to me that he was not able to resist Communist wishes in connection with the appointment of their party men in the foreign service, because of the precedents created by the Smallholder and Social-Democratic parties. Since I was a civil servant without party affiliation, Gyöngyösi tried to persuade me to enter the Smallholder party. I refused and expressed the opinion that a civil servant must consider the general interests of the nation and should not be influenced by allegiance to a party and participation in party politics. Although this reasoning seemed outlandish at that time, he respected my view. I argued that my position would be stronger both domestically and internationally if I remained a non-party man.

Reflecting on the political stumbling blocks in peace preparations, I first informed Prime Minister Tildy in mid-December 1945 that the peace preparatory work had reached a deadlock, and on December 28, I presented to him an exhaustive memorandum. The memorandum described the history, progress, and actual state of peace preparations, analyzed the main problems, and very frankly discussed some of the outstanding political difficulties. As already mentioned, I explained my views concerning the handling of Hungary's war responsibility and dealt at some length with a decree concerning the expulsion of the Germans from Hungary issued on December 22, 1945. I thought it necessary to emphasize the danger of accepting the doctrine of collective responsibility in regard to any group of Hungarian citizens. The memorandum pointed out that it was not sufficient to make decisions concerning our peace aims and the arguments to be used, but it would be necessary to concentrate our efforts upon carrying out the accepted policies. In this connection I referred to the lack of governmental experience on the part of the coalition parties, especially conspicuous in the handling of foreign affairs. I developed my objections to the disintegration of Hungarian foreign policy under the coalition regime, especially some abuses in party political appointments in the foreign service. I summed up the urgent agenda in the following points:

1. The Government's decision concerning our Peace aims and argumentations. Once such decisions are taken, we should manifest a consistent conduct with regard to accepted moral, political and legal principles.

2. The immediate appointment of experts to be sent to the Peace Conference so that they could begin the study of the material as soon as possible.

3. The establishment of an adequate Peace preparatory organization and of provisions assuring that the execution of the Peace preparatory work under the guidance of the Foreign Ministry should not have to be interrupted from time to time or limited to an insufficient framework because of technical reasons or constant lack of funds. Not only pengö, but also foreign currency must be provided for in time.

4. The Ministry of Industry as well as the Ministry of Finance should be advised by the Government to complete without delay their peace preparatory work.

5. All government agencies should be instructed with regard to our peace aims and accordingly an agreement should be made between the political parties aiming at uniform and consistent public policies under the guidance of the Foreign Ministry. The same unity of view should prevail on the radio, in the press and other publications, in the activities of the parties and in the course of official and semi-official travels abroad.

6. The elimination of petty personal and party political influences with respect to the organization of our foreign service and especially in connection with the selection of delegates to be sent to the Peace Conference.

I ventured to mention above a few viewpoints which, in my modest opinion, are important in connection with the preparations for peace. I wanted to be absolutely straightforward in pointing out difficulties and causes of trouble because this is a primary duty to all those who took risks in difficult times for the establishment of a democratic Hungary.

Finally, I would like to emphasize that Hungary, after a war which was lost politically, militarily, and to some extent even morally, is confronted with better prepared states whose diplomatic position is incomparably more favorable than ours. In addition, the rehabilitation of the country is being carried out amidst a great economic crisis and other difficulties by political parties which — without their own fault — have not, thus far, had any governmental experience.

We must sincerely admit that the unfavorable diplomatic position of ours, and the difficult internal conditions of the country frequently hinder correct actions. Thus, it will not be easy to achieve success. Notwithstanding difficulties, however, all of us, and first of all the responsible Government have to do all possible for the promotion of the Hungarian case at the Peace Conference. The future of Hungarian democracy depends largely on the success of this work.

Mister Prime Minister, I am awaiting your effective and urgent actions, and those of the Hungarian Government, and remain,

Respectfully yours,
(signed) István Kertész[17]

For a short time this memorandum caused consternation in high governmental circles, and as a result I received promises from the prime minister and the foreign minister that they would take steps to eliminate the difficulties. They authorized me to prepare new peace preparatory notes that had to be in line with the general views of the government in foreign affairs. Yet difficulties did not cease. Friendly pledges could not change the fact that the coalition parties could not agree on principles in foreign policy—particularly as to our specific aims at the peace conference.

Tildy eventually called an interparty conference in mid-January 1946, which I attended as the official in charge of peace preparations in the Foreign Ministry. The conference was frustrated by the dynamism and dialectics of the Communist leader Rákosi whose obvious goal was to prevent any decision. The representative of the Social Democratic party, Szakasits, supported him with enthusiasm. The issue that occasioned the longest debate involved the decree of December 22, 1945, concerning the deportation of the Germans from Hungary. I pointed out that this decree was a fundamental mistake from the point of view of our peace preparations and national interests and asked for its revision. In my opposition to the indiscriminate expulsion of the Germans, I was supported only by the Smallholder undersecretary of state, István Balogh. The other Smallholder representatives and the Social Democrats sided with Rákosi or remained silent. In regard to other issues connected with our preparations for the peace conference, the representatives of the Smallholder party (Tildy, Gyöngyösi, and Balogh) remained passive. The representative of the Peasant party, Imre Kovács, firmly stated that we must take a stand for the claims vitally affecting the nation. Otherwise, he added, the Peasant party would be obliged to reconsider its participation in the coalition government. This was a strong statement, but most participants in the meeting suspected that the Peasant party was infiltrated by Communists, and in case of a showdown would not follow Kovács. Eventually the interparty conference ended without having made any substantial decisions.

In addition to the territorial and nationality questions, it was necessary to decide upon economic problems to be submitted to the peace conference, as well as the manner of their presentation. In this respect Soviet and Communist interventions again frustrated progress. Envoy Pushkin said that the Hungarian territorial and political grievances and claims were vestiges of the Horthy regime, and refused to consider them. He urged the "democratization" of Hungary and acceptance of the Czechoslovak demands concerning the exchange of population and transfer of Hungarians from Czechoslovakia to Hungary. He suggested, confidentially, that Hungary should stress territorial claims against Rumania, which as a former satellite was in the same political category as Hungary. Marshal Voroshilov intimated to Prime Minister Tildy that Hungary might obtain territorial compensation from Rumania if it behaved well and accepted the Czechoslovakian proposals concerning the Hungarian question in Czechoslovakia.

Pushkin was more concerned that the Hungarian government might reveal the country's plight to the Western public — especially the Soviet methods for exploiting devastated Hungary. When he discovered that the Hungarian government was compiling data on war damages by means of detailed questionnaires, to be answered by all inhabitants of Hungary, he preemptorily demanded the cessation of this work and destruction of the data. He asserted that the ACC had not authorized this action and charged that the questionnaires clearly indicated that the goal was to establish statistics concerning damage caused by the Soviet army. In due course the Foreign Ministry transmitted the Soviet protest to the Ministry of Finance. Eventually an elaborate reply to Pushkin explained that the war was caused by German aggression, and therefore the Hungarian government intended to attribute war damage to the Germans. Because the questionnaires covered different periods during which the damages occured, those caused by the Germans and the Soviet army were easily distinguishable. The balance was decidedly unfavorable to the Soviet army.

In harmony with Soviet policy, the Communist party made efforts to sabotage preparations of economic questions for the peace conference. Communist cabinet ministers hindered nomination of the chief economic delegate to the peace conference. I initiated the appointment of Arthur Kárász, director and former president of the National Bank of Hungary. Time and again, Gyöngyösi brought up the matter in cabinet meetings, but the Communist ministers always asked for time to consider the problem. Finally, when Kárász was about to leave the country on an official mission, the Council of Ministers agreed to his appointment. After his return he prepared a memorandum revealing the economic situation of the country and proposing that we should ask for a reduction of reparation payments. When this memorandum was read in the peace prepatory ad hoc sub-committee of the parliament's Committee on Foreign Affairs, the Communists reacted violently. Chief Communist delegate to peace preparations, Joseph Révai, launched a sharp attack and concluded: "Because of this memorandum a head must fall," adding obligingly, "of course, only politically." The political decapitation of Kárász took place promptly. General Sviridov demanded that the president and managing director of the National Bank and Kárász be removed and prosecuted because of mismanagement of the ruble fund in the National Bank. The charges were absurd and the Hungarian government resisted for some time. Eventually the three leading officials were dismissed but not prosecuted.[18]

In a note dated Januray 25, 1946, I found it expedient to request the three major powers to appoint a committee of experts to investigate problems connected with the Hungarian peace settlement.[19] The memorandum attached to this note pointed out some of the mistakes and errors at the peace conference after the First World War and suggested that the organizational weakness of the conference in 1919 facilitated and partly explained why the Treaty of Trianon incorporated exaggerated claims against Hungary.

In a note dated February 1, 1946,[20] it was possible to insert passages describing the anti-Nazi conduct of the Hungarian people during the war and to make statements on Hungary's responsibility in the sense I had indicated in my memorandum addressed to Tildy. A later memorandum dealt in detail with Hungary's responsibility in the Second World War. Another explained the handling of the Jewish question in Hungary. Both memoranda were handed later to the powers participating in the Paris Conference.[21]

The note of February 1 pointed out that the Hungarian problem after the Second World War must not find an isolated solution. A proper solution would consider the interests of all Danubian peoples in an institutional reorganization of the Danubian basin. The note emphasized that the settlement of Southeast European problems did not present "insurmountable difficulties," and remarked that

similar conditions of life brought about by geographic factors, the influence which for centuries one nation had been exercising over the other, the effects of intermarriage and more especially the cooperation of the long period preceding the epoch of exaggerated nationalism had long ago produced forms of life which bore a certain resemblance to each other. The small states are in fact separated from each other only by differences of language and an exaggerated and improper interpretation of their historical traditions, and the chauvinist propaganda to which the former gave rise. Large sections of the population, above all the working classes and the peasants who struggle against the same social evils, have no difficulty in understanding each other. The first step towards the furthering of mutual prosperity through peaceful cooperation would be an honest and institutional attempt to uproot the nationalism which, for the last century, has been fostering the growth of differences.

After such explanations the note concluded that the settlement of Southeast European problems should be based on the following principles:

1. Harmonization of questions of territory and nationality.
2. Establishment of economic and cultural cooperation.
3. Elimination of factors that give rise to political and social discord between countries.

Not until May 1946 were we able to present a note to the three major powers that put forth more detailed propositions. In the interval several incidents characteristic of our situation occurred. In early February 1946 the Social Democratic party delegate to the peace preparatory work, Sándor Szalai, called at my office to inform me in the name of his party that the peace preparations under my direction had become partly useless and partly harmful. He accused me of nationalism and suggested that the Foreign Ministry try to find a practical solution by removing the Hungarian minority from Czechoslovakia, thus assuring amicable relations with our northern neighbor. I rejected his suggestions and replied that the peace preparatory work was not my personal enterprise; if there were such essential political objections, they should be raised at a higher level and reported to the foreign minister and prime minister. Simultaneous with the move of the Social Democratic party and the Communist party, the Soviet envoy, Pushkin, expressed dissatisfaction with the peace preparatory notes. He pointed out to Gyöngyösi that our notes had the character of policies followed under the Horthy regime and could have been sent by that regime. A few days later the Social Democratic press launched a campaign against the foreign minister.[22]

Gyöngyösi then refused to sign a note he had previously approved, which dealt with territorial and ethnographic questions, particularly with problems of Transylvania. He called an interparty conference in the Foreign Ministry and submitted the text of the note to the representatives of the coalition parties.

At this interparty meeting the delegates of the Communist party, supported by Vilmos Böhm, delegate of the Social Democratic party, refused to accept the ideas and terms of the proposed note. The Communists did not offer any specific suggestions. They stated only that the note contained veiled revisionist tendencies against Rumania, that Hungary should by no means weaken "Groza's democracy," and that before a stand could be taken Soviet support must be sought. Our actions, they said, must be governed by Soviet advice. The interparty meeting eventually accepted this suggestion and advised the foreign minister to find out more about Soviet intentions as to the peace settlement. I could not make it known that it was Voroshilov and Pushkin who had suggested that Hungary should raise territorial claims against Rumania.

The draft note rejected by the interparty meeting developed the idea that the Hungarian nation should have a territory corresponding to the proportion of the Hungarian population in Danubian Europe. It was reemphasized that the conditions brought about by Trianon had contributed greatly to the dissatisfaction of the Hungarian nation and had developed the revisionist and irredentist movements. As to the future, the note again proposed the setting up by the victorious powers of an expert committee whose duty would be to examine the nationality and territorial problems. The Hungarian government declared it was willing to accept a plebiscite regarding the fate of any territories affected by a new settlement. The Communists and Socialists especially objected to the following passage of the note dealing with Transylvania:

> For the present, the Hungarian Government only wishes to point out that a territorial rearrangement affects Hungary most closely where the question of Transylvania is concerned. With the satisfactory solution of the problem of Transylvania—by settling equitably the political and economic claims of Hungary and Rumania—this territory could form a connecting link, rather than a dividing line between the two states. In any case, the solution must be such that any division of the mountainous region of Transylvania lying between the areas of the original settlement of these two neighboring nations—both of which have populations of about the same size, 11-12 million Hungarians, 13-14 million Rumanians, of whom the greater part inhabit the Great Plain—should be affected in such a manner that it should complete most advantageously the economic systems of both countries, and

that, from a national point of view, it should also create a state of equilibrium.

After the interparty meeting the peace preparatory work came to a standstill. The Smallholder party did prepare a memorandum concerning peace aims, but the party leaders did not want a showdown with the Communists since it might have caused the breakdown of the coalition government.

Meanwhile the technical part of the peace preparatory work was nearing completion. All important problems that could have been dealt with at the peace conference were worked out in detail by competent experts and then synthesized. There were hundreds of memoranda and other materials brought into a comprehensive system.

Because of lack of peace aims on the part of the government and the breakdown of cooperative efforts by the parties, we could not use the materials for any specific purpose; in this situation I felt that my duties had been fulfilled and I could do nothing more. On March 13, 1946, I asked the foreign minister for release as head of the division for peace preparation and suggested the division be dissolved. I explained that the division had accomplished its mission, and the necessary political decisions must be made by the government. Since my request went unheeded I sent a letter to Prime Minister Ferenc Nagy on April 5, 1946, informing him of the deadlock in peace preparations and expressing disagreement with the government's dilatory policy. I stated that under the circumstances I could do no more useful work and requested that the government release me from my assignment.

Shortly after I dispatched this letter to the prime minister, the foreign minister informed me confidentially that perhaps the situation was not hopeless. He told me that leading members of the Hungarian government, following an invitation of the Soviet government, shortly would visit Moscow. He asked me to prepare material for the delegation and asked me to accompany them as their political adviser. Next day the embarrassed foreign minister regretfully informed me that Pushkin had removed my name as well as the name of the economic adviser[23] from the list, stating that the conference would negotiate issues of great political importance and therefore only leading politicians were needed and experts were unwanted. Under the circumstances, this was scarcely bad news for me.

I found it amusing that the delegate of the Social Democratic party to the peace preparations called on me again and excitedly asked for maps and materials concerning territorial claims against Rumania.

This was the same man, Szalai, who a few weeks before had characterized the peace preparatory work as partly useless and partly dangerous. He now explained enthusiastically that this material would be needed by the Social Democratic party leader, Szakasits, in Moscow. He indicated that the chances of regaining territories from Rumania were good and this would strengthen Hungarian democracy.

Faced with dissatisfied public opinion and strong Smallholder pressure, the government decided to ask for Soviet support concerning the settlement of the problem of Transylvania. The Communist party apparently received the green light from Moscow, reversed its attitude toward national aspirations, and suddenly became the champion of Hungarian territorial claims against Rumania, an attitude previously branded as Fascist and reactionary.

The government delegation under the leadership of Prime Minister Ferenc Nagy left on April 10 and was received in Moscow with boundless hospitality. Stalin devoted several hours to discussions with the members of the Hungarian delegation. The atmosphere seemed friendly, and Stalin's benevolent attitude inspired optimism for a favorable solution of Hungary's territorial claims in Transylvania.[24] Besides the friendly atmosphere, the meeting produced some positive results. The period for the fulfillment of the reparation liabilities was extended from six to eight years. Stalin promised an early return of the Hungarian prisoners of war and recognized the validity of the Hungarian claim for equal rights of Hungarians in Czechoslovakia. The Soviet demand for $15,000,000 for the restoration of Hungarian railroads was cancelled,[25] and the delegation believed that the Soviet leaders showed understanding for Hungary's territorial claims against Rumania. Although the Soviet negotiators made no promises, as a first step they recommended bilateral negotiations with the Rumanian government.

After the Moscow visit some confident politicians concluded that Stalin seemed to be a reasonable man of good will with whom the Smallholder politicians would be able to negotiate without the mediation of the Hungarian Communists. (It should be noted parenthetically that Stalin made similar favorable impressions on several Western politicians.) This optimism vanished when the leaders of Rumania refused to discuss Hungary's territorial claim with a special Hungarian envoy, Paul Sebestyén, dispatched to Bucharest. The Foreign Ministry promptly forwarded on April 27 a note defining Hungary's territorial claims to representatives in Budapest of the three major victorious powers.[26]

Because of dissatisfaction and reproaches from many quarters and because of the general depression of public opinion caused by inactivity of the government in foreign affairs, the foreign minister decided to send me to Paris where at that time the Council of Foreign Ministers was in session preparing drafts for the peace treaties. Pushkin once more refused to grant me permission to travel abroad, saying I would not be needed for peace preparation in Paris. Gyöngyösi — under attack at that time even in the Smallholder party — was adamant and told Pushkin that if he was not allowed to send a high official of the Foreign Ministry to Paris to make preparations for the peace conference, he would no longer consider himself as foreign minister and would act accordingly. Not wanting to make a political issue of this trifle, Pushkin suggested I be appointed counselor to the Hungarian legation in Paris. He explained that such an appointment would enable him to grant me the necessary permit to leave the country.(Later Moscow reprimanded Pushkin because he gave me permit to leave for Paris.) Gyöngyösi promptly appointed me minister-counselor to the Hungarian legation in Paris and asked me to assume the role of the secretary-general of the Hungarian peace delegation. I left by plane on May 9, 1946. Shortly before my departure news arrived that the Council of Foreign Ministers at a meeting on May 7 had decided to accept the Trianon boundary between Hungary and Rumania as final.

A few days before I left, the president of the republic, Zoltán Tildy, asked me through a confidential go-between, Béla Demeter, whether I would be willing to lead the Hungarian peace delegation as foreign minister. Demeter informed me that a group of Transylvanian politicians had discussed with Tildy the problems connected with the peace settlement. In the course of these conversations they had criticized the weaknesses of Hungarian foreign policy, and Tildy himself expressed concern because of the general discontent with Gyöngyösi. He was considered pro-Soviet even in his own party. Inasmuch as national unity was of utmost importance before the peace conference, they had agreed with Tildy that I, as a civil servant without party affiliation, should take over the portfolio for the period of the peace conference. I replied that I was a government official and as such would do my best as administrative leader of the Hungarian peace delegation, but I would not consider accepting a cabinet position as long as the country was under Soviet occupation. I added that probably a few things could have been done differently in the past, but it was questionable whether the Russians would have tolerated a more assertive Hungarian foreign policy. Through military occupation and the camouflage of the ACC, Hungary was practically under Soviet rule. Since the Western powers did not mean business in Danubian Europe, no Hungarian foreign minister could have changed this situation. It is difficult to play cards if you do not have a partner and your opponents hold all the aces. Moreover, the Smallholder party was playing for time and wanted to avoid a showdown. Thus no one could have followed a foreign policy substantially different from that of Gyöngyösi. The only question was whether someone was willing to play a political role under such circumstances. I did not feel suited for this role and was convinced I could do more useful work in my administrative capacity.

Another surprise was in store for me. Ossukin, the English-speaking counselor of the Soviet legation, asked me to visit him. After a conversation about travel formalities concerning my trip to Paris, he suddenly opened a drawer of his desk and took out a thick folder. He explained that the files in it contained documentation of atrocities committed by the Hungarian army in the Soviet Union. After reading the dates, names, and other particulars of a few cases, he pointed out that it would not be prudent for the Hungarian delegation to bring up in Paris some of the alleged abuses of Soviet soldiers in Hungary because the Soviet government could make public much worse atrocities committed by the Hungarian army in Russia. I told Ossukin that I was not in a position to discuss such cases since I had no knowledge of them. I added that at the Paris Conference our object was to argue our peace aims along the lines we had developed in notes addressed to the three major victorious powers. He hardly reacted to my statement. As we were talking about different things and no meeting of minds was in sight, I used an excuse and left. Ossukin was considered the most powerful man at the Soviet legation, allegedly an intelligence operative disguised as diplomat. This strange threat, or blackmail, might have originated from his real profession. It was difficult to understand his motive because the atrocities committed by the Soviet army in East European countries were well known in Western Europe, and it would not have served our interests to bring them up in Paris.

5

Territorial and Nationality Problems

Before discussing the Hungarian case at the Paris Conference, one must examine a delicate problem of postwar Hungary: the fate of Hungarian minorities numbering over three million people in neighboring states, that is, almost one-third of the Hungarian nation.

The coalition parties did not want to support any policy similar to the revisionism of the Horthy regime, which was anathema both in the East and in the West. The Hungarian people had been exhausted by the war years, frustrated by Nazi and Soviet devastation of the country; they wanted peace and a fair settlement with all neighbors. Most politicians realized that the country was close to a political, economic, and social collapse, similar to that of Germany in 1945. In Hungarian politics in 1945–46 there were no traces of revisionist or imperialist tendencies.

Yet mistreatment and persecution of Hungarians in neighboring states had been a reality, and the fact remained that the peace treaty after the First World War had attached a large number of Magyar people, against their wishes, to neighboring states. The Hungarian peace delegation in 1920 had vainly proposed a plebiscite for the territories in dispute. It was obvious after the Second World War that to raise territorial claims against victorious states like Yugoslavia and Czechoslovakia would be futile. Without support of some of the victorious Great Powers, such claims would have met with general disapproval in Allied countries, and in home politics would not have been feasible anyway because of the opposition in the coalition parties, not to mention the ACC and the occupying Soviets.

In view of this predicament, it is pertinent to examine the wartime American approach toward Hungary's territorial and nationality problems, the American ideas of 1941–45. During the war, the State Department prepared several memoranda concerning Hungary's relations with its neighbors, and the briefing papers prepared for the second Quebec and Yalta conferences set out succinctly the American position. A briefing paper of September 1944 stated:

In regard to the territorial settlement, the United States favors, as a matter of principle, the restoration of the pre-Munich frontiers, and any consideration of the boundary disputes between Hungary and its neighbors should start from that point. However, we do not regard the pre-Munich boundaries as unchangeable and believe certain changes to be desirable in the interest of a stable settlement.

Thus, in the case of the frontier with Czechoslovakia, if an opportunity arises for revision by agreement which would leave to Hungary certain overwhelmingly Magyar-inhabited districts, the United States would favor such a solution. In the case of the frontier with Yugoslavia, the United States sees some merit in a compromise solution which would leave to Hungary the northern part of the Voyvodina, although this Government should not, we feel, press for such a solution. In the case of the frontier with Rumania, the American position will be more or less frozen by our agreement to the armistice terms for Rumania which provide for the restoration to that country of "all or the major part of Transylvania, subject to confirmation at the peace settlement." In the final settlement the United States would favor, at the least, a revision of the pre-war frontier on ethnic grounds, transferring to Hungary a small strip of territory given to Rumania at the end of the last war.[1]

The same briefing paper declared that the "United States does not contemplate participation in military operations in Hungary or in the occupation of that country. American troops in that area could probably be used more effectively, in the political sense, than either British or Soviet armies, but such participation would inevitably involve this Government as an active agent in the political questions of Southeastern Europe."[2] This statement left unanswered the question of how United States influence could be effective in territorial or other important issues in the area without being involved politically. Idealistic thinking in Washington seemed hardly sufficient under the circumstances. The briefing paper's solution was to send political representatives to Hungary in the period after surrender. It was thought that such representation would be able to support the general American objectives of "promoting a just and stable political and territorial settlement, as well as securing accurate first-hand political and economic information, and protecting American interests."[3]

A summary of the briefing paper on Hungarian problems prepared for the Yalta Conference suggested, in a similar fashion, that it would be desirable to secure agreement of the British and Soviet governments to three principles, of which the third was as follows:

The desirability of reaching a settlement of the Hungarian-Rumanian frontier dispute and of encouraging an eventual settlement between

Hungary and Czechoslovakia and perhaps between Hungary and Yugoslavia by friendly mutual negotiation, which would take into account the Hungarian ethnic claims.[4]

Subsequently the paper characterized the motives of the American position:

> The long-range interest of the United States in Hungary centers in our desire to see established peaceful and stable relationships among European nations. The United States has an interest in the achievement of solutions of Hungary's boundary disputes and its political and economic problems which will promote orderly progress and peace with neighboring states. We believe this interest would be served by a territorial settlement which would rectify the frontier with Rumania in favor of Hungary on ethnic grounds. While Hungary must of course renounce the territorial gains made at the expense of Czechoslovakia and Yugoslavia with German help, the United States would favor, for example, an eventual negotiated settlement which would transfer to Hungary some of the predominantly Hungarian-populated districts of southern Slovakia.[5]

A further suggestion was made that it was not in the interest of the United States "to see Hungary deprived of its independence or of any of its pre-1938 territories or saddled with economic obligations which would cripple its economy and thus delay general European recovery."[6] Then the paper set out American policy in the armistice period:

> While the United States would not, of course, take the position of supporting Hungary against the Soviet Union, it is possible that American and Soviet policies toward Hungary during the armistice period may not be in harmony. . . .
>
> The United States Government recognizes that the Soviet Union's interest in Hungary is more direct than ours. We have had no objection to the Soviet Government's taking the lead in the negotiations for the armistice and in the control of Hungary in the armistice period until the surrender of Germany. We do not, however, consider that the Soviet Union has any special privileged or dominant position in Hungary. . . .
>
> The interests of the United States would be served by the conclusion of peace with Hungary at the earliest practicable date. Such a step would put an end to many of the powers of control which under the armistice will be exercised by the Soviet Union, and by opening the way to the resumption of normal diplomatic relations between the United States and Hungary would give the United States Government a better opportunity to protect American interests in that country.
>
> It is also in our interest that free elections be held and that Hungary be left to manage its own internal affairs as soon as possible.[7]

The briefing paper on Rumanian problems also spoke of "the desirability of finding a solution of the Hungarian-Rumanian frontier dispute which will give some satisfaction to Hungary's legitimate claims and promote peaceful relations between the two states."[8] The paper thoughtfully suggested that

> It would be advantageous if reassurances could be obtained from the Soviet Government that: . . . The Soviet Government will agree to work with the other principal Allied Governments for a just and stable solution of the boundary dispute between Rumania and Hungary.[9]

From briefing papers and other more extensive documents available in the National Archives it appears that policymakers in the State Department were influenced by reasonable ideas. They defined the American objectives in rational, benevolent terms. They desired "peaceful and stable relationships among European nations." Friendly relations between Hungary and its neighbors were part of this scheme.

The State Department was looking for just solutions of long-standing conflicts in Danubian Europe. The idea was the application of distributive justice under the assumption that the Soviet Union and the minor victorious powers, such as Czechoslovakia and Yugoslavia, would be interested in a just territorial settlement based on ethnic principles. The assumption might have been realistic if leaders of the Soviet Union had been enlightened archangels or if American troops had participated in the occupation of Danubian Europe beyond Austria. But such involvement was considered and rejected in Washington. Probably it was thought in the State Department that a general peace conference would allow a reasonable application of the principle of self-determination. In reality things have worked out differently.

The Sub-Carpathian Territory

The postwar Hungarian government first confronted the problem of Sub-Carpathian Ruthenia. According to a Soviet-Czechoslovak agreement of June 29, 1945, this region and thirteen communities from Slovakia had been annexed to the Ukrainian Soviet Socialist Republic. In this area according to the 1930 Czechoslovak census were 123,129 Hungarians, the majority of whom lived in territories contiguous with Hungary.[10] In the course of the execution of the Soviet-Czechoslovak agreement, the Soviet envoy Pushkin demanded that Hungary recognize and welcome the union of the Sub-Carpathian region with the Ukraine. This Soviet demand was satisfied by a public statement of the foreign minister. In connection with this event the peace preparatory division of the Foreign Ministry raised the possibility of reunion of the southern part of Sub-Carpathian Ukraine with Hungary; this area was overwhelmingly inhabited by Hungarians and was geographically part of the Hungarian Plain. The Trianon Treaty of 1920 had annexed it to Czechoslovakia, partly for economic reasons but mainly to secure the east-west railroad and a highway connection with Slovakia and between Rumania and Czechoslovakia. After the attachment of the Sub-Carpathian territory to the Ukraine, these reasons no longer existed. The valleys between the mountains, running north-south, provided excellent lines of communication and transportation with the Ukraine. From the point of view of transportation, the Soviet Union — in contrast to Czechoslovakia — had no need for the plain at the foot of the mountains.

We realized in 1945 that defeated Hungary, at the mercy of occupying Soviet forces and the ACC, could not make such a claim publicly against the Soviet Union. Yet it was our obligation to raise the issue, pointing out that this slight territorial concession, unimportant to the vast Soviet Empire, would have a tremendous psychological effect on the Hungarian public. When our memorandum was completed on this subject the foreign minister gave it to Pushkin, inquiring whether the Soviet Union would be willing to consider the cession of that narrow strip inhabited by Hungarian as a friendly gesture toward Hungary. Pushkin advised the foreign minister not to raise the question. He asked whether the Hungarian government wanted the same thing to happen in Sub-Carpathia as was happening in Czechoslovakia, where thousands of Hungarians were being expelled; such would be the case, he said, if the Hungarian government should raise the fate of the Hungarians living in Sub-Carpathia.

Shortly after this rejection, the Foreign Ministry was informed through private channels that the Soviet Union intended to annex the small portion of territory between Sub-Carpathian Ukraine and the Tisza River, inhabited by Hungarians and belonging to Hungary. Soon the Soviet army invaded that territory from Sub-Carpathia and took measures indicative of a permanent occupation. The Hungarian government protested this action to Marshal Voroshilov, who promised to investigate, and a few days later the Soviet army withdrew. Hungarian authorities never received an explanation. So ended the Soviet-Hungarian pourparlers over the fate of more than 100,000 Hungarians in Sub-Carpathian Ukraine.

One should mention that a State Department memorandum of

May 27, 1944, had discussed American policy toward Czechoslovakia and proposed that the United States "should favor the restoration of Ruthenia to Czechoslovakia with the frontiers established in 1920, subject to such frontier adjustments as Czechoslovakia might be willing to make as a part of a broader settlement of the issues in dispute between it and Hungary."[11] The memorandum marshalled arguments against incorporation of Ruthenia into the Soviet Union and pointed out that "Although the Ruthenians are ethnically related to the Ukrainians, the Soviet Union apparently favors the restoration of Ruthenia to Czechoslovakia."[12] Despite this assumption it concluded that

> If the Soviet Union should annex Ruthenia, however, the United States should favor the establishment of an ethnic line which would leave the great body of Magyars, in the valley of the Upper Tisza River, to Hungary, since Ruthenia would then be a part of the Soviet economy and its communications with the west would be less important.[13]

I could not find any evidence that the United States suggested to the Soviet government the establishment of a new boundary that would have attached to Hungary the great body of Magyars in the valley of the upper Tisza River.

Relations with Yugoslavia: 1945–1946

Then there was the post-1945 question of the approximately half a million Hungarians in Yugoslavia. After the First World War the boundary proposed by the United States at the Peace Conference in 1919–20 would have left much of the Magyar population in Hungary.[14] Such was not the case, and they went to Yugoslavia. The peace preparatory division, in 1945–46, as a matter of routine prepared some reasonable plans for boundary revision on ethnic grounds and considered the possibility of a mutually advantageous exchange of territory; but such projects never entered the realm of practical politics. The coalition parties agreed unanimously that Hungary should not raise territorial claims against Yugoslavia. Under the existing political circumstances such claims would have boomeranged.

Hungary's position toward Yugoslavia after the Second World War was complicated for several reasons. A pact of eternal friendship was signed with Yugoslavia on December 12, 1940, and Prime Minister Teleki hoped that this bilateral agreement would strengthen Hungary's position by leaving open possibilities for the future. Hungary and Yugoslavia could have formed a neutral bloc, but these hopes were destroyed by the course of events. On March 25, 1941, the Yugoslav government adhered to the Tripartite Pact, and two days later the Cvetković government was overthrown by a coup d'état. Germany considered this move a hostile act, and Hitler promptly demanded Hungarian approval for the passage of his troops as well as active military cooperation against Yugoslavia.[15] This demand was preceded by direct and confidential parleys between the German and Hungarian general staffs, without knowledge of the Hungarian government. General Paulus later testified in Nuremberg that he arrived in Budapest on March 30 and had a conference with the chief of the Hungarian General Staff, General Henry Werth, and with Colonel László, chief of the operational group of the Hungarian General Staff, discussing deployment of German troops on Hungarian territory and participation of Hungarian troops in the forthcoming attack on Yugoslavia. Paulus noted that these conferences were brief and orderly and achieved the desired results.[16]

Quick understanding between German and Hungarian high army officers was not an accident. The chief of the German General Staff, General Franz Halder, had informed General Werth as early as November 1940 — that is, before the conclusion of the pact of eternal friendship between Hungary and Yugoslavia — that in the spring of 1941 Yugoslavia "would have to be compelled, if necessay by force of arms, to adopt a definite position in order to exclude, at a later date, the menace of a Russian attack from the rear. In this preventive war, possibly against Yugoslavia and definitely against Soviet Russia, Hungary would have to participate if only in her own interests."[17] Werth had agreed with Halder and asked that Germany complete the Hungarian rearmament program. A Hungarian armament commission thereupon was invited to Berlin, and close contact was maintained between the two general staffs. In March 1941, Halder urged Werth to mobilize certain army corps in order that Hungary be prepared for war against Yugoslavia and Soviet Russia.[18]

The Hungarian General Staff wholeheartedly supported the German plans, made the necessary preparatory steps, and thus confronted the political authorities of the country with a fait accompli. When the decisive moment arrived the Hungarian government had little leeway. Unable to alter the course of events, Prime Minister Teleki committed suicide on April 3, 1941, the eve of the crossing of Hungary's boundary by German troops marching to attack Yugoslavia.[19] On the evening of April 2, he received a telegram from the Hungarian envoy in London stating that the British Foreign Office had informed him that if Hungary took part in any German action against Yugoslavia, she must expect a declaration of war upon her by Great Britain. Winston Churchill noted in his memoirs: "His suicide was a sacrifice to absolve himself and his people from guilt in the German attack upon Yugoslavia. It clears his name before history. It could not stop the march of the German armies nor the consequences."[20]

With the death of Teleki a new era began. Up to that time the Department of State and the British Foreign Office had appreciated the merits of Hungary's moderate and dilatory policy, particularly during the sad days of the invasion of Poland. This appreciation was repeatedly asserted to the Hungarian ministers in Washington and London. The ambassador of France in London, M. Charles Corbin, characterized the Hungarian attitude as an *acrobatie diplomatique digne de toute éloge*. Teleki's successor was his foreign minister László Bárdossy, a professional diplomat, but a man of scant political experience. Death had prepared the way for his ill-fated career.[21] He had been Hungarian minister to Rumania at the time of the second Vienna Award and upon the sudden death of Count Csáky in January, 1941, had succeeded him as foreign minister. Although a patriot and originally an anti-Nazi, he followed a pro-German policy. Impressed by the successful pro-Nazi policy of the Rumanian dictator General Jon Antonescu, he believed that a limited cooperation with Germany was the only means for maintaining some independence for Hungary. In the course of this policy he committed grave mistakes and proved especially weak in his dealings with the Hitlerite element in the Hungarian army.

Germany attacked Yugoslavia on April 6. A death blow was soon administered to the Yugoslav army in the south by German troops previously massed in Rumania. On April 10 the independence of Croatia was proclaimed in Zagreb. Thereafter Regent Horthy declared that, since Yugoslavia had ceased to exist, the Hungarian army would protect the Magyar population living in territories taken from Hungary by Yugoslavia in 1918. Between April 11 and April 14, and without serious fighting, the Hungarian army occupied part of the former Hungarian territory attached to Yugoslavia by the Trianon Treaty.[22]

Besides Hungary's violation of the eternal friendship pact, a tragic incident exacerbated relations with Yugoslavia in January 1942, during the last weeks of Bárdossy's premiership. In some areas reattached to Hungary from Yugoslavia, Tito's partisans were particularly active and repeatedly carried on raids against units of the Hungarian armed forces. The military commanders in the area received orders to take punitive measures against the partisans, and under the pretext of reprisals the Hungarian army and gendarmerie carried out organized massacres of the Serbian and Jewish populations, especially in the triangle of Zsablya and in Ujvidék (Novi Sad). The army instituted a regime of terror and isolated the area, while local civilian authorities were intimidated and blocked from all intervention. The indiscriminate murders were accompanied by extensive looting. The numbers of victims totaled over three thousand, many of whom were thrown into the Danube through holes in the ice. This was the figure established by the investigating interministerial committee appointed by the Kállay government in 1943. Although the local population had nothing to do with these massacres, one of the results was reprisal by Tito's partisans who in 1944–45 tortured, murdered, and deported innocent Hungarians by the thousands. In some villages the Hungarian population was wiped out, and the victims greatly outnumbered those of Ujvidék and Zsablya. These appalling massacres against the Hungarians were considered by the Yugoslav authorities as a just punishment for misdeeds or ideologically motivated class persecutions. The Tito regime did not officially make a distinction between nationalities, except the Germans, but persecuted all social classes and individuals considered politically dangerous.

After the massive atrocities of the early postwar period, persecutions of ethnic groups took place increasingly within the framework of Communist ideology. Anyone could be severely punished if he was considered dangerous by Tito's partisans. Alas, the coalition parties in Hungary followed an ostrich-like policy toward abuses in Yugoslavia. They simply chose not to notice any of the atrocities and other anti-Hungarian actions of the Tito regime. Of course it was next to impossible to check the data the Foreign Ministry received through private channels. Moreover, in legal terms Hungarians were not persecuted because of their ethnic backgrounds. The Yugoslav government — unlike the new regime in Prague — expressly recognized the equality of all nationalities, except the Germans.

There were rumors in early 1946 that Yugoslavia intended to claim some boundary readjustments from Hungary. Later the Foreign Ministry in Budapest understood that the Yugoslav government had abandoned those plans. The Hungarian Communist party alleged that Belgrade dropped these claims because of the intervention with Tito. The Yugoslav delegation at the Paris Conference did not raise territorial claims but proposed voluntary exchange of population and agreement on hydraulic questions.[23]

6

The Fate of Transylvania

The Peace Treaty of Trianon had transferred to Rumania a larger territory than that retained by Hungary and, according to the Rumanian census, one and a half million Magyars remained in Transylvania. The Hungarian government could not disregard the fate of this large Hungarian population. Despite the minority protection clauses of the Trianon Treaty, the Magyars in Rumania had suffered degrading and pauperizing discriminations in the interwar years. During the Second World War both Germany and Russia used Transylvania as a stick or carrot in their relations with Hungary and Rumania. Hitler alternated promises and threats to keep Hungary and Rumania in line. Then Article 19 of the Rumanian armistice agreement made it possible for the Soviets to encourage territorial claims in Budapest. Actually the Soviet government transferred northern Transylvania to the Groza government in March 1945 and in the Council of Foreign Ministers refused to consider an American proposal aiming at a slight boundary modification on ethnic grounds. Since the question of Transylvania played a foremost role in Hungarian politics during the war and in the armistice period, this chapter also will examine some general aspects of Hungarian foreign policy.

It is a curious fact that the Soviet Union was the first Great Power during the Second World War that showed a willingness to support revision of the frontier between Hungary and Rumania. When Soviet troops occupied Bessarabia and part of Bucovina at the end of June 1940, and during the following days and weeks, Foreign Minister Vyacheslav Molotov made several friendly statements and promises to the Hungarian envoy in Moscow, József Kristóffy, who reported them in telegrams to Budapest. He later summed up Molotov's statements in a report: the Soviet Union has no claims whatever against Hungary; is striving to establish good neighborly relations with Hungary; considers Hungary's territorial demands against Rumania well founded and will support them at the peace conference; its attitude will remain as explained above, in case of a conflict between Hungary and Rumania; is ready to begin negotiations for a trade treaty with Hungary.[1]

Molotov's expressions of good will toward Hungary and his promise of support were not new in Soviet diplomacy. His predecessor, Litvinov, in the mid-1930s showed much understanding of Hungarian political aspirations and promised support. But such conversations took place between the Hungarian envoy and the Soviet foreign minister or his deputy within the Kremlin's walls.

The summer of 1940 was an exceptional period because the Soviet army occupied Bessarabia and part of Bucovina. Those days Moscow not only encouraged Hungary through diplomatic channels, but the Soviet radio and Tass reports were unexpectedly friendly toward Hungary. Erdmannsdorff, the German minister to Hungary, reported on July 1, 1940, a conversation with Foreign Minister István Csáky, during which Csáky stated that

> The political director in the Foreign Commissariat had expressed to the Hungarian Minister in Moscow spontaneously and as his personal opinion [his Government's] disinterest in Transylvania and the trans-Carpathian territory. It was striking how the Soviet Minister here was encouraging Hungary to take armed action against Transylvania. The Soviet Minister had expressed himself to me in a similar vein.[2]

Hungary established diplomatic relations with the USSR in April 1934, and Moscow severed diplomatic relations in February 1939 because Hungary adhered to the Anti-Comintern Pact. Diplomatic relations were renewed between the two countries in September 1939. At that time the extreme right in Hungary praised the wise cooperative policy of the two greatest powers in Europe—Nazi Germany and Soviet Russia. Telegraphic communications and railway connections were established between Hungary and the Soviet Union. The Hungarian government in October 1940 released two Hungarian Communist leaders, Mátyás Rákosi and Zoltán Vas, then in a Hungarian jail. In March 1941 the Soviet government returned to Hungary the banners taken by the Russian army in 1849, when it intervened on behalf of Austria in crushing the war of independence in Hungary. Despite such gestures, the anti-Soviet attitude of the Hungarian public was virulent, expecially during the Russo-Finnish war (November 1939–March 1940) when demonstrations were held and collections organized for Finland, and Hungarian volunteers fought in Finland against the Soviet aggressor.

In late 1939 Rumania began to worry about the possibilities of a

Soviet attack, and an emissary of the Rumanian king asked the Italians to "work on the Hungarians," because any Hungarian threat on the Rumanian rear would "oblige the Rumanians to come to an agreement with the Russians."[3] Foreign Minister Csáky assured the Italian foreign minister, Galeazzo Ciano, that "Hungary will not take the initiative in the Balkans and thus spread the fire."[4] He emphasized Hungary's demand for equality of treatment for the Hungarian minorities in case Rumania should cede territory to Russia or Bulgaria without fighting.[5] Hungarian policy was expressed even more clearly by Prime Minister Count Pál Teleki on a visit to Rome in March 1940; Ciano noted that "he [Teleki] will not do anything against Rumania, because he does not want to make himself responsible, even indirectly, for having opened the doors of Europe to Russia . . . Teleki has avoided taking any open position one way or the other but has not hidden his sympathy for the Western Powers and fears an integral German victory like the plague."[6] Later Teleki told Ciano that he hoped for "the defeat of Germany, not a complete defeat—that might provoke violent shocks—but a kind of defeat that would blunt her teeth and claws for a long time."[7]

Shortly thereafter Hungarian hopes for possible Italian help against the Germans diminished. On the pretext that Russia would soon move into Bessarabia, Germany intended to occupy the Rumanian oil fields. The German General Staff approached the Hungarian General Staff and requested passage through Hungary and possibly Hungarian military participation. The reward for Hungary's cooperation allegedly would have been Transylvania. The Hungarian government sent a special messenger to Rome who explained that "For the Hungarians there arises the problem either of letting the Germans pass, or opposing them with force. In either case, Hungarian liberty would come to an end."[8]

During these Hungaro-Italian negotiations the Germans began the occupation of Denmark and Norway, and the Italian ambassador to Germany, Bernardo Attolico, denied the rumor of a German attack on Rumania. The Duce advised the Hungarians to "keep calm and moderate, and . . . accede to the German requests." Ciano commented: "This was not the answer the Hungarians expected and hoped for. They went so far as to ask whether, in case of military resistance, they could count on Italian help. Mussolini smiled; "How could this ever be," he said, "since I am Hitler's ally and intend to remain so?"[9]

The spectacular occupation of the smaller Western European states by Germany, and the unexpected collapse of France, deeply impressed the Hungarian public and, in fact, caused general consternation. The government press maintained a dignified reserve, and when Italy declared war on France and Great Britain, Csáky stated that Hungary would continue its non-belligerent status.

Soviet Russia reacted to the German victories in the West by the incorporation of the Baltic states and Rumanian territories. Following a Russian ultimatum, Rumania evacuated Bessarabia and northern Bucovina and ceded these territories to the Soviet Union. Simultaneous with these events, Hungary made military preparations along the Rumanian frontier and decided to solve the question of Transylvania by force if necessary. Hitler vetoed Hungarian military action and invited Teleki and Csáky to a conference in Munich, where they met on July 10 in the presence of the German and Italian foreign ministers, Joachim von Ribbentrop and Ciano. Hitler warned against unilateral action, advised the Hungarians to initiate bilateral negotiations with Rumania, and promised to support their initiative in Bucharest. The Rumanians procrastinated and would have preferred Hitler's arbitration instead of bilateral negotiations with Hungary. King Carol informed the Germans of Rumanian willingness to return to Hungary 14,000 square kilometers of the territory the Trianon Treaty transferred to Rumania.

In August the Rumanian government agreed in principle with Bulgaria concerning retrocession of South-Dobrudja, but declined to entertain the Hungarian claims. The Hungarian government could not accept the negative Rumanian attitude; eventually the Rumanian government agreed to bilateral negotiations, but when the Hungarian and Rumanian delegations met in Turnu-Severin (August 16–24) they could not find a basis for agreement.[10]

Meanwhile Rumania renounced the Anglo-French guarantee of Rumania's political independence (July 1940), and some great powers expressed approval or understanding of the Hungarian thesis. As noted, Molotov declared to the Hungarian envoy, Kristóffy, on July 7, 1940, that the Soviet government considered the Hungarian claims well founded and would support them at the peace table. At the time of the negotiations in Turnu-Severin, Molotov again stated to Kristóffy that the Hungarian claims were justified.[11] According to reports of the Hungarian envoys in London and Washington, George Barcza and John Pelényi respectively, high officials in the British Foreign Office and in the Department of State showed an understanding of Hungary's policy in the Transylvania dispute.

After failure of the bilateral negotiations both Hungary and Rumania mobilized, and a conflict seemed imminent; under these circumstances Hitler resolved to take a direct hand in the affair since conflict in southeastern Europe would have complications for Germany and hinder the flow of Rumanian oil. The possibility of Russian intervention in a Hungarian-Rumanian conflict also existed. Later the German leaders repeatedly pointed out to the Hungarians that Germany had to settle the Hungaro-Rumanian conflict in order to save Rumania from collapse and from Russian intervention.[12] The German and Italian governments invited representatives of the Hungarian and Rumanian governments to Vienna. The day before the meeting Hitler told Ciano that he was leaving the decision up to him and Joachim Ribbentrop; the only thing he had at heart was that "peace be preserved there, and that Rumanian oil continue to flow into his reservoirs."[13]

The Vienna Award and German Domination

The Hungarians thought the Axis powers would mediate but were not prepared to submit the issue for arbitration. Ribbentrop assailed the recalcitrant Teleki in Vienna; he accused Hungary of having adopted anti-German policies on more than one occasion and his words were "rather threatening."[14] Finally the Hungarian delegation asked Budapest for full powers to submit the issue to Italo-German arbitration; the document was deposited at the German legation in Budapest only half an hour before the second Vienna Award was delivered on August 30, 1940. A Crown Council in Bucharest similarly authorized the Rumanian delegation to accept the arbitration. Based mainly on ethnographical considerations, the award restored the northern part of Transylvania to Hungary. At the same time Germany and Italy guaranteed the territorial integrity of Rumania, which retained the major and economically more important part of Transylvania with a minority of more than a half million Hungarians.[15] There was an outcry in Rumania against the award, and at the same time disappointment in Hungary, for the new frontier created difficulties from the point of view of communications, and it left under Rumanian control the most important mineral assets and major resources of Transylvania such as the district of Meggyes-Kissármás with mineral, oil, and natural gas deposits. King Carol resigned in favor of his son Michael and left the country. Thereafter Prime Minister Marshal Ion Antonescu became the dictator of Rumania.

The award caused serious friction between Moscow and Berlin. Germany informed the Soviet Union only after the Vienna decision had been delivered, and Molotov claimed that Germany violated the Nonaggression Pact providing for consultation in questions of common interest to both countries. Molotov declared that the German government "could not have been in doubt that the Soviet Government was interested in Rumania and Hungary."[16]

Hungary's position was made more difficult by the pro-Nazi reorientation of Rumania's foreign policy, a change achieved with amazing speed. Rumania resigned from the League of Nations and the Balkan Entente and began to transform the internal structure of the country according to National Socialist principles. The most dangerous step was the invitation extended by Rumania in early October 1940 to the German "instructor corps." General Friedrich Paulus stated in his deposition at Nuremberg that an entire panzer division was transferred to Rumania, manifestly as a training unit but actually for the purpose of preparing the Rumanian army for war. These troops had to cross Hungary, and some military personnel remained in Hungarian railroad stations "to maintain the lines of communication between Rumania and Germany."[17] Although Teleki restricted the Germans to a few important railroad stations, this was the beginning of German military penetration into Hungarian territory. Shortly after these events Hungary adhered to the Tripartite Pact (November 20, 1940) concluded on September 27, 1940, in Berlin between Germany, Italy, and Japan. This was considered a way to maintain the relative independence of Hungary in Axis Europe.[18] But the Hungarian government refused to accept a secret additional protocol that aimed at the implementation of the pact for newspapers and propaganda. Such cooperation would have ended anti-Nazi opposition newspapers in Hungary.[19]

Hungary's adherence to the Tripartite Pact was followed by catastrophic events. Prime Minister Teleki committed suicide on April 3, 1941, the eve of the crossing of Hungary's boundary by German troops marching to attack Yugoslavia, and his successor was Foreign Minister László Bárdossy. Under him Hungary's international position rapidly deteriorated. On April 8, 1941, Britain severed diplomatic relations with Hungary. Following the outbreak of the German-Russian war, Bárdossy was induced by the General Staff to declare war on Russia on June 27, without consulting parliament. The town Kassa (Košice) allegedly had been bombed by Soviet planes on the preceding day, and Bárdossy considered this action a *casus belli*.[20] The declaration of war caused violent protests from the opposition parties. At the time the chief of staff of the Hungarian army, General Henry Werth, suggested that war against Russia would be just a matter of weeks and Hungary must not be late this time. He had announced the forthcoming attack on the Soviet Union at a secret meeting of Hungarian army corps commanders in May 1941, and stated that Rumania and Hungary would take an active part on the side of Germany.[21]

The British declaration of war against Hungary (December 6, 1941)[22] and severance of Hungarian diplomatic relations with Washington (December 12, 1941) was followed by an Axis-enforced declaration of war against the United States.

Hungary's entry into war with the English-speaking powers was not without dramatic incidents. When the American minister to Hungary, Herbert Pell, representing also British interests in Hungary, handed over on November 29, 1941, the British ultimatum, Bárdossy according to his own record of the conversation replied: "Your information comes as a surprise. I never believed it would go that far, nor that England could help the Soviets, only by declaring war on us. . . . There are no Hungarian forces fighting in Russia now. We have withdrawn our forces from the front. The Hungarian Government is not participating in any direct military action. . . . Most of the Hungarians placed their faith in English fairness to judge the present situation. They will feel hurt by such a decision of the British Government."

In the course of the ensuing conversation Pell showed an understanding attitude toward Hungary. Counselor Howard K. Travers stated that the American legation tried every means to prevent a declaration of war by England on Hungary, after the first rumor of such a decision, and Pell said that he considered the decision of the English government as his own defeat.[23]

After Pearl Harbor, Hitler declared in the Reichstag that a state of war existed between Germany and the United States. As a subterfuge the Hungarian government simply stated its solidarity with the Axis and severed diplomatic relations with the United States. According to the files of the Hungarian Foreign Ministry, in answer to the question of Minister Pell, "Does it mean war?" Bárdossy replied with a categorical, "No."

The Italian minister and the German chargé d'affaires at Budapest called next day on Bárdossy, urging the Hungarian government to declare war on the United States,[24] and the Hungarian declaration of war was dispatched. This declaration, together with those of the other satellites, was accurately characterized later in a note of the American government delivered in Budapest by the Swiss legation on April 7, 1942. This note considered the satellite declarations of war as made "under duress, and . . . contrary to the will of the majority of the peoples of the countries in question." Similarly President Roosevelt stated in a message to Congress on June 2, 1942, that although the governments of Bulgaria, Hungary, and Rumania had declared war against the United States, "I realize that the three governments took this action not upon their own initiative or in response to the wishes of their own peoples but as the instruments of Hitler." On recommendation of President Roosevelt, Congress declared war on Bulgaria, Hungary, and Rumania on June 4, 1942, and the next day Roosevelt signed the declarations of war.[25] The state of war with the United States and Britain was considered a great misfortune in Hungary, yet it proved to be a blessing in disguise at the armistice and peace negotiations, for without it the affairs of the Danubian countries would have been settled unilaterally by the Soviet Union.

The reluctance of Hungary and the other Danubian satellites to declare war on the United States reflects the limited options of small nations in a world conflagration. Bárdossy aptly described the tragic dilemma of Hungarian statesmen when he told Mussolini's representative in Budapest, Filippo Anfuso: "God confronted us with Hitler. If the Germans demand something, I always give a quarter of it. If I refused categorically, they would take everything, which would be worse."[26]

From the autumn of 1941 onward the German attitude toward Hungary stiffened, for up to that time Hungarian military help in Soviet Russia had been of token value. Time and again the Nazis pointed out that the Rumanians, Slovaks, Czechs, and Croats were more cooperative and Hungarian unfriendliness might have unpleasant consequences. Ribbentrop himself came to Hungary in January 1942 to convey Hitler's insistence upon 100 percent mobilization of Hungarian resources needed for speedy termination of the war. He dangled the idea of Transylvanian territorial concessions, their magnitude depending on the amount of Hungarian support. This, combined with threats, was the usual German method. Ribbentrop extolled Antonescu, the Rumanian dictator. He pointed to Rumania's full participation in the war as a shining example for Hungary to follow.

Seeking to reduce to a minimum Hungarian participation in the war, Bárdossy refused to yield to German pressure for complete mobilization and argued with Ribbentrop that Hungary could not send all its military forces abroad, leaving the frontiers undefended. This had been the main cause of Hungary's First World War catas-

trophe. Germany's interests, he said, could not be served by an un-
ruly Hungary, in which all production would be seriously curtailed.
Ribbentrop expressed regrets about this unexpected reply, intimating
that it was likely to lessen Hitler's good will toward Hungary. Eventually Bárdossy agreed to Hungary's increasing participation in the
war, and Hitler's next move was to dispatch General Keitel to Budapest with a large military suite to discuss details. Even so, for the
spring offensive in Russia he could bring about the mobilization of
but one-third of Hungary's military forces.[27]

Because Regent Horthy was dissatisfied with Bárdossy's policy, he
had to resign in March 1942. His successor, Miklós Kállay, sought to
extricate Hungary from the German grasp—no easy undertaking as
the country was encircled by German satellites and German-occupied
territory. In the face of the growing assertiveness of Hungarian independence, the Germans whipped up interest in the formation of
a Rumanian-Croat-Slovak bloc against Hungary. Hungary's relations
with the two German-protected puppet states, Monsignor Tiso's
Slovakia and Ante Pavelić's Croatia, were unfriendly, and relations
with Rumania were even worse, having at times approached the point
of a severance of diplomatic relations. Both Hungary and Rumania
were manifestly preparing for a private showdown at the end of the
general war, if not sooner.

As first secretary of the Hungarian legation in Bucharest in 1942,
I had a special assignment regarding the affairs of the Hungarian
minority in southern Transylvania,[28] and thus I witnessed the Antonescu regime apply ruthless measures against members of the
Hungarian minority group. Thousands of tragic cases accumulated in
the files of our legation and consulates. I received dozens of desperate
people daily who came to the legation, but we had only limited
means to help. The Rumanian authorities confiscated all food, and
the destitute Hungarians could not feed their children. Diplomatic
protests had no results. The Rumanian government complained about
persecution of the Rumanians in northern Transylvania. The whole
situation seemed utterly hopeless. We proposed to Budapest severance of diplomatic relations.

Hitler envisaged a war between Hungary and Rumania but desired
to postpone it and explained his views on the matter to Mussolini,
recalling how he had stated to the Rumanians and Hungarians that

> if, at all cost, they wanted to wage war between themselves, he would
> not hinder them, but they would both lose by it. However, it would
> be a problem if both countries now withheld petroleum for the war

which they wanted to fight between themselves later. It would be the duty of the Foreign Ministers of the Axis to deal with both countries persuasively and calmly so as to prevent an open break.[29]

To avoid an open conflict in the Axis camp, Berlin and Rome decided in the summer of 1942 to appoint an Italo-German commission headed by a German and an Italian plenipotentiary minister (Hencke and Rogeri) to study the complaints of the Hungarians in southern Transylvania and those of the Rumanians in northern Transylvania. I was recalled to Budapest and then sent to northern Transylvania to prepare memoranda on the political and economic situation of the population. I composed a questionnaire which was sent by the minister of interior to the chief official of each county (főispán). When I visited them in their county hall office, the collected materials were handed to me and in a day or two I prepared a memorandum on conditions in the county to be presented to the Italo-German Commission. In some cases one of the officials attached to me by the central government made inquiries on the spot. The Italo-German Commission spent almost two months in southern and northern Transylvania, investigated hundreds of cases, and prepared a long report that recommended several measures to the Hungarian and Rumanian governments to ameliorate the situation of the minorities.[30] Italo-German military commissions established in northern and southern Transylvania informed the German and Italian governments of discrimination against minorities and other troubles and tried to improve the situation by intervention with the local authorities.

By the end of 1942, the Rumanian deputy prime minister and foreign minister, Mihai Antonescu, under a strange misunderstanding, initiated a conciliatory policy toward Hungary, and the Hungarian government reciprocated. Both governments made some small conciliatory gestures and prepared a list of questions to be settled through bilateral negotiations. Kállay appointed a Transylvanian and former foreign minister, Count Miklós Bánffy, to begin informal negotiations with a Rumanian representative. Bánffy's official mission was connected with another Rumanian initiative. The Transylvanian leader of the democratic opposition in Rumania, Iuliu Maniu, believed in early 1943 that British and American paratroops would be sent to Danubian Europe and he wanted to meet secretly with a former prime minister of Transylvanian origin, Count István Bethlen, to discuss Hungaro-Rumanian cooperation against Germany. Bethlen received Maniu's confidential message and wanted contact with him, but he had apprehensions that the Germans would learn of the meeting and therefore asked Bánffy to get in touch with Maniu. As mentioned, Bánffy traveled legally to Bucharest to discuss specific problems of the Hungarian minority in Rumania and those of the Rumanian minority in Hungary. He arrived on June 18, 1943, and met a few days later with the Rumanian negotiator, G. Mironescu, a former prime minister and foreign minister. Bánffy was unable to discuss problems designated in the memoranda of the two governments because Mihai Antonescu instructed Mironescu to discuss only territorial questions, while he was authorized to negotiate solely measures for improvement of the minorities situation in the two countries. Mironescu informed Bánffy that the Rumanian government had denounced in Berlin and Rome the Vienna Award[31] and was unwilling to negotiate on the basis of the status quo. The Hungarian and Rumanian positions were irreconcilable and there was no reason to continue the meetings.

The indomitable Bánffy got in touch with opponents of the Antonescu regime, and his most important conversation was with Maniu who came to Bucharest to meet him. Since a police car watched Maniu's residence until 11:00 P.M., Bánffy visited him during the darkness of night. The two Transylvanians agreed that military cooperation between Hungary and Rumania would be desirable against the Germans, but Maniu wanted to include the Yugoslavs and emphasized that Rumania would never recognize the Vienna Award. While Bánffy proposed the maintenance of the status quo until the peace conference, Maniu demanded immediate recognition of the Rumanian territorial claims and suggested that with the expected coming into being of large economic units the frontiers should lose importance. Failure of Bánffy's mission on both official and opposition levels demonstrated the intractable nature of the conflict between the two countries. The policy of rapprochement came to an inglorious end.[32] Mihai Antonescu changed his mind and the Germans continued their squeeze play, using to advantage the conflicting territorial aspirations of Hungary and Rumania.

In Transylvania the Italo-German conciliatory efforts proved to be palliatives, and the Germans supported the Rumanians almost openly. This policy was reinforced in Hungarian-Rumanian relations in that Rumania had a key role in the war against Soviet Russia; it had carried out full mobilization and contributed to the German war efforts incomparably more than had Hungary. Hitler's dislike of Hungary was well known and has been verified by many documents.[33] He had a great liking for the Rumanian dictator, Ion Antonescu. As

Hitler's interpreter Paul Schmidt later put it, Antonescu was "one of Hitler's closest intimates and was even kept more closely in the picture than Mussolini. He was the only foreigner from whom Hitler ever asked for military advice when he was in difficulties. . . . He made long speeches just like Hitler, usually starting off at the creation of Rumania, and somehow relating everything he said to the hated Hungarians, and the recovery of Transylvania. This hatred of Hungary, too, made him congenial to Hitler, for the Fuehrer despised the Magyars."[34] Antonescu indicated his determination to recover northern Transylvania by force of arms, and "Hitler took a secret pleasure in Antonescu's outbursts against the Hungarians, and even went so far as to hint that he might perhaps give him a free hand later in his plans of conquest."[35]

Surrounded again by a sort of revived Little Entente, protected this time by Germany, the Hungarian government tried to rely on Italy. The policy was bound to fail because Italy gradually declined to the status of Hitler's vassal, and Mussolini decided to fight along with Hitler until the very last. Despite disappointments, the Hungarians tried to win Italy's support because they saw no other alternative.

The Hungarian government sought to explore the possibilities of electing an Italian king. The advanced age of the regent was reason for such soundings. The duke of Aosta, cousin of Victor Emmanuel III, a possible candidate for the throne of St. Stephen died in March 1942. The Hungarians then sought to strengthen Hungary's independence by a personal union with Italy under King Victor Emmanuel. The Duce reacted adversely to this plan, saying he had entertained a similar proposition in regard to the duke of Aosta, "but with him dead, nothing else will be done."[36]

Prime Minister Kállay was anxious to clarify the delicate political problems in Rome and arranged for a visit to Italy in November of 1942, but the trip was postponed by Mussolini because of the collapse of the Libyan front. "In fact, this is not the moment to welcome any guests," remarked Ciano.[37] Eventually Kállay visited Rome in early April 1943, to gain Italian support for resistance to Germany. When Kállay referred to the fact that the Axis was retreating on every front, Mussolini interrupted him saying that "Hitler had assured him that in the summer he would settle with the Russians once and for all." Kállay replied that he could only discuss the present situation and pointed out that "Hungary could not give a single soldier for this offensive."[38] He avoided the question of a separate peace but brought up the possibility of a separate common policy within the Axis of Italy, Hungary, and possibly Finland and extolled the benefits of a common Italo-Hungarian policy on the Balkans. He explained to the Duce that he wanted to extricate Hungary from the war and lead it back into nonbelligerency. Mussolini assured Kállay of friendship, tried to justify Italy's foreign policy in a historical context, and warned Kállay that "We cannot even think of a separate peace."[39]

During this period there was some similarity between the foreign policies of Hungary and Rumania. Both countries overestimated Italy's capability to resist Germany and Mussolini's willingness to change his pro-Axis policy. Rumania's deputy prime minister and foreign minister, Mihai Antonescu, followed a strong pro-Italian policy, for he had hoped that Italy would establish contacts and conclude an armistice with the Western powers. He had maintained close relations with Bova Scoppa, the Italian minister to Rumania since July 1941, and had hoped that under Italy's leadership Rumania, and possibly Hungary, Finland and other small states, could cooperate and conclude an armistice and change sides during the war. In his memoirs[40] Bova Scoppa described Antonescu's ideas and endeavors in this respect. While visiting Rome in early June 1943, Scoppa submitted a *Promemoria* to Giuseppe Bastianini, Ciano's successor as foreign minister since February 1943, reflecting the Rumanian evaluation of the military and political situation and Antonescu's ideas as to the steps to be taken.[41] Scoppa met Ciano who told him frankly: "Con Mussolini non c'e niente da fare. E'un muro chiuso." (Nothing can be done with Mussolini. He has a closed mind.)[42]

Finally Bastianini informed Scoppa on June 15 that the Duce agreed with Mihai Antonescu on many points but would like to wait two months with the suggested diplomatic initiative when the military situation would be better. He invited Antonescu for an exchange of views, and a visit took place at the end of June with Antonescu warmly received and Mussolini emphasizing again that negotiations should start in two months, when the belligerent and neutral states would be brought to a conference—by Hitler or without Hitler—to decide Europe's future. Antonescu finally realized that Mussolini had replaced policy by pipe dreams.[43] Events in Italy soon took a different turn; the English and the Americans landed in Sicily in July 1943, Mussolini was forced to resign, and Marshal Badolgio's government signed an armistice on September 3, made public five days later.

Another common error of this period was the belief in Budapest and Bucharest the British and American troops would occupy the Danubian countries in the last stage of the war. Hungarian and Rumanian politicians assumed that the United States at the peak of its power would not tolerate Soviet hegemony in Danubian Europe. Hungary had established contacts in 1942 and 1943 with British and United States representatives, and Hungarian and Rumanian diplomats and special emissaries in neutral countries put forth peace feelers in 1943 and 1944. Appraisal of these moves are outside the scope of this book, but one should note that the British and the Americans faithfully informed the Soviet government of the Hungarian and Rumanian approaches.

Armistice in Russia's Europe

The parallelism between Hungarian and Rumanian politics changed drastically in 1944 when Hungary was occupied by German troops on March 19, according to a carefully prepared plan, Marghareta I. The looming shadow of the Nazi dictator became a cruel reality. Hitler's promise to Horthy concerning the exclusively military character of the occupation proved worthless. The Gestapo started its usual work. Prominent Hungarian patriots were jailed, deported, or forced underground. Persecution and mass deportation of Jews began. Prime Minister Kállay never resigned formally and found asylum in the Turkish legation. The new head of the government, Döme Sztójay, a former general and Hungarian minister to Germany, had always advocated a policy of submission to Nazi Germany, and in close collaboration with the Germans carried out the Nazification of Hungary. Horthy assumed an ostensibly passive attitude in the first months, later resisting more or less openly the occupying Nazi forces and their Hungarian accomplices. Since the Germans did not take over direct control of major government agencies some possibilities for the future were left open. The attempt to kill Hitler on July 20, 1944, created confusion among German authorities in Hungary, momentarily increasing Horthy's freedom of action. He dismissed the pro-Nazi Prime Minister, Sztójay, and replaced him with General Géza Lakatos; General Gusztáv Hennyey, another faithful servant of Horthy, became foreign minister.[44]

But then Rumanian politics suddenly took an unexpected turn. On August 23, King Michael dismissed and arrested Marshal Antonescu and Mihai Antonescu, proclaimed Rumania's surrender, and appointed a government of national unity with the nonpolitical General Constantin Sanatescu as premier. Rumania declared war on Germany and the Rumanian army changed sides with lightning speed and fought against the Germans. The quick action of the Rumanian army was an immense benefit to the Russians. The German plan for occupation of Rumania, could not be carried out and the German army, in disorderly retreat, did not even defend the passes in the Carpathian mountains.

The movement of the Soviet army and the regular Rumanian divisions into northern Transylvania was followed by the "Voluntary Guards" of Maniu who introduced a regime of terror in regions inhabited by Hungarians. In view of large-scale atrocities and lootings the Soviet High Command in some instances intervened to protect the Hungarian population, and the Allied Control Commission in Bucharest on November 14 ordered the returned Rumanian functionaries and the "Maniu Guards" to evacuate northern Transylvania. From this time on the autochthon population, Hungarians and Rumanians together, organized an autonomous administration with the approval of the Soviet High Command, and for a few months northern Transylvania enjoyed an exemplary public order with constructive cooperation of the native population. The Soviet army needed orderly conditions behind the front.

The Italian and Rumanian cases were warnings to Hitler, who decided to prevent similar events in Hungary and concentrated German armored divisions on the outskirts of Budapest. When Regent Horthy's armistice proclamation was read on the Budapest radio on October 15, these divisions moved into the capital. The Germans arrested pro-Horthy military commanders, deposed the Lakatos government, and installed an Arrow Cross government under Ferenc Szálasi. Horthy was taken prisoner and deported with his family to Germany. A chapter of Hungarian history came to an end. Battles were fought all over Hungary for several months and the siege of Buda lasted over seven weeks. Gradually, however, German resistance collapsed, and the last German troops were driven out from western Hungary on April 4, 1945.

A new order began in Russia's Europe with the ensuing armistice period. The rules of international and domestic politics were fundamentally changed in countries occupied by the Soviet army. An armistice was signed with Rumania on September 12, 1944 and its Article 18 stated:

> An Allied Control Commission will be established which will undertake until the conclusion of peace the regulation of and control over the execution of the present terms under the general direction and orders of the Allied (Soviet) High Command, acting on behalf of the Allied Powers.

The Bulgarian armistice agreement was signed on October 28, 1944 and its Article 18 (identical with Article 18 of the Hungarian armistice agreement of January 20, 1945) set forth:

> For the whole period of the armistice there will be established in Bulgaria an Allied Control Commission which will regulate and supervise the execution of the armistice terms under the chairmanship of the representative of the Allied (Soviet) High Command and with the participation of representatives of the United Kingdom and the United States.
>
> During the period between coming into force of the armistice and the conclusion of hostilities against Germany, the Allied Control Commission will be under the general direction of the Allied (Soviet) High Command.

There are two major differences between the two texts. The Rumanian armistice simply stated that the ACC would be under direction and control of the Soviet High Command, acting in behalf of the Allied powers during the whole armistice period. The Bulgarian and the identical Hungarian texts provided that the ACC would "regulate and supervise the execution of the armistice terms under the chairmanship of the representative of the Allied (Soviet) High Command *and with the participation of representatives of the United Kingdom and the United States.*" (Emphasis added) A second paragraph of Article 18 in these two armistice agreements restricted the general direction of the Soviet High Command to the period between coming into force of the armistice and the conclusion of hostilities against Germany. The United States proposed that in the post-hostilities period tripartite control should replace Soviet dominance, but this proposal was not accepted by the European Advisory Commission in London because of Soviet opposition. These changes were supposed to secure greater British and United States influence in the Bulgarian and Hungarian ACC. This formula was worked out by Foreign Secretary Anthony Eden and Molotov on October 11, 1944, when the definitive percentage figures for influence in the Balkan countries and Hungary were established.

These were some of the diplomatic agreements and military developments which determined Hungary's and Rumania's international situation at the close of hostilities.

The ink had hardly dried on the Yalta agreements when Soviet Deputy Commissar of Foreign Affairs Andrei Y. Vyshinsky went to Bucharest and compelled King Michael to dismiss General Nicholas Radescu's coalition government and appoint Petru Groza as premier. When Groza presented a solid National Democratic Front (FND) government—the FND was a Communist sponsored organization—the king refused to appoint the designated cabinet members. Vyshinsky reportedly stated that this was an unfriendly act to the USSR and Rumania might cease to exist as a sovereign state. The king had no choice and the FND came to power. Within three days the Russians restored northern Transylvania to Rumanian administration so as to demonstrate Soviet support of Groza's government. Although Groza tried to introduce a conciliatory policy toward the Hungarian minority, his success was limited, abuses continued, and all benefits of the autonomous position of northern Transylvania came to an end.

The Role of Transylvania in Soviet Policy

As the armistice agreement declared the Vienna Award of August 30, 1940, to be null and void, the Hungarian government looked for a solution of the Transylvanian problem along new lines. The revival of the ethnographic arguments, which were the basis of the Vienna Award, was considered unwise and was rejected at the outset. Although a variety of projects were prepared for solution, I would have preferred a general rather than specific demand until we ascertained what support Hungary could get from the Great Powers. I was overruled, and the foreign minister decided to accept a plan worked out by Imre Jakabffy, a member of the Pál Teleki Institute for Political Science. This plan envisaged the return of 22,000 square kilometers to Hungary with roughly 1,600,000 inhabitants. According to the 1930 Rumanian census, this territory was inhabited by 865,620 Rumanians and 495,106 Hungarians. In the 1941 census the proportion of Hungarians was higher, but this difference did not change the basic disproportion. Meanwhile, over a million Hungarians would have remained under Rumanian sovereignty. The idea was to balance the Hungarian and Rumanian minorities in Hungary and Rumania. It was assumed that these conditions would result in better treatment for minorities in both countries.

In early April the Soviet government invited leading members of the Hungarian government to Moscow, and this was considered a good occasion to raise the question of Transylvania. A meeting held under chairmanship of the president of the republic on the eve of the departure for Moscow endorsed the Jakabffy plan, but at the same time also decided that the delegation should have an alternative solution in reserve that included only the border districts with a clear Hungarian majority. After the meeting, I was ordered to prepare the alternative plan that night. Although presentation of two proposals to the Russians—without knowing their intentions—did not strike me as a good idea, I discussed the matter with Transylvanian experts in the Teleki Institute and they worked out another plan proposing to return to Hungary 11,800 square kilometers and 967,000 people. According to the Rumanian figures of 1930 the Hungarians had a slight majority in this territory, 442,000 compared to 421,000 Rumanians. The delegation presented both proposals to the Russians.

The delegation returned from Moscow full of optimism, for it had been well received. Soviet hospitality knew no bounds and the Hungarian delegation had been lavishly entertained. Stalin seemed benevolent and made concessions in several areas. Gyöngyösi then explained to the leading officials of the Foreign Ministry how the discussion developed concerning Transylvania. According to him Stalin listened to the Hungarian arguments and requests, turned to Molotov and asked if there was a basis for territorial claims, and Molotov correctly replied that Article 19 of the Rumanian armistice agreement opened the way for Hungary's territorial aspirations regarding Transylvania. Next day Deputy Foreign Minister Vladimir G. Dekanozov advised the Hungarian foreign minister that before raising territorial claims, direct negotiations should be attempted with the Rumanian government. Molotov later repeated this advice. The atmosphere of the conversations seemed so friendly and Stalin's attitude so benevolent that the delegation took Soviet support for granted. Stalin's toast delivered at a dinner for the Hungarian delegation on April 16 inspired understanding and good will. The following excerpts are characteristic:

> At present it seems that many medium and small countries are afraid of the Soviets. This fear is unjustified. Lenin stated that all nations, large or small, have their particular value and importance from the point of view of humanity. This principle still rules in Soviet policy. More than half of the Soviet population is non-Russian, and consists of many nationalities. These nationalities enjoy complete autonomy and freedom.
>
> The Soviets have always had sympathy for Hungary and always wanted to be on friendly terms with her. This was true even when the Hungarian regime was not democratic. [Stalin then spoke about the Hungarian flags of 1849 which had been returned to Hungary by the Soviets in 1941.] At that time declarations made by Hungarians induced the Soviets to believe that Hungary was a real friend. In their simplicity the Soviet leaders did not know that this was only a fake. A few months after the flags had been returned, Hungary declared war

on Russia. The fight was long and bloody, Horthy later was prepared to make an Armistice, but he had no character and energy. Szálasi continued the fight. Under such circumstances the Red Army could do nothing else than to fight too.

The Russian people have a debt towards Hungary. The Armies of the Czar helped the Austrians in 1849 to defeat the revolutionary Hungarian army. However, the Soviet Union, who executed the last Czar, Nicholas II, is not responsible for the sins of the Czarist regime.

[He is now glad to know that the leaders of the Hungarian nation are democrats and that they have come to Moscow. He emphasized the fact that the Soviet Union always wanted friendship with Hungary, regardless of the latter's government.]

[He then emptied his glass to the health of the friendly relations between Russia and Hungary.]⁴⁵

Besides the friendly atmosphere there was another reason why Moscow's apparent good will toward Hungarian claims appeared credible. As mentioned, Voroshilov and Pushkin had encouraged Gyöngyösi and Tildy that Hungary should raise territorial claims against Rumania, another former German satellite. In reality, both before and after the Moscow visit of the Hungarian delegation, in the Council of Foreign Ministers Molotov had resolutely opposed an American proposal looking to slight modification in the Hungarian-Rumanian boundary. Although nothing was promised to the Hungarians in the Transylvanian question, the Soviet suggestion for bilateral negotiations with the Rumanians seemed encouraging to the delegation as a first step in the resolution of the boundary dispute. Not a hint was made about the real Soviet policy that opposed even the study of boundary revision between Hungary and Rumania in the CFM. The camouflage in Moscow was complete. By handing over all of Transylvania to the Groza government in March 1945, the Kremlin politicians played their trump card, consolidating that puppet regime and refusing to discuss boundary modification. To them the important consideration was control over Rumania. Article 19 of the Rumanian armistice agreement set forth that:

> The Allied Governments regard the decision of the Vienna Award regarding Transylvania as null and void and are agreed that Transylvania (or the greater part thereof) should be returned to Rumania, subject to confirmation at the peace settlement, and the Soviet Government agrees that Soviet forces shall take part for this purpose in joint military operations with Rumania against Germany and Hungary.

The parenthetical phrase was used by the Russians as a club held over the Rumanians and as encouragement to the Hungarians in

Budapest. The British and Americans proposed the expression, "subject to the confirmation at the peace settlement," thinking this insertion would keep the whole question open for reconsideration at the peace conference. But the Soviets refused to discuss at inter-Allied meetings the meaning of the parenthetical phrase. And "subject to confirmation at the peace settlement" meant to the Soviets automatic confirmation of what they had done.[46]

After the Moscow visit the Communist party in Hungary made a turnabout and began to support Hungarian territorial claims; one of the leading Hungarian Communist authorities in foreign affairs, József Révai, delivered an irredentist speech on April 26, demanding that all territory along the Rumanian borders inhabited by Hungarians be returned to Hungary, together with such cities as Arad, Szatmárnémeti, Nagybánya, and Nagyvárad. He asserted that the Communists in the emigration between the two World Wars were true representatives of Hungary's national aspirations but that their efforts were annihilated by the suicidal pro-Nazi and anti-Soviet policy of the Horthy regime. A few weeks before this speech Révai had wanted every "reactionary" who dared ask for territory from Groza's Rumania to be brought before the People's Court. "We cannot weaken Groza's democracy," he had said at that time.

This reversal of Communist policy concerning Hungary's territorial claims gave a basis for optimistic speculation, but later it became evident that the motive behind the change in Communist tactics was hope of winning the support of Hungarian public opinion. The Communists apparently did not want to burden the Party by opposing national aspirations; they preferred to ride a popular bandwagon. The leaders of the Hungarian Communist party might have believed that after the Moscow visit the Soviet government would support some Hungarian territorial aspirations. According to my observations, Soviet authorities gave orders and instructions to the Muscovite Communists in Budapest but did not inform them of the real objectives and tactics of Soviet foreign policy.

On May 5, at Székesfehérvár, the prime minister, and at Szolnok the foreign minister, delivered addresses outlining in vigorous terms the peace aims of Hungary. Public opinion was optimistic for a short time although the first disappointment occurred a few days before the delivery of these addresses. In accord with Moscow's advice, a high official of the Foreign Ministry, Paul Sebestyén, went to Bucharest to initiate negotiations. Prime Minister Petru Groza and Foreign Minister Gheorghe Tatarescu gave him courteous reception but refused to discuss Hungarian territorial claims; Sebestyén immediately returned and on April 27 a note was dispatched to representatives of the major victorious powers in Budapest.[47] This note was based on the above-described proposal prepared in the Pál Teleki Institute, which had been presented in Moscow by the Hungarian delegation. The Hungarian government requested return of 22,000 square kilometers to Hungary, that is, 20 percent of the total area of 104,000 square kilometers transferred to Rumania by the Treaty of Trianon.

The optimism that followed the Moscow visit soon vanished, if only because of the negative response of Rumanian statesmen to Hungarian overtures. The shrewd Tatarescu would not have refused negotiations with Sebestyén had the Rumanian government lacked assurance of Soviet support. Groza and Tatarescu hinted as much to the Hungarian envoy. The coalition parties and the Hungarian people became disappointed when it appeared that members of the delegation to Moscow could not support with facts the optimism they had expressed in speeches. A last effort in the Transylvanian dispute was made at the Paris Conference.

7

Conflict with Czechoslovakia

Of all the difficult substantive issues the postwar government of Hungary had to face, none was more intractable than relations between Budapest and Prague. This was an unexpected and disastrous development for the new leaders of Hungary who planned and eagerly wished to establish good neighborly relations with Czechoslovakia. Democratic parties represented in the coalition government had for a long time advocated cooperation between the two states. In the 1920's and early 1930's, Eduard Beneš and other Czechoslovak politicians frequently stated that concessions to the Hungarians met but one obstacle: a reactionary regime in Hungary. This was not the case any more in 1945, not even in the eyes of the Czechoslovak leaders. The armistice agreement declared null and void the Vienna Award of November 2, 1938, and reestablished the frontier between Hungary and Czechoslovakia as laid down in the Peace Treaty of Trianon.[1] Hungarian politicians believed there would be nothing to prevent friendly relations and possibly institutionalized cooperation with Czechoslovakia.

In the course of the Second World War emigré Czechoslovak politicians on several occasions had praised the Hungarian population in Slovakia. The Slovak Communist leader, Vladimir Clementis, extolled the behavior of the Hungarians in Czechoslovakia in the following manner:

> Whoever experienced the period preceding Munich in the Magyar districts of Slovakia knows what a fundamental difference there was between them and the Sudeten regions.The majority of the Magyar workers and peasants not only appreciated the political and cultural progress which the Republic had brought them, but these classes also had an accurate view of Czechoslovakia's position in the European situation, and of her significance for the hopes of their comrades in Hungary, and thus for the whole Magyar nation.[2]

The Hungarians in Slovakia proved more anti-Nazi than the Slovaks. Beneš pointed out in his memoirs that the attitude of the

Slovak people was one of the factors in the destruction of Czechoslovakia.[3] Many Slovaks had supported the pro-Nazi Tiso regime wholeheartedly. The Hungarian party was the only one that voted against the Hitlerite anti-Semitic laws in the Slovak parliament. It seemed incredible to the Hungarians that they might be punished on the basis of collective responsibility after reestablishment of Czechoslovakia.

During the war Nazi Germany placed Slovak behavior as an example before Hungary. Slovak newspapers accused Hungary of pro-Western sympathies and of promoting a double-dealing opportunistic policy. Some of Monsignor Tiso's supporters advocated expulsion of Hungarians. Czech agrarian and industrial production also was highly praised by the Germans. Czech farmers won highest prices in the German production race. As early as 1943 the powerful German minister of economics, Karl Clodius, hinted to the Hungarian prime minister, Kállay, that Hungary's economic sabotage might lead to military occupation since the Germans could get much more out of the occupied countries. As an example, Clodius mentioned the output of Czech industry and agriculture.

The Czechoslovak emigré government in London enjoyed a privileged position among the United Nations. The bad consciences of Western powers because of Munich was important, overshadowing objective facts. Hungarians were not responsible for the Runciman mission, and the Munich Agreement was accepted by Czechoslovakia, France, and Britain.[4] The London *Times* wrote on September 28, 1938: "Self-determination, the professed principle of the Treaty of Versailles, has been invoked by Herr Hitler against its written text, and his appeal has been allowed." But in the growing anti-Munich political atmosphere in London, the Czechoslovak emigré government felt free to designate scapegoats for the disintegration of Czechoslovakia and decided that after the war they would get rid of non-Slav minorities. The radical transformation of Beneš's policy during the war was aptly characterized by Wenzel Jaksch, the leader of Sudeten German Socialists in London.[5] Slovak peasants who for centuries had worked peacefully as neighbors of Hungarian peasants, were incited by propaganda both from overseas and by Slovak-Nazi propagandists at home. A twofold propaganda machine stirred up the feelings of the Slovak people and explained to them that they could no longer live in the same state with the Hungarians.

The postwar coalition government of Hungary refused to believe that the Czechoslovak state would deviate from the principles of its founder, Thomas Masaryk, indulging in persecution and racial hatred similar to that of Nazi Germany. In early 1945 they were inclined to attribute anti-Hungarian atrocities to irresponsible elements. This wishful thinking was supported by news of a few manifestations of Hungarian-Slovakian friendship, but gradually it became clear that persecution of Hungarians in Slovakia was being planned and carried out systematically by the government.

In January 1945, the Czechoslovak ambassador to the Soviet Union suggested to the Soviet People's Commissariat for Foreign Affairs the inclusion of several points in the Hungarian armistice. It was proposed that "Hungary take on certain obligations with respect to Magyars who possessed Czech citizenship but who will be transferred to Hungary."[6] Although this proposal was not included in the armistice agreement, Prague apparently thought that the expulsion of Hungarians would be a simple affair. Under secretary of state in the Foreign Ministry, Vladimir Clementis, told the French chargé d'affaires, Keller, on August 25, 1945, that the expulsion of the Hungarians differed from the expulsion of the Germans. It will be more of an exchange than transfer of population because the Slovaks from Hungary and the Hungarians expelled from Slovakia would be repatriated simultaneously, said Clementis. He explained to Keller that the transfer of Hungarians would not depend on the good will of the three Great Powers, but solely on approval of the Russian military authorities who alone were responsible for order in Hungary. The Czechoslovak government would send a mission to Budapest in the near future to work out with the Soviet commission the material conditions of transfer. As soon as agreement was reached with the Soviets, Prague would deal directly with Budapest to determine the dates and places of transfer and the destination of each group. On this occasion Clementis himself intended to travel to Budapest to regulate the transfer within the general framework of an accord of good neighborhood. Keller thought that he understood Clementis to say that he envisaged to raise the question of rectification of the Slovak frontier.[7]

Clementis's explanations to the French chargé d'affaires revealed his determination to expedite the expulsion of Hungarians through an agreement with Soviet authorities in Budapest. Although Prague received Soviet diplomatic support, things did not work out entirely according to Clementis's expectations. The process of ridding Czechoslovakia of minorities began by a "voluntary" cession of Sub-Carpathian Ukraine to the Soviet Union by the Czechoslovak-Soviet Treaty of June 29, 1945. This was not an unexpected development. Beneš indicated as early as 1939 that he would be willing to cede this territory to the USSR.[8] During his visit in Moscow in December 1943, he told

Molotov that "in regard to issues of major importance, [the Czechoslovak government] . . . would always speak and act in a fashion agreeable to the representatives of the Soviet government." And he pledged "loyal collaboration and concerted action in all future negotiations."[9] It is not surprising that Moscow appreciated this policy of *Vorleistung* and the Soviet government gave support to the Czechoslovak policy of persecution and expulsion of Hungarians. Soviet officials pointed out on numerous occasions, particularly in connection with the Czechoslovak demand for transfer of the Hungarians, that the Czechoslovak government had earned support by its reliable attitude in the past.

The Potsdam Conference authorized Czechoslovakia to expel her citizens of German nationality, and the transfer took place rapidly. By the autumn of 1946, 2,165,000 Germans had been expelled. Having gotten rid of the Germans and most Ukrainians, Czechoslovakia probably would not have been endangered if the Hungarian minority had been treated in the spirit of Masaryk's democracy. If Czechoslovakia preferred to become a purely national state, without a Hungarian minority, it would have been possible to solve this problem by moderate territorial cessions, for most of the Hungarians lived on territory contiguous with Hungary.

The ethnic boundary line had not undergone significant changes between Hungarians and Slovaks in centuries. That the southern part of Slovakia was not "Magyarized" territory was stated by one of the scholars on this subject, Alexej Petrov, of Russian descent, who made a detailed study of ethnic development of this region and whose works were published in Prague by the Czech Academy in 1928. Petrov reached the conclusion that "The frontier of homogeneous Slovakia has, to all intents and purposes, remained constant for the past 100 and 150 years." This statement implied recognition that the territory below this line had been Hungarian. "The picture of the Magyar-Slovak lingual frontier has, along a stretch of frontier about 400 km. in length and 10-25 km. in depth, scarcely been affected by the development of the two nations."[10] As there was no massive "Magyarization" on these territories,"[11] it was a perverted argument of postwar Slovak politics to speak about "reslovakization" of the Hungarian population. In 1945 any reasonable settlement would have provided the basis for cooperation between the two countries. Instead Czechoslovakia started a brutal persecution of Hungarians with expulsion as the ultimate goal.

A proclamation of April 2, 1945, in Košice (Kassa) announced that Czechoslovakia was going to be a national state. President Beneš emphasized in a speech of May 9, 1945, in Bratislava, that Czechs and Slovaks did not want to live in the same state with Germans and Hungarians. It became evident that the elimination of the Hungarian population constituted a major program of postwar Czechoslovakia. Hungarians were deprived of their citizenship, of all political and elementary human rights by a series of legal measures, administrative steps, and even by officially tolerated malicious actions of private groups and individuals. Hungarians were sent to concentration camps by the thousands. The state dismissed Hungarian officials, stopped payment of pensions to retired Hungarian civil servants, disabled men, war widows and sick people, and obliged private concerns to do likewise. Hungarian schools were closed and private education banned for Hungarian children. Ownership of radios or publishing and selling of Hungarian printed materials was banned. Use of the Hungarian language on the streets of some cities as well as use in postal communication and religious services was forbidden by law. For example, Decree no. 253/1945 of Sept. 10, 1945, stated in regard to the Evangelical church: "German and Hungarian parishes and seniorates lose their independence; their assets are transferred to the Slovak churches. The clergy are to be dismissed and services held only in the language of the State." A Hungarian was not allowed to have employees or to be employed. Private property was confiscated in many cases and licenses withdrawn. Hungarian cultural and welfare institutions were dissolved and activities of this kind prohibited. Within a short time an entire legal system had been devised that discriminated against Hungarians in political, administrative, economic, cultural, religious, and other matters.[12] Hungarians were placed almost entirely outside the law.

It is characteristic of this legislation that a constitution law, passed by the Provisional National Assembly on April 11, 1946, declared the following:

> Only Czechoslovak citizens of *Czech, Slovak* or other *Slav race* possess the suffrage. (Clause 3)
> Only Czechoslovak citizens of *Czech, Slovak* or other *Slav race* may be elected. (Clause 4)

When these provisions were promulgated, the Hungarian authorities had proof of the purpose of Czechoslovak policies and changed their attitude. On April 5, 1945, the Hungarian government protested to the ACC against the anti-Hungarian discriminatory provisions of the decree concerning agrarian reform issued on February 27,

1945, by the Slovak National Assembly.[13] In a note dated July 4, 1945, to the Soviet government, the Hungarian government summarized anti-Hungarian decrees and atrocities and asked for intervention.[14] Between April 1945 and July 1946 the Foreign Ministry sent 184 notes to the ACC protesting Czechoslovakian abuses against Hungarians.[15]

Because the protests did not bring results, the Foreign Ministry sent memoranda to the three major victorious powers with detailed descriptions of anti-Hungarian measures. In a note of September 12, 1945, the Hungarian government asked to be heard by the Council of Foreign Ministers on the situation of the Hungarians in Czechoslovakia. This step was prompted by an action of the Czechoslovak prime minister, Zdenek Fierlinger, who had requested the Allied powers to agree to removal of Hungarians from Czechoslovakia. The Hungarian government proposed an international Commission of Inquiry, composed of delegates of Britain, the United States, the Soviet Union, and France, to investigate controversial issues between Hungary and Czechoslovakia, notably the following:

(a) To ascertain the accurate ethnic facts and economic conditions of the regions of Southern Slovakia inhabited by Hungarians.
(b) The record of the attachment of the Hungarian regions to Czechoslovakia at the Peace Conference after the First World War.
(c) The attitude adopted by Czechoslovak statesmen in the past regarding this territory
(d) The attitude adopted by the Czechoslovak government prior to the Vienna Award of November 2, 1938.
(e) The Hungarian government's treatment of the Slovak and Czech settlers and of the indigenous population in the territories ceded to Hungary.
(f) The position of the Hungarians in Czechoslovakia since its liberation by the Russsian army.[16]

In view of the fact that after the dispatch of this note the position of the Hungarian minority in Slovakia worsened, the Hungarian government reiterated its request on November 20, 1945.[17] This note argued that the Czechoslovak government would have been obliged to restore the legal position of the Hungarians as of December 31, 1937, including protection of minority rights, and requested that districts of Slovakia inhabited by Hungarians be placed under international control pending appointment of a Commission of Inquiry. A memorandum attached to the same note furnished information on the situation of the Hungarian minority.

The Soviets did not reply to these notes. The British and American reactions were not favorable either, and eventually written refusals arrived in February and March 1946.

The American reply remarked that

> In present circumstances the Gorvernment of the United States does not consider feasible the formation of an international commission to examine the Hungarian-Czechoslovak minority problem or to supervise any exchange of population. The Government of the United States cannot support a request for the establishment of international control of the districts inhabited by Hungarians in Slovakia. The Government of the United States will recognize and support a humane settlement freely agreed to between the Government of Hungary and the Czechoslovak Republic.[18]

The British reply informed the Hungarian government that

> His Majesty's Government would be unwilling to participate in any international commission for the examination of the problem of Hungarian minorities in Czechoslovakia or for the supervision of any Czechoslovak-Hungarian exchange of population on the lines proposed by the Hungarian Government. His Majesty's Government are of the opinion that this question should be settled on a bilateral basis between the two Governments concerned. Further, they would not be prepared to try to persuade the Czechoslovakian Government to agree to any frontier rectification in favour of Hungary though they would not withhold recognition of any changes freely agreed to between the two countries concerned.[19]

The United States was the only power that gave indirect support to Hungary's protest against the application of the principle of collective responsibility. The American political Mission in Budapest handed the Hungarian government a memorandum on June 12, 1945, containing principles for a humanitarian transfer of population.[20] This memorandum took a stand against the principle of collective responsibility.

> The United States Government would not consider it justified to deal with all members of an ethnic group who constitute a minority as criminals against the state and as subject to expulsion from its territory, only because of their ethnic origin.

The memorandum emphasized that removal of minorities could take place only in accord with international agreements and "in an orderly way." It quoted the foreign minister of Czechoslovakia who had said on May 21, 1945, at San Francisco that

> punishment would be imposed only upon Hungarians who had conspired against the Czechoslovak Republic and who had fought on the

side of the Nazis, but that those Hungarians who had shown friendliness to the cause of Czechoslovakia might remain in that country with the full rights of citizens of that Republic.[21]

In reply to the American note the Hungarian government stated that, without wishing to oppose severe punishment for Magyar war criminals in Czechoslovakia, it was obliged to protest against collective persecution of the Hungarian minority, which recalled anti-Jewish measures of the Nazis. It could not be said that all the Hungarians were to blame for disintegration of Czechoslovakia; after World War I nobody asked the opinion of Hungarians in territories attached to Czechoslovakia as to what state they wished to belong; the same thing had happened in 1938. On both occasions the Hungarian government proposed plebiscites. Hungarians in Slovakia surely could not be stamped as war criminals because they were satisfied to be reattached to Hungary in 1938. The note pointed out that

recent events in Slovakia demonstrate that the Government unfortunately is still pursuing the same Nazi principles which gave rise to the "Hlinka-Guard" movement and to other similar organizations partly established to terrorize the Hungarian community. Those who are today persecuting the Hungarians in the name of democracy have done so for many years with the approval and at the instigation of the Third Reich under the pretext that in the "new order" for Europe the Hungarians could not be relied upon.

The fact that the Hungarian Party formed the only opposition in Tiso's Fascist Slovakia shows how little the Hungarian minority was in sympathy with the Nazi ideology. The leader of the Party, John Esterházy, was the only member of the Slovak Parliament who voted against the anti-semitic laws and strongly criticized them as not being in accordance with humanitarian principles.[22]

Negotiations in Prague

Dalibor Krno, representative of the Czechoslovak government with the ACC, proposed to the Hungarian government on October 9, 1945, that negotiations should begin in Prague on the exchange of population. Similar proposals were made in November 1945 to a delegation of the Hungarian Social Democratic party attending the Social Democratic Congress in Prague.[23] Hungarian Socialists supported the suggestions and after return advocated in Budapest the idea of a population exchange as a step toward better relations between Hungary and Czechoslovakia. Under both internal and external political pressures, the Hungarian prime minister, Zoltán Tildy, informed the Czechoslovak representative with the ACC that in the first days of December 1945 the Hungarian government would be prepared to open negotiations in Prague. At the same time he pointed out that the Czechoslovak government had taken new anti-Hungarian measures and that the Slovak press, with its magyarophobe propaganda, had created an atmosphere not likely to facilitate negotiation.[24]

At the invitation of the Czechoslovak government, a small Hungarian delegation negotiated in Prague, December 3–6, 1945. I accompanied the foreign minister with two specialists in Czechoslovak affairs, Alexander Vájlok and Lehel Farkas. In an address at the opening of the negotiations, Vladimir Clementis, under secretary of state in the Czechoslovak Foreign Ministry and head of the Czechoslovak delegation (in view of Jan Masaryk's absence he was also acting foreign minister), insisted upon the responsibility of Hungary in the war and emphasized that Hungary had not complied with certain provisions of the armistice agreement. He put forward a proposal as a basis for negotiation[25]: in exchange for Slovaks from Hungary who spontaneously declared their wish to be transferred to Czechoslovakia, the government of Prague would have the right to select and transfer an equal number of Hungarians from Czechoslovakia to Hungary. The Hungarians not subject to exchange would be removed to Hungary and their goods confiscated. Hungarians to whom Czechoslovak citizenship would be granted could enjoy the rights of citizens but would not have any minority rights.

These proposals seemed preposterous, for it was well known that Czechoslovak authorities granted Czechoslovak citizenship only to Hungarians who declared themselves Slovak. Clementis stated on September 16, 1946, at the Paris Conference, that those "who are shown in the Czechoslovak census return as Magyars, are not really of Magyar ethnic origin, but are partly of Slovak origin. Those of them who speak Slovak and have now declared their nationality to be Slovak have been granted the right to acquire Czechoslovak citizenship by a special law."[26]

Hungarians in Slovakia outnumbered several times the Slovaks in Hungary. This latter group voluntarily moved from Upper Hungary to the Hungarian Lowland in the eighteenth century, after expulsion of the Turks, and had lived ever since among Hungarians and in considerable distance from the bulk of the Slovak people. Czechoslovak statisticians estimated in 1945[27] that 652,000 Hungarians remained in Czechoslovakia while Hungarian estimates ran between 700,000 and 800,000. In Hungary the individuals who declared Slovak as their mother tongue were 104,819 in 1930 and 75,920 in 1941. Even if all Slovaks of Hungary would have declared their wish to be transferred it would have left unsolved the fate of more than half a million Hungarians in Slovakia. It is true that Clementis and other Slovak nationalists claimed there were 450,000 Slovaks in Hungary but such assertions were not supportable by facts—as pointed out by objective foreign experts[28]—and proved in error by the result of the population exchange.

After two days of negotiations in Prague, the two delegations decided on December 4 to put into writing the views expressed and the solutions envisaged. Papers were exchanged the next day. Although the Czechoslovak aide-memoire[29] made minor concesssions, it still reiterated the original proposal for negotiation.

The Hungarian protocol, which I drafted, was a condensation of views expressed by the Hungarian and Czechoslovak representatives.[30] It stated that the Hungarian government found itself unable to approve the exchange of population because it was not in conformity with the principles of humanity and democracy. In view of an atmosphere more favorable to friendly relations between Hungary and Czechoslovakia, Hungary would agree to the exchange under certain conditions. The delegation proposed to count among Hungarians to be transferred those who were expelled from Czechoslovakia or unable to return as a result of Czechoslovakian measures—although they were Czechoslovak citizens on November 1, 1938. Outside those categories, the exchange would include persons whom judicial authorities qualified as hostile to the Czechoslovak state. When these categories had been exhausted the parties would agree on the choice of other Czechoslovak citizens of Hungarian ethnic origin, taking into consideration domicile, occupation, material situation, etc. The commissions supervising the exchange would have an international character; apart from representatives of interested states they would include representatives of the Soviet Union, Britain, and the United States.

The Hungarian proposal provided for immediate abolition of all discriminating measures applied to Hungarians, plus integral restitution and compensation. As to the Czechoslovak proposal that after exchange the Hungarian population in Czechoslovakia should be expelled from that country, the Hungarian delegation was not even willing to enter into negotiation. Transfer of these Hungarians to Hungary could only be effected with simultaneous cession of territory in which they lived. The Hungarian delegation declared that the principle of exchange of populations appeared admissible only if the fate of Hungarians in Czechoslovakia would be regulated by appropriate measures.

After exchange of the Czechoslovak aide-memoire and the Hungarian draft protocol it became evident that no agreement was possible. The Czechoslovak delegation rejected all Hungarian proposals. Negotiations broke off on December 6 with a statement of the Hungarian foreign minister[31], who asked the Czechoslovak government in the name of democracy and the spirit of humanity not to apply new discriminatory measures to Hungarians in Slovakia, and above all to end persecution. The delegations could not agree even on the text of a communiqué, and the two governments published separate statements.

Two episodes pertaining to usual diplomatic contacts remain vivid in my memory because they characterize the atmosphere of Prague in December 1945.

The representative of Hungary in Czechoslovakia, Francis Rosthy-Forgách, arranged for me a private meeting with the head of the economic division of the Czechoslovak Foreign Ministry, whom he considered a friend of Hungary. I told the Czech diplomat that we would like to establish close cooperation with other Danubian nations, especially Czechoslovakia, and explained our ideas. His reply was that as a first step we should accept the political demands of Prague concerning the settlement of the Hungarian question in Slovakia, then we should fulfill the financial obligations provided in the armistice agreement; and if all these and other pending problems were settled the Czechoslovak government might consider putting into operation the excellent commercial treaty concluded between Czechoslovakia and Hungary in 1938. After this reply not much remained for discusssion.

A conversation of mine with Clementis was surprising in a different sense. At the farewell party given the Hungarian delegation he asked me for an eye-to-eye exchange of views, in the course of which he explained that it would serve the cause of Hungaro-Czechoslovak reconciliation if Hungary eliminated from its historical coat-of-arms the stripes and hills symbolizing rivers and mountains in Slovakia. I expressed surprise and told him that Hungary's coat-of-arms was not a negotiable question. It was grotesque to see that amidst cruel persecution of Hungarians, one of the promoters of the persecution — and a leading Communist — wanted to improve Hungaro-Slovak relations by such a queer proposal. He apparently thought it possible to wipe out the memory of ten centuries through heraldic changes in a historic emblem.

I left Prague with the conviction that between Slovak jingo-nationalism and helpless Czech bureaucracy not much space remained for statesmanship and common sense, necessary elements of lasting political settlements.

The much criticized nationality policy of Hungary had many defects but remained a far cry from, and could not even be compared with, systematic government-controlled persecutions in the new Czechoslovakia. Extravagant racial hatred became the central idea in post-World War II Czechoslovak politics, instead of the humanism of Masaryk. It was obvious that Czech and Slovak political leaders were abusing their favorable power position and were destroying the possibility of cooperation with neighbors, especially Hungarians. In the course of negotiation I reminded Clementis that the wheel of history was turning rapidly, there had been ups and downs in the history of all Danubian nations and it was time now to look for a long-range settlement in Hungaro-Slovak relations. Clementis's answer was that Czechoslovakia, enjoying support of both the Soviet Union and the Western powers, would remove all Hungarians in one way or another. President Beneš went even further and declared to Foreign Minister Gyöngyösi that the victorious powers had agreed in principle at Potsdam on removal of Hungarians from Czechoslovakia and seemed astonished to see our "stubborness" in this matter, I expressed the opinion to Gyöngyösi that the Czechoslovaks would not negotiate with us if Beneš's allegations were true.

After returning to Budapest, I went to see the American minister, Schoenfeld, and asked him about the validity of Beneš's statement. He categorically denied an agreement was reached at Potsdam on removal of Hungarians. Although such an agreement was not in the published text, the official denial was reassuring because tacit and unpublished understandings are not unknown in diplomacy.

Second Negotiations in Prague

In early January Dalibor Krno, the Czechoslovak representative accredited to the ACC, invited me for luncheon to discuss the possibilities of a population exchange agreement. Krno was an influential member of the Slovak Communist party and suggested with authority that instead of demanding withdrawal of anti-Hungarian legislation, we should be satisfied with de facto improvement of living conditions of Hungarians and emphasized that the Czechoslovak government must have discretionary power for selection of Hungarians to be transferred from Slovakia. When I expressed disagreement, he argued that the population exchange was in Hungary's interest as well. In case of Hungarian unwillingness to cooperate, they would organize a worldwide diplomatic and propaganda campaign against Hungary and establish several hundred Slovak schools in Hungary, following the model of the Alliance Française possibly in cooperation with other Slavic people so that Hungary might have a Slavic population of a million in fifty years.[32]

Like Clementis, Krno had personal grudges against the Hungarians that originated back in pre-1918 Hungary. I realized in the course of my contacts with both men that they lived under the impact of alleged persecutions suffered by them or their families and wanted to retaliate. This lust for revenge caused frustration and imbalance in their thinking and approach toward present-day problems connected with Hungary. Slovak leaders whom I met were either incapable or unwilling to envisage realistically Hungarian-Slovak relationships. All were convinced that they could obtain anything because they enjoyed support of the Soviet Union and the Western powers.

The Hungarian government informed the three major powers of the Prague negotiations on December 11.[33] The usual silence of Moscow and the negative replies of the Western Powers justified the boast of Clementis and other Slovak leaders concerning the sympathy enjoyed by Czechoslovakia. Hungary asked again for Western cooperation in settlement of our conflict with Prague. The Hungarian proposal concerning participation of Western representatives in the international commission to be established in connection with the population exchange was opposed by Czechoslovakia and rejected by the Western powers.

After failure of the Prague negotiations the Russians increased pressure on the Hungarian government for acceptance of the Czechoslovak proposals with respect to settlement of the Hungarian question in Slovakia. Pushkin complacently explained to Foreign Minister Gyöngyösi that the clumsy Czechoslovak politicians had committed a serious mistake in not removing the Hungarians from Slovakia at the close of hostilities. An accomplished fact would have been created that would have solved the chief difficulty between Hungary and Czechoslovakia, and negotiations between the two countries would have been easier. Pushkin repeatedly made clear that Czechoslovakia enjoyed unqualified support of Moscow because in the past it had proved a reliable friend; Hungary should accept the Czechoslovak thesis and should look for compensation from Rumania, a country that had been in the same boat as Hungary.

Along with most Czechoslovak experts in the Foreign Ministry, I advised Gyöngyösi that Hungary should delay negotiation and submit the whole problem to the peace conference. But Gyöngyösi felt that this policy would run against Western advice and provoke Soviet retaliation. All the powers remained unresponsive to Hungarian proposals and complaints concerning persecution of Hungarians, and the Hungarian government had no way of defending its persecuted kinsmen or to hinder mass expulsions or internal removals to the Sudeten territories. Clementis made it clear that the persecution of the Hungarians would be continued on an increasing level until the conclusion of the population exchange agreement. In this situation the foreign minister saw no possibility for protecting the Hungarians in Slovakia. He was convinced the population exchange would prove that Czechoslovak allegations of the several hundred thousand Slovaks in Hungary were without foundation. He was afraid the Czechoslovak government with its great propaganda facilities might convince the peace conference of the validity of these allegations and hoped that results of the population exchange would show the situation realistically and strengthen Hungary's position at the peace table.

At the end of January 1946 the Hungarian government decided to accept with some modifications a Czechoslovak proposal presented to the Hungarian delegation in Prague on December 5, 1945, and rejected by the latter. I gave this compromise proposal to Krno on January 30, 1946, and stated that in event the Czechoslovak government accepted it as the basis for negotiation the Hungarian delegation was prepared to go to Prague.[34] The most important Hungarian modification stipulated that, concerning the criteria of Hungarians in Slovakia to be transferred in exchange, a decision would be taken by a special Hungaro-Czechoslovak commission, as soon as it was informed of the number of Slovaks in Hungary who presented themselves for transfer.

Three days later the Foreign Ministry received an invitation from Prague through Krno which implied the acceptance of our conditions. The Czechoslovak government invited the Hungarian delegation, which arrived in Prague on February 5, 1946.[35] The same delegation was led again by the foreign minister and included the secretary general of the Foreign Ministry, Paul Sebestyén, an experienced negotiator and legal expert.

Immediately upon arrival in Prague, Krno called on me at the

Hotel Alkron and stated he had to clear up an unfortunate misunder-standing—namely, that to his great regret it had not been possible to transmit in Budapest the full reply of the Czechoslovak govern-ment to our communication of January 30. Handing over a document in English he explained that it ought to have been sent by the cypher service of the Czechoslovak Foreign Ministry as early as February 2 to the Czechoslovak misssion in Budapest and that delay was due to an error on the part of the cypher service.

After reading the text I informed Krno that we had arrived in Prague with the conviction that the Czechoslovak government ac-cepted the conditions of the Hungarian government as a basis for negotiation. Now the Czechoslovak position as elaborated in the En-glish text deviated in fundamental questions. I expressed my opinion that in the circumstances there seemed litttle likelihood of agreement.

As appeared from the text handed over by Krno, the Czechoslovak government wished to have free hand in regard to selection of Hungarians to be exchanged for Slovak volunteers from Hungary and refused to accept the Hungarian proposal looking to a Hungaro-Czechoslovak commission to select Hungarians in Slovakia for trans-fer. The Czechoslovak text rejected again the American and British representatives on the international commission and proposed in-stead a representative of the ACC in Hungary.[36]

Against my advice the foreign minister decided to begin negotia-tion on the basis of the Czechoslovak surprise note. This meant prac-tical acceptance of the Czechoslovak thesis on selection of Hungarians to be transferred from Czechoslovakia to Hungary. It is true that in subsequent negotiations the Czechoslovaks accepted an obligation to see that the choice of Hungarians to be transferred under the agree-ment should correspond on general lines—proportionally—to the social structure, profession, and material situation of the Hungarian population of Czechoslovakia.[37] This general statement was nothing but face-saving formula.

In a plenary sesssion Gyöngyösi agreed that the two delegations should work out a draft convention concerning the population ex-change and appointed Sebestyén and myself to a committee of four to discuss details. The Czechoslovak members of this committee were Arnost Heidrich, secretary-general of the Foreign Ministry, and Juraj Slavik who later became ambassador to the United States. The com-mittee considered the drafts proposed by the Hungarian and Czechoslovakian governments respectively for the treaty, and major disagreements were decided by the heads of the two delegations, Gyöngyösi and Clementis. Finally Sebestyén and a legal expert of the

Czechoslovak Foreign Ministry were charged to draft the text of the treaty and the attached declarations and exchange of letters. They completed this work with amazing rapidity in a few hours before our scheduled departure on February 9. We hardly had time to compare the various drafts. I did not believe that the text, prepared with such haste and without the consultation of financial and other experts, would be final. The Czechoslovaks agreed that Sebestyén would return, if needed, with observations of the Hungarian government.

Before our departure I had an exchange of views with leading officials of the Czechoslovak Foreign Ministry; one of them mentioned that at the close of hostilities Hungary was almost in the same political situation as Germany and thus it did not seem probable that the solution of the Hungarian problem in Czechoslovakia would present more difficulties than that of the Sudeten German. Now we were in the process of formal diplomatic negotiation, he added, and asked how it was possible to improve our international position so rapidly. I could not take this diplomatic complacency and replied that since the conclusion of the armistice agreement we did not have an independent foreign policy because we lived under the guardianship of the ACC. If our international position improved it was to a large extent the result of Czechoslovak political mistakes, especially the persecution of Hungarians. Anti-Hungarian and anti-Jewish excesses in Slovakia had international repercussions, I said, and we were bound to reap benefits. This did not change the basic weaknesses of our international situation.

On our return trip to Budapest I pointed out to the foreign minister that the hastily drafted convention was a typical unequal treaty. It contained discrimination against Hungarians and unilateral benefits to Czechoslovakia because contrary to our preliminary condition to resume negotiations in Prague, only Czechoslovak authorities would select the Hungarians to be transferred from Slovakia. Prague's acceptance expressed in Budapest for establishment of a Hungaro-Czechoslovak Commission for the selection of Hungarians to be transferred for Slovak volunteers in Hungary was only a trap to make possible our trip to Prague. I added that the economic and financial clauses of the draft treaty had been loosely formulated in the course of our speedy negotiations without participation of experts. On the basis of our agreement, Sebestyén could return to Prague with observation of the Hungarian government concerning clarification of financial treaty clauses and he should do so after consultation with experts in the Ministry of Finance. We could possibly continue negotiations until the peace conference settled all outstanding problems between

Hungary and Czechoslovakia. In any case, it seemed doubtful that we could complete the exchange before the peace conference.

Although Gyöngyösi agreed with my contention concerning the unequal nature and other flaws of the draft treaty, he replied that he wanted to sign the treaty as soon as possible because the population exchange would prove that Czechoslovak allegations of 450,000 Slovaks in Hungary were without foundation. Otherwise the Czechoslovak government with its propaganda facilities might convince the peace conference of the correctness of their allegations. He estimated the number of Slovaks in Hungary who would volunteer for transfer would be around 30,000 or 40,000. Gyöngyösi resided in Békéscsaba, the chief town of the Slovaks in Hungary, and his wife was of Slovak origin. He considered himself an expert on Slovaks in Hungary and would not accept much advice in this respect. His major argument was that in view of Western passivity, the conclusion of the treaty was the only available means to secure physical survival of Hungarians in Czechoslovakia until the peace conference. Although I recognized the validity of Gyöngyösi's argument, I felt strongly about the flaws of the treaty and asked him to relieve me from further participation in the negotiation concerning the population exchange. He graciously respected my position and agreed. Gyöngyösi's decision was probably unavoidable because of external pressure and persecution of Hungarians in Slovakia, but even in this difficult situation some financial and other technical provisions of the agreement should have been improved through further negotiation.

In Budapest I did not hide my opposition to the population exchange agreement as formulated in Prague. My argument was that Hungary should not enter into an agreement providing for unequal treatment of Hungarians. I considered the removal of Hungarians from Czechoslovakia without their consent as a dangerous precedent. The peace treaty could have imposed such an obligation, but this would be a different matter.

The population exchange agreement was strongly opposed also by the Ministry of Finance because of the unclear financial clauses that later caused many difficulties. The senior expert of Czechoslovak affairs in the Foreign Ministry, Alexander Vájlok, prepared a memorandum summarizing the arguments against the population exchange treaty and it was transmitted to the president of the republic, the prime minister, and the leaders of the coalition parties, but without effect. The Council of Ministers unanimously consented to the agreement. The firm attitude of the foreign minister prevailed. The agreement was signed in Budapest on February 27, 1946, and ratified by the National Assembly on May 14, 1946. I did not attend the diplomatic events connected with signature of the treaty and did not participate in the post-signature negotiations.[38]

Debate in the National Assembly took place on May 10, 11, and 14, 1946, in the course of which some speakers attacked the agreement and exposed its weaknesses and its discriminatory provisions against Hungarians. Changes were proposed but none accepted and the agreement was ratified in its original form. In a closed session the foreign minister explained the circumstances that compelled the government against its better judgment to conclude the agreement.[39]

In accordance with provisions of the protocol, in a letter of February 27, 1946, addressed to Gyöngyösi, Clementis stated in the name of the Czechoslovak government that the agreement for the exchange of populations represented only a partial solution of the problem of the Hungarian minority in Slovakia because even after the restoration of Czechoslovak citizenship to persons of Slovak ancestry, the remainder of the Hungarian population there would still be 150,000 to 200,000 persons whom the Czechoslovak government wished to transfer to Hungary. The Czechoslovak government, while not unaware of the gravity of this problem for Hungary, considered the transfer absolutely necessary in order to be able to improve Czechoslovakia's relations with Hungary.[40]

In reply the Hungarian foreign minister informed the Czechoslovak government that its proposals relating to partial reslovakization and transfer of Hungarians were unacceptable. The Hungarian government demanded that

the Hungarian population remaining on Czechoslovak territory should, after the annulment of all the exceptional discriminatory measures . . . recover its Czechoslovak citizenship and its equality of rights with other Czechoslovak citizens, and that the Czechoslovak Government ought to assure the enjoyment of the human rights guaranteed by the Atlantic Charter and the Charter of the United Nations, in order that they may live without fear and without want.[41]

The Hungarian government in a note of May 6, 1946, informed the representatives of the Great Powers in Budapest of the development of Hungaro-Czechoslovak relations and of the Czechoslovak proposals for the settlement of the Hungarian question in Slovakia.[42] The note requested the powers to ensure the rights laid down in the Charter of the United Nations calling for a special minority protection system under international guarantees and proposed that

The Czechoslovak Government should give back their Czechoslovak citizenship to those of Magyar nationality, and accord them equal treatment with citizens of Czechoslovak nationality. It should afford the Magyars also all the nationality rights which it has granted to its Ukrainian minority. The Hungarian Government asks in the first place for the positive guarantee of the following rights:

1. Freedom for the extension of the popular democratic administrative and cultural institutions accepted in Czechoslovakia;
2. Organisation of political parties and trades unions;
3. Freedom to employ and to be employed;
4. Freedom of economic organisation.[43]

Aftermath of the Exchange Agreement

A volume would be necessary to tell of the execution of the population exchange, in the course of which both the Hungarian and Czechoslovak governments accused each other of violations of the agreement and bad faith.

A Czechoslovak commission of some two hundred members was sent to Hungary with headquarters in Budapest to promote and implement the exchange, and during three months every facility was put at its disposal to propagandize the Slovaks and register people of Czech and Slovak origin in Hungary who wished transfer to Czechoslovakia. Troubles soon began. General Francis Dastich, the newly appointed delegate of the Czechoslovak government to the ACC, on May 20, 1946, addressed a letter to the Hungarian foreign minister in which he charged that neither the Hungarian press nor radio adopted an affirmative attitude toward the transfer of population. He complained because of the alleged negative and hostile attitude toward the agreement of Hungarian political leaders, administrative authorities, and private individuals. He enumerated a series of concrete cases and quoted the speeches of the Communist leader Rákosi, Prime Minister Nagy, and Foreign Ministery Gyöngyösi. He demanded a more efficacious execution of the agreement.

In reply the Hungarian foreign minister emphasized that the authorities had loyally fulfilled all obligations agreed upon. He quoted statements from the Czech and Slovak press, according to which the attitude of Hungarian administrative organs had been found satisfactory even by members of the Czechoslovak commission sent to Hungary. The note charged that the Czechoslovak commission had not respected certain articles in the agreement, notably that the Czechoslovaks abstain from any activity or conduct incompatible with the sovereignty of Hungary or hostile to the Hungarian people. To clarify the issues Gyöngyösi included the passage of his speech objected to by the Czechoslovak government:

> The Hungarian Government opened negotiations in Prague, and as a result of these—in order to prove the endeavours of our country to find agreement and its peaceful intentions—we accepted the Agreement for the exchange of population on the basis that we are willing to take over from Slovakia the same number of Hungarians as there are Slovaks who voluntarily declare for removal in Hungary. We conducted these negotiations and also made this Agreement on the advice of the Great Powers, although the idea of an exchange of population is contrary to our conceptions, because we do not consider it democratic or humane to force people like the Hungarians of Slovakia to leave their ancestral homes.[44]

In conclusion the note drew attention to the fact that, contrary to the letter and spirit of the agreement, the Czechoslovak government was continuing to take measures prejudicial to the interests of the Hungarians in Czechoslovakia.[45]

This exchange of notes was only the beginning of a long and bitter controversy over actions of the Czechoslovak government considered by the Hungarian government to be new methods of persecution. The agreement for population exchange made possible the expulsion of major war criminals of Hungarian nationality guilty of offenses under Article 1-4 of the Decree No. 33 of 1945 of the Slovak National Council, which expired on May 15, 1946. Such expulsions could take place in addition to the equal number of Slovaks, Czechs, and Hungarians to be exchanged. This provision was inserted into the population exchange agreement on the express wish of Czechoslovak negotiators who claimed that the number of persons involved was insignificant.

The issue of the war criminals was discussed again at the Paris Conference where the Hungarian delegate, Aladár Szegedy-Maszák, stated in the Political and Territorial Commission for Hungary on September 18, 1946,[46] that the Czechoslovak government intended to "foist on Hungary not less that 23,192 Hungarians as major war criminals. These, together with their families will make some 80,000 persons and would arrive in Hungary with only a single suit of clothes, deprived of their property and of all their goods and chattels." Szegedy-Maszák mentioned that in Košice (Kassa), 750 Hungarian cases were decided in eight days in July 1946, so that 40–50 people an hour were condemned as major war criminals. As Clementis questioned the accuracy of this statement,[47] the Hungarian delegation on September 30, 1946, in a communication to Siniša Stanko-vić, president of the Political and Territorial Commission for Hungary, gave details based on Slovak sources.[48] It quoted the organ of the Communist pary, *Pravda*, appearing in Bratislava, which on July 25 published on its front page an article headed: "On Friday of this week the case was opened at the People's Court in Košice against 750 Hungarians." According to this article they were accused of having been members of Hungarian political parties. The note addressed to Stanković further explained:

> On the 14th of August the *Vychodoslovenská Pravda* of Košice, in a special edition, gave an excerpt from the judgment in the case, which had finished on 2nd August. According to the judgment, the majority of the accused were sentenced because they were members of the National Hungarian Christian Socialist Party, or the Hungarian National Party, or the United Hungarian Party, the Hungarian Union for the League of Nations in Czechoslovakia, or the League of Nations Union. I must here stress that all these associations were formed with the permission of the Czechoslovak government and functioned perfectly legally in Czechoslovakia. Moreover, representatives of the parties concerned had sat, during the existence of Czechoslovakia, as deputies in the Czechoslovak Parliament.
>
> Another important circumstance is that a large majority of the accused were indicted and sentenced not for their individual acts or crimes, but exclusively for having belonged to the above-mentioned legally authorised and legally functioning Parties or Associations. Thus this judgment is a glaring example of indictment of grounds of collective responsibility, and throws a characteristic light on the way in which tens of thousands of Hungarians are today being sentenced within a few days as war-criminals in Czechoslovakia. These sentences, besides imprisonment, also involve confiscation of all property and expulsion from the country.

In an exchange of letters between Clementis and Foreign Minister Gyöngyösi at the Paris Conference, Clementis agreed that persons subject to transfer as major war criminals should be fixed at 999 but demanded the exchange of 30,000 Magyars from Czechoslovakia by the end of 1946 without regard to discussion in the Hungaro-Czechoslovak Mixed Commission.[49]

The Hungarian foreign minister refused to agree to the proposed accelerated informal exchange, and insisted upon the execution of the agreement signed in February 1946. He charged that

> the Czechoslovak Government has modified the text of the Slovak decree No. 33 of 1945 and prolonged its validity, in order to employ

the Decree thus modified as a weapon to persecute tens of thousands of innocent Hungarians by having them declared, by methods so far unknown in criminal procedure, war-criminals or fascists, confiscating their goods and ordering their expulsion to Hungary. In the view of the Hungarian Government, these measures constitute such a breach of the Agreement as to render its execution impossible for it until the Czechoslovak Government decides to adopt the conception which constitutes the very basis of *raison d'être* of the Agreement, by putting an end to the mass political trials directed against Hungarians with a view to their expulsion and annulling by appropriate measures the political penal and material effects of the sentences already imposed.

He reminded Clementis that

the Czechoslovak Government has not fulfilled the engagements which it assumed with a view to putting a stop to the persecution of the Hungarians in Slovakia and of giving social assistance to Hungarians who have been deprived of their employment or their pensions, which also constitutes a breach of the Agreement.[50]

During the Conference of Paris, Gyöngyösi and Clementis did not succeed in settling the differences blocking the execution of the population exchange agreement, and the Paris Conference did not insert in the peace treaty the Czechoslovak amendment that would have authorized Czechoslovakia "to transfer 200,000 inhabitants of Magyar ethnic origin from its territory to that of Hungary." The peace treaty obligated Hungary to enter into bilateral negotiations with Czechoslovakia to solve the problems of Hungarians remaining in Czechoslovakia after the population exchange. This rebuff exasperated Clementis. On October 31, speaking on the removal of Hungarians in the Committee for Foreign Affairs in the Czechoslovak parliament, he threatened the Hungarian government with a unilateral action. He stated that the manner of solution of the question of Hungarians in Slovakia was in the hands of the Hungarian government, adding that for definitive solution "we can, if the worst comes to the worst make arrangements according to our methods."[51] On November 4, 1946, the Settlement Office for Slovakia issued a confidential order to Slovak authorities, No. 12, 771, concerning "regrouping of the Hungarians in Slovakia" and their transfer from their home to Bohemia and Moravia. According to these instructions, the compulsory transfer was to be carried out in twenty-three Hungarian districts of Slovakia by application of Public Labor Decree No. 88. Clause 4 provided that property of the transferred persons was to be confiscated.

On November 13, 1946, the newspaper of the Slovak National Council used violent language: "We have the right to assimilate the Hungarians, and to create a national state in Czechoslovakia by any means. As the Hungarians cannot lay claim to minority rights, our ultimate move will have to be to disperse the Hungarians in various parts of Czechoslovakia."[52] Shortly after the Czechoslovak minister of agriculture, Július Ďuriš, announced that a definitive solution of the questions of Hungarians in Slovakia would take the form of transfer of the Hungarians to Sudeten-German areas.[53]

Although the Hungarian government in a note of November 16, 1946, again expressed willingness to negotiate the problems of Hungarians remaining in Czechoslovakia, the Czechoslovak government was not satisfied and started an arbitrary unilateral solution. Deportation of Hungarians began on November 17, 1946. Slovak authorities used as a pretext Public Labor Law No.88 promulgated in 1945. Under it, men between ages of 16 to 55 and women from 18 to 45 could be obliged for urgent public work for a maximum period of one year. There was no urgent agricultural work in the depth of the winter when Hungarian peasants were forced to leave their homes. Entire families, comprising children, old people, expectant mothers, and disabled men were indiscriminately deported from Hungarian districts designated for evacuation.[54] Hungarian villages were surrounded by the army or gendarmery and forceful removals took place amidst tragic scenes, similar to those of Jewish deportations by the Nazis. Removed people had to sell their belongings on short notice, or their properties were seized and confiscated. Slovak settlers moved into their houses without ado. Approximately 100,000 Hungarians were deported during the winter months of 1946–47, mostly into Sudeten German districts of Moravia and Bohemia, or sent as farmhands or servants to landowners and farmers.[55]

Deportations aiming at dispersion of Hungarians violated the pledges of the Czechoslovak government given simultaneously with signature of the population exchange agreement. These and other violations of the agreement were repeatedly pointed out by Hungarian representatives in sessions of the Mixed Hungaro-Czechoslovak Commission.[56] They brought up, by way of example, the decision, dated September 25, 1946, of the National Council of Rimavská Sobota (Rimaszombat) which declared the Calvinist church a Fascist organization and therefore ordered the confiscation of its property. As no satisfactory answer came, the Hungarian government interrupted negotiation for the population exchange on December 16, 1946.

An exchange of notes between Budapest and Prague and a meeting between Gyöngyösi and Clementis in Bratislava, on January 26, 1947, failed to promote a solution. The Hungarian government asked for the immediate cessation of deportations, but the Czechoslovak government was unwilling to give such a pledge. Under these conditions the Hungarian government refused to negotiate and in a memorandum informed the Great Powers of the situation brought about by the deportations of Hungarians.

In the middle of February 1947 the Yugoslav government intervened in Prague and asked for discontinuance of the dispersal of Hungarians living in Slovakia. Following this intervention, the Czechoslovak government suspended the removals of Hungarians on February 25. Conditions for intergovernmental negotiations were created, and a Hungarian delegation, headed again by Foreign Minister Gyöngyösi, traveled to Prague.

At the Prague negotiations, March 2–7, no agreement was signed because the Czechoslovak delegation was unwilling to discuss the Hungarian proposal concerning restitution of property to Hungarians removed from Slovakia or damages caused by removals. The Hungarian delegation regarded these deportations as violations of an international obligation accepted by the Czechoslovak goverment at the conclusion of the population exchange agreement. The Czechoslovak delegation declared that removals were executed according to legal provisions concerning compulsory labor and remained within the domestic jurisdiction of Czechoslovakia. This vital problem remained unsolved, but an agreement was concluded on controversial financial, economic, and technical questions.[57]

The population exchange began on April 11, 1947, with understanding that the Hungaro-Czechoslovak Mixed Commission would settle some pending questions. In following months, simultaneous with sessions of the Mixed Commission, intergovernmental negotiations took place in Bratislava, Piestiany (Pöstyén), and Budapest. Although the negotiations failed to solve fundamental problems, the population exchange continued. Economic and financial problems were not settled according to the exchange agreement and even some decisions of the Hungaro-Czechoslovak Mixed Commission were disregarded for the sake of prompt execution of the transfer. There were Slovaks of all political persuasion in Hungary who took a stand against the population exchange.[58]

As a result of the population exchange—according to Hungarian sources—53,000 Hungarians were transferred from Czechoslovakia to Hungary, and 53,000 Slovaks left Hungary voluntarily for resettlement in Czechoslovakia. 7,000 Slovaks — mainly miners — moved to Czechoslovakia before the exchange agreement was carried out. Outside the bilateral exchange 39,000 Hungarians left Czechoslovakia for Hungary. Some were expelled, others wanted to avoid persecution. Altogether, 60,000 Slovaks moved from Hungary to Czechoslovakia and the Hungarian population of Czechoslovakia was diminished by 92,000 — almost twelve percent of the Hungarian minority.[59]

On the basis of the archives of the Slovak Communist party, Juraj Zvara stated that 73,273 persons left Hungary for Slovakia, but only 59,774 persons were included in the exchange of population. From Slovakia, 68,407 persons were transferred to Hungary within the exchange of population, and approximately 6,000 persons left voluntarily. Zvara did not mention the number of Hungarians expelled. He estimated that the exchange of population affected approximately twelve percent of the Hungarians in Slovakia,[60] and so the Hungarian and Slovak data about the result of the population exchange seem comparable.

A considerable number, if not the majority, of Hungarians deported to Bohemia, returned; but no restitution was made and they received no compensation. The number of major war criminals expelled to Hungary was limited to 184[61] at the Prague-Budapest negotiation in 1947; that is, it was limited to Hungarians sentenced before May 15, 1946, the expiration date of Decree No. 33 of 1945 referred to in the population exchange agreement. But the tens of thousands of Hungarians declared war criminals by Slovak courts were deprived of all their property and received no compensation, although they were allowed to remain in Czechoslovakia. Primarily those Hungarians were transferred who owned a house or landed property. In the latter case, properties were in most cases over 15–20 hectares. The purpose of this policy was to create gaps in Hungarian regions with Slovak settlements. Although there were teachers and other intellectuals among the transferred, many of them were expelled earlier or left because of persecution.

After the Communist seizure of power in Prague in February 1948, the persecution of Hungarians became worse. Many anti-Hungarian measures promulgated but not enforced were executed with utmost rigidity. This policy changed in October 1948 when the Czechoslovak parliament restored Czechoslovak citizenship to Hungarians who were resident in Slovakia on November 1, 1938, and who had not been convicted of crime. This latter provision excluded from restitution the Hungarian "war criminals," a category that embraced a large number of Hungarians; members of Hungarian cultural or social associations or of Hungarian political parties; people connected directly or indirectly with the Hungarian administration in the years 1938 to 1944; people who waved handkerchiefs when Hungarian troops moved into Slovakia after the first Vienna Award; or those who wore Hungarian national costumes at any time. Practically all manifestations of Hungarian nationality were considered by Slovak judges as crimes. In all these cases property was confiscated and sentenced persons remained without citizenship and without property even after the so-called restitution of October 1948. Later it was announced that, Hungarians removed to Bohemia could return to their homes and receive the same or better property. But no provisions were made for removal of Slovak settlers who in 1946–47 had been installed in the property of the deported Hungarians.

Hungarian-language Communist newspapers have been published in Slovakia since 1949, and Hungarian teaching was authorized in 1949–50. But the great majority of Hungarian teachers had been expelled or otherwise dispersed in the previous years. One can hardly imagine orderly Hungarian teaching without trained Hungarian teachers.

In 1950 the Presidium of the Slovak Communist party condemned the anti-Hungarian measures, and in 1952 the equality of Hungarians was recognized. In 1963 the Central Committee of the Slovak Communist party exercised self-criticism and openly admitted that the anti-Hungarian measures taken in 1945-46 were not correct and that they committed the mistake of anti-Magyar nationalism.

Postwar conflict between Hungary and Czechoslovakia clearly showed that in Soviet-bloc countries political reliability was the decisive consideration for Moscow. As long as Hungary and Czechoslovakia were not ruled by Communist governments, persecution of Hungarians in Slovakia was an effective antidote against rapprochement between these Western-oriented countries. After the Communist coups in Budapest and Prague, both countries became "democracies" in the Soviet sense, and Hungarians no longer were considered a danger for Czechoslovakia. A treaty of alliance concluded in April 1949 between Budapest and Prague demonstrated the Soviet-engineered new reality along the Danube.

In conclusion one may say that the population exchange and the many anti-Hungarian measures weakened considerably the Magyar population but did not change fundamentally the ethnic boundaries in southern Slovakia. Under duress many Hungarians declared themselves Slovaks. Forced declarations, however, have about the same moral value as Nazi or Soviet-style elections. The number of Slovaks who volunteered for exchange put an end to the myth, claimed so emphatically by Clementis and other Slovak leaders, of 450,000 Slovaks in Hungary. The emergence of truth did not compensate for the economic spoliations and immense human suffering of hundreds of thousands of Hungarians in Czechoslovakia. The sad truth is that these Hungarians became second-class citizens. Through a combination of persecution, expulsion, and transfer many potential leaders of the Hungarian minority had been removed from Slovakia to Hungary and the remaining population reduced to poverty.

Stephen Kertesz, Rome, 1947

The Royal Palace before and after the siege of Buda

The interior of the Palace

Above, Buda after the siege, 1945. *Below*, the fate of a Nazi plane

Left, the Hungarian Foreign Ministry in Buda, 1945. *Below*, the garden of the Hungarian legation, Rome, 1947 (left to right): Ambassador Marchese Taliani, Envoy Kertész, Foreign Minister Carlo Sforza, Count Mihály Károlyi, Countess Judith Károlyi, Italian Socialist leader Pietro Nenni.

DIVISION OF
COMMUNICATIONS AND RECORDS
TELEGRAPH BRANCH

ACTION COPY

DEPARTMENT OF STATE

INCOMING TELEGRAM

ACTION-TRO——
INFO:
A-C   JSP -C-N   4439
EUR   Paraphrase before com-
NEA   municating to anyone.   Budapest
DC/L
ITP   Dated May 9, 1946
FC   SECRET
DC/R   Rec'd 9:30 a.m., 12th

SECSTATE

PRIORITY

871, May 9, (?)

MYTEL 774, April 25.

Kertesz of FOROFF told me today FORMIN desired me to
know privately and unofficially that Russians are taking
very stiff opposition line re operational landing rights
for American aircraft. Pushkin argues that inasmuch as
it is unthinkable that Soviet aircraft would be granted
such rights in American Zone in Germany or in Italy and
since Russian aircraft have allegedly been shot down
in American Zone, Soviet Government is not willing to
permit aircraft to fly (presumably without Russian clear-
ance in each case) in any zone under Soviet control.
Pushkin reportedly added that American aircraft would not
be permitted to fly operationally in areas such as Hungary
within five hours flying time of Moscow.

Kertesz emphasized this was an authorized intimation
from Gyongyosi and that Hungarian Government is completely
at loss to answer our note requesting landing rights which
is admittedly reasonable and logically correct.

Sent Dept, repeated London as 217, Berlin as 53,
Moscow as 198, and Paris for Secretary as 129.

DES

SECRET

MESSAGE UNSIGNED

Schoenfeld's cable regarding Soviet opposition to American landing rights in Hungary.
Russian intransigence to reasonable requests was to be a hallmark of the Paris Conference.

Part III

FINALE

8

The Framework of Peace

The drawing up of the Charter of the United Nations and conclusion of the peace settlement with the five ex-enemy states turned out to be two separate processes. The victorious nations prepared the final draft and signed the Charter of the United Nations in June 1945. Peacemaking began at the Potsdam Conference of the Big Three (July 16–August 2, 1945).

The leaders of the American delegation to Potsdam, President Harry S. Truman and Secretary of State James F. Byrnes, had had little experience in international negotiation, although Byrnes had been a member of the Yalta delegation. They faced veterans of wartime conferences. The British were led by Churchill, ably supported by Foreign Secretary Eden, his close wartime collaborator. The Labor party leader Clement Attlee accompanied them, to ensure continuity of negotiation whatever the outcome of the parliamentary elections. In the midst of the conference, Churchill and Attlee flew back to London on July 25 to learn that the Conservative party had lost. Attlee returned to Potsdam as head of the British delegation, joined by the new foreign secretary, Ernest Bevin. But this change did not affect British policy; the secretary general of the British delegation, Sir Pierson Dixon, told me years later that Attlee and Bevin used the position papers prepared by the Foreign Office for Churchill. The Soviet delegation at Potsdam was dominated by Stalin and his henchman Molotov, the foreign minister. The Russians were in a triumphant mood and advocated aggrandizement; they had the feeling that they were not getting recognition for their victory over the Germans and for the immensity of their wartime losses. Stalin impressed the leaders of the British and American delegations. One day Churchill kept repeating to Eden, "I like that man." Eden quickly wrote a memorandum in which he reminded Churchill that the Soviet goal was not only revision of the restrictive Montreux Convention and access to the Mediterranean but placing Constantinople under Russian control as a first step in the subjugation of Turkey. Soviet policy, he wrote, was becoming "more brazen every day" and aspired to positions in Lebanon, Egypt, even Tangier.[1]

In the war against Napoleon, Russian troops had marched over Europe, and the Czar himself had arrived in Paris with his army. But at the subsequent Congress of Vienna, Russian ambition had received satisfaction with Polish territories, and the Russian army withdrew from other European countries. Although Western nations hoped in 1945 that the Soviets would imitate this precedent, Stalin had no such intention. When Ambassador Averell Harriman met him at Potsdam, he said that it must be gratifying to be in Berlin after all the struggle and tragedy of the war. Stalin hesitated a moment and replied, "Czar Alexander got to Paris."[2] He possibly meant that Soviet troops in 1945 had not reached the Atlantic, despite the epic struggle and gigantic sacrifices of the Soviet people. Stalin's remark was characteristic of the Soviet way of thinking at the close of hostilities. Soviet leaders remembered the London treaty of 1915 that promised Constatinople and the Straits to the ramshackle Tsarist Empire and hoped to achieve something along such lines. Churchill had encouraged Stalin, saying at Teheran in 1943 that a large land power such as Russia deserved access to warm water ports, and he expressed hope that he would see Russian fleets, both naval and merchant, on all seas of the world.[3]

After the first conversation with Stalin, Truman noted in his diary: "I can deal with Stalin. He is honest—but smart as hell."[4] After his first meeting with Churchill and Stalin at Potsdam, Truman later wrote in his memoirs: "I returned to my temporary home at Babelsberg with some confidence. I hoped that Stalin was a man who would keep his agreements. . . . Because the Russians had made immense sacrifices in men and materials. . . we hoped that Russia would join wholeheartedly in a plan for world peace."[5]

The secretary of the British delegation, Sir Pierson Dixon, evaluating the balance of the Potsdam Conference,[6] recognized that Stalin's great victory at Potsdam came over Poland—its frontiers and government. "Not only did Poland acquire from Germany all the territories up to the Oder/*Western* Neisse: Russia acquired Koenigsberg and a large slice of East Prussia. "But in other respects the Soviets gained little at Potsdam, Dixon noted. Stalin received only token reparations from the Western zones of Germany, and they came to an end in May 1946. "The Ruhr was kept firmly in Western hands: the Anglo-Americans held on to the Berlin enclave in Eastern Germany; they would not allow the Russians to acquire a similar enclave in western Germany."[7] Italy and Austria were protected. Churchill in a series of sallies on July 23 and 24 "put a stop to Russian penetration in six areas: Tangier, Libya, Turkey, Syria, Persia and Suez." A few days later Attlee and Bevin "stopped all further discussion of Stalin's designs on Trieste and Greece."[8]

Dixon admitted that "by being tougher the British could have extracted concessions from the Russians over eastern Germany and the Satellites. But to achieve this they would have had to make concessions in western Germany and the Middle East." Then Dixon asked two rhetorical questions: "Was it worth pushing the German frontier well east of the Oder if that meant having the Russians on the Rhine? Was it worth having democracy in Eastern Europe if that meant having the Russians in the Mediterranean?"[9]

Meanwhile the victors at Potsdam planned for future cooperation. The conference established a Council of Foreign Ministers of the five principal victors: China, France, the Soviet Union, the United Kingdom, and the United States. The CFM's purpose was to undertake the preparatory work for the peace settlement. The council was to draw up peace treaties primarily with Italy, Rumania, Bulgaria, Hungary, and Finland. In discharge of these tasks the council was to be composed of members representing states signatory to the surrender of enemy states. Although there was no French government recognized by the Allies at the time of Italy's surrender, France was recognized as one of the signatories of the armistice agreement with Italy. This meant that Britain and the Soviet Union prepared the treaty for Finland. For the three Danubian countries it was Britain, the Soviet Union, and the United States. For Italy, France and the Big Three. Here was the origin of the 4-3-2 formula of peace making, but it was assumed that all five members of the council would participate in discussions. Western expectation was that the Council of Ministers at an initial meeting would agree on basic issues, and their deputies would cast the agreement into comprehensive form and draft the details and provisions of lesser importance. At a second meeting the council would consider these drafts and decide controversial questions. Texts prepared by the council would be submitted to "the United Nations," and their recommendations would be considered by the council when approving the final version of the five treaties.

France and China did not participate in the Potsdam Conference, and so the United States ambassador to France, Jefferson Caffery, addressed a series of notes to the French minister of foreign affairs, George Bidault, transmitting some agreements concluded at Potsdam before they were published. He also asked for French participation in the Council of Foreign Ministers and agreement with the principles accepted by the Big Three concerning Germany and other matters.[10] The French government accepted the invitation to participate in the CFM and emphasized that France was "interested in all important questions concerning Europe in any region of Europe. This applies particulary to the settlements concerning Rumania, Bulgaria, Hungary and Finland.[11] China also accepted membership in the council.

The structure for peacemaking seemed clear and simple, and yet this process was soon blocked by surprising developments. The first session of the CFM met in London on September 11, 1945, to provide directives for deputies in the preparation of the five treaties. The first session accepted France and China as full participants in all discussions, and sessions were held for nine days with substantial progress made on the Italian, Finnish, and Bulgarian treaties. But on September 22, Molotov alleged that the procedure violated the Potsdam Agreement. It was illegal, he said, because it permitted the Chinese and French foreign ministers to participate in discussion of treaties on which they would not vote. He demanded exclusion of the Chinese foreign minister and partial exclusion of the French foreign minister.

Although the Western and Chinese foreign ministers were baffled by Molotov's interpretation of the Potsdam Agreement, in a spirit of compromise they showed willingness to accept Molotov's proposal. Byrnes suggested acceptance of the Soviet interpretation, provided that at the same time the council agreed that a truly representative peace conference should meet before the end of the year. This conference should include the five members of the council, all European members of the United Nations, and all non-European members that had supplied substantial military assistance in the war against European members of the Axis.

Instead of accepting the concession, Molotov put forward a more extreme demand: he proposed to change retroactively all records of the conference, eliminating any indication of Chinese and French presence in the sessions on the basis of the 4-3-2 formula. Molotov in effect demanded falsification of the record. The Soviet proposal was rejected, and on October 2 the council adjourned *sine die* without agreement.

With the procedural demand Molotov apparently wanted to retaliate because the council was unwilling to consider some far-reaching Soviet aspirations. He had proposed the transfer of Trieste to Yugoslavia and establishment of a Soviet base on the Mediterranean through Soviet trusteeship over Tripolitania and raised the issue of Soviet participation in the occupation of Japan. Rejection of such demands and Western unwillingness to recognize the unrepresentative governments of Rumania and Bulgaria challenged the Soviet position in the Balkans, and Molotov decided to terminate the session through a procedural demand.[12]

At the London session of the CFM, Byrnes had proposed consideration of a modest boundary revision in favor of Hungary, to decrease the substantial Hungarian minority in Rumania. When Molotov heard this proposal he turned to one of his advisers and asked: "Are there Hungarians in Transylvania?"[13] The Soviet delegation opposed the American proposal, and the British delegation supported the Soviet position.

Another Hungary-related incident in London was Byrnes's declaration that the United States would not sign treaties with the unrepresentative governments of Rumania and Bulgaria, but was ready to recognize the broadly based coalition government of Hungary on receipt of a pledge of free elections. An American note to Budapest indicated readiness to establish diplomatic relations and negotiate a treaty with the provisional government, provided it would give a full assurance "for free and untrammeled elections for representative government." As the Hungarian government offered the guarantee, Molotov countered the American move by an immediate and unconditional recognition of the provisional government.

In his report on the first session of the Council of Foreign Ministers (October 5, 1946), Byrnes emphasized that the American government "shared the desire of the Soviet Union to have governments friendly to the Soviet Union in eastern and central Europe" and reaffirmed the pledges made in the Declaration on Liberated Europe. In a book published in 1947 Byrnes gave extensive explanation for failure of the London meetings.[14] He was aware that any failure of peacemaking would be attributed to him and so decided to make a gesture toward Moscow. In a speech before the *Herald Tribune* Forum in New York (October 31, 1945) he drew a parallel between the role of Soviet Russia in Eastern Europe and that of the United States in the Americas, pointing out that the United States could not and would not deny to other nations the right to develop a good-neighbor policy.

> Far from opposing, we have sympathized with, for example, the effort of the Soviet Union to draw into closer and more friendly association with her central and eastern European neighbors. We are fully aware of her special security interests in those countries, and we have

recognized those interests in the arrangements made for the occupation and control of the former enemy states.[15]

One of the apparent reasons of the failure of the London Conference was United States reluctance to recognize the governments of Bulgaria and Rumania, and Byrnes decided to ask the publisher of the Louisville *Courier-Journal,* Mark Ethridge, to examine political conditions in those two countries. Molotov in London had alleged that the American government was misinformed about conditions in Bulgaria and Rumania, indirectly accusing American representatives in Sophia and Bucharest. An independent investigation by a non-diplomat liberal Democrat seemed desirable. Ethridge knew little about the Balkans, but he was a perceptive journalist and, in company of a specialist in Balkan affairs, Cyril E. Black, visited Bulgaria, Moscow, and Rumania. In the two Balkan countries he interviewed members of government, opposition leaders, and public figures of various persuasions. In Bucharest the Moscow-trained Ana Pauker frankly told him that non-Communists were allowed to participate in the government only if they accepted Communist policies. Early in December, Ethridge submitted a "Summary Report on Soviet Policy in Rumania and Bulgaria," together with a cover letter. His report was critical of conditions in Bulgaria and Rumania, and the secretary decided not to publish it.[16]

Byrnes meanwhile initiated a reconciliation with Moscow. Ambassador Harriman visited Stalin at Gagra in the Crimea on October 24 and transmitted a message from President Truman that reviewed disagreements of the London Conference, offered compromises, and assured Stalin that the president remained faithful to the Yalta accords and the policies of Roosevelt. Harriman was surprised that Stalin was less interested in the Balkans than in control of Japan. He realized that Byrnes's refusal to discuss Japanese affairs at London was the main reason for Molotov's behavior. In two long meetings Stalin agreed to reconvene to CFM to draft five treaties, with a peace conference to follow. The number of participating states in the conference remained open, and Stalin linked the control of Japan with the political future of the Balkan countries. Harriman then opened a series of talks with Molotov, on the question of Russia's role in Japan.[17] Amidst these negotiations Byrnes instructed Harriman to propose a mid-December meeting with Molotov and Bevin in Moscow on the basis of the Yalta Agreement that called for periodic consultation of foreign ministers of the Big Three. This he did without consulting the British foreign secretary, Bevin. Molotov was delighted to accept, but Bevin was offended because of ex post facto notification. When he objected to the suddenly called meeting, Byrnes threatened to go to Moscow without him.

The tripartite Moscow Conference created ill-feeling in France. Byrnes explained to Ambassador Henri Bonnet that the tripartite conference would discuss primarily questions connected with the atomic bomb, Russian-American problems in the Far East, and the setting of the peace conference proposed by Byrnes in London, but not with questions touching French interests, notably affairs of Germany. Bonnet expressed dissatisfaction and asked Byrnes to arrange an invitation of the French government to Moscow.[19] None was arranged.

The Moscow meeting of the foreign ministers (December 16–26) resolved that draft treaties prepared by the CFM on the basis of the 4-3-2 formula should be submitted to a conference, not of all the United Nations, as mentioned in the Potsdam Agreement, but of five members of the council and sixteen other Allied nations that had fought in Europe with substantial contingents. The conference, to meet in Paris before May 1, 1946, could discuss drafts of the peace treaties, express opinions, and make recommendations. The Soviet government had opposed a more substantial conference with wider jurisdiction and would have preferred a peace settlement exclusively by the Great Powers.

At the Moscow meeting Byrnes gave the Ethridge report to the Russians and by way of compromise showed willingness to recognize Soviet-installed governments in Bulgaria and Rumania, provided these governments took in two representatives of "democratic parties not hitherto participating in them." The Big Three agreed on a commission to advise the Rumanian king on broadening the Groza government. Token representatives of the Liberal and National Peasant parties were duly admitted to the cabinet, but dropped after the Rumanian elections of January 1947. It was agreed that in Bulgaria the Soviet Union should advise the government to broaden its base, but this scheme did not work because the Bulgarian government rejected conditions of the opposition.

Besides preparation of peace treaties and reorganization of governments in Bulgaria and Rumania, the Moscow Conference agreed on a Far Eastern Commission and an Allied Council for Japan, on some Korean and Chinese questions, and establishment by the United Nations of the Commission for the Control of Atomic Energy.[20] Byrnes noted in his memoirs that in Moscow he still hoped that the Soviet Union and the United States had "a common purpose."

Former Undersecretary of State Sumner Welles, out of office since

August 1943, blamed Byrnes for failures at the Potsdam, London, and Moscow conferences and criticized his willingness to recognize the unrepresentative Rumanian and Bulgarian governments. He suggested that such "a face-saving device" was counter to the Yalta agreement. Byrnes, he said, "paved the way for the immediate consolidation of Soviet domination over eastern Europe and the Balkans."[22] There is truth in Welles's allegation, but he was not aware of such events as the Anglo-Russian percentage agreement of October 1944 in which Britain recognized Soviet predominance in Rumania, Bulgaria, and Hungary.

Hungary was not involved in the distribution of power in the Black Sea countries. Its position seemed different to foreign observers because it was the only country under Soviet occupation where free national elections took place in November 1945, elections in which the Communist party obtained only 17% of the vote. For centuries Rumania and Bulgaria had been on the highway of Russian expansion, and installation of Communist-dominated governments in Bucharest and Sophia was an urgent matter for the Kremlin. Yet the absence of Western assertiveness over Bulgaria and Rumania showed a pattern that foreshadowed events in Hungary. In the Anglo-Soviet percentage agreement Hungary had the same position as Bulgaria, an 80-20 percentage division in favor of Russia, but this fact was not known until the opening of British Foreign Office records in 1973.

After the Moscow Conference of 1945 the head of the European division of the State Department, H. Freeman Matthews, visited the secretary—general of the French Foreign Ministry, Jean Chauvel, to transmit Byrnes's assurance that the American government considered very important France's adherence to the proposed plan for preparation of the five peace treaties. He informed Chauvel of questions discussed in Moscow and did not conceal that the Russians opposed a genuine peace conference and insisted that peace treaties should be prepared by the Big Three. Consequently, the Moscow formula for a conference was a compromise laboriously established. Matthews reassured Chauvel that the role of the CFM remained as established at Potsdam and that deputies of the foreign ministers should meet soon in London.[23]

French diplomats had a dim view of France's exclusion from peacemaking along the Danube, and Ambassador Maurice Dejean in a telegram from Prague reported a conversation with Masaryk who told him that elimination of France from the general peace settlement was "un véritable disastre" for Czechoslovakia. Why did Byrnes not understand that in barring France he abandoned all Europe to a single power, Masaryk asked? According to reports received in Prague, Molotov had displayed the greatest cordiality toward Byrnes at Kremlin receptions, while ostensibly neglecting Bevin to show that the British foreign secretary was only tolerated in the company of the Big Three.[24] Dejean noted that the Moscow Conference evoked more the meeting of Tilsit that gatherings of the Yalta style.[25] Simultaneous with this telegram he dispatched a long report to Paris about the impressions the Moscow Conference had produced in Prague. He explained that for the Czechoslovaks, the exclusion of France from negotiations of the Hungarian and Balkan treaties meant that, except for the Italian treaty, Paris would have only a consultative voice in the peace settlement and that this had created a belief in Prague that France had become a second-class power.[26]

About this time Bonnet reported from Washington that a member of the American delegation in Moscow had told him that the Russians had accepted without objection the American proposal that the peace conference should be in Paris and that in Secretary Byrnes's opinion this meant recognition of the European role of France. The American delegate informed Bonnet of questions discussed in Moscow and called attention to the fact that France had not declared war on Bulgaria and Rumania, hence weakening its negotiating role.[27]

Ambassador Caffery transmitted Secretary Byrnes's message to the French foreign minister *ad interim,* Francisque Gay, whose answer reiterated that France was interested in all important questions concerning Europe and asked for clarification and assurance on several points decided at Moscow.

Secretary Byrnes, now representing the Big Three, gave the following explanations to the French government: The Moscow Agreement in no way altered the understanding in regard to preparation of the peace settlement with Germany; on the basis of the Potsdam Agreement the CFM retained authority to invite other states when matters concerning them were discussed; a broad and thorough discussion would take place at the forthcoming conference, and final drafts of the treaties would be made only after fullest consideration to recommendations of the conference; the draft treaties would take into account the views of enemy states, and adequate opportunity would be given to them to discuss the treaties and present their views.[28]

This statement assured the French government that the states participating in the conference could debate the treaties, that the council would consider recommendations of the conference, and that the defeated states would receive a hearing. France was apparently anxious to avoid even the appearance of dictation, in view of what had happened after the First World War. The French government then decided to participate in the conference as host country.

The Moscow Conference caused friction not only with the British and French but between Truman and Byrnes. Truman apparently believed Byrnes in December 1945 had become soft on the Soviets and resented that he had not kept him informed while in Moscow. He seems to have told Byrnes this in a meeting late in December on the yacht *Williamsburg,* and again at the White House on January 5, 1946, when he read from a handwritten letter addressed to Byrnes (but not given to him). The letter concluded: "I'm tired of babying the Soviets."[29]

Deputies of the foreign ministers began work in London on January 18, 1946, and the several decisions accepted at the first conference of the council formed the basis of their deliberations, which strictly followed the 4-3-2 rule. They discussed primarily such issues as the fate of the Italian colonies, the Italo-Yugoslav frontier, the Trieste problem, and reparations. Soviet draft treaties for the Danubian countries were put forward in a session of the deputies in early March. The texts were shorter than the armistice agreements and contained sketchy economic and military clauses; territorial provisions were not included, with exception of restoration of northern Transylvania to Rumania. The United States delegation proposed that the council either make an investigation of the boundary problem or ask the Rumanian and Hungarian governments to take up the dispute. The Soviet delegation refused to discuss the matter.[30]

The Council of Foreign Ministers met again in Paris, for a second session — which itself was in two parts, the first on April 25–May 16 and the second on June 15–July 12, 1946. Molotov proposed at the outset that the four foreign ministers participate in all sessions, quietly eliminating the stumbling block he had created at the London session. France being the host country, Bidault chaired the opening meeting, and the French noticed with satisfaction Molotov's changed attitude. Except for this gesture, the Soviet delegation returned to wrangling on procedural matters. Time-consuming Soviet tactics exasperated the Western delegations, and on one occasion Bevin became so irritated when Molotov attacked Britain for past sins in international affairs that he

> rose to his feet, his hands knotted into fists, and started toward Molotov, saying, "I've had enough of this, I 'ave," and for one glorious moment it looked as if the Foreign Minister of Great Britain and the Foreign Minister of the Soviet Union were about to come to blows. However, security people moved in. . . .[31]

The United States proposed in February 1946 that the Austrian treaty be prepared along with other treaties, and Byrnes submitted a treaty draft to the council on April 26, entitled, "For the Reestablishment of an Independent and Democratic Austria."[32] Byrnes at last had realized that as long as Soviet troops were stationed in Austria, Danubian Europe would remain under Soviet occupation. Two days later a bilateral American-Soviet meeting took place, before and after a dinner given by Byrnes for Molotov, in which they discussed the Austrian treaty and a twenty-five-year quadripartite treaty on disarmament and demilitarization of Germany. Byrnes told the Russians that in December 1945 he had discussed the German treaty with Stalin who had expressed himself strongly in favor, but the Soviet government did not even acknowledge the draft treaty transmitted to the foreign ministry in Moscow. Despite Stalin's alleged approval, Molotov was reluctant to discuss Austrian and German matters. He felt that the five peace treaties were more than enough for that session of the council. He argued that in Germany an immediate disarmament was the important task, although in principle he favored twenty-five-year treaties for demilitarization of Germany and Japan. Vyshinsky added that in Austria denazification had not progressed far enough to consider a final settlement with that country. In the council, Bidault and Bevin supported the American initiative concerning the Austrian and German treaties, the debate continued through several sessions, and Molotov eventually agreed to discussion of Austrian questions, not the treaty, after completion of drafts of the five peace treaties. This meant a postponement until November. Byrnes argued politely with the Russians but did not put up a fight, though he noted the anomaly of leaving Austria in a worse situation than the ex-enemy countries, particulary in view of the Moscow Declaration. Molotov indicated it might be necessary to leave troops in Austria for another year—that is, two years after the end of hostilities.[33]

The council examined thoroughly boundary disputes outside the Soviet zone, such as the controversy between Yugoslavia and Italy. Both governments argued their cases before the council four times. There were hearings on the Franco-Italian and Italo-Austrian boundaries, in addition to spot investigations of all three boundary disputes affecting Italy. Even Australia, New Zealand, and the Union of South Africa presented their views to the council concerning the Italo-Yugoslav boundary quarrel. While Italy was permitted to present its case orally before the council, similar requests by other ex-enemy states were turned down.

Amidst controversies, during a short period of concessions, Byrnes wanted to give satisfaction to the Russians, and in the council on May 7 proposed the annulment of the Vienna Award and restoration of the 1938 frontier between Hungary and Rumania.[34] He had realized that the Russians were unwilling even to study boundary changes between these countries and decided to eliminated conflicts so as to expedite the convocation of the Paris Conference.

The deputies of the foreign ministers met again between May 16 and June 15, 1946, to prepare for resumption of meetings of the CFM, and eventually the council reached agreement upon a large number of treaty articles. The Soviet delegation insisted that the conference could not be convoked before agreement on all treaty clauses. The American delegation explained that the Potsdam and Moscow conferences had charged the council to prepare treaty drafts and submit them to a conference of Allied nations, but complete draft treaties were not required. As soon as agreement was reached on Italy's reparation deliveries to the Soviet Union, the Soviets agreed to set the opening date of the conference for July 29.[35] This was another example of a procedural objection dropped when the Soviet Union received a concession. There remained twenty-six points upon which members of the council could not agree, which delayed the sending of invitations to the conference. The Soviet delegation opposed dispatching invitations until the council had accepted the Soviet draft of conference procedure. Byrnes explained repeatedly that the council could not impose rules of procedure on an assembly of sovereign states. Molotov insisted that conference recommendations be made by two-thirds majority. Eventually a compromise was reached; draft rules of procedure, enclosed with the invitations, suggested decisions of the conference by a two-thirds majority vote.[36] Byrnes emphasized that the suggested procedural rules did not represent a hard-and-fast agreement comparable to agreed treaty clauses—an essential distinction because the foreign ministers agreed to support at the conference the treaty clauses they accepted in the council. The Soviets were convinced that the only important task of the Conference of Paris was prompt approval of the council's agreements. After further argument on organizational questions, the council recommended a commission structure for the conference.

Delegations of twenty-one nations at long last assembled at the Luxembourg Palace on July 29, 1946, and as agreed by the foreign ministers of the Big Three at their Moscow meeting in December, 1945, the participating states were the United States, United Kingdom, Soviet Union, France, China, Australia, Belgium, the Byelorussian Soviet Socialist Republic, Brazil, Canada, Czechoslovakia, Ethiopia, Greece, India, the Netherlands, Norway, New Zealand, Poland, the Ukrainian Soviet Socialist Republic, the Union of South Africa, and Yugoslavia. Separate representation of the Ukraine and Byelorussia was in accord with the Yalta arrangement whereby Britain and the United States promised to support a proposal to admit to original membership in the United Nations these two Soviet Socialist Republics.

Machinery of the conference consisted of a General Commission, a Legal and Drafting Commission, Military Commission, five Political and Territorial Commissions, and two Economic Commissions — one for Italy, and the other for Finland and the three Danubian countries. The General Commission (which never met), the Military Commission, and the Legal and Drafting Commission were composed of representatives of the twenty-one nations participating in the conference. Five Political and Territorial Commissions had representatives from those nations actively at war with the enemy states concerned. In these commissions, Communist states and non-European countries prevailed. Members of the Hungarian Political and Territorial Commission were the United States, United Kingdom, the Soviet Union, France, the Byelorussian SSR, the Ukrainian SSR, Australia, Czechoslovakia, India, New Zealand, Canada, the Union of South Africa, and Yugoslavia.

The conference set up the usual Credentials Commission and elected a Commission on Procedure. Debates on procedure lasted over a week. The majority of delegates opposed the council's proposal that required a two-third majority for a recommendation and agreed on majority decision. Byrnes and Bevin supported the majority's desire to allow the conference to make recommendations to the council by two-thirds vote or by majority. After long argumentative sessions this motion was accepted by a 15-to-6 vote; the "Slav bloc" (Soviet Union, Byelorussia, Ukraine, Poland, Czechoslovakia, Yugoslavia) voted against it, and Molotov accused Byrnes and Bevin of violating council agreements. Byrnes explained again that there was no obligatory agreement on procedural questions and announced that at the forthcoming meeting of the council the United States would support any recommendation accepted by two-thirds vote even if the American delegation voted against it at the conference. Subsequently the conference accepted fifty-three recommendations by two-thirds majority and forty-one by simple majority.

On Byrnes's proposal the press was admitted to all meetings of commissions and the plenary sessions, an unfortunate innovation in peacemaking as most speakers addressed their remarks to public opinion in their own country, and some sessions became unproductive examples of public diplomacy. In the United Nations, propaganda speeches are boring and ineffective but usually harmless rhetorical exercises, but the Paris Conference of 1946 had to discuss issues to be settled by treaty provisions.

The conference had a narrow focus, and it was almost out of context if a delegate brought up constructive ideas. Herbert V. Evatt of Australia introduced several amendments to bring the treaties more in line with concepts of peace and justice. Among them was the establishment of a European Court of Human Rights that could have given realistic meaning to treaty clauses on human rights and fundamental freedoms. The proposed court could have extended protection to minorities under alien rule. Evatt proposed commissions to study territorial disputes and convocation of a conference within five years to consider revision of the peace treaties. Such proposals were in harmony with American thinking, but the United States delegation voted against them because of a council agreement. Molotov accused the Americans and British of being behind amendments he did not like, apparently believing that the United States controlled small states in the same fashion as he controlled the "Slav Bloc." Reasoned discourse between the two blocs seldom was possible. Quiet diplomacy facilitates compromises, but was rarely used in Paris. Propaganda speeches at open meetings had the opposite effect; once a public stand is taken, it is difficult for governments to make concessions. Open meetings widened the gulf between East and West. Marxist oratory did not serve the cause of understanding, and it became clear that Moscow's goals were incompatible with those of the Western Allies. World opinion was excited by propaganda speeches that took little account of the substance of issues and application of principles accepted by the Allies during the war.

Negotiation at the council and the Conference of Paris was part of a worldwide struggle that could not be divorced from the political ambitions and events dominating the world scene. A Communist objective was to increase tension because it was easier to obtain concessions in an atmosphere of uncertainty and surprises; tactics included obscuring issues by emphasis on procedural questions and irrelevancies. The Soviet idea about peacemaking was simple: Moscow wanted to transform the armistice agreements into peace treaties. Molotov made clear that he considered the armistice agreements as final settlements and proposed that the peace treaties confirm them. As noted, the Soviet government would have preferred a peace settlement exclusively by the Big Three.

Although the Paris Conference did not discuss German affairs, an unusual incident concerning Germany almost caused Byrnes's resignation. During the summer the controlled press in the Soviet zone misrepresented American views on Germany, referring to the so-called Morgenthau Plan that would have turned Germany into agricultural land, and Communists spread rumors in Berlin that the United States had decided to withdraw from Europe. To make clear American policy, Byrnes delivered an address in Stuttgart on September 6 in which he said that "Germany is part of Europe, and European recovery . . . will be slow if Germany with her great resources of iron and coal is turned into a poor house." He expressed hope for an economically united and democratic Germany and assured his audience that American forces would remain in Germany for a long time. The United States, he said, wanted to return the government of Germany to its people and "help them win their way back to an honorable place among the free and peace-loving nations of the world."[37] The speech had wide repercussions. On September 12, Secretary of Commerce Henry A. Wallace delivered an address in New York in which he denounced Byrnes's "Get tough with Russia policy." The speech caused consternation and had a bombshell effect at the Paris Conference because it was unprecedented that the policy of a foreign secretary negotiating abroad was publicly attacked by a member of the cabinet. Byrnes asked the president to accept his resignation, but Truman asked for and received Wallace's resignation.[38]

The noncooperative Soviet attitude stirred crises and blocked serious negotiation. A member of the American delegation, Philip E. Mosely, remarked retrospectively that in negotiation of this kind the most reluctant government determines the maximum rate of progress.[39] In this bewildering atmosphere even minor Soviet concessions brought relief. Fundamental problems were avoided, and participants limited the issues and range of discussion. Most delegations were in a hurry to attend the General Assembly of the United Nations in New York, postponed from September 23 to October 23. The CFM decided that the closing session of the conference should be on October 15. Byrnes and Molotov in a private meeting on October 3 agreed on a simplified procedure for the forthcoming plenary sessions and Byrnes inquired what Molotov thought would be done "if despite all efforts the conference had not voted on all questions before it by October 15." Molotov said the work "must be finished by that day." Byrnes raised the possibility that the work would not be finished. He recognized that Molotov wanted to return to Moscow before coming to New York but felt that "if absolutely necessary the conference should stay in session a few days more in order to complete its work." Molotov repeated that "they should make sure that the conference complete its work by the fifteenth."[40] That is what happened.

A British observer of the Paris Conference of 1919 and veteran member of his country's foreign service, Harold Nicolson was present throughout the Paris Conference of 1946. He had devoted his life to the study and practice of diplomacy and characterized the pace of negotiations as follows:

> It is the way of every conference to begin like a tortoise and to end like a greyhound. But no conference that I have ever attended showed a greater disparity of progress between the commencement and the finish. During the first six weeks the Conference dragged itself along painfully at the rate of an inch an hour; during the last four weeks there was a breathless scramble to conclude. In frantic haste the delegates rattled off their final speeches, the concluding votes were registered in an indecent rush, and so anxious were the statesmen not to miss the *Queen Elizabeth* that there was no time at the end for the customary courtesies and farewells.[41]

The final text of the five peace treaties was drawn by the third session of the CFM in New York on November 4–December 12, 1946. At the outset, Molotov's cordial and cooperative attitude seemed to show he was satisfied. Then for weeks he repeated Soviet proposals he had offered at previous meetings, disregarding recommendations of the Paris Conference. During the fourth week of the exasperating New York session, in a private meeting, he asked Byrnes what could be done to make progress, and Byrnes replied that since Molotov had rejected practically all recommendations of the Paris Conference, he saw no hope to agree upon the treaties and nothing remained but to admit failure and disband. Molotov in bewilderment said Byrnes was unduly pessimistic and asked him not to take hasty action and observe developments at the next meeting. Because Moscow had much to gain by concluding the treaties, Molotov then reversed his policy and at subsequent meetings "handed out concesssions like cards from a deck."[42] The council approved forty-seven of the fifty-three recommendations adopted by two-thirds majority at the Paris Conference and twenty-four of forty-one adopted by a simple majority.[43]

Here was another demonstration that Molotov under pressure reversed inflexible policies, and the sudden volte-face raised the question of lost opportunities because of lack of Western assertiveness. If Byrnes had taken a firm attitude earlier, say at the Potsdam Conference, concerning primacy of a state treaty with a liberated country, Austria, peacemaking could have taken a more constructive turn for the Danubian nations, even within the narrow Potsdam scheme.

The peace treaties signed on February 10, 1947, implicitly gave the stamp of legality to the Soviet position established in Eastern Europe at the close of hostilities. The gradual seizure of power by the Communists in Hungary in 1947, incorporation of Czechoslovakia into the Soviet sphere in February 1948, and exclusion of the Western powers from the Danube by the Russian-dictated Danubian convention signed at the Belgrade Conference in the same year—all these were logical consequences of a determined Soviet policy. As Stalin explained it to Milovan Djilas in April 1945; "This war is not as in the past; whoever occupies a territory also imposes on it his own social system. Everyone imposes his own system as far as his army can reach. It cannot be otherwise."[44]

In postwar planning it probably was a major mistake to conclude peace treaties with the five less important ex-enemy states before concluding a treaty with Austria and reaching at least a policy agreement on Germany.[45] The German question was by far the most difficult issue between the Western democracies and Russia, but according to conventional wisdom, an agreement on its solution should have created better conditions to tackle less difficult problems. The assumption that conclusion of peace with the lesser enemy states would help the settlement of the German question was an illusion because it disregarded the nature and purpose of Soviet foreign policy.

One of the consequences of the Potsdam schedule of peacemaking was postponement of the major peace conference *ad Graecas Calendas*, and this meant shelving if not burying a basic policy assumption of the Roosevelt administration. Peace preparations in the State Department had assumed that a major conference would follow hostilities. This plan was abandoned and replaced by a piecemeal approach at Potsdam, and this change was favorable for Soviet designs. Little give-and-take was possible because four out of five ex-enemy states were in the Soviet sphere. The CFM decided that Italian sovereignty should be restored at the conclusion of peace and consequently foreign troops should be withdrawn. Molotov, in turn, reluctantly agreed to withdraw troops from Bulgaria. A better arrangement would have been a linkage between the Italian peace treaty and an Austrian state treaty and simultaneous withdrawal of foreign troops from both countries. The Moscow Declaration of 1943 had recognized that Austria was an occupied country to be liberated, and a treaty with Vienna should have brought simultaneous evacuation of foreign troops from Danubian Europe.

If Moscow would not have accepted a reasonable order of peace-making, the Western powers could have concluded a separate peace with Italy, as they did with Japan in 1951, and the British and American sections of the ACC would have remained in the Danubian ex-enemy countries. In this way the West could have preserved a bargaining chip lost by conclusion of peace treaties. In the framework created by the Potsdam and Moscow Conferences in 1945, the Western powers were primarily interested in consolidation of Italy's international position. Nominal sovereignty was of little value for states in the Soviet orbit. Independence of Hungary and Rumania remained fictitious because the peace treaties authorized the Soviet Union to keep un-limited forces in those countries for maintenance of lines of communication with the Soviet army in Austria.[46] In early September 1946, Ambassador Walter Bedell Smith assured Prime Minister Ferenc Nagy that withdrawal of occupation forces was the "foremost objective" of the United States. Although Secretary Byrnes emphasized this policy goal even in private sessions of the American delegation, he did not take a stand to achieve this objective. Western acceptance of the Soviet timetable and priorities in peacemaking helped consolidate Soviet power in East Central Europe.

During the period between the Yalta Conference and the Japanese surrender, the United States was the strongest world power, but at the time of the Paris Conference of 1946 the demobilized Western nations had only weak occupation forces in Europe, and more importantly, lacked political will to make a meaningful European settlement. They wanted to finish an unpleasant business in Paris. Even in this mood and with restrictions of the Potsdam and Moscow agreements, Western peacemaking was less than satisfactory. Despite Soviet occupation of the Danubian area and presence of a strong Soviet army in Central Europe, it was frustrating to witness the overcautious attitude of Western delegates. Wartime concessions to Moscow were understandable. But at the peace table only determined resistance to unjustified Soviet demands could have a result. There were exceptional delegates like Evatt of Australia, but their proposals were like voices in the wilderness. The approach of the Western Great Powers was similar at best to the old Austrian policy of *weiterwursteln* — muddling through.

The monotonous repetition of Communist views throughout the negotiations in the council and at the Paris Conference was far different from the Atlantic Charter and the Declaration on Liberated Europe, documents endorsed by the USSR. Elevation of public discussion to a higher level might not have impressed Molotov, but it would have provided appealing and uniting ideas and swayed public opinion of countries participating in peacemaking. Separate handling of issues coupled with separate votes in committees and plenary sessions of the Paris Conference, without reference to overriding principles proclaimed in the war years, offered a chance for a field day for Molotov. Time and again he merely repeated slogans, while bickering about procedure exhausted Western representatives; they were relieved by any small Soviet concession. Negotiation about freedom of navigation on the Danube is a case point. At dozens of meetings the CFM discussed Danube River problems, and eventually Molotov's stubbornness prevailed. Western delegates withdrew elaborate proposals, and Molotov rejected the article on the Danube adopted by the Paris Conference. At the New York session, the CFM accepted a general declaration on freedom of navigation on the Danube without provision for enforcement or reference to the 1921 Danubian Convention. The council agreed on a special Danubian conference of representatives of riparian states and the four council members. The apparent nonchalance of Western diplomacy prepared the way for a Soviet-dictated Danubian treaty at the Belgrade Conference in 1948, a treaty that practically abolished the international regime of the Danube first established by the Treaty of Paris, nearly a century before, in 1856.

Wartime agreements and especially the Yalta Declaration on Liberated Europe were made in the hope that the Soviet Union would keep its promises. Philip Mosely, a member of the American delegation at wartime and postwar conferences, noted:

> By the end of 1946, against unyielding Soviet insistence on transforming East Central Europe into a closed preserve, the American government had a heap of broken Soviet promises to point to as a reminder that hope divorced from power is not a policy.[47]

It is clear that the weak negotiating position of the Western Allies was one of the consequences of wartime strategy and policy. The ex-enemy states could not influence the course of events; they were at the receiving end of the system of peacemaking established at the Potsdam and Moscow conferences.

9

The Paris Conference: Part One

Vicissitudes of Peacemaking

I arrived in Paris on May 9, 1946, as minister-counselor of the Hungarian legation, with the understanding that I would be secretary-general of the Hungarian peace delegation. Soviet authorities in the ACC delayed an exit visa to Paul Auer, designated Hungarian minister to France, so he could get to Paris only a few days before my arrival. When we met, he was in a pessimistic mood because the Council of Foreign Ministers recently had decided to reestablish the Trianon boundary between Hungary and Rumania. We agreed promptly on diplomatic steps to be taken in the period preceding the Conference of Twenty-One Nations. In following weeks the substantial material I took with me made it possible to address notes to the British, French, United States, and Soviet representatives on the Council of Foreign Ministers. Until that time such notes had been addressed only to envoys of the three principal victorious powers in Budapest.

On June 4, 1946, the legation forwarded to the council, with a covering letter, the ten most important peace preparatory notes and aide-memoires that were originally sent between August 14, 1945, and May 20, 1946, to the British, Soviet, and United States representatives in Budapest. A followup note asked the council to grant a hearing to Hungary's representative in connection with two questions: (1) persecution of Hungarians in Czechoslovakia; and (2) the May 7 decision of the council concerning reestablishment of the Trianon boundary between Hungary and Rumania.[1]

After dispatching these notes I visited the council's secretary-general, de La Grandville, and inquired about the prospects of our request for a hearing and generally the prospects of our proposals. Grandville could not give me an official answer, but in the course of our private conversation I learned about the council's working method and policies. I understood that a hearing of Hungary's representative was not in the cards. Grandville indicated that the coun-

182

cil was unwilling to create a precedent in view of the requests for hearings submitted by governments of several states. Governments of ex-enemy countries would be invited to state their cases at the Conference of Twenty-One Nations. Another discouraging piece of information was that the council would examine only the draft peace treaties prepared by the deputy foreign ministers. This meant that the council would not consider our carefully and sometimes boldly prepared proposals.

The meeting with Grandville clarified some other questions. I had heard of an initiative to establish a permanent international committee to evaluate Italy's capability to pay reparations and inquired about the possibility of creating a committee of this nature for the other ex-enemy states. Examination by an international body of Hungary's ability to pay reparations would have revealed our catastrophic financial situation and the need of lowering reparation payments. Grandville relied that Molotv opposed the creation of a committee to evaluate Italy's financial capability, probably for two reasons — that such a committee would secure for the Anglo-Saxons a lasting influence in Italy, and it also would become a precedent for the other ex-enemy countries.

Finally, I asked Grandville about the council's channels of information to the press, for the benefit of countries not participating in CFM deliberations. He replied that joint communiqués would be in order, but if such were not forthcoming, each delegation might inform the press. He pointed out that a daily press conference took place at the United States embassy.

Information from Grandville made clear the stark realities of peacemaking in 1946, and contacts with several Western representatives corroborated and supplemented this information, deflating any hope for constructive negotiation. Sometimes even knowledgeable people are inclined to assume that reasonable arguments and "justice" prevail at a peace conference. In reality after both World Wars the major victorious powers discussed the terms of peace settlement among themselves, and the outcome depended on their respective power, national interests, and ideologies. We had received desperate letters from Hungarian citizens of Czechoslovakia and Rumania. The writers believed that their better future depended on our steadfast stand and pleading for their cause at the peace conference. It was heartbreaking to know that we could do very little for them. Even if defeated countries stated their cases in Paris, without support of principal victorious powers their proposals and claims remained voices in the wilderness. Peacemaking after both World Wars was a far cry from the Congress

of Vienna in 1814–15, when France was admitted to the high council
of the victors, and the resultant Vienna settlement secured general
peace in Europe for a century.

During my first days in the familiar atmosphere of Paris I felt like
Rip Van Winkle in political matters. During the war and especially
after the German occupation in March 1944, we had received little
reliable information about inter-Allied agreements, and in our
isolated situation in 1945–46 we did not have a clear idea of the
peacemaking machinery established by the Potsdam and Moscow
conferences. Our legation in Washington had suggested that I go to
London in the spring of 1946 because the deputy foreign ministers
would meet there to prepare draft peace treaties for the CFM.
Pushkin had refused to give me an exit visa to Switzerland, where our
peace preparatory material had been deposited early in 1944. He told
Gyöngyösi that such material would not be needed. So it was hopeless to ask for a visa to London.

I had hoped that the Western powers — especially the United
States — would support our proposals, primarily economic and cultural, for cooperation in Danubian Europe. It seemed to me that an
honest presentation of some longstanding problems of the Danubian
nations would serve the general interests of Europe and would be a
first step toward reconciliation, cooperation, and integration in this
long-suffering area. But Moscow opposed regional integration in its
sphere of influence.

I note at this point that in Hungary such leading statesmen as
Count Pál Teleki had been convinced even in the mid-1930s that the
United States would play a decisive role at the next peace settlement
in Europe. He expressed this view to me before I left for Yale as a
Rockefeller fellow in 1935. During the war the officials in charge of
peace preparations in the Foreign Ministry had assumed that the
United States, as the strongest world power at the close of hostilities,
would exercise a decisive influence for economic reorganization of the
Danubian region. At the Paris Conference in private conversation
American and other Western representatives recognized the rational-
ity of our proposls. But after observing the Soviet attitude and policy
in CFM conferences they questioned their feasibility. The Kremlin
would champion all integration in favor of Moscow and would not
tolerate any Danubian integration until they had control of the whole
area, and then only in associations in which the USSR was a member.
Such considerations were the reason for the subdued Western attitude at the conference table, both in the CFM and the Paris Conference. Tito's Yugoslavia, Groza's Rumania, and Beneš's Czecho-

slovakia were all competing, caps in hand, for Moscow's favor. Under such conditions it could have been self-defeating to initiate a movement for an institutionalized cooperation of the Danubian countries. The Eastern European experts of the Western Great Powers were well informed in Danubian affairs, but in light of their experiences with Moscow, they were convinced that for countries under Soviet occupation Moscow would call the tune.

If the CFM was unwilling to grant a hearing to the Hungarian government, it still seemed important that Auer and I visit, together or separately, the ambassadors of selected countries. To them we explained Hungary's political and economic predicament, gave out memoranda, and asked support. While I was engaged in these activities, Foreign Minister Gyöngyösi informed me, first in a cipher telegram and then in a letter, that he had designated me as chief political delegate of Hungary to the Paris Conference. I declined this position, and he wrote another letter on July 15 in which he said he did not understand the reason of my refusal because things had developed more favorably than we expected, adding:

> You may claim with satisfaction that the evolution of domestic politics has justified both of us; myself as politician who assumed responsibility, and yourself as public servant and a good patriot who accomplished honorably your task. Everybody refers now to the note of last August 14, [1945] as a unanimous decision of the coalition, whereas the two of us know best that this was not at all the case and that we went those days much beyond the position of the coalition and the government. So far this has been a great satisfaction to both of us and I admit with pleasure the fact that first of all to you who all the time represented the standpoint of national honor and common sense . . .

I could not share Gyöngyösi's optimism, based on momentary superficial improvements in Hungarian politics. National unity seemed greater at that time because the Communist and Socialist parties, contrary to their initial positions, openly supported national aspirations, especially in the Transylvanian question. Yet the country's predicament remained the same. As long as Hungary was occupied by Soviet troops and practically ruled by the Soviet chairman of the ACC, I did not want to accept a political position, preferring to remain secretary-general of the Hungarian peace delegation. This position had secured me more influence, through behind-the-scenes operations, than would the conspicuous title of a political delegate. I could achieve more through quiet diplomacy; in a political position I would have become a hostage of the coalition parties which often worked at cross purposes.

I suggested to Gyöngyösi that a chief political delegate was super-fluous because the foreign minister himself would be the political leader and chairman of the Hungarian delegation. If the government wished to appoint a chief political delegate he should not be a civil servant but a prominent political figure, preferably a leading member of the Communist party. I made this latter suggestion in view of Auer's suspicion that Communists did not want to participate in the peace negotiations. Absenteeism would have made it possible for them to blame the punitive peace treaty on the Smallholder party. When the Communist deputy foreign minister, Elek Bolgár, refused to accompany the delegation to Paris, because of illness, Auer informed Frederick T. Merrill of the United States delegation that this was a diplomatic illness, as Communist policy was "not to participate in presenting the Hungarian case to the Conference." Auer had "wired the Prime Minister recommending that a leader of the Communist Party be included in the Delegation in order that all members of the coalition and not the Smallholder Party alone should bear the onus of a failure to modify a proposed treaty now considered by most all [sic] Hungarians as little less than catastrophic."[2]

The twenty-one victorious states at last formally opened the peace conference at the Luxembourg Palace, on July 29, 1946, in response to an invitation from the governments of Great Britain, France, the United States, and the Soviet Union. By this time the Soviet delegation was ready and confident for whatever might result. For several days prior to the session of the conference, members of the delegation arrived from Budapest. Gyöngyösi and his entourage came a few days before the initial meeting.

Our delegation came together for two conferences each day—one political, the other administrative. Gyöngyösi chaired the political conferences in which Paul Auer usually participated, together with Aladár Szegedy-Maszák, minister to the USA; Gyula Szekfű, minister to the USSR; Paul Sebestyén, envoy extraordinary and minister plenipotentiary; László Faragó, director of the Financial Institutions Center in Budapest, chief economic delegate; Colonel István Szemes, delegate for military affairs; and various short-term visitors. Depending on questions under discussion, specialists attended political sessions.

As secretary-general, each morning I chaired a conference in the secretariat at 9:00 A.M., a meeting dealing with schedules and other administrative matters and drafting of texts. I participated in the daily policy session for which I prepared the agenda and substantive materials and carried out decisions through the secretariat and with collaboration of select members of the delegation. This meant drafting notes, aide-memoires, memoranda, speeches and preparing diplomatic moves.

Coordination of all these activities was time-consuming. In view of short deadlines on several occasions I had to be "the whip." I maintained contact with the conference secretariat and the secretariat of the CFM. As a rule Auer or other members of the delegation, sometimes including myself, accompanied Gyöngyösi when he visited the chairmen of delegations, ambassadors, foreign ministers, or other dignitaries. I negotiated specific questions with other delegations or asked a member of the Hungarian delegation to perform such tasks. Szegedy-Maszák maintained contact with several members of the American delegation. Denis Nemestóthy, counselor to the Hungarian legation in Paris, was most helpful and acted as liaison between the legation and the delegation. Finally, my responsibility was to sign or forward for Gyöngyösi's signature the outgoing notes, aide-memoires, and memoranda.

The first administrative conference established sections of the delegation and determined activities, priorities, and plans. Sections of the secretariat dealt with Rumanian, Czechoslovak, economic, and military affairs, and there was a section for miscellaneous categories. The drafting committee and the group of translators played an important role. Iván Boldizsár was in charge of public information and press affairs. In addition to resident members, visitors attended some sessions of the delegation, and István Bede, Hungarian minister to the United Kingdom, visited Paris on two occasions (August 6–10 and September 7–21).

Eventually a leading Communist, Ernő Gerő, minister of commerce and transportation, replaced Bolgár as deputy chairman of the Hungarian delegation. While in Paris, August 22, to September 9, he attended some of the political conferences and expressed a nationalistic view concerning our conflicts with Czechoslovakia and Rumania. After the Moscow visit of the government delegation in April 1946, the Hungarian Communist party took up this line.

Gerő strongly supported our claim for boundary rectification with Rumania, and in connection with Auer's address in a joint session of the Hungarian and Rumanian Territorial and Political Commissions he emphasized that even a small territorial gain would demonstrate that the new democratic regime of Hungary was able to revise the Trianon Treaty in ways that Horthy's Hungary could not have achieved. Rumor circulated that during the darkness of night Gerő visited Communist dignitaries, including Molotov, members of the

Yugoslav delegation, and the head of the Ukrainian delegation, Dimitrii Z. Manuilsky, formerly his colleague in the Comintern. Such visits probably occurred, but Gerő did not inform me of his nocturnal and other activities, and after his departure Molotov's negative policy had not changed in questions affecting Hungary's interests.

One of the short-term visitors in Paris was Count Mihály Károlyi, provisional president of the Hungarian republic in 1918. In 1946 the Hungarian government appointed him envoy extraordinary and minister plenipotentiary as well as a member of the peace delegation. His lack of comprehension of postwar Europe's political conditions and Hungary's problems at the peace table was pathetic. He reflected the atmosphere of the 1918 revolution and was pro-Communist and anti-American. When Károlyi attended one of the daily political conferences, he suggested that we emphasize that "the counts and bishops" had caused Hungary's catastrophe. Apparently he did not realize that nobody was interested at the peace table in the Hungarian counts and bishops; the issue for us in Paris was Prague's proposal to expel 200,000 Hungarians. Gyöngyösi stated at the plenary session of the conference, August 14, 1946, that if Czechoslovakia insisted on forcible removal of the Hungarian minority, "the Hungarian Government would be compelled to maintain the principle that the land is the people's." Károlyi commented in his memoirs that Gyöngyösi's speech was addressed to the Hungarian nationalists." He often visited Jan Masaryk and appealed to him "to use his influence on behalf of the 500,000 Hungarians outlawed by the Slovaks." Masaryk, sharing his indignation, said; "How can you imagine that I approve such inhuman proceedings? Don't forget that I am Thomas Masaryk's son. But it is not me you should try to persuade, but Clementis."[3]

The status of the delegations of defeated countries was much more liberal in 1946 than after the First World War, for representatives of the ex-enemy states could move around freely without control or special permission. They were not confined to their headquarters, as were the delegations of ex-enemy states in 1919–20. The Quai d'Orsay had assigned hotels to delegations, and ours was the Claridge on the Avenue des Champs-Elysées. We lived there with the delegation of the Union of South Africa, the chairman of which was Field Marshal Jan Christiaan Smuts who had participated in the peace conference after the First World War and was familiar with Hungary's problems and especially the situation of Hungarians in Czechoslovakia. I had several pleasant and informative conversations with him, but politically he could not help much.

A problem at the Claridge was overbooking; it was impossible to get the rooms we needed. Our large conference room was satisfactory for daily meetings, but the delegation's secretariat was squeezed into two small rooms. We had to leave the bulk of our material at the Hungarian legation where conferences of a confidential nature were held. The dual location of background papers caused much waste of time.

The French government courteously put at our disposal several weatherbeaten automobiles, with Algerian chauffeurs, a great help in view of the scarcity of automobiles in 1946. The Algerians were well-trained but reckless drivers who casually disregarded traffic regulations in Paris. One day I wanted to have a confidential conversation with Gyöngyösi, and we decided to take a walk in the Bois de Boulogne. We boarded the best automobile assigned to the foreign minister and reached the Bois after a hair-raising ride. Suddenly flames appeared at the front of the automobile, and we got out. The driver did not seem disturbed. Waving his hand in a gesture of futility he explained in broken French, "This happens all the time." When we returned from our walk the necessary repair had been made; we got into the automobile with some misgivings and returned to the Claridge.

Members of an ex-enemy delegation could attend conference sessions only when invited. The ex-enemy countries were not negotiating partners; they played roles comparable to those of defendants in criminal proceedings. Nemestóthy and János Erős, counselors to the legation in Paris, attended sessions of the conference and prepared reports for the delegation. Boldizsár also supplied information, as he and a limited number of his confreres from the Hungarian press were permitted to attend any session.[4]

The interests and policies of the ex-enemy countries, of course, differed greatly. Italy was recognized as a co-belligerent and enjoyed Western support, especially in Trieste-related questions, and was granted hearings by the CFM on several occasions. Although the fate of many more people was affected by the peace settlement in Transylvania or Slovakia than on the Italian-Yugoslav border, the Trieste area became one of the most important issues because Trieste was on the frontier between the Soviet and Western zones. All Hungarian problems were in the Soviet zone, where the Western powers had little influence.

The Rumanians were self-confident because they enjoyed all-out Soviet support. The Groza government was Communist-dominated, and Rumania had ceded Bessarabia to the Soviet Union. The army had followed King Michael's order when Rumania changed sides suddenly in August 1944; the new government declared war on Germany, and Rumanian divisions fought alongside Soviet troops. All these events might have influenced Soviet policy in the Transylvanian question.

Bulgaria, as Germany's ally, had been at war with Britain and the United States but had maintained diplomatic relations with the USSR. Moscow declared war on Bulgaria in early September 1944, followed by a peaceful march of Soviet troops into Bulgarian territory and transfer of the armistice negotiations from Egypt to Moscow. The Soviet Union emerged as the main actor in Bulgarian affairs.[5] A new Bulgarian government declared war on Germany and the Soviet Union recognized Bulgaria as a co-belligerent. In the fight against Germany, Bulgarian troops lost about 32,000 men. In view of these events and the historically strong pro-Russian feeling in the country, Bulgaria expected forceful Soviet support at the peace table. The Bulgarian minister to France, Ivan Marinov, informed me that his government was not going to sign the peace treaty unless Bulgaria received access to the Aegean Sea. The peace treaty did not give the Bulgarians any satisfaction on their claim.

The Finns thought at the outset that they might argue their case seriously at the peace table. Prime Minister Mauno Pekkala had arrived with three cabinet ministers, leading representatives of political parties, and a galaxy of experts, prepared to negotiate any questions connected with the proposed peace treaty. Pekkala went with members of his delegation to the press gallery at the first session of the Political and Territorial Commission for Finland. Although it was an open meeting, their group was asked to leave, but Finnish journalists were permitted to stay. The Finns realized the nature of the conference, and most of the delegation returned to Helsinki, Foreign Minister Carl Enckell remaining with a few officials of the Foreign Ministry.[6]

Finland's situation was exceptional among the ex-enemy countries. The Finnish army had fought bravely but had not penetrated deeply into Russian territory. The country possessed experienced political leaders and a less important geographical location, from the Soviet point of view, than countries on the highway to Central Europe or Istanbul. Last, but not least, the treaty with Finland was prepared almost entirely by the Soviets. Britain played a small part in it. Finland was not at war with the United States. When I visited Finland's envoy to France, Johan Helo, he told me his government would accept the peace treaty without much discussion. He implied that the Finns were not in a good position to resist Soviet demands.

In the plenary session of the conference, the foreign minister of Finland, Enckell, pointed out that cooperation with Moscow was the basis of his country's foreign policy. He asked for modification of territorial clauses of the treaty and made a mild plea for a one-third reduction in the $300 million reparation.[7] Molotov saw no reason for modification and said Finland had not been occupied, implying that, unlike Hungary and Rumania, Finland had not had to bear occupation costs and other inconveniences of occupation.[8]

One may conclude that delegations of the ex-enemy states came to the Paris Conference with a variety of political aspirations and expectations. In view of their divergent interests they had hardly any contact with the other ex-enemy delegations.

My personal situation was exceptional. As minister-counselor to the Hungarian legation, I was accredited to the French government; consequently, I enjoyed all privileges of resident diplomats and was invited to French and other diplomatic receptions. From the French point of view, I was not a representative of an ex-enemy state since Hungary was not at war with France. French soldiers who had escaped from Germany had found refuge in Hungary during the war.[9] All members of the Hungarian delegation enjoyed personal freedom, but we had to struggle with many handicaps. Several experts we needed in Paris were not permitted to leave Hungary. The chief delegate for economic affairs, Arthur Kárász, was dismissed for political reasons, although he was able to come to Paris for a short visit in connection with an official trip to Switzerland.

We had some outstanding experts for territorial and ethnic problems, crucial in debates over Transylvania and the fate of Hungarians in Slovakia. They produced reliable memoranda under the leadership of István Révay, head of the Teleki Political Science Institute. Specialists drafted most of the texts in Hungarian, and ranking officials of the Foreign Ministry prepared the French and English translations. I usually checked the text in the language in which it was delivered or dispatched. Short deadlines made thorough checking of translations in the second foreign language impossible. There was a shortage in typists and translators, and on some occasions the collaboration of the bilingual French professor Aurélien Sauvageot was a great help. In several instances members of the secretariat had to work twenty-four hours and, in a few cases, over forty-eight hours without letup. They did their best, cheerfully, in conditions of great discomfort.

Among our operational difficulties were belated notifications from the conference secretariat. Several times we received information at the last minute concerning a deadline for notes or invitation to sessions of the conference. The Hungarian delegation was notified by telephone on August 18, at 8:00 P.M., that the deadline for Hungarian observations concerning the proposed peace treaty was August 20, midnight.[10] I telephoned the conference secretariat for written confirmation, which we received after the deadline on the morning of August 21. When Foreign Minister Gyöngyösi paid a courtesy call on Secretary Byrnes on August 19, he expressed hope that Hungary would have full opportunity of presenting her views on the peace treaty in the Political and Territorial Commission, but "noted with some dismay that comments on the Treaty must be in by tomorrow night." Byrnes explained that this would not be the final opportunity for Hungary to comment on the treaty; he expected the committee to consult the Hungarian delegation on disputed points and give every opportunity for presentation of Hungarian views.[11]

Gyöngyösi was sensitive to this matter since similar difficulty had developed in connection with his address at the plenary session on August 14. Because of the short notice, his speech and the translations had been completed just before delivery; the usual distribution in advance in two languages was possible only at the last minute.[12] I protested repeatedly the short deadlines, but the secretariat could not be blamed. The conference wasted precious time on procedural points, and only a limited time remained for discussion of questions of substance. The secretariat simply carried out instructions from the committees of the conference.

As soon as committee chairmen realized how little time remained for substantive questions, the procedure became speedy, if not erratic. Ex-enemy countries were at the bottom of the totem pole. Under these conditions it was a great help to have the full peace preparatory material in Paris. Without it we would have been unable to draft notes and addresses in a few hours. We were well prepared for discussion of any Danubian problem. It was handy to have a 73-page index of peace preparatory material.

Technical inconveniences appeared insignificant in comparison to our difficult political situation. Within a lifetime, Hungary had appeared for the second time as a defeated country at peace negotiations following a world war. In the First World War the major ally of the Austro-Hungarian Empire was the German Reich, which was declared undemocratic and imperialistic. But in the Second World War, Hungary was considered a junior partner of Hitler's Germany, and the Nazis had committed horrendous crimes well publicized after the war. Representatives of the victorious powers repeatedly reminded the Hungarians of this situation. We would have liked to discuss the circumstances of our involvement in the war, but such topics could not be clarified. Even outsiders came to see me and offered materials in this category. They presumed that this matter would be discussed. But responsibility for the war or for wartime behavior was hardly mentioned in Paris. We had submitted a substantial aide-memoire on Hungary's responsibility and hoped it would be read and discussed.[13] Responsibility for the war was not debated; perhaps this was not desirable, because the Soviet Union had negotiated the Molotov-Ribbentrop Pact of August 23, 1939, which made possible the German Blitzkrieg against Poland.

The Soviet bloc countries considered the active contribution to the military defeat of Germany more important, and from this point of view Hungary was in a less favorable position than the other ex-enemy countries whose peripheral location made possible their early surrender. Although the provisional national government of Hungary declared war on Germany on December 28, 1944, reorganizing the Hungarian army took time. In the session of the ACC on June 5, 1945, Voroshilov pointed out that Hungary had supplied two full and one incomplete infantry divisions, but only the First Division saw any active service against the Germans.[14] He might have added that Soviet authorities were not in a hurry to give weapons and equipment to Hungarian divisions.

In this difficult situation the Hungarian delegation had to find ways to present Hungary's international problems and at the same time defend the vital interests of the nation. Here, again, an important task was to protect the mistreated Hungarian population in neighboring states. Our peace preparatory notes discussed the pertinent problems and proposed measures for correction of intolerable situations. Auer and I presented these questions orally to several ambassadors before the conference. When Gyöngyösi visited the heads of delegations and asked support, he emphasized the predicament of Hungarians in Czechoslovakia and Rumania. In the course of such visits we met with much good will, but also with an amazing ignorance in regard to conditions in Danubian Europe in general and in Hungary in particular. Several delegations showed interest in Hungary's predicament. The American delegation was understanding and American support was crucial, but it was restricted to a few important cases. When Yugoslavia and Czechoslovakia proposed the transfer of materials from Hungarian archives, and Envoy Gyula Szekfű asked General Walter Bedell Smith, American representative in the Hungarian Committee, for support, Smith pointed out that it was more important to avoid human suffering with expulsion of

Hungarians from Czechoslovakia than to block transfer of archival materials.[15] It was clear that the United States did not want to appear in the role of Hungary's protector against Allies. As John C. Campbell put it:

> In general, the United States sought fair terms for Hungary, but it did not want to place itself in the position of Hungary's champion against Allied nations. American relations with Czechoslovakia had to be considered. Furthermore, Hungary's record as a junior partner of the Axis, both before and during the war, hardly entitled her to over-sympathetic treatment at the peace settlement. That was the main reason why the Hungarians, despite the validity of many of the arguments they presented, found so few friends at Paris, even among the democratic nations outside the Soviet bloc.[16]

We forwarded through the conference secretariat to all twenty-one delegations fifteen peace preparatory notes together with geographic and ethnographic maps.[17] Such unsolicited documents, emanating from an ex-enemy state, were not officially considered but some of our arguments proved to be effective. Several delegations, especially the Australians, studied our notes carefully and made proposals along the lines of our reasoning. But such interventions seldom brought practical results.

Besides notes of protest against the persecution of Hungarians in Czechoslovakia and Rumania, the Hungarian government pointed out the importance of reviving and strengthening provisions for international protection of minority rights. The Hungarian delegation submitted an elaborate draft treaty for protection of minority rights, with a system of regional mixed commissions and tribunals to enforce them under supervision of the United Nations.[18] This draft treaty was similar to ideas and proposals expressed in a State Department memorandum on "The Problems of Minorities in Europe," prepared and approved by the Inter-Divisional Committee on the Balkan-Danubian Region, Russia-Poland, and Greece on November 21, 1944.[19] This material was not used in the post-Potsdam era. It was regrettable that the CFM inserted in the draft peace treaty only an ineffective clause concerning human rights and fundamental freedoms. The council decided that special provisions on the protection of minorities were not necessary. It was unrealistically believed that protection of minorities was not a matter for the peace treaties but for the recently established United Nations. Our extensive draft treaty on protection of minorities was not considered.

Relations with the Great Powers

All the while, as the business of settling affairs for the Paris Conference of the Twenty-One Nations was going along, it was necessary to keep up diplomacy with the major powers, and there was a considerable activity. Our relations in this regard with the Soviets, Americans, British, and French were delicate and difficult, and almost unending before and during the peace negotiations.

The French government hosted the Paris Conference and in most cases took a neutral attitude. Although France had not participated in the preparation of the Hungarian Peace Treaty, French diplomats in Paris occupied key administrative positions in the Council of Foreign Ministers and in the secretariat of the conference. We established good working relations. Auer had been legal adviser of the French legation in Budapest during the interwar period and was *persona grata* not only in the French Foreign Ministry but also in French political circles. Through his interventions, the Quai d'Orsay and other offices made several gestures toward us. Thanks to a private arrangement, I could use the apartment of a distinguished French family to meet inconspicuously members of delegations participating in the conference. From the legation, Nemestóthy handled the invitations for these gatherings, and the secretariat at Claridge was not involved in this activity. On one occasion I could not accept Molotov's invitation for the luncheon he gave for the Hungarian delegation because I had invited to this apartment several ranking diplomats. Samuel Reber came from the American delegation. American opposition to expulsion of Hungarians from Czechoslovakia was all-important. But at the same time we had to obtain the support of as many countries as possible, large or small, because Secretary Byrnes pledged the United States would automatically accept any decision voted by two-thirds majority in the plenary session of the conference, where Czechoslovakia had many friends.

The negative Soviet attitude toward Hungarian interests had indeed made clear before and during the conference that our diplomacy must look for Western support. Although events had shown that in the Soviet zone of Europe the Western powers had little influence and in some cases their policy seemed uncertain if not counterproductive, Hungarian policy in the course of peace preparatory activities had continued to appeal to the West, in the face of Soviet opposition. Of course, we were aware of the new power equation along the Danube but it was a question of national honor to take a stand for our own sake, irrespective of outside support. As it turned out, this attitude was no exercise in futility. Without strong United States opposition, 200,000 Hungarians would have been expelled from Czechoslovakia. In this case and in connection with a Czechoslovak claim to a piece of Hungarian territory opposite Bratislava across the Danube, we had close contacts with the American delegation. John C. Campbell characterized this relationship:

> On these questions, with my colleagues Philip Mosely and Fred Merrill, I was in close contact with Stephen Kertesz and with Aladar Szegedy-Maszak, the Hungarian Minister to the United States. We consulted. They asked our advice about their delegation's draft statements, about what they should say that might have a chance of getting support and acceptance by the United States, what might be the best strategy at the conference meetings in dealing with what the Russians and the Czechs might do, and so on. There was perhaps, something incongruous in this business of representatives of a defeated enemy state and of a victorious allied state getting together to concert a strategy against other victorious allied states, but that's the way it was . . .
>
> And it was right, I thought at the time and I still think now, for the United States to support the Hungarian position on those issues. We were trying to save whatever chance there might be for the democratic elements in Hungary to prevail or at least to survive in their country, and there were questions of principle involved in the question of the expulsion of Hungarians from Czechoslovakia. We stood, as Hungary stood, for the principle that there is no collective guilt, and no collective punishment, for those of a particular ethnic group for whatever reason. It was a principle, incidentally, which we had already violated at the Potsdam conference with respect to Germans from eastern Europe, but that was no reason why we should violate it again.[20]

The United States proposed in the Council of Foreign Ministers and at the Paris Conference to reduce the total amount of reparations to be paid by Hungary from $300 million to $200 million. These efforts failed.

It was obvious that the Kremlin had a clear line of policy toward the Danubian countries from the beginning of Soviet occupation. The result of the Hungarian elections in October and November 1945 baffled the Soviets and probably delayed the Communist seizure of power at least by one year. Unlike the coup in Czechoslovakia in February 1948, the Communist seizure of power in Hungary did not take place by one stroke; it was a gradual process which continued during the Paris Conference.

It was exceptional at the peace table that a country in the Soviet zone would request support of the Western powers concerning issues in which Moscow was following a different policy. Since in such matters there were no secrets in Paris, I thought it advisable to inform the Russians personally about our objectives. I visited the Soviet embassy several times before the opening of the conference and talked with Alexander E. Bogomolov and Fedor T. Gusev, ambassadors to the French and British governments respectively, and with A. A. Lavrishchev, head of the Southeastern European division in the Soviet Foreign Ministry. I outlined Hungary's political and economic problems, emphasizing our conflicts with Czechoslovakia and Rumania, and described our proposals for reorganization of the Danubian region on the basis of self-determination. I received polite, stereotyped answers, mainly about the general purposes of Soviet foreign policy. This was a graceful form of evasion. On one occasion I reminded Bogomolov of Lenin's doctrine of self-determination of peoples and quoted Lenin's severe criticism of the Versailles Treaty and argued that a genuine Danubian settlement should be made on the basis of self-determination of all nations. Bogomolov introduced his lengthy, philosophical, but entirely negative answer with the statement that principles have only a relative meaning. Conditions change. What seemed just and true after the First World War may no longer be true, he said. While Gusev appeared to be a reserved and taciturn Russian type, Bogomolov was more outgoing and willing to argue.

After the liberation of France, Bogomolov established close relations with de Gaulle's government, and it is worthwhile to recall his checkered background. At the outbreak of the war he was Soviet ambassador to France and followed the French government to Vichy, remaining there until the Nazi attack on the Soviet Union. When the Vichy government severed relations with Moscow, Bogomolov was transferred to London. He functioned there as Soviet representative to the French National Committee. In this capacity he established friendly relations with General de Gaulle and his entourage. Since de Gaulle's position was precarious and he had been involved in controversies with Churchill and rebuffed by Roosevelt, the French appreciated Bogomolov's courtesies and friendly gestures. He handled de Gaulle as a chief of state, despite Stalin's contempt for France. In the spring of 1943 Bogomolov was sent to Algiers, where he was loosely attached to Eisenhower's headquarters as ambassador to represent the Soviet Union in relations with France. Ambassador Murphy noted that "Bogomolov deserves a major share of credit for de Gaulle's tolerance toward—sometimes practically an alliance with—French

Communists in Algiers and later in France in 1944–45."[21] When the Moscow Conference of Foreign Ministers of the Big Three created in October 1943 an advisory council for matters relating to Italy, Bogomolov became Vyshinsky's deputy as Soviet representative. His success in France was facilitated by his education in pre-revolutionary Russia, his gracious manners and refined taste in food and other amenities of life.

Lavrishchev belonged to a younger generation. He was a typical Soviet-educated diplomat, reportedly with secret service background. He had been an envoy to Bulgaria for five years, and after the war became political adviser to the ACC in Sofia. He was familiar with anti-Hungarian measures in Czechoslovakia but questioned the mistreatment of Hungarians in Rumania. I explained that after a period of atrocities and merciless persecution under the preceding governments, Groza was trying to alleviate the fate of Hungarians in Transylvania, but his endeavors were often sabotaged by a reactionary chauvinistic administration and by many local abuses. I gave some recent examples to illustrate my contention.

The Soviet diplomats always received me in the same room at the embassy, where most probably our formalistic conversations were recorded. It was easier to have interesting discussions with them around a white table, but they accepted social invitations only in groups. On one occasion Lavrishchev politely accompanied me into the corridor of the embassy, and I invited him to have lunch with me. He became embarrassed and could hardly mumble an evasive answer. French colleagues were amused because they had similar experiences with Soviet diplomats.

We did our best to smoke out the Russians, but real human contact did not develop on any level, although even Molotov was friendly and sometimes cracked jokes at diplomatic receptions. On social occasions liquor made communication with Soviet diplomats easier, but small talk was of no consequence. A lunch Auer gave at the Hungarian legation in honor of the Soviet delegation was instructive. As usual in the course of such contacts with Russians, everybody had to join in the toast game, and after several drinks the atmosphere was rising. As the round of toasts were delivered, my assignment was to greet Lavrishchev. I expressed hope that his work would contribute to peaceful and cooperative relationships in the Balkan peninsula and referred to the role of Balkan problems in European politics. Molotov, my vis-à-vis at the table, laughed in a slightly inebriated state, while pounding the table with his glass and saying cheerfully, "The Balkans, the Balkans are very important." Vyshinsky in his toast emphasized that we should forget bygone unpleasant aspects of Soviet-Hungarian relations and talked in glowing terms about the promising future of Soviet-Hungarian friendship. Remembering that at conference sessions he had strongly attacked Hungary's case, when the clinking of glasses subsided, I could not help remarking to Molotov that "Pilate also washed his hands." Molotov burst into laughter and retorted, "Young man, be careful, there are dangerous comparisons."

My neighbor at the table, Bogomolov, was in a more relaxed mood than any time I saw him at the Soviet embassy. Apropos Vyshinsky's friendly toast I related to him a story about the famous Hungarian playwright, Ferenc Molnár, who met by chance in the washroom of a hotel the critic who had published an unfavorable review of the premiere of his play. The critic started to apologize and praised the play, saying that he had a bad headache, felt miserably, and left after the first act and had to write the review at home in a hurry. Next day he read the play carefully and was most favorably impressed. Molnár replied, "This is fine. But I hope next time you will praise my play highly in the newspapers and criticize it severely in the washroom." Bogomolov was amused by the story and suddenly began to make allusions to some phases of my career. Among other things, he mentioned my Rockefeller Fellowship at Yale in 1935–36 and in Oxford and Geneva the following year. Apparently his purpose was to let me know that he had a file on me. Perhaps his disclosure was a warning.

When we visited the Ukrainian and Byelorussian delegations the reception was friendly, the hospitality first class, the discussion long and frustrating, and the result from our point of view, negative. We received a lot of information about their suffering during the war. What they said was true enough but did not alleviate our problems. The heads of the Ukrainian and Byelorussian delegations were not professional diplomats. They were talkative and colorful people and ranking Communists. They informed us about the Soviet position in very different surroundings from those of the diplomats of the USSR. We would receive an appointment at the Byelorussian delegation at 9:00 P.M. The head of the delegation, Kuzma V. Kiselev, would receive us courteously and offer seats around a white table where he was sitting with his advisers. First he offered a variety of cold cuts, exquisite fruits, cheese, then plenty of vodka. When we characterized the plight of Hungary and suggested a substantial reduction of our reparation payments, Kiselev described in detail the suffering of Byelorussians during the military operations. He said that entire villages were destroyed and people still lived in caves and dugouts.

After a long discussion of Hungary's and Byelorussia's problems, we left empty-handed. Dimitrii Z. Manuilsky, head of the Ukrainian delegation, handled us in similar fashion. Such was the usual result of our visits at Soviet headquarters.

As noted, Gerő's visit in Paris and our efforts did not influence Soviet policies one iota. The Soviet line increasingly reflected self-confidence and rigidity. Molotov's trip to Moscow between August 31 and September 5, and the instructions he received from Stalin, may have played a role in this process. According to a United States observer in Paris, "Soviet policy, as evidenced by their actions here and elsewhere, since visit of Molotov to see Stalin, is that of interim change in emphasis on objectives, tending for the moment to put in secondary emphasis their efforts to strengthen Communism in Germany, France, and Italy while making first priority the firming up of control over and more strongly supporting Slav nations inside curtain."[22]

It should be brought up at this point that the routine peace preparatory activities in Budapest and Paris were supplemented by visits of a government delegation to the capitals of the three major victorious powers. The April visit in Moscow was followed in June by visits to Washington and London, with a stopover in Paris on the return trip. These visits preceded the Paris Conference and their purpose was to present Hungary's problems and ask for support at the peace table. The delegation, under leadership of Prime Minister Ferenc Nagy, included Deputy Prime Minister Mátyás Rákosi, representative of the Communist party, Minister of Justice István Riesz, representative of the Social Democratic party, and Foreign Minister Gyöngyösi. The delegation arrived in Washington on June 11, 1946, stayed in Blair House, and departed New York on June 19.[23] President Truman, Secretary Byrnes, and after his departure, Acting Secretary Dean Acheson and other officials in the State Department received the Hungarian delegation. Nagy described the economic plight of Hungary and peace aims of the government and asked for political support and economic aid. Byrnes informed him that last autumn in London he had proposed that in the case of Transylvania the boundary should follow ethnic lines so far as possible, but the Soviets wanted all of Transylvania to be transferred to Rumania and he eventually yielded. In a followup conversation with the deputy director of the Office of European Affairs, John D. Hickerson, Gyöngyösi summed up the Hungarian position regarding Czechoslovakia and Rumania and suggested several categories of economic aid. The Hungarian government asked for restitution of displaced goods located in the American zones of occupation in Germany and Austria, including the gold reserve of the Hungarian National Bank amounting to $32,000,000, stock of the Hungarian state railroads, and ships belonging to Hungarian steamship companies; an increase in the amount of UNRRA assistance; a loan through the Export-Import Bank; an increase to $20,000,000 of the $10,000,000 surplus property purchase credit.

Next day Nagy submitted the same requests to Acting Secretary Dean Acheson, who in turn indicated that "it would be easier for his government to consider such matters with sympathy if a similarly helpful approach were forthcoming on certain matters of interest to the United States in Hungary." He noted that his government had endeavored to obtain information from the Hungarian government concerning the country's economic situation but such information had not been furnished. Similarly his government had endeavored to obtain landing rights for American aircraft in Hungary, which request had been denied by the Hungarian government. Nagy replied that information concerning Hungary's economic situation was common knowledge, but the government was precluded from meeting the American request by regulations issued by the ACC. As to landing rights, Hungary would be happy to welcome American aircrafts as soon as the occupation ceased. Landing rights were under exclusive jurisdiction of the High Command of the occupying power. The acting secretary at a subsequent meeting gave Nagy a memorandum that contained the department's replies. It was important for Hungary that Washington was prepared to return the gold reserve of the Hungarian National Bank, a necessary step to stabilization of the monetary system. American commanders in Germany and Austria were instructed to proceed with restitution of some categories of displaced property. The United States government was prepared to consider sympathetically the Hungarian request for increase in existing credits to Hungary for purchase of surplus property. The memorandum recognized that implementation of an air transport agreement might require arrangements between the United States and the military force occupying Hungary. The necessity of such arrangements did not preclude Hungary from an agreement with the United States. The memorandum emphasized that access to official information concerning all aspects of Hungary's economic condition and commercial relations would facilitate consideration of Hungarian requests.

Nagy was appreciative of the American action. He regarded the American position on landing rights for American aircraft as reasonable, and said he again would raise this question with the cabinet and requested that the United States approach the ACC once more concerning freedom of the Hungarian government to give economic information.[24] The Americans stated they would do so.

Gyöngyösi held a press conference at Blair House, and Nagy made a statement over the State Department's International Broadcasting Division. The delegation visited the Tennessee Valley Authority and spent three days in New York before leaving the American shores.

In London the cabinet and a group in the House of Commons entertained the delegation, but politically the visit was less rewarding. Hungarian peace aims did not impress British statesmen. In connection with the minority rights of Hungarians in Czechoslovakia, Philip Noel-Baker asked the question: "Don't you find it slightly unusual that you desire support for a defeated nation at the expense of a victorious one?"[25] Prime Minister Clement Attlee lectured on the criteria of democracy and pointed out to the delegation of the Hungarian coalition government that a true democracy needed an opposition in Parliament. This statement was odd because Attlee, as a member of the war cabinet, was informed of the Churchill-Stalin percentage agreement concluded in October 1944, which gave Russia 80 percent influence in Hungary. Fortunately, Attlee did not oppose the return of Hungarian property from the British zone of occupation in Austria and Germany.[26].

During a short stopover in Paris on June 25, the delegation paid a courtesy call to Foreign Minister Georges Bidault and visited Foreign Secretary Ernest Bevin. Prime Minister Nagy brought up the May 7 decision of the CFM that reestablished the Trianon boundary, disregarding the large number of Hungarians under Rumanian rule. He called Bevin's attention to the fact that 650,000 Hungarians were in Czechoslovakia and approximately 50,000 persons might be exchanged. This meant that 600,000 Hungarians would remain in Czechoslovakia, deprived of human rights. Nagy asked that the peace treaty guarantee equal civil rights to the Hungarian minority and expressed hope that the Great Powers would settle pending questions according to the Atlantic Charter.

Bevin replied that at the London session of CFM he was inclined to support the American secretary of state's proposal concerning revision of the boundary between Hungary and Rumania, but the CFM realized that in that region of Europe it was impossible to establish satisfactory boundaries. After Rumanian elections and settlement of other complex problems, it would be easier to work out a sensible solution through bilateral negotiations. As to the question of Hungarians in Czechoslovakia, Bevin believed that there were plans for transfer of a large number of people and this action would cause enormous economic dificulties. The peace treaties contained a clause for the protection of human rights, and he was hopeful the United Nations would develop a moral code of universal validity for the protection of minorities. This would be a better solution than specific agreements. Bevin pointed out that during the war he had tried to convince the leaders of the East European governments in London, among them Beneš and General W. Sikorski, that establishment of a customs union would serve the interests of all of them. For the same reason he emphasized freedom of navigation on the Danube and stated that after conclusion of peace and normalization of conditions it would be possible to give Hungary some badly needed economic aid and find solutions for the common problems of all nations in the Danubian Valley.

Nagy informed Bevin that for the solution of the boundary question the Hungarian government had proposed bilateral negotiations in Bucharest. Since the Rumanian government was unwilling to negotiate, the CFM should reconsider the Hungarian-Rumanian boundary. If that would not be possible, the Hungarian government requested insertion in the peace treaty of an article providing for reexamination of the boundary between Hungary and Rumania by an international forum. Bevin replied that he would consider this question.[27]

The Hungarian government delegation also used their stay in Paris to call on Molotov to inform him that the Americans would be willing to support revision of the boundary with Rumania if the Soviet Union would take the initiative. When after friendly conversation about the American trip Nagy referred to the boundary revision, Molotov's friendliness disappeared. He assumed his habitual stone face and simply referred to the CFM's decision accepting the proposal of Secretary Byrnes that reestablished the Trianon boundary.[28]

All the while Soviet pressure was increasing in Hungary.[29] The leading Smallholder politicians saw the handwriting on the wall, became desperate, and Gyöngyösi suggested that Prime Minister Nagy again visit the delegates of the Great Powers in Paris. Nagy arrived in early September and called on General Smith, the United States ambassador to the Soviet Union and United States representative in the Hungarian Commission. The prime minister described the difficult and delicate political course he had been forced to take to preserve a Western form of democracy in a country almost entirely surrounded by Communist-controlled states. He "intimated quite clearly that unless Hungary could get Western support for the easement of the treaty provisions, he could not hold out much longer as prime minister."[30] Ambassdor Smith replied that it was Secretary Byrnes's "firm opinion that *the ex-enemy states of Eastern Europe must be given a chance to breathe again and that this was not possible until the occupation forces were withdrawn. This was the foremost objective of the United States Government.*" (Emphasis added) He pointed out that the American government had taken a great interest in Hungary, particularly in economic matters. The United States always believed in the right of all nations to trade freely and had advocated that international waterways such as the Danube should be accessible to all on an equal basis. Finally he asked what Hungary wanted specifically. Nagy emphasized that it was important that part of Transylvania be returned to Hungary and went on to say that it would be impossible for Hungary to accept the transfer of 200,000 Hungarians from Czechoslovakia. Ambassador Smith reassured Nagy that the United States opposed the expulsion of Hungarians. During the ensuing discussion regarding the Czechoslovak territorial claim on Hungary, the so-called Bratislava "bridgehead," the ambassador expressed hope that this demand might serve as a basis for some give-and-take and that both sides should be willing to make concessions in order to reach an agreement.[31]

Subsequently the Prime Minister had conversations with Secretary Byrnes and, in Molotov's absence, with Andrei Vyshinsky, deputy foreign minister. According to Ambassador Jefferson Caffery's report, Nagy pointed out to Byrnes that "he was one of the few Peasant leaders left in Europe leading fight against eastern interpretation of democracy and then elaborated on Soviet pressure on Hungary as well as Communist domination of neighboring states." He noted that Hungary had not gained much by holding a free election in November 1945. Byrnes replied that "Hungary unlike other satellites had advantage of being a sovereign state and had more independence. . . . He greatly sympathized with Hungary's problem and hoped to hear of progress made to overcome economic difficulties and further developments towards attainment of political freedom."[32] According to Nagy's version, Byrnes said to him that it would be in Hungary's best interest to sign a peace treaty as soon as possible. "If we introduce the Transylvanian question and cause difficulties regarding a settlement, peace with Hungary will be delayed. We are doing everything in our power to free you both politically and economically as soon as possible. For this reason we are expediting a peace treaty . . . once the independence of Hungary is assured, a firm economy will follow. We will assist you in this also." Vyshinsky, in turn, brought up the possibility of negotiations with Rumania about Transylvania after the peace treaty had been signed.[33]

Because of such inconsequential conversations in Paris, Nagy returned to Hungary in a dispirited and deeply pessimistic mood, prepared to resign if the conference voted for expulsion of the Hungarians from Czechoslovakia. His conclusion was that the Western democracies either were unwilling or unable to oppose Soviet policies in Eastern Europe. Of course Bedell Smith's statement that withdrawal of the occupation forces was "the foremost objective of the United States Government" had sounded like music to Hungarian ears. Unfortunately, there was little reality behind this assertion.

10

The Paris Conference: Part Two

Dispute with Rumania

In postwar Hungarian politics the revision of the boundary with Rumania or some other settlement of the Transylvanian question, and the protection of Hungarian minorities in Rumania, remained the foremost consideration. The Hungarian government informed the Great Powers and the other participants in the Paris Conference in aide-memoires of the grievances of the Hungarian minority in Transylvania and pointed out that the redressing of these grievances and the securing of satisfactory conditions for the Hungarians were the sine qua non of the reconciliation between Hungary and Rumania. A booklet[1] submitted to the conference provided an overview of the situation in Transylvania since 1918 and enumerated the anti-Hungarian discriminations and atrocities committed between August 1944 and May 1946. For the future the Hungarian government proposed the application of the principles of self-determination and the institutionalization of the protection of minorities under the aegis of the United Nations.

In Budapest we were forced to live behind a diplomatic iron curtain and knew little of the CFM activities, but in Paris I gradually reconstructed the chain of events in the Transylvanian question. Despite Voroshilov's and Pushkin's encouragement given to President Tildy and Gyöngyösi concerning Hungary's territorial claims in Transylvania, the Russians had been unwilling to consider the modification of the Trianon boundary in the first session of the CFM and at the subsequent meeting of the deputy foreign ministers in London. In view of the unyielding Soviet position, an American document submitted in the second session of the CFM in Paris, on May 7, 1946, proposed restoration of the Hungarian-Rumanian frontier as it existed on January 1, 1938. In the report of the deputy foreign ministers on the Rumanian treaty (April 18 and 19) the article on Rumania set forth:

The decision of the Vienna Award of August 30th, 1940, is declared null and void. The frontier between Rumania and Hungary existing on January 1st, 1938, is hereby restored, [the whole of Transylvania being thus included in the territory of Rumania.] [Nevertheless, the Allied and Associated Powers would be prepared to recognize any rectification of the Roumanian-Hungarian frontier that may subsequently be mutually agreed between the parties directly concerned and which would substantially reduce the number of persons living under alien rule.]

The brackets in the text indicate unagreed provisions in the article. The first bracket was a Soviet proposal, and the other delegations suggested deletion of that addition. The second bracket was an American proposal. Then Byrnes stated in the May 7 session of the CFM that the United States would withdraw the sentence in the second bracket if the Soviet delegation would withdraw the words in the first bracket. He thought the article would be improved as a result of the withdrawals. Molotov and Bevin agreed and accepted the text preceding the brackets.[2]

Byrnes's proposal meant that the American delegation gave up its tentative endeavors for a modest rectification of the Hungarian-Rumanian boundary on ethnic grounds, fully accepting the Soviet position in the Transylvanian question. Four months later, in the Rumanian and Hungarian commissions respectively, Harriman and Bedell Smith vainly tried to revive the idea of bilateral negotiations between Hungary and Rumania for settlement of outstanding questions. These belated actions had a gesture value at best, in view of Byrnes's withdrawal of the original American proposal for bilateral negotiations. One should recall at this point that Molotov and Dekanozov had strongly recommended bilateral negotiations to the Hungarian government delegation in Moscow in April 1946. Soviet duplicity in this case was a prize example of the seamy side of Muscovite diplomacy.

Because in the CFM the four powers made all decisions unanimously, and the Russians were unwilling to consider any boundary rectification, the council's action was final, according to information I received from official sources in Paris. But in Hungarian politics it was impossible to accept this verdict as definitive. The delegation led by Prime Minister Nagy continued to bring up the Transylvanian question in encounters with Soviet, United States, and British representatives. Auer and I did the same when we visited ambassadors in Paris. Such visits brought a few surprises. At the Polish embassy the ambassador interrupted our presentation to tell us that our colleague from London had visited him recently and had given him all information about the Transylvanian problem. We suggested that this was impossible because the Hungarian envoy to Britain would have informed us of his visit to the Polish embassy. We continued to explain the intricacies of the conflict between Hungary and Rumania. The ambassador interrupted again and said, "Gentlemen, I will call my secretariat and will prove to you that your colleague from London visited me a few days ago and gave me the same information." He went to the telephone and after a brief conversation said, "I apologize. My visitor was the Rumanian ambassador from London." On several occasions we witnessed such a lack of knowledge about Danubian affairs.

Despite hopeless political conditions the Hungarian delegation decided to raise the Hungarian-Rumanian frontier question at the conference, and for this purpose we needed American support. Auer and I visited Philip E. Mosely, the foremost East European expert of the American delegation, on May 17, and he told us that at the London meeting of foreign ministers, Secretary Byrnes "had not advanced any proposal for a revised frontier but had merely pointed out that the question existed and should be studied to see if the boundary could be improved over that established in 1920 and of which the United States Government had been critical at that time." Mosely pointed out that "the Soviet Delegation had been unwilling at all times to admit even that the question deserved study." To the question whether Hungary would have an opportunity to raise the question at the conference, Mosely stated his personal understanding that "Hungary would be free to present its view on any aspect of the treaty which affected its position or interest." Concerning Hungarian suggestions for boundary readjustment, he avoided detailed discussion but stated that the concept of a numerical balancing of minorities on opposite sides of the frontier "might seem somewhat mechanical in approach and might be interpreted to imply a willingness to provide for large-scale exchanges of population." He stated as his strictly personal view that "a moderate suggestion for rectification based mainly on ethnic and economic factors might have a better hearing.[3]

Mosely's cautious statements reflected the American position, of which he had been one of the architects. When the Hungarian government asked for a hearing, the Soviet bloc countries opposed even a debate about the frontier between Hungary and Rumania, but strong American support of the Hungarian request prevailed.

When Foreign Minister Gyöngyösi visited heads of delegations he brought up the frontier dispute with Rumania, and in a plenary session of the conference on August 14 he asked reattachment to Hungary of 22,000 square kilometers of Rumania, that is, he repeated the request expressed in the Hungarian note of April 27. As Mosely had told us in cautious diplomatic terms three months earlier, this proposal had no chance although a position paper of the State Department had considered a similar solution among several alternatives.[4]

At the meeting of the Political and Territorial Commission for Rumania on August 29, Mr. Officer from the Australian delegation proposed that the commission hear the views of Hungary on Article 2 of the draft treaty, which dealt with the boundaries of Rumania. Bogomolov of the USSR saw no need to consult the Hungarian government, since the text of Article 2 had been agreed to by the CFM. After a long debate, a Czechoslovak motion for adjournment was defeated by 8 votes to 4 and the Australian proposal carried by vote of 8 to 4.[5] The commission decided that both the Hungarian and Rumanian delegations be invited to appear to express their views on Article 2, the Hungarian delegation speaking first.

On August 31, in a joint session of the Hungarian and Rumanian Commissions, Auer delivered an address. In view of the unfavorable decision of the CFM and in harmony with Mosely's personal view, he asked the reattachment to Hungary of only 4,000 square kilometers along the boundary; this would have meant reattachment of approximately a half million persons—about two-thirds of whom were Hungarians—and with them some major cities along the boundary. Auer emphasized the necessity of international protection of Hungarians remaining in Rumania.[6] The foreign minister of Rumania, Gheorghe Tatarescu, opposed Auer's proposals in a speech at a joint session of September 3, arguing for the maintenance of the boundary established by the Trianon Treaty.[7]

Such addresses had only symbolic significance, because the conference had no power to change the decisions of the CFM. When the Hungarian delegation asked the Russian delegation for support in the Transylvanian dispute, their answer was that they could not do anything because Secretary Byrnes had withdrawn his proposal concerning revision of the boundary between Hungary and Rumania. Technically this was true. But Byrnes had acted this way because the Soviet Union was unwilling to consider a boundary change, and he decided to eliminate a point of friction between the United States and the USSR to expedite the convocation of the Paris Conference. Invitations could not be sent without Soviet agreement. In view of the fact that both Hungary and Rumania were occupied by Soviet troops and unanimity in the CFM was necessary for all decisions, American diplomacy had little clout in the Transylvanian question.

At the meeting of the Rumanian Commission on September 5 the Australian delegate, Officer, wanted to hear from the representative of one of the states responsible for drafting Article 2, so the commission would know the reasoning that guided the council. Harriman, responding to the Australian request, said that

> the United States had not been a strong supporter of the proposed text but wished to make it clear that he would vote for it since it had been agreed by the Council. He said that during the discussions in the Council the United States Delegation had made certain proposals for a study of possible modification of the frontier which might, by reducing the number of persons under alien rule, contribute to stability and to mutual cooperation between Hungary and Rumania. The other members of the Council of Foreign Ministers had not shared this view and, in view of the desirability of reaching unanimous agreement, the U.S. had not insisted on its position. Mr. Harriman reiterated his statement that he would vote for Article 2 as drafted but wished to take the occasion to say that, in view of the differences on various subjects evident in the statements of the Hungarian and Rumanian representatives, the United States hoped that progress might be made through direct negotiations between them toward a mutually satisfactory settlement of the outstanding questions.[8]

After statements by the Soviet, British, and French delegates, Officer proposed that Article 2 be adopted "with a rider in the form of a recommendation that the Council of Foreign Ministers, before putting it into the final treaty, make a further effort to secure, in cooperation with the two interested parties, an adjustment by which some additional Hungarian centers might be incorporated in Hungary." This proposal was not accepted, and eventually Article 2 was adopted by 10 votes, with 2 abstentions.[9] Thus Australian attempts to reopen the Transylvanian question failed.

The American position concerning the dispute between Hungary and Rumania was reiterated on September 23 in the Hungarian Commission by Bedell Smith, who read into the record a statement similar to that by Harriman in the Rumanian Commission "regarding the desire of Rumania to sign a protocol with Hungary or any bilateral arrangement which the United States Delegation felt would tend to improve relations and good understanding between the two countries."[10]

Meanwhile the Hungarian territorial claim presented by Auer on August 31, had been evaluated by a senior East European specialist of the American delegation, John C. Campbell, in a memorandum of September 2. He pointed out that this claim was based purely on ethnic considerations; it was about the same as the hypothetical ethnic line worked out in the Department of State. He made some additional suggestions for the case of a review of the frontier between Hungary and Rumania. Discussing the pros and cons of the Hungarian proposal, he concluded that if there was any disposition on the part of the other members of the CFM to make any change in the frontier, "we might give as our view that the Hungarian claims appear reasonable with the exception of the claim for Arad and the immediate vicinity." Campbell also raised the possibility of direct Hungarian-Rumanian negotiations.[11]

At the plenary meeting of the conference on October 10, Molotov stated that "the treaty with Rumania was a matter of great importance for the peace of Europe. Rumania was now a democratic state and it was essential that the question of Transylvania be settled to the satisfaction of the Rumanian people.[12]

The Hungarian government addressed a note on November 8, 1946, to the Council of Foreign Ministers which was deliberating the final text of the peace treaties in New York during November-December 1946. This note proposed that the third article of the Rumanian draft peace treaty should be supplemented by a clause, according to which the rights of the Hungarian minority in Rumania should be defined through direct negotiations between Hungary and Rumania. "Should these direct negotiations between Hungary and Rumania result in failure, the Hungarian government should be given an opportunity to apply to the Council of Foreign Ministers for a final adjustment of this problem."[13] The council disregarded the Hungarian note.

The Czechoslovak Amendments

The greatest direct threat to the Hungarian nation at the Paris Conference was the Czechoslovak proposal for transfer of 200,000 Hungarians from Slovakia to Hungary. Because the Hungarian government refused to considered a bilateral agreement on the transfer of Hungarians from Slovakia, the Czechoslovak delegation on August 21 proposed the following amendment to the peace treaty with Hungary.

Czechoslovakia is authorized to transfer a maximum number of 200,000 inhabitants of Magyar ethnic origin from its territory to that of Hungary and the latter is bound to receive these persons on its territory and to recognize them as nationals.

When the Czechoslovak government proposed transfer of Hungarians, the Hungarian answer was that the territory in which the Hungarian people had lived for centuries belonged to them. The ethnic boundary between the Hungarians and Slovaks has not changed for centuries. At a plenary meeting of the conference on August 14 the foreign minister of Hungary again expressed willingness to accept the Hungarians together with the territory in which they lived. He formulated the Hungarian position in the following terms:

> The forcible eviction of the Hungarians from Slovakia is not only morally and politically unjustifiable, it would confront Hungary with an economic, social and political problem which she is unable to solve. It must not be forgotten that the problem involves the eviction and resettlement of the rural population uprooted from their ancestral homes and land.
>
> Gentlemen, however serious and desperate our position may be, the defeated party can never be denied the right of believing that such a demand is contrary to morality and humanity. And if a Hungarian Government could be found willing to accept it under outside pressure, it would be digging its own grave and the grave of Hungarian democracy by so doing. The land and the people who have tilled it for centuries and implanted their civilization therein, are indissolubly linked together. Such a bond could only be forcibly broken by violation of the fundamental laws of human existence. Czechoslovakia wants to keep territory inhabited by Hungarians. In that case let her keep the Hungarians also and give them the full rights of the individual and the citizen. If for any reason Czechoslovakia refuses to do so and insists on the forcible removal of the Hungarian minority, the Hungarian Government would be compelled to maintain the principle that the land is the people's.[14]

Next day the foreign minister of Czechoslovakia, Jan Masaryk, accused Gyöngyösi of keeping his speech a well-guarded secret until the last moment, contrary to usage.[15] He declared that the address reminded him of Hungarian revisionist speeches of 1918–38 and asked, "Who won this war—the United Nations or Hungary?" Kiselev, chief of the Byelorussian delegation, together with Vyshinsky, supported Masaryk's contentions.[17]

Simultaneous with the proposal for expulsion of the Hungarians, Czechoslovakia demanded in a second amendment transfer of five Hungarian villages for enlargement of the Bratislava bridgehead on the right bank of the Danube. At the seventh meeting of the

Hungarian Commission (September 6), the Czechoslovak representative, Juraj Slavik, contended that this territory was necessary for proper development of the city and port of Bratislava. The Hungarian delegation was invited into the session, and Paul Sebestyén requested the commission to reject the Czechoslovak claim on the grounds that Bratislava's development had never been in the direction of the south bank and the existing bridgehead had not been used for this purpose; that that claim was contrary to the Atlantic Charter and to ethnic principles and that the people living in the territory had no desire to be attached to Czechoslovakia; and that it would be an economic hardship to Hungary to construct a detour of 25 kilometers for the main highway to Vienna.[18]

At the ninth meeting of the Hungarian Commission (September 9), General Smith stated that the Czechoslovak proposal deserved some sympathetic consideration, but he added that reduction in the size of the territory might help meet the economic and ethnic objections raised by the Hungarian delegation. He pointed out that the proposal involved transfer of Magyars to Czechoslovakia at a time when that country was proposing to transfer Magyars to Hungary. He concluded that "the two Czechoslovak amendments were a part of the larger and unsettled problem between the two countries and should be examined simultaneously." He emphasized the strong feeling of the United States delegation that the principle of forced transfer of population should not be inserted in a peace treaty. After long debate, the commission accepted an Australian proposal to set up a subcommittee that would not only study the facts in the dispute but maintain close connection with the Hungarian and Czechoslovak delegations. The subcommittee included Australia, New Zealand, Canada, the Ukraine, and Czechoslovakia.[19]

The thirteenth meeting of the Hungarian Commission (September 18) was devoted to a speech by the Hungarian representatives, Aladár Szegedy-Maszák, who replied in detail to the Czechoslovak argument for transfer and pointed out that after the dissolution of the Austro-Hungarian empire Hungarian minorities were incorporated in neighboring states without being consulted. Now only Czechoslovakia expressed a desire to get rid of these minorities by such drastic means. Czechoslovakia was endeavoring to have the Potsdam decision include Hungarians. No other country "had requested that 200,000 innocent people accept the stigma of collective responsibility or had attempted to persuade other hundreds of thousands of its inhabitants to deny the nationality of their forefathers by accepting Slovak citizenship in order to assure right of life and liberty." Instead of Munich,

Szegedy-Maszák urged the commission to remember "the Atlantic Charter and the Four Freedoms, for which the war was fought."[20]

At the fourteenth meeting of the Hungarian Commission (September 20), Clementis spoke in refutation of Szegedy-Maszák's statement, questioning Hungary's statistics, and came to the conclusion that revisionism still existed in that country. General Smith explained that

> the United States was trying to avoid a situation where it would be necessary to vote against the Czech proposals, which it would have to do if it were necessary to incorporate in a peace treaty the principle of a forced transfer of populations. This principle was unacceptable.

Then he urged a bilateral approach and proposed that the question be referred to the commission's subcommittee for a constructive solution.

Vyshinsky spoke in support of the Czechoslovak amendment. He saw nothing unethical about a transfer of population and felt that "the return of people to their Motherland should be encouraged and that the best solution of the nationality problem is to free a given state of the nationals of another state." He stated that "500,000 people had been moved from Hungary to Germany, as General Smith knew, so there was lots of room in Hungary and even a forced transfer would not be inhumane."[21]

At the fifteenth meeting of the Hungarian Commission (September 23), the Yugoslav delegate traced the history of revisionism in Hungary from 1919 and took note of the same spirit of revisionism in certain circles of the new democratic government in Hungary. He reminded the delegates of the Bačka massacres and "twenty years of plotting on the part of the Horthy Government" and pointed out that Yugoslavia had solved its minority problems by giving rights to its minority peoples. "Here was the chance for the sons of the mother country to return on an organized basis and the net result would be to remove a lack of confidence in Hungary which now existed." The delegate of Byelorussia in a long speech supported the Czech amendment. He stressed that Hungarians were "in the process of expelling half a million Germans. Should the Hungarians refuse to accept the return of the Hungarians now living in Slovakia, it would demonstrate that they did not wish to cooperate with their neighbors."

Viscount Hood of England expressed sympathy with the aims of the Czechoslovak delegation but pointed out that "unilateral solutions cannot and should not be imposed." He hoped "the problem could be solved by bilateral agreement; it was the only way."

Masaryk stated that he had resolved to erase hatred from his heart and wanted nothing more than friendship among the nations of Central Europe. "The Czechoslovak Delegation had believed that the transfer of 200,000 Hungarians would be the beginning of a new era and that they would be received in Hungary with open arms as Slovakia would receive its returning sons." He mentioned that Potsdam solved the problem of the German minority in Czechoslovakia and asked why the problem of Hungarians could not be solved at Paris. He pledged to proceed in an attempt to solve the problem in the best way but described the transfer "as the removal of a cancer by surgery, quickly and cleanly." Masaryk agreed to refer the matter to the subcommittee.[22]

The Czechoslovak and Soviet delegates time and again used the argument that transfer of 500,000 Germans from Hungary would make plenty of space for Hungarians from Slovakia. Yet the number of the Germans in Hungary was less than half a million and a considerable group of them had moved to Germany with the retreating German army in 1944.[23] Although the Hungarian government protested against the application of the Nazi principle of collective responsibility, the recurring use of this argument explained why the Soviet authorities in Budapest had pressed the Hungarian government since the spring of 1945 for expulsion of all Germans from Hungary. To increase pressure on the Hungarian government, at the Potsdam Conference the Soviets, in a surprise move, had proposed the transfer of the Germans from Hungary. Although the British and Americans at Potsdam would not contemplate such action, they did not oppose the Soviet proposal. Cavendish-Cannon, President Truman's senior adviser, tried to warn the president not to accept the sudden addition of the Germans from Hungary,[24] but his intervention was of no avail. After this Soviet maneuver the tripartite agreement stated that "transfer to Germany of German populations, or elements thereof, remaining in Poland, Czechoslovakia and Hungary, will have to be undertaken. They agree, that any transfers that take place should be effected in an orderly and humane manner."

On November 20, 1945 the Allied Control Council in Berlin approved a plan for transfer of Germans and allocation between zones of occupation including a schedule of movement of the German population. According to this plan 500,000 Germans from Hungary were to be admitted into the American zone.[25] American and British diplomacy seemed embarrassed if not hypocritical in this matter.[26]

Returning to the Paris Conference, it is worthwhile to note that at the outset Masaryk showed a willingness to make territorial concessions in connection with transfer of the Hungarians. Visiting the American delegation on August 3, 1946, he informed Samuel Reber

> in the strictest confidence that he is prepared to consider an adjustment of the frontier with Hungary if such a cession will solve the questions of the transfer of Hungarian minorities. As this is contrary to the expressed views of the Czechoslovak Government, he does not wish anything said about it at this stage of the Conference but has indicated that if Czechoslovakia does not receive satisfaction with regard to the expulsion of the Hungarian minorities this may provide a solution.[27]

In the course of direct negotiation between the Czechoslovak and Hungarian delegations in the subcommittee (September 29), the Hungarian delegation declared readiness "to admit Hungarians on her territory partly with, partly without territory." At this meeting Masaryk was unwilling to consider any territorial adjustment. He pointed out that his government had bound him concerning that principle of transfer.[28] A few days before the Czechoslovak-Hungarian direct negotiation, members of the Hungarian delegation discussed with the Canadian delegation in Hotel Crillon, with the United States delegation in Hotel Meurice, and with the British delegation in Hotel George V the Hungaro-Czechoslovak conflict and particularly the combination of a territorial settlement with an exchange of population. On September 28, a member of the British delegation, James A. M. Marjoribanks visited the Hungarian delegation and discussed with our specialists the conditions of a territorial settlement. Next day Marjoribanks gave a memorandum with British suggestions to Gyöngyösi and Masaryk before the subcommittee meeting in the Luxembourg Palace. In the course of these contacts the Hungarian delegation put forward proposals; regrettably such backdoor endeavors had no result.

In the last stage of the bilateral negotiations with the Czechoslovaks, the Hungarian delegation offered (private session of the subcommittee, September 30) to accept two-thirds of the Hungarian minority with the territory in which they lived and one-third without territorial compensation and expressed willingness to give the frontier rectification a reciprocal character.[29] Such an appeal to reason did not succeed, because the Czechoslovak delegation was dominated by jingo-nationalists unable to think in long-range historical perspective. They felt powerful because of all-out Soviet support.

During the critical period of negotiations I was involved in semi-official conversations that threw light on the way of thinking of several delegations. My reports, expecially those concerning negotiation with the delegates of Canada and New Zealand, showed that several delegations had recognized the validity of the Czechoslovak proposal. General Pope, representative of the Canadian delegation in the Hungarian subcommittee, invited me to luncheon in his Hotel Crillon apartment on September 15, and during our long conversation tried to persuade me of the necessity of compromise in connection with transfer of Hungarians from Czechoslovakia.[30] I explained to him the reasons of our position and was glad to see that Canada eventually refused to support the Czechoslovak amendment.

A few days later Lord Hood invited me to visit him at the headquarters of the British delegation in Hotel George V. He was interested in my evaluation concerning the probable votes of various delegations with respect to the Czechoslovak amendment, and I shared with him all the information we had. Then he asked me what the Hungarian delegation would do if the conference accepted the amendment. I told him that the Hungarian government would send new instructions and added that personally I would buy a railroad ticket to Budapest because I did not see any reason why the Hungarian delegation should remain in Paris after such a catastrophic decision. I pointed out that the coalition government surely would collapse. On September 23, Hood opposed the imposition of unilateral solutions concerning the Hungarian minorities in Czechoslovakia. After some hesitation Britain and later Canada decided to follow the United States in opposing the Czechoslovak amendment.

Costello, a delegate of New Zealand, rapporteur of the Hungarian subcommittee, came to see me unexpectedly in the Claridge on September 29 and informed me during luncheon that his government had instructed his delegation to support the Czechoslovak amendment for expulsion of Hungarians. He pointed out that the United States, Britain, Australia, and the Union of South Africa were against the amendment, but that the five Slav states together with France and New Zealand would vote for it. With possible support of India, Canada, and some other states, the amendment might obtain the two-third majority that would change the position of the United States. In view of this possibility he recommended a compromise, the transfer of Hungarians in ten years, with a yearly quota of 20,000. He expressed fear that in the case of our refusal the Hungarian population of Slovakia would be transferred to remote parts of the USSR. I refused to entertain this possibility and told him we were not willing to accept the transfer of Hungarians from Czechoslovakia under any conditions, in any shape or form. Costello became strikingly depressed during our conversation and concluded that he was "frightfully sorry" because of the negative result of our exchange of views.[31]

Foreign Minister Gyöngyösi, Auer, and I visited Foreign Minister Georges Bidault and asked for French support against the expulsion of Hungarians from Czechoslovakia. Bidault replied that he told the Czechoslovaks that he didn't like it. Auer asked him: "Does this mean that France would vote against the Czechoslovak amendment?" Bidault answered in the affirmative and we were greatly relieved. A few days later I understood through the grapevine that France would support the Czechoslovak amendment and suggested to Auer that he clarify the French position at the Quai d' Orsay. He was reluctant to do so and asked me: "Didn't you hear what Bidault said?" When I detected in Lord Hood's attitude that he seemed certain that France was supporting the Czechoslovaks, I asked Gyöngyösi to instruct Auer to go to the Foreign Ministry to ascertain the French position. He did so and the secretary-general informed Auer that in case of a vote France would support the Czechoslovak amendment. This incident showed a strange communication gap between Bidault and his Foreign Ministry.

Eventually the conference did not accept the Czechoslovak amendment concerning transfer of 200,000 Hungarians, but the peace treaty obligated Hungary to enter into negotiations with Czechoslovakia to solve the problem of the latter's inhabitants of Magyar ethnic origin (Article 5). United States policy and in the last stage British opposition to the transfer of Hungarians was decisive at the Paris Conference.[32]

Molotov was aware from the outset of the importance of American policy in this case. President Beneš in a conversation with the American ambassador, Lawrence Steinhardt, on May 7, 1946, stated that

> in the course of the talks between the Czech representatives in Paris and Molotov, when the former had stressed the desire of the Czech Government to transfer its Hungarian minority to Hungary, Molotov had indicated his acquiescence but had added, "I must first find out how the Americans feel about it as without the Americans I can do nothing." Beneš added with obvious relish that he had repeated Molotov's remark at a cabinet meeting yesterday for the benefit of the Communist members of the Government who had been visibly "shocked" to learn that the Soviet government did not regard itself as omnipotent.[33]

As we have seen, as soon as the Kremlin installed reliable Communist governments in Budapest and Prague the Hungarians no longer were considered a threat to Czechoslovakia, their equal rights for citizenship were recognized, and the bilateral negotiations provided in the peace treaty to solve the problem of the Magyar population in Slovakia were not considered necessary.

The other Czechoslovak amendment, which demanded transfer of five Hungarian villages for enlargement of the Bratislava bridgehead on the right bank of the Danube, ended with a compromise. Although it was difficult to find compelling reasons for this Czechoslovak proposal, except expansion for expansion's sake, the peace treaty transferred three villages to Czechoslovakia: Horvátjárfalu, Oroszvár, Dunacsún. The conference would not approve the Czechoslovak amendment for expulsion of 200,000 Hungarians, and the Allied powers, in a spirit of diplomatic compromise, apparently wanted to give some satisfaction to Prague.

Encounter with Yugoslavia

During the busiest days of the conference the Yugoslavs, in a surprising ultimatum, demanded that the Hungarian delegation sign within forty-eight hours an exchange of population agreement and an agreement on hydraulic questions. This incident occurred under curious circumstances. The secretary-general of the Yugoslav delegation, Jože Vilfan, urgently asked me to meet him on August 17, that is, three days before the August 20 deadline for proposal of amendments to the draft peace treaties. Vilfan informed me that unless the Hungarian delegation was willing to sign the two agreements within forty-eight hours, the Yugoslav government would ask the conference for insertion of the amendments in the peace treaty. In the course of a hurried conversation I tried to convince him that without adequate preparatory work, including consultation of experts from Budapest and Belgrade, it seemed next to impossible to negotiate agreements, let alone sign them, in a couple of days. It was my impression that the impromptu proposals were results of a sudden decision in the Yugoslav delegation, but according to more pessimistic interpretations the Yugoslav pressure was unusual, and Szegedy-Maszák expressed our apprehensions to the American delegation.

Vilfan apparently knew little of the intricacies and technical problems in the proposals. He did not bring background paper to our meeting. Although it was necessary to gain time, I did not want to antagonize Vilfan, because our important issue at the conference was the Czechoslovak amendment aiming at expulsion of 200,000 Hungarians. To neutralize the Yugoslavs as much as possible in our conflict with Prague, I assured Vilfan of our willingness to consider the proposals and suggested further negotiation.

The Yugoslav delegation had submitted amendments to the conference and the Hungarian government's Observations on the Draft Peace Treaty had commented on this Yugoslav initiative as follows:

> The Hungarian Delegation welcomes the initiative of the Yugoslav Delegation and adheres, in principle, to the Yugoslav proposal, under which Hungary and Yugoslavia should settle hydraulic questions affecting both countries by an agreement. It wishes to point out, however, that the matter has a wider scope, and that a satisfactory solution can only be arrived at if the countries of the Carpathian Basin settle these questions by joint action. It feels that the Conference would reach the desired results if all the Danubian countries were to participate in this settlement.[34]

The chairmen of the two delegations, Foreign Minister Gyöngyösi and the Deputy Prime Minister Edvard Kardelj, exchanged letters in September concerning the questions raised by Vilfan and agreed that on the basis of a *voluntary* exchange of populations, Hungary and Yugoslavia could exchange a maximum of 40,000 inhabitants from each country.[35] This exchange agreement was born in the muddled atmosphere of the Paris Conference and never carried out. Ambassador Caffery in a succinct telegram informed Washington of withdrawal of the Yugoslav amendment and included the statement by the Hungarian legation concerning the agreement between Hungary and Yugoslavia.

Another agreement dealt with hydrographic questions. It proposed a two-man bilateral committee for maintenance and improvement of hydrographic installations divided by the boundary between Hungary and Yugoslavia. A technical agreement seemed to serve the interests of both countries.[36] Well before the conference, the Hungarian government in a memorandum of November 12, 1945, addressed the three principal victorious powers on problems arising from the hydrographic unity of the Carpathian Basin and the Danubian waterway to the sea. This memorandum proposed a treaty with all the neighbors of Hungary. Such a Danubian and hydrographic treaty would have guaranteed the international status of the Danube and served the interests of all states in the Carpathian Basin.[37]

Human Rights without Enforcement

The peace treaties obliged the defeated states to take all measures necessary to secure to all persons under their jurisdictions, "without distinction as to race, sex, language or religion, the enjoyment of human rights and of the fundamental freedoms including freedom of expression, of press and publication, of religious worship, of political opinion and of public meeting.[38] International control for the enforcement of these rights, or an adequate machinery for the settlement of disputes concerning the execution and interpretation of the peace treaties, was not established. An Australian proposal aiming at the creation of a European Court of Human Rights was rejected.[39] The British, United States, and French delegations proposed that any dispute concerning the execution or interpretation of the peace treaties, which could not be settled by direct negotiation, might be referred to the International Court of Justice at the request of any party to the dispute.[40] This proposition, strongly opposed by the Soviet delegation, was accepted at the conference by a vote of 15 to 6. The Council of Foreign Ministers, however, under Soviet pressure, eliminated from the final draft all reference to the International Court.

The course of events demonstrated that the system for solution of disputes inserted in the peace treaties did not prove satisfactory in the face of the tactics of the Communist-dominated Danubian countries. Their sabotage was supported, if not instigated, by the Soviet Union.[41] When Great Britain and the United States in 1948 charged Bulgaria, Hungary, and Rumania with having violated their obligations under the respective peace treaty provisions requiring them to secure to all persons under their jurisdiction the enjoyment of human rights and fundamental freedoms, they refused to recognize the existence of a dispute. The Danubian countries denounced the English and American notes as illegitimate interferences in their domestic affairs and stated that they had complied with the human rights provisions of the peace treaties. Subsequent proceedings before the General Assembly of the United Nations and the International Court of Justice brought no result.[42]

The Danube Question

Because the Danube is the only waterway to the sea for landlocked Hungary, it was natural that Budapest suggested that the prewar system of guaranteed free international navigation be reestablished and strengthened by provision for changes required by new conditions.

Along these lines the Hungarian government, in a note of November 15, 1945, advocated full freedom of navigation on the Danube and proposed changes in the Danube Convention, signed in Paris in 1921, reinstating the International Danube Commission and the European Danube Commission, possibly in a merger. Article I of the Danube Convention of 1921 provided that "navigation is to be unrestricted and open to all flags, on a footing of perfect equality, on the entire navigable portion of the Danube, *i.e.*, from Ulm to the Black Sea." When the Hungarian delegation visited Washington in June 1946, Prime Minister Nagy announced that he favored international control of the Danube. Secretary Byrnes noted that this was "a surprising demonstration of independence on the part of a satellite state."[43]

Freedom of navigation on the Danube was debated time and again in the CFM and in the Paris Conference, and Molotov insisted that the question should not be settled in the peace treaties with Rumania, Hungary, and Bulgaria but that after the conclusion of peace all riparian countries should participate in the settlement of Danubian problems. It was obvious from the outset that Molotov's purpose was to secure exclusive control over the Danube for the riparian states, including the USSR and the Ukrainian SSR. Bevin remarked that Britain, as a victorious state, wished to reestablish the position with respect to the commission of the Danube which existed in 1939, but he was not proposing that the Soviet Union be excluded from the regime of the Danube. The thrust of his proposal was the reestablishment of the regime which provided for freedom of trade and various shipping rights. Byrnes at one point suggested the following language: "Navigation on the Danube River, its navigable tributaries and connecting canals, shall be free and open on terms of complete equality to the nationals, merchant vessels and goods of all states."[44]

The Soviet delegation proposed a restricted *modus vivendi* with validity "so long as Allied forces are stationed on the Danube."[45] A British proposal combined features of the American and Soviet ideas.[46] The repetitious debates continued without resolving the conflicting views.[47]

In the Economic Commission of the Paris Conference five votes were cast in favor of the Soviet proposal (Byelorussia, Czechoslovakia, Ukraine, USSR, and Yugoslavia) and nine against (Australia, Canada, France, Greece, India, New Zealand, Union of South Africa, United Kingdom, and USA). Both the United Kingdom and the USA delegations withdrew their elaborate proposals and accepted a new proposal tabled by the French delegation, a compromise solution for the much debated questions. The first paragraph was a declaration of principle on the freedom of navigation on the Danube, and the second proposed the convocation of an international conference with the object to establish an international regime for the Danube. The commission cast eight votes for the French proposal and five against, with one abstention.[48] The plenary session of the Paris Conference accepted this proposal, fourteen votes to six, with one abstention.[49]

At the New York session of the CFM, Molotov opposed the article on the Danube in the form adopted by the Paris Conference, but after much delay and postponements he was willing to sponsor a general declaration on the Danube.[50] The council agreed to adopt the following Soviet text, amended by the United Kingdom delegation, for inclusion in the treaties with Bulgaria, Hungary, and Rumania:

> Navigation on the Danube shall be free and open for the national vessels of commerce, and goods of all states, on a footing of equality in regard to port and navigation charges and conditions for merchant shipping. The foregoing shall not apply to traffic between ports of the same State.

This watered-down declaration was far from reestablishing the international regime of the Danube; no enforcement mechanism was attached to it and no reference was made to the validity of the 1921 Danube Convention. But the CFM agreed at the same time to call within six months of the coming-into-force of the peace treaties with Rumania, Bulgaria, and Hungary, a conference to work out the new convention regarding the regime of navigation on the Danube to be composed of the representatives of the Danubian states: USSR, Ukrainian SSR, Bulgaria, Rumania, Yugoslavia, Czechoslovakia, and Hungary, and representatives of the USA, United Kingdom, and France.[51] The peace treaties came into force on September 15, 1947, and the United States proposed then the calling of a conference.

The conference met in Belgrade in the summer of 1948 and practically abolished the international regime of the Danube which was institutionalized by the Treaty of Paris in 1856 and further developed by the Danube Convention of 1921. The conference accepted by majority vote the text of the new Danubian treaty Vyshinsky brought from Moscow; he controlled the seven votes of the riparian states. Arguments and proposals of the three Western powers were disregarded. It was a Soviet concession that Austria participated in the conference "in a consultative capacity." At the opening session Vyshinsky proposed the exclusion of English as an official language, and the satellite majority voted for it. Next day Vyshinsky told the Western delegates: "The door was open for you to come in; the door is open for you to leave, if that is what you wish." Negotiations did not take place at the conference, and the seven-vote majority automatically rejected the 28 Western amendments and accepted the Soviet draft. The international regime of the Danube came to an end. The new Danube Convention was signed on August 18, 1948, without participation of the Western delegates.[52]

L'Europe s'en va

When I left Hungary for Paris I was still optimistic despite many disappointments, hoping that the principles proclaimed by the Allied powers during the war would influence peacemaking at the conference table. In this spirit our aide-memoires and notes addressed to the victorious powers considered not only the affairs of Hungary, but the conditions necessary for a lasting peace in Europe. During the conference I went through periods of acute despair. It became clear that we had to play the game without much hope for a just and constructive peace along the Danube. During my return trip to Budapest I recalled Mallet du Pan's saying in a different context in 1792, *l'Europe s'en va* —Europe is vanishing. Europe certainly was vanishing for nations beyond the Iron Curtain. The conflicting ideologies and values and Soviet imperialism made impossible constructive negotiations. The differences between East and West had not been eliminated by Western concessions, and it was discouraging to see the lack of purpose and stamina in Western policies.

11

The Aftermath

After my return to Budapest I attended Marshal Voroshilov's reception at the end of October and was cornered by Ossukin, the English-speaking and gregarious counselor of the Soviet legation. Helped apparently by a fair amount of liquor, he was in a talkative mood. When he cheerfully congratulated me on our success at the Paris Conference, I expressed astonishment and told him that none of our major proposals was considered in Paris; our reparation burden was not alleviated; on some important issues that Soviet delegation opposed us, while the United States and other Western countries supported us. Ossukin replied that he was familiar with these problems and added, "We know that you were Pál Teleki's man, but you have always played straight and have not lied to us." I remarked that I did not lie to anyone and added that only a fool would divulge all he knows, but it was important in international relations that whatever we say correspond to facts. I explained that it was especially important in Paris in my contacts with many delegations to state our position clearly, to friends and foes; that there were few secrets at the peace conference; that leaks and sensational news items spread with lightning speed; that it was not difficult to discover the source of any indiscretion in the conference circuit; and that I understood the Soviet embassy had a first-class intelligence network. This was my last encounter with Ossukin. A few weeks later he left Budapest unexpectedly and all kinds of sinister rumors circulated in connection with his disappearance. This was not unusual in the Soviet service.

At home the deterioration of the domestic political situation shocked me. Communist aggressiveness increased in interparty relations, and that could not have occurred without Soviet approval. I wondered what was going to happen and, in particular, how long the Smallholders could resist. During this period of increasing tension, Gyöngyösi took a stronger stand than before the Paris Conference. Apparently the sojourn in a free political atmosphere and his contacts with Western statesmen strengthened his self-confidence. He ap-

pointed me head of the newly established Division for International
Relations, to deal with Hungary's participation in the United Nations
and other international organizations. Because our participation in
most of these august bodies was a distant aspiration, I considered
publication of our peace preparatory material and an account of activities of the Hungarian peace delegation at the Paris Conference an
urgent task, and my plan was to prepare five volumes to appear in
English, French, Russian, and Hungarian under the title, *Hungary
and the Conference of Paris.*

Meanwhile, the foreign minister asked me about my preference for
a post abroad, and I told him that after the strenuous work and
vicissitudes of the last three years I would like to represent Hungary
in a congenial quiet post and indicated my preference for the
Netherlands. I had been at The Hague several times for extended
periods in the 1930s, at sessions of Mixed Arbitral Tribunals and the
Permanent Court of International Justice, and had friends from my
student days at the Académie de Droit International. Gyöngyösi proposed my designation to the Council of Ministers, but the Communist party vetoed it. I all but expected this outcome and continued
to concentrate on publication of the peace conference material. As I
had some forebodings, I wanted to expedite this work, a historical
evidence of our endeavors. Time was important because a shift to the
political left would have made publication impossible. I was thinking
of the possibility of a Soviet-engineered Communist coup after ratification of the peace treaty. Gyöngyösi recognized the urgency of publication, approved my scheme, and then in early 1946 informed me
he had decided to propose my accreditation to the Italian republic.
I raised the likelihood of another Communist veto, but he asserted
that this would be a different case because the post in Rome had
been reserved for him by the coalition parties, and he would transfer
the designation to me. He told me frankly he had no experience in
foreign lands and would prefer to remain in Hungary. The Council
of Ministers accepted the proposal in January 1947 and in March of
that year the president of the republic appointed me Hungarian minister to the Italian republic (at that time Hungary did not appoint
ambassadors).

It was a relief to see my life coming into some order. I handed
over the affairs of the Division for International Relations to Zoltán
Baranyay, assistant under-secretary of state in the Foreign Ministry
and a veteran of the Hungarian diplomatic corps. As former head of
the cultural division, he had special qualifications for editing the
volumes pertaining to Hungary and the Conference of Paris. Volume

IV, containing documents relating to the Czechoslovak amendment aiming at expulsion of 200,000 Hungarians from Czechoslovakia, appeared in April. Unlike the others, this volume still mentioned my name. The following month volume II appeared with documentation on the exchange of population and other aspects of Hungaro-Czechoslovak relations. The two volumes were in English and French. Volume I was published only in French in September 1947 with our major peace preparatory notes and material concerning Hungaro-Rumanian relations, protection of minorities, and notes addressed to the Council of Foreign Ministers. I established the priorities according to the importance of topics, but it was to Baranyay's credit that at least three volumes appeared before the Communist takeover of the Foreign Ministry. Volumes III and V, containing miscellaneous materials and economic clauses, were not published.[1]

As my departure approached, my days were busy. The prime minister and the foreign minister, both Smallholders, suggested that I should explore in Rome the possibility of renewal of diplomatic relations with the Vatican and conclusion of a concordat. They advised me, however, to discuss some major problems with President Tildy who gave me ambiguous, noncommittal answers. When I asked for written instructions, he said that in the times in which we lived it was better not to set our policies in written form. László Bánás, the bishop of Veszprém and a former member of the Vatican diplomatic staff, was led to believe that the Communists and Russians supported the plan and, in a state of high emotion, asked me to expedite renewal of official relations with the Vatican. Cardinal Mindszenty was not encouraging; he remained skeptical of Communist intentions. Consent of the Soviet-dominated Allied Control Commission was necessary to the planned diplomatic move. Consequently, I decided to clarify Soviet intentions about which conflicting opinions were circulating in governmental and ecclesiastical circles. In a meeting with Pushkin I brought up the problem of exchanging envoys with the Holy See and argued that Hungary had a large Catholic population and it would be advisable for the new regime to settle Church-State problems by the intervention of an experienced papal diplomat. The Soviet Minister replied: "The Vatican is an agency of American interests in Europe, financed by American capitalists. The new Hungarian democracy does not need the representative of such reactionary forces." Pushkin's position was in harmony with Rákosi's opposition to the renewal of diplomatic relations with the Vatican—he said that a nuncio would act the same way as Mindszenty but in a more sophisticated form.

Pushkin's blunt answer corresponded to his nature and methods. He was a cool, calculating professional and more outspoken in personal contacts than most Soviet diplomats. He was aware of the anti-Soviet feelings of the Hungarian population and not impressed when politicians extolled the achievements of the liberating Soviet army. He preferred business-like, matter-of-fact language. On the same occasion, after expressing opposition to a nuncio to Budapest, he warned me that I should not follow the pro-Italian line of my predecessors. I replied that we understood the changed power situation in Europe but that it was next to impossible in Hungary to find popular support for a pro-Soviet foreign policy because of the many unpleasant things and political mistakes after the Soviet army occupied the country. Pushkin admitted errors but said they were immaterial; it was not the present but the future that counted; one should educate the new generation properly and they would cooperate. This conversation occurred March 1947; in less than a decade students and workers led a revolution in Hungary against the regime that educated them, and the Communist party disintegrated like a house of cards. Pushkin, then ambassador to East Germany, was perhaps surprised that history was not working along the lines he predicted.

My last months in Hungary were marked by a series of dismal events. They started with the arrest of many army officers, politicians, and officials, including a member of my division, Domokos Szentiványi. Newspapers announced the discovery of a large-scale conspiracy against the Hungarian republic. As far as I could ascertain, the principal accusation was preparation of political plans for the post-armistice period. Almost everybody believed that after the coming-into-force of the peace treaty, Soviet forces would withdraw from Hungary as provided by Article 22. They overlooked the fact that the same article authorized the Soviet Union to keep on Hungarian territory unlimited armed forces for the maintenance of the lines of communication of the Soviet army with the zone of Soviet occupation in Austria.

Secretary of State Byrnes in the Council of Foreign Ministers had proposed the reduction of occupation forces throughout Europe; this proposal would have limited Soviet forces to 5,000 in Hungary as well as in Rumania, but Molotov was not prepared to consider this question. When Secretary of State George C. Marshall presented the same proposal at the Moscow meeting of the foreign ministers in March 1947, Molotov did not agree. This meant that the Soviets could keep unlimited forces in Hungary until the conclusion of a treaty with Austria.[2]

After my return from Paris several people inside and outside of the Ministry for Foreign Affairs asked about the deadline for withdrawal of Soviet forces. My answer was the clause of the Roman law: *Incertus an et quando*, that is, uncertain when, if at all. My interlocutors were appalled. But I could not honestly say anything else. Conclusion of the Austrian treaty was in the nebulous future and even after that Moscow could make an arrangement to station Soviet forces in Hungary. The situation was clear to anyone who cared to think about it, but people do not like to envisage unpleasant realities and prefer to indulge in wishful thinking. Ferenc Nagy's book[3] relates his conviction in 1947 that Soviet forces would withdraw after ratification of the peace treaty. Many non-Muscovite Communists shared this view. Before I left for Paris a ranking Communist official of the Foreign Ministry told me indignantly that Fascists and reactionaries were spreading rumors that the Russians would not evacuate Hungary after the conclusion of peace.

The Conference of Paris and the peace treaty had made clear Hungary's predicament, and under these circumstances group planning for the period following withdrawal of Soviet forces was not prudent, but it was not a conspiracy, it was an exercise in futility. During those days personal security hardly existed, and many people speculated about a better future when a majority government would govern the country. The Communists had obtained only 17 percent of the vote in November 1945, and the idea of their exclusion from government was in their eyes the supreme crime. Persons arrested in the alleged conspiracy confessed under torture anything necessary to justify the accusations and involvement of others. On the basis of loose and less-than-prudent talk many people were or could have been arrested throughout the country. But the "conspirators" had no arms or plan for a coup d'état.[4]

The purpose of the mass arrests became obvious when Communist newspapers connected the conspiracy with the Smallholder party—a Smallholder minister and several members of the party were arrested and their "confessions" implicated Béla Kovács, the secretary-general of the Smallholder party. This strange Orwellian scenario implied that members of the majority party conspired against the regime, that is, against themselves. After much pressure, Béla Kovács went on leave and later resigned as secretary-general of the party. Although parliament refused to suspend his immunity, he offered to give evidence to the political police. Upon return from this hearing, Soviet authorities arrested him, February 25, 1947, on a charge of espionage against the Soviet army.

The United States on March 5 addressed an energetic note to the British, Soviet, and Hungarian governments on the basis of the Yalta Declaration and as a participant in the Allied Control Commission, against "foreign interference in the domestic affairs of Hungary in support of repeated aggressive attempts by Hungarian minority elements to coerce the popularly elected majority." The note emphasized that Soviet occupation forces had arrested Kovács on the basis of unwarranted charges and proposed a collective investigation of the so-called conspiracy and the Kovács case by the Allied Control Commission in cooperation with the Hungarian prime minister, the minister of defense, minister of the interior, minister of justice, and the president of the National Assembly.[5]

A Soviet note from the acting chairman of the ACC, General Vladimir Petrovich Sviridov, rejected the American allegation, claiming that the prime minister and the Smallholder party had recognized the existence of an anti-constitutional plot and that the Smallholders voluntarily had agreed to deprive the plotters of parliamentary immunity. The note emphasized that Soviet authorities had a legal right to arrest Kovács for crimes against the Soviet occupation forces. Hence Sviridov rejected the American proposal for a collective investigation.[6] The Hungarian press published these notes and a subsequent exchange of notes[7] showing the Hungarian nation American interest in their predicament. In the persistent political crisis the cabinet was reorganized, three Smallholder ministers resigned and were replaced by left-wing Smallholders, with Lajos Dinnyés appointed minister of defense and Ernő Mihályfi, minister of information.[8]

This distressing case was a continuation of Communist salami tactics against the Smallholders. The process had begun in March 1946 when the Smallholder party leaders under Communist pressure advised twenty-two Smallholder members of Parliament, the group of Dezső Sulyok, to leave the party. The Communists declared these politicians "rightists" and demanded their exclusion from the Smallholder party. Creation of a leftist block within the coalition greatly helped such tactics. In some cases, early in 1947, Smallholder resistance was effective; for example, in the refusal to suspend Béla Kovács's parliamentary immunity. But Tildy and Ferenc Nagy advocated concessions because the examples of Poland, Bulgaria, and Rumania frightened them, and they wanted to avoid a similar fate. They played for time, in hope that Soviet occupation would end after ratification of the peace treaty, and on some occasions Western leaders fostered this hope. Western support was not forthcoming, and the ACC disregarded American and British notes of protest. Under these conditions the Smallholder leaders' ability to endure, while swallowing insults and injuries, seemed a way to survive in hope that Western policy would change. American policy did change with the Truman Doctrine in March 1947, but it was late for Hungary and the policy of containment meant just that — it did not alleviate the fate of countries already within Russia's Europe.

A few days before my departure, the director of the Pál Teleki Institute, István Révay, came to inform me that the political police discovered in his organization a spy for Czechoslovakia. In connection with this affair all employees of the institute were summoned to the political police, but when they appeared the police interrogated them about my activities, especially my contacts with Géza Teleki and his confidential undertaking. Simultaneous with this, a Communist periodical, *Képes Figyelő*, published an article against a "high official of the Foreign Ministry" because his testimony made possible the favorable screening of Colonel István Szentmiklósy, arrested in the conspiracy case. Although my name was not spelled out, it was clear I was involved. I had known Szentmiklósy when he had been a liaison officer in northern Transylvania attached to the Italo-German military commission in 1942–44, and during this period he had initiated and directed a risky intelligence operation that would have provoked German retaliation if discovered. I had emphasized this case in my written and oral testimony during his screening.

These episodes showed that someone was collecting data and trying to build a case against me, but the political police did not summon me. I paid farewell visits to party leaders, called on representatives of the Great Powers, and had frequent official and social contact with the Italian legation. The ACC gave me an exit permit, the Hungarian authorities agreed to the schedule of my departure, and the Italian government was notified of my arrival. There would have been unnecessary sensation if the police had stopped me for whatever reason. I left the country without difficulty.

In Rome I was warmly received by officials in the Palazzo Chigi. My conversation reflected feelings of traditional friendship between our countries. After presentation of my letter of credence to the provisional head of state, Enrico de Nicola, a lawyer and former mayor of Naples, I had a private audience with this warm-hearted and forthright man, and we discussed the postwar problems of Italy and Hungary and our traditional relations. Exchange of anecdotes and easy laughs made our conversation lively.

In the course of visits to the heads of diplomatic missions, I introduced myself to the apostolic nuncio, Francisco Borgongini Duca, accredited to the Quirinal since 1929. He also was the doyen of the diplomatic corps. I informed him of my verbal authorization to negotiate for the renewal of diplomatic relations with the Vatican and conclusion of a Concordat and explained that during the armistice period we would need approval of the Allied Control Commission for such a step. Relating Pushkin's opposition, I proposed to begin formal negotiation after ratification of the peace treaty. The nuncio understood our predicament and took note of my communication to be forwarded to the Vatican.

Soviet Ambassador Mikhail Kostylev told amusing stories about his return to Italy after the war. As a specialist in economics affairs he had served at the Soviet embassy in Italy in the 1930s. As Stalin did not hesitate to send him back to Italy without informing Washington and London, he became the first ambassador accredited to the Badoglio government in April 1945. He witnessed the slow development of Italian administration in Caserta and saw Badoglio take his letters personally to the post office. I recounted my experiences during the siege of Buda and the miraculous revival of Budapest.

The Austrian minister, Johannes E. Schwarzenberg, was most helpful. Some problems of our neighboring countries were comparable. But Austria was a liberated country, not an ex-enemy state, and the four-power occupation gave the Austrians more flexibility and hope for the future.

The easy-going life of the Italians contrasted with terror-stricken, uncertain conditions in Hungary. Although Italy had been a poor country and there was an open black market, I remembered what Cardinal Mindszenty told me after his first visit to Rome in November 1945. He wanted to see how people lived and had visited a street full of butcher shops, commenting that in the same street he never saw so much meat and that most of it had come from the United States.

It was a pleasure to watch the enjoyment of life and vitality of simple Italians always ready to sing Verdi or Puccini arias. In my house the chef and supervisor of servants was Peppino, a dignified old Italian employed by the legation for many years. I decided to hire a cook, a specialist in sophisticated French meals, who was to come twice or three times a week. When I asked him about his salary he indicated a ridiculously low amount. I was surprised and asked him how could he make a living on this small salary. He replied: "Excellency, I am an honest man and confess to you that in a cook's life the salary is insignificant. I make real money when I buy things for you in the market." That time there was still rationing in Italy, and he received valuable coupons from the legation. Of course, the major beneficiary of this system was Peppino, who handled the coupons at the legation.

Composition of personnel at my legation reflected conditions in Hungary. I was a civil servant without party affiliation, but most of the staff belonged to a political party in the coalition. My Counselor was a non-Muscovite Communist. We had good relations, but I knew that he had to send reports to the Communist party. In addition to the reporting of party members, there were spies at the legation. When I was informed that my personal steward who had been employed for many years by the Foreign Ministry was looking into files and sending reports to the political police, I let him overhear conversations and sometimes "forgot" notes and files on my desk—a convenient way to send to Budapest the kind of information I wanted. As soon as the situation became critical, I deposited my confidential documents at the house of an Italian friend and received certain visitors there.

Besides increasing official and social duties and visits to Hungarian cultural and ecclesiastical institutions in Rome, I spent much of my time with a variety of Hungarian visitors such as scholars, priests, actors, politicians. At the end of April a delegation of Hungarian parliamentarians arrived who under Count Mihály Károlyi's chairmanship had participated in the Conference of the Inter-Parliamentary Union in Cairo. I was pleased that members of our National Assembly had attended a conference of this time-honored institution and invited the group for dinner and a reception. Károlyi remained in Rome for a few days, and I made appointments for him with leading figures of Italian politics. I invited Foreign Minister Carlo Sforza, the former foreign minister and Socialist leader, Pietro Nenni, and a few high officials from the Palazzo Chigi, to have lunch with Károlyi and his charming daughter Judith. Since Károlyi wanted to see Prime Minister Alcide de Gasperi, I made the arrangements and accompanied him. During a memorable visit Károlyi questioned de Gasperi's pro-American policy. Familiar with Károlyi's background, de Gasperi smiled and quietly enumerated the economic aid and other assistance Italy received from the United States and asked Károlyi where Italy could turn for similar support. There was no answer. When we left, Károlyi muttered: "What Gasperi said was interesting but I still don't agree with his pro-American policy." The United States was Károlyi's *bête noire* and nothing could shake this obsession. He was in many ways a pleasant and gentle man, but the bitter years of exile had taken their toll and influenced his thinking. He wanted to be ostentatiously more leftist than anyone else. Perhaps this was his way of reacting against his past when he had been one of the richest aristocrats in the Habsburg Empire. Allegedly Károlyi once said that he could accept Communist ideas, but he never would enter the Communist party because no one should tell him what to do or say. In early June he surprised me with an elaborate thank-you letter. He expressed appreciation that I had made it possible for him to see in a short time the most important personalities in Roman politics and concluded: "At last, a right man in the right place." It was almost amusing to read his compliments because at that time I was in the midst of a political crisis and knew that my days in Hungarian diplomacy were numbered.

The first news of political troubles in Hungary reached Rome by the end of May, when rumor spread that all Hungarian envoys had been ordered home to report. Newspapermen stormed the legation. I instructed my press attaché, George Kósa, to inform them that I did not have knowledge of such an order and did not plan to travel to Budapest. Since I had not received authentic information about events in Hungary, I addressed a cipher telegram to Budapest on May 31:

> Fantastic news is appearing in world press concerning crisis and alleged Soviet note. Please inform me about real situation. Kertész. Code telegram No. 15.

I understood through newspaper reports that Prime Minister Nagy had been forced to resign while in Switzerland and in the new government the Smallholder minister of defense, Lajos Dinnyés, became prime minister. Gyöngyösi was not included in the cabinet, and it was announced that I would be foreign minister. One of the most reliable newspapers in Europe, the *Neue Zürcher Zeitung*, published a long front-page article on June 2, entitled, "Transformation of the Government in Hungary - The New Dinnyés Cabinet." Two passages of this article discussed my "appointment" as follows:

> The new Foreign Minister, Stephen Kertész, at the present time envoy in Rome, was secretary general of Hungarian Delegation at the peace conference. He directed the preparation of the first official publication on the peace treaty under the title, "La Hongrie devant la Conférence de Paris." Kertész, already active in the Foreign Ministry in previous times and in charge of several special tasks, participated in the resistance movement against Germany . . . Until entering in office of the new foreign minister, which will be possible only some time later, the Minister of Propaganda, Ernő Mihályfi, will handle current affairs."[9]

I was less surprised by the prime minister's forced resignation than by the dismissal of Gyöngyösi, whose reputation had been pro-Russian in the sense that he realized that without a cooperative attitude toward the Soviet Union, Hungary's survival might be in danger. It is true that after the peace conference he had shown more independence and defied the Communists, particularly in the Béla Kovács affair when he opposed suspension of parliamentary immunity. After Gyöngyösi's dismissal the appointment of a non-party man of Western orientation would have been only a front to mislead the West and the Hungarian public. I was destined to be window dressing, to demonstrate to the West that nothing serious had happened or changed in Hungary. Later I could have been dropped from the cabinet without the slightest difficulty. Although Communist designs in connection with my proposed appointment were obvious, I would have been willing to take the chance if I could have expected a forceful American intervention to carry out the Yalta Declaration on Liberated Europe. In the spring of 1947, the Truman Doctrine had foreshadowed a stronger foreign policy, but I was aware of the limitations of the policy of containment.

Meanwhile I had contacts with Hungarian envoys in several capitals. I sent a cable to my colleague in Washington, Aladár Szegedy-Maszák, a close friend since our student days in Paris. My cable crossed his message in which he asked me to call him by telephone. We had a long conversation on the night of May 31–June 1, and he informed me of his intention to resign because events in Hungary — like the German occupation of the country on March 19, 1944 — meant the end of Hungary's independence. With dismissal of Nagy and Gyöngyösi, Hungary would be dominated by the Soviet Union militarily, politically, and economically. Dinnyés was no guarantee, and the question of personalities was similar to the choice in March 1944 between Imrédy and Sztójay as prime minister. Under the circumstances he did not recommend that I accept the position of foreign minister. I replied that I did not intend to rush home to accept the portfolio, but I questioned resignation as a right course at the present time. Hungary had lost independence in March 1944 and never regained it. Soviet and Communist pressure took place repeatedly, and Prime Minister Nagy made concessions time and again and proved especially weak in the Béla Kovács affair. But the legal and political situation was very different in March 1944, for German troops had invaded the country, the government had been deposed, politicians arrested, and yet Germany's defeat was only a question of time. After the cessation of hostilities with Hungary the basis of Soviet intervention had been the armistice agreement. The peace treaty would by ratified soon. I suggested a wait-and-see policy and raised the question what would happen to the Hungarian people if all decent men left their posts. After our conversation I sent Szegedy-Maszák a cable in which I marshalled additional arguments and asked him to reconsider his decision.

My colleague in Paris, Paul Auer, called me on June 1 to persuade me to accept the portfolio of foreign minister. He said that resignation would not be justified because Dinnyés, though not a man of the right caliber for a high office, was an old and reliable Smallholder politician and if I accepted the portfolio there would be no reason for resignation. The Hungarian envoy in Switzerland, Francis Gordon, called twice to inform me that he would resign because he had been recalled to report and was unwilling to do so. Resignation became the pattern. I understood only the Social Democrat Vilmos Böhm returned to report. Auer changed his mind and resigned, as did most Hungarian representatives abroad. Together with my colleague in London, István Bede, I continued a wait-and-see policy.

At this juncture it was necessary for me to ascertain the position of the Western powers, that is, the support Hungary could get from them. At the British embassy I received only vague, noncommittal answers to my inquiry. My conversations with Edward Page, the political officer in charge of East European affairs at the United States embassy (later envoy to Bulgaria), were more helpful. I explained my situation and said that I did not have the ambition to become foreign minister because since the war Hungary had not been an independent state and lived under the Soviet-dominated Allied Control Commission. In the existing conditions I, as foreign minister, would only be window dressing. Yet if I could expect energetic Western action for the implementation of the Yalta Declaration on Liberated Europe, I would be willing to take any personal risk and play for time in Budapest until the next session of the Council of Foreign Ministers, scheduled for November. We agreed to meet again in a few days to receive answers to the questions I raised.

I consulted colleagues in the diplomatic corps and especially Selim Sarper, the ambassador of Turkey to Italy, formerly ambassador in Moscow and familiar with Soviet methods. His first question was who would support me in Hungary. I explained that probably nobody would if the chips were down, because I was a non-party civil servant and the coalition regime was vanishing. I added that under the peculiar political situation in Hungary this might be an advantage in the short run, but then a few months later I could be dropped without much ado. A show trial might be possible also. I would be willing to take these risks, I told him, if I could get substantial Western support for maintaining Hungary as part of Europe and if an evolution toward genuine parliamentary democracy could take place. Sarper thought that solid Western support for such developments in Hungary was not in the cards. He did not see much possibility of dislodging the Soviet-supported Communists in the country and advised against accepting the cabinet post.

Shortly after my conversation with Sarper I received information from Page, who told me frankly that along the banks of the Danube within the near future there was no hope for an energetic political action such as I suggested. At that time the United States intended to concentrate on strengthening Greece and Turkey, afterward Western Europe and Austria, and if these countries were rehabilitated and made safe for democracy, Hungary's turn might come. This timetable seemed reasonable from the American point of view, but the time span was too long for my purposes.

I asked Budapest repeatedly for information concerning political events and the rumors that were flying in Italian and other Western newspapers. An explanatory telegram I received was humorous in light of the depressing events. It said, with studied naivete, that resignation of the prime minister did not affect the coalition, that the Hungarian people had received it with indifference, that supplies in the markets were abundant, and that food prices were low.

My wife Margaret arrived at the end of May, and Kostylev and his wife invited us for lunch on June 4. Probably he wanted to find out my position concerning events in Hungary. I remained noncommittal and kept the conversation in generalities. The same day we had dinner at the Austrian legation, and I discussed with Schwarzenberg the possible consequences of political changes in Hungary. One of the guests, Joseph Alsop, chimed in and said that the Communist endeavor to seize power in a country like Hungary was similar to pregnancy, in that one could not stop it in the fourth month.

On June 5 a cipher telegram told me in a very polite way that I was wanted in Budapest for consultation, and the same day the head of the political division in the Foreign Ministry asked me by phone to return; he explained that I had been designated for the portfolio of the Foreign Ministry because in the opinion of leading politicians a diplomat without party affiliation could conduct foreign affairs much better than a party politician during the present quiet political period. I replied that I could not accept the portfolio; I had to open the Hungarian pavilion at the Milan fair on June 14 and could not

leave Italy before that date. Two days later I received a strictly personal secret cipher telegram that ordered me to send an open
telegram to the Hungarian government strongly condemning the
resignation of my colleagues, Szegedy-Maszák and Gordon, Hungarian ministers to the USA and Switzerland, respectively. I immediately sent my answer, in which I refused to follow the order and
declared that I would go on leave and did not intend to deal with
politics as long as an independent government, able to defend the
vital interests of the Hungarian people, could not function in Hungary. The same day I handed over affairs of the legation to my Communist counsellor, László Pödör. In the Palazzo Chigi I had a talk
with Foreign Minister Carlo Sforza. I described my situation and told
him frankly that I might be obliged to ask for asylum in Italy. His
answer was most understanding and promised full support if and
when I would need it. I did not ask Sforza to keep my request confidential and realized that he would report it to the Council of
Ministers and the news would spread in political and diplomatic
circles. This meant that Budapest would be informed in no time. I
did not mind; at this stage I decided to play with open cards.

Two courses were open at that moment: to resign with a denunciation of the Hungarian situation or to try diplomatically to influence
events from Rome. I was inclined to follow the second alternative.
Newspaper headlines did not interest me and would not have been
useful to the Hungarian people. The resignation of Hungarian envoys in March 1944 did not help Hungary's case at the peace table.
At his press conference on June 5, 1947, President Truman characterized the situation in Hungary as an outrage and stated that the
United States would not stand by idly.[10] Yet in practice nothing was
done, although it would have been possible to reduce diplomatic
relations with Hungary to the level of a chargé d'affaires. Envoy
Schoenfeld was scheduled to relinquish his post on May 31, and he
departed from Budapest the following day. Selden Chapin's nomination as minister to Hungary had been confirmed by the Senate on
April 9, and he arrived in Budapest on July 2. His schedule was not
altered, and appointment of a chargé d'affaires as an expression of
disapproval of events in Hungary was not even considered. The State
Department decided to send to Budapest one of their best men, and
this decision was not changed because of Nagy's unceremonious
resignation. When Szegedy-Maszák inquired in the State Department on June 5 concerning American intentions with regard to
Minister-designate Chapin, "Mr. Hickerson expressed the opinion
that Mr. Chapin would proceed to Budapest and take up his position

as Minister as planned."[11] I was not aware at that time of Szegedy-Maszák's inquiry in the State Department because we did not have contact after our telephone conversation. All the while I tried to convince the Western powers of the necessity to take Soviet abuses in Hungary to the United Nations and prepared a strong denunciation of the Hungarian situation for this purpose.[12] After a few days, however, I again received a negative answer through Page, with whom I remained in contact. He assured me that the United States would not cease to support democratic principles in the Danubian area as expressed in the Yalta Declaration on Liberated Europe, but when I asked him about the steps they could take immediately in Hungary, he replied that according to his personal opinion the withdrawal of Western representatives from the ACC might be considered in the case of Soviet violation of agreements. He recognized that this would mean little in terms of practical politics.

In view of the passivity of the Western governments I did not think that a spectacular resignation would bring any benefit to my countrymen. I felt that for a limited time I was in an advantageous position toward the Hungarian government because my designation as foreign minister had been made public in Budapest. I was in a better position abroad than a recalcitrant envoy usually would have been and decided to make the most of the situation. The resignations of my colleagues were greatly publicized and helped open the eyes of the Western world, but did not make the heavy lot of the Hungarian people easier. Influenced by these considerations, I decided to try to exert pressure on the government so as to assure freedom for all political parties before the national elections scheduled for August 31. Considering the desperate situation in Hungary, action along this line seemed the only one that could have brought some benefit to Hungarians, who could not resign or protest but had to live under conditions created by the Soviet occupation. Several of my friends participated in the elections despite physical threats and other risks, and my heart went out for them.

My supposition that Budapest would act for a limited time in a cautious way toward me proved justified by the reaction of the Foreign Ministry to my refusal to obey orders. The acting foreign minister, Ernő Mihályfi, in a new cipher telegram of June 11 annulled the order to condemn my colleagues. The head of the political division of the Foreign Ministry offered to come to Rome and explain the "misunderstanding." But by no means did I want to negotiate with him in Rome as his host and suggested that we meet in Switzerland.

A few hours before my departure to Switzerland, Borgongini Duca telephoned me for an urgent appointment. He came immediately and informed me that a prominent person living in a foreign country had sent me a message through a nunciature. The message was a warning that I should not accept the portfolio of the foreign ministry. He was aware that as a good Catholic I was willing to make this sacrifice for my country, but it was too late at that time for such an undertaking and it would not make sense under the present conditions. I thanked the nuncio for transmitting the message and assured him that things being as they are I had no intention of accepting a cabinet position. To this day I do not know who sent me the message.

I met in Zurich on June 14 the head of the political division and outlined the political conditions under which I would be willing to represent in Rome the new government. I asked for the formation of a real coalition government and guarantees of political freedom and civil liberties during the electoral campaign. Moreover I asked for the real reason of removal of the prime minister and the foreign minister. My colleague from Budapest, apparently instructed to deal with me in a friendly way, promised fulfillment of all my political conditions but emphasized that my influence would be much greater if I would return home for consultation and repeatedly almost implored me to do this. It was clear that he had to follow orders. He said that Gyöngyösi during his last weeks in office had behaved as if he were Truman's foreign minister and referred particularly to his speech at Nagykanizsa on May 12, 1947. As for Ferenc Nagy, he was not a Fascist but had planned to exclude Communists from the government after the Russian evacuation, and this was equivalent to fascism. This was the enlightening information concerning the removal of Nagy and Gyöngyösi.

After my return to Rome, I thought it safer to send the terms of my political conditions and some suggestions to the president of the republic in a cipher telegram. Technically this was difficult because I was on leave and only the Communist chargé d'affaires could forward an official message. I decided to cope with the situation and prepared the following text:

> Envoy Kertész asks Foreign Minister to transmit the following message to the president of the Republic:
>
> Every good Hungarian is filled with deep anxiety because of the repercussions of the last weeks' events abroad and in the masses at home. I feel it my duty to propose to the President and to the Leaders of the Parties the following:
>
> 1. I agreed in Zürich with the Head of the Political Division that the government should announce in a public declaration all guaran-

tees necessary to assure the purity of the elections, and further announce agreed concrete particulars concerning the independence of Hungarian foreign policy. It is desirable that this should be done as soon as possible and in a very definite form.

2. The coalition government should be enlarged with politicians of the opposition and with non-party men, against whom Soviet Russia could not raise objections and who would represent a guarantee towards the West as well.

3. The police should be reorganized by reliable experts of the Social Democratic and non-labour parties. The present police, and particularly the political police, have the characteristics of a Communist party-formation, which actually, is not a benefit to the Communist Party either.

4. Freedom of the press, of opinion and freedom to form associations should be gradually assured.

5. For the sake of our international prestige it would be important to keep our press and radio up to a reputable standard. It is regrettable that the evergrowing cursings and incitements remind us of the bygone Arrow Cross regime.

The government could regain the confidence of the Hungarian people and of foreign public opinion through the enactment of the above proposed measures and through some energetic reforms putting an end to the abuses of party politics and corruption. Otherwise the abyss between the government and the large masses of the people will but increase. This will make it impossible to govern in a democratic way. Hungary will sink to the level of a dictatorial police-state. This is the unanimous opinion I heard about Hungary in the last weeks from persons with the most varied allegiances.

The recommended reforms are all the more important since cooperation on a realistic basis with our neighbours, and first of all with Soviet Russia, is Hungary's vital interest. This, however, could be achieved only by a democratic government based on the large majority of the Hungarian people. A government without popular support might provoke ultra-nationalist movements. These would shake the confidence in Hungary.

Please present this telegram to the Prime Minister and Deputy Prime Ministers. Repeated London and Washington. Kertész. Code telegram No. 23.

I handed this text to Pödör on June 21 and asked him to forward it immediately. After reading it he turned pale and stuttered that he did not think he could forward such a text. I replied cheerfully that in that case I would send it as an open telegram. This possibility prompted him to immediate action, though I understood later that he did not send copies to our legations in London and Washington and he changed the text slightly by putting my request for presentation of the telegram to the prime minister and deputy prime ministers in the first part of the message rather than at the end. Thus the first sentence of the transmitted version asked the foreign minister to transmit the message not only to the president of the republic but to the prime minister and deputy prime ministers. He undoubtedly performed this manipulation in deference to his Communist boss Rákosi, one of the deputy prime ministers, to make sure that Rákosi got the text at the same time as the president of the republic.

In fact it did not matter much whether the helpless president of the republic received my message. It was more important to impress the Communist leaders, the real masters of Hungary, with the necessity of granting some freedom to the people before the elections, which eventually became the second great anti-Communist demonstration by Hungarians against Soviet communism. To influence the Communists, I pointed out in the telegram that these freedoms were necessary for cooperation on a realistic basis with our neighbors and especially with Soviet Russia. Of course the expression "realistic basis" had a different meaning in my mind than in theirs. "Cooperation" with Russia was a necessity, not of our choosing. We were thinking in the postwar years of a cooperation similar to the model developed in Russo-Finnish relations. Although Hungary was between Czechoslovakia and Yugoslavia on a highway toward western Europe, such wishful thinking was encouraged by the result of free elections in 1945 and the survival of a coalition government for over two years.

On June 25, I received the following answer from the acting foreign minister:

> In reference to your cipher telegram No. 23: In accordance with your proposal made to the head of the Political Division, the Prime Minister will deliver a speech on Sunday afternoon. The Civic Democratic Party is again a member of the National Council of Hungary, following the Thursday decision of the latter. Thus it is a member of the National Independence Front. Mihályfi. Code telegram No. 32.

This reply did not impress me because the Civic Democratic party was insignificant in postwar Hungary's political life and had obtained only two seats in parliament at the 1945 elections. Thus I did not react.

On July 2 the acting foreign minister contacted me by telephone and said that on Sunday the prime minister had delivered a speech containing the announcements for which I had asked in Zurich and in my telegram. He explained that it appeared from my telegrams that I had not properly evaluated recent events in Hungary, and he emphatically demanded in the name of the government that I return for consultation. I replied that from Rome I naturally saw events in a different light than did people in Budapest and expressed my views accordingly. I stated that I did not see any reason for return to Hungary before the general election and did not intend to do so in any case before September. Mihályfi said that he would give my answer to the prime minister and promised to inform me in a personal letter about the political situation in Hungary. I understood later that he actually wrote the letter but it was forwarded to the competent Communist party organ, not to me.

A few days after my conversation with Mihályfi, I had a slight hope that Hungary might again become part of the Western community of nations. On July 4 the head of the British political mission in Budapest transmitted to the Hungarian government a joint Anglo-French invitation to take part in the Marshall Plan conference that was to open on July 10 in Paris. Having received this piece of news on July 5, I reassumed my duties at the legation because I intended to exert all possible influence in favor of Hungary's participation in the preparatory conference in Paris. This seemed the last chance for cooperation with the West. In the first days of July this endeavor did not appear hopeless, and in any case this was the only thing that I could do for my country, for it had been made clear to me that the Western powers were not able or willing to give any effective political support to Hungary.

I was informed from various sources that Czechoslovakia and Poland had decided to take part in the conference and that the other Eastern European states did not reject possibility of participation. It was significant that in Prague even the Muscovite Communist members of the government concurred in a unanimous decision of July 4, 1947, to accept the joint British-French invitation to the preparatory conference in Paris. The Western powers hoped at that time that Russia would allow participation of the satellites, at least for tactical reasons. Thus, on the very day of taking over again my position as minister to Italy, I addressed the following cipher telegram to Budapest:

> I visited today leading officials of Palazzo Chigi. In the course of my visit, I was informed that the central problem of Italy's foreign policy was full participation in the Marshall Plan. The Italians prepare memoranda concerning Italy's participation in the European reconstruction and concerning her need for the rehabilitation of her own economy. The other states follow a similar procedure and they will organically

complement each other's economy. The deficiencies in the final balance will be covered by the U.S. The head of the political section pointed out to me that they expect from the realization of the Marshall Plan, an unprecedented European collaboration. The Italian government is hopeful as to Hungary's participation. Otherwise Hungary would be completely isolated from the western European states. In view of our difficult situation, we really could not put forward any serious arguments for a refusal to take part in an economic plan which could only help us. If there were difficulties, we could apply for the permission of the ACC. This step could be motivated by our restricted sovereignty. Kertész. Code telegram No. 31.

With my last proposition I intended to convey a hint to the acting foreign minister that in case of Soviet opposition our request to the ACC would automatically involve the American and British sections of the ACC.

On July 7 a rather encouraging announcement was made in Budapest—the Official Telegraphic Agency reported that great interest was being taken in the Marshall offer and in proposals for a European economic program, adding cautiously that Hungary "would have great difficulties in taking an attitude different from other southeast European ex-enemy states." In view of our political situation, this reservation was not out of place. It was also reported from Budapest that the prime minister had decided to ask the ACC for permission to accept the invitation to the Paris conference on United States aid to Europe.[13] Having received this information I felt justified in sending another message about our need for Western help:

> In reference to the decision to be taken concerning the Marshall Plan, I have the honor to recommend for consideration the fact that among the Eastern European states, Hungary is the most vitally interested in the renewal of its industrial equipment. This cannot be carried out without Western help. With our ruined industrial equipment, we shall not be able to fulfill our international obligations. Our isolation from the West could have incalculable disadvantages for our whole economy. Kertész. Code telegram No. 36.

Unfortunately the East Central European delegations were unable to participate in the Paris Conference, because of Russian pressure. On July 8 a Moscow radio broadcast said that Poland, Rumania, and Yugoslavia had decided against participating.[14] Next day the Finnish, Polish, and Rumanian diplomatic representatives in Paris denied that their countries had rejected the invitations. Warsaw, Bucharest, and Belgrade remained silent or issued denials concerning the Moscow radio statement.[15] Nevertheless that same day the Polish, Bulgarian, and Rumanian governments decided to decline the invitation to Paris. The next day Budapest, Prague, and Belgrade made similar announcements, and Helsinki concurred on July 11.

In the case of Czechoslovakia, violent pressure was brought on a delegation which left for Moscow on July 8 "to discuss a trade treaty." The delegation consisted of the prime minister, foreign minister, the minister of justice, and the secretary-general of the Czechoslovak Foreign Ministry. Stalin received the delegation in the Kremlin on July 9, 11 P.M. Dr. Arnost Heidrich, secretary-general of the Foreign Ministry, made the following report on their discussion with Stalin:

> Stalin explained that the aim of the Soviet policy was to get the Americans out of Europe and Asia. Stalin emphasized that the United States pursues, through the Marshall Plan, political and economic aims which are opposed to those of the Soviet Union. This is the reason why Czechoslovakia cannot and should not participate in the Marshall Plan. For the United States the Marshall Plan is only a means to solidify its political and economic influence in Europe. Stalin mentioned that the Soviet Union and its allies cannot have any interest in increasing the political and economic influence of the United States in Europe. Czechoslovakia, therefore, must not assist in the realization of these American plans. The Marshall Plan will lead to a situation in which Germany would be used either as a military or industrial basis against the Soviet Union. Czechoslovakia, which is an ally of the Soviet Union with the aim to prevent any resurrection of German aggressive power, cannot be both an ally of the Soviet Union and a participant in the Marshall Plan. It is a question of compatibility. The interest of the Soviet Union and its allies, according to Stalin, is to force the United States to abandon its positions in Europe and, step by step, in other parts of the world. Great Britain and France, if they have to rely on their own resources, are — according to Stalin — too weak to resist the interests of the Soviet Union and its allies. Stalin then emphasized that the United States will be obliged to evacuate its position in Europe, Asia and elsewhere, as a consequence of a deep economic crisis which the American system will be unable to avoid. Stalin did not make any mention of military measures. On the contrary, Stalin emphasized that these actions, the aim of which is to destroy the American power in the world, must not have any military character and must, therefore, not appear in such a way that would awaken the American public opinion — as happened after Pearl Harbor — and, consequently, allow the American Government to start military counter measures.

On July 10, it was announced in Prague that "the Government held an extraordinary meeting today at which Czechoslovak participation in the Paris conference was again discussed. It was ascertained that a number of countries, especially all Slav States and other countries of central and eastern Europe have not accepted the invitation. Consequently, these countries, with which the Czechoslovak Republic maintains close economic and political relations based on treaty obligation, will not take part in the conference. In these circumstances, Czechoslovakia's participation would be interpreted as an act directed against the friendship with the Soviet Union and our other allies. For this reason the Government decide unanimously not to take part in the conference.[16]

The Hungarian reply handed over to the British political mission in Budapest on July 10 emphasized that

> The Hungarian Government fully appreciated the importance of the efforts of European reconstruction, but to its greatest regret, does not see the possibility of being present at the Paris Conference. The previously held French-British-Soviet Conference proved that the Great Powers could not come to an understanding concerning the plan, which will be the object of the Paris conference. The Hungarian Government maintains that it cannot take part at a conference on the object of which the Great Powers concerned could not come to an understanding. This decision of the Hungarian Government does not mean that it wants to keep outside of the great task of European reconstruction and nothing could be farther from its intentions than to reject the principle of mutual aid of nations.

According to this text and a communiqué on the same day, the Hungarian government could not send delegates to Paris because of disagreement between the Great Powers. Allusion to the "disagreement" in practical terms meant the Soviet veto. Prior to this veto the Smallholder and Socialist parties had decided that Hungary should send representatives to Paris, and reportedly the Communist party had designated tentatively Ernő Gerő as head of the Hungarian delegation.

On July 13, I was surprised to receive from the acting foreign minister the following inquiry concerning the Marshall Plan:

> In reference to your code telegrams nos. 31 and 36, I ask you to indicate the sources of your information concerning the Marshall Plan, and to explain your information in concrete form. Notably, I ask you to let me know the motives of your suppositions in reference to
>
> 1. The U.S. willingness to help the reconstruction of Hungary with industrial equipment or foreign exchange.
>
> 2. In which respect could our participation in the Marshall Plan facilitate the realization of the Three Year Plan?

3. What would be the conditions of the supposed help? Through which organizations would it be remitted, within what period of time, and in which form?

All these facts were not clarified in the press communiqués, in the invitation, and in your telegrams. Mihályfi. Code telegram No. 44.

Here, of course, was a display of anger and ignorance. But it offered a gleam of hope in the sense that participation of the satellites in the Marshall Plan was still a possibility. I decided to send the following detailed cipher to Budapest:

In reference to your code telegram no. 44, I inform you that I received information concerning the Marshall Plan in the Italian Foreign Ministry, as it appears from my cipher-telegram no. 31. The Secretary General as well as the heads of the political and economic divisions gave me information concerning the Italian views and preparations. A special commission is working day and night in the Foreign Ministry to prepare the material for the Paris Conference.

Economic experts would find an answer in my cipher-telegram no. 31. for the first and second questions. Notably, the European states first will clarify among themselves the possibilities of mutal assistance and the need for the maximum utilization of their economic resources. Thus the European countries first will establish an integrated economy among themselves and will receive help from the U.S. only to cover the remaining needs and necessities. The U.S. gave help until now through UNRRA and through other similar methods. This would be done in the future within a European planned economy. The head of the political division pointed out to me that the Marshall Plan might result eventually in a European cooperation which would not be in America's interest because it would make the European states to a large extent independent of the U.S.

According to the above explained plan, the Hungarian government was expected to make a statement in Paris concerning our capacity to give assistance to the rest of the European states and concerning our need in industrial equipment, capital, and raw material for the increase of our economic output. Hungary, like the other participating states, was supposed to get help from the U.S. only for those necessities which could not be covered in Europe.

For Hungary it is of vital importance to take part in an integrated European economy. Irrespective of our serious war damages, it is well known that we were not able to renew the industrial equipment of our factories and mines at least in the last 10 years, and that only the West could supply us with machines and capital, necessary for the modernization of our productive capacities. Soviet Russia needs the very same things; we cannot get from her anything but raw materials and orders for hired work. Stabilization was made possible only with the

help of the gold and other goods returned from the West and through
the strenuous efforts of the Hungarian people. I refer to the last information bulletin prepared by the National Bank to our foreign representatives. This states that the gravest problem of our heavy industry
is the considerable deficit of the factories, which is mainly caused by
the deterioration of our tools of production and the present methods
of production. The same bulletin designates as the cause of the deficit
in coal production the obsolete state of equipment and the lack of important raw materials. The production increases are necessary because
of the reparation and for other reasons as well. This will even more deteriorate the machines and will cause a crisis sooner or later. Our high
prices of production and, in connection therewith, our weak exporting
capacities towards the West, are seriously alarming phenomena.

The renewal of our industrial equipment is all the more important
since we pay the major part of our reparation with industrial products.
Finland and Rumania deliver more raw materials.

The third question cannot be answered at present, because the USA
cannot make a statement before the decisions of the Paris Conference
concerning the methods of giving help to the European states. I shall
make inquiries in this respect with the Economic Counselor of the
American Embassy. Kertész. Code telegram No. 40.

A few days later I sent the following supplementary cipher:

Referring to the third point of your cipher no. 44 and to my cipher
no. 40:

According to information received from the Economic Counselor of
the American Embassy, the government of the USA would like to help
the European states mainly through the UNO. However, the opposition of the Soviet Union may hinder this. In this case, the USA will
give help to those European countries which establish cooperation
among themselves in the sense proposed by Marshall. The USA in no
way intends to interfere with the methods of organization of the economic cooperation of the European states. However, help could not
be given but within the framework of a reasonable economic plan. The
U.S. Congress would not accept a plan which would only consist in the
payments of the bills presented by European countries. This is one of
the reasons why the Americans cannot accept Molotov's proposal.
Kertész. Code telegram No. 48.

After my exchange of telegrams with the government, the foreign
minister ordered me on July 22 to return to Budapest for consultation. I again refused and asked in a cipher telegram rather to be
relieved from my post. Although the consequence of my attitude was
clear to me from the outset of the crisis, it was a traumatic feeling to
sever relations with my fatherland. I had served to the best of my

ability, and I preferred the government cut the umbilical cord.

On the same day, the Soviet ambassador to Italy, Mikhail Kostylev, was my guest for lunch. I explained to him the economic plight of my country and our need for industrial equipment and capital from the United States and called his attention to the fact that the USSR would need the same assistance and thus was in no position to help Hungary. Without American aid it would be difficult for Hungary to pay reparation and fulfill other financial obligations as well, I concluded. In his lengthy reply Kostylev forcefully stated that I was wrong. Real planning and economic integration, he said, could not take place in capitalistic countries. The Marshall Plan could not help Hungary because in the capitalistic world only a few capitalists made huge profits and had no regard for the good of the people. Thus the Marshall Plan would be useful for a few American capitalists because it would create markets, but it could not and would not help the masses of people in European countries. Real planning took place only in Soviet Russia and in countries that were its neighbors, and eventually it would help the people much more effectively than intervention of American capitalists, who decided to find an outlet in Europe for their products and create industrial colonies there. It was difficult to argue with him seriously along these lines. Kostylev was an experienced economist and fully understood Hungary's plight and the problems I raised. He concluded with a significant smile that no matter what our personal opinion might be, we were government officials, and thus we had to obey the orders of our governments. Since his allusion to the official party line was clear, there was no reason to continue the discussion. I simply offered a toast to his good health. It was my last contact with him.

In this period, two Communist emissaries arrived and sought to persuade me to return. I said again that I preferred to be relieved of my post rather than return before the elections. I did not want to hide my feelings and explained that I had undertaken to represent a coalition government; now there were signs that the coalition was to be broken by force. I intended to await the elections, the result of which would show whether there were any possibilities for a real coalition government.

I was able to refuse to return to Hungary because, by fortunate coincidence, my family was abroad. My elder daughter Marianne was in a boarding school in France. My younger daughter Agnes had to finish school in Budapest, and my wife wanted to rent our apartment and arrange other affairs before joining me in Rome in late June. I persuaded her to come for a short visit and decide what sort of personal effects to bring to Rome. Although my residence at the legation was fully furnished, a few paintings and some small objects would have created a more homelike atmosphere. And so Margaret and Agnes arrived in May a few days before the beginning of the political crisis in Budapest. Had they remained at home, it would have been necessary for me to return when recalled, and the course of my life would have taken a different turn. As Providence arranged, my refusal to return to Budapest had become a new departure in our life.

The Hungarian government waited four more weeks before I was relieved of my post on August 20 — not long before the national elections scheduled for August 31 on the basis of a modified electoral law. The government probably suspected that after August 31 I would denounce the result of the elections and many electoral abuses.

While I made farewell visits in Rome, a new foreign minister was appointed in Budapest, Erik Molnár, a member of the Communist party. I left the legation on September 12, and my successor arrived soon afterwards. László Velics, a distinguished senior diplomat in the Hungarian foreign service. I went to see him on September 26 to hand over my letter of resignation from the foreign service. Velics asked me to reconsider my decision, emphasizing that he brought promises from President Tildy and Deputy Prime Minister Rákosi that after my return I would receive an outstanding position corresponding to my rank and later a post abroad. Velics added that he personally was willing to guarantee my safety. I asked him what he would do if something should happen to me. He replied that he would immediately resign.

In separate sessions Velics and his vivacious wife tried to persuade me with a variety of arguments. They referred to my personal relations with Cardinal Mindszenty and other Catholic leaders and argued that it was my patriotic duty to go home and cooperate in the integration of non-Communist forces in Hungary. Mrs. Velics pointed out that her husband was an old reactionary and that he represented the Hungarian people and not the Communists. I replied that I was not a reactionary but that I declined to represent a government unwilling or unable to grant basic human rights and political freedoms to the Hungarian people. Our discussion lasted four hours, during which Velics repeatedly refused to accept my letter of resignation. Referring to our old friendship he asked me to reconsider my decision and to come to see him in three days. In view of the futility of further exchange of opinions I departed and sent him a letter of resignation through one of the secretaries of the legation, Count Andor Esterházy. This was our last contact.

I understood that Velics's ambition in Rome was to bring about an agreement with the Vatican. This is what he told to several of his colleagues. Hungarian authorities apparently made him believe such an agreement was possible. Early in 1949 he was recalled for consultation and not allowed to return to Rome, and later was pensioned. In 1951 during the barbaric mass removals of people not considered useful in the capital of the country, he was deported from Budapest. Shortly afterward he died in the village to which he was sent.

Epilogue

The Hungarian government ordered its diplomats who resigned abroad to return and report to the state security police. The announcement indicated that punishment for refusal to return was deprivation of citizenship and confiscation of property and other belongings in Hungary. Although confrontation with the political police, famous for brutality and torture, was a tempting proposition, to my knowledge nobody accepted the invitation.

Despite a new electoral law that facilitated abuses, during the elections held in August 1947 the Communist party had polled only 22 percent of the votes. After this electoral failure the Communists set out to liquidate the opposition parties and void the parliamentary mandates of opposition members. Many deputies escaped from Hungary to avoid arrest. The Smallholder president of the republic, Zoltan Tildy, was forced to resign, and his son-in-law, Viktor Csornoky, was executed for treason. Single-list elections were held in May 1949, and on August 20 Hungary was declared a People's Republic. Despite the inglorious end of the Hungarian Republic, an important psychological factor remained: the Hungarian people had defeated the Communists in elections and acquired some practice in the ways of democracy under very difficult conditions.

Simultaneous with seizure of political power, the Communists applied their usual methods in banking, industry, commerce, collectivization of agriculture, in religious and cultural affairs. Prominent Catholic and Protestant churchmen were intimidated, forced to resign, or jailed. Joseph Mindszenty's trial and imprisonment for life in February 1949 had particularly strong repercussions.[1] A merger of the Socialist and Communist parties eliminated old-time Socialist leaders and created the Hungarian Workers party[2] in June 1948. As the Cominform rift with Tito became more embittered, a sweeping purge began in the Hungarian Communist party. A former minister of interior and foreign minister, László Rajk, and other potential

252

leaders of a national Communist movement were executed. A large number of Communists were jailed for years and some of them tortured, including János Kádár, a former minister of interior, who was jailed from 1951 to 1954.

Political and social changes in Hungary were directed by a small group of Moscow-trained Communists under the leadership of Mátyás Rákosi. This Soviet-dictated reign of terror lasted until the political "thaw" that followed Stalin's death in 1953. The new masters of the Kremlin realized the necessity of political changes in Hungary, and summoned the leaders of the Hungarian Communist party to Moscow in June, blamed Rákosi for worsening conditions in Hungary, and ordered Imre Nagy to form a government and inaugurate new policies.[3] In July 1953, in his first public address as prime minister, Nagy confessed the overall failure of Communist policies and outlined a "New Course." He ended deportations and emptied concentration camps, freeing Communists and non-Communists alike. Peasants were allowed to leave collective farms, which they did on a large scale. A People's Patriotic Front was established to win popular support. Nagy, however, did not enjoy Moscow's support for long. Rákosi remained first secretary of the Communist party, and by the end of 1954 had undermined Nagy's position in Moscow; he branded the "New Course" as "right-wing deviationism." Nagy had to resign and later was expelled from the Politburo and the Central Committee and, in November 1955, from the Communist pary. His successor, András Hegedüs, by that time Rákosi's puppet, modified the new course by placing emphasis on heavy industry and farm collectivization. But there was no complete reversal, and a measure of criticizm continued within the Communist party.

While the struggle of the pro- and anti-Stalinist groups raged in the Hungarian Communist party, the Hungarian press echoed Moscow's propaganda against colonialism and foreign intervention. The Bandung Conference, Khrushchev's and Bulganin's trip to India, their spectacular reconciliation with Tito and the Declaration of Belgrade, which emphasized every country's right to choose its road to socialism, and above all, Khrushchev's condemnation of some of Stalin's crimes at the Twentieth CPSU Congress, February 24–25, 1956, strengthened the anti-Stalinist and liberalizing trends in Hungary. Opposition to Rákosi became more vocal, and an almost inevitable rapprochement took place between Communist intellectuals and the Hungarian people.

The Central Committee elected a new Politburo, which

rehabilitated several hundred party officials. Hungary's chief prosecutor admitted that hundreds of people had been unjustly jailed
and executed. Communist intellectuals expressed criticism: the
Writer's Union, and later the Petőfi Circle, (authorized as a debating
club in March 1956) and students' organizations, demanded punishment of Rákosi, calling for his resignation and Imre Nagy's return to
office. In one meeting of the Petőfi Circle, Rajk's widow demanded
punishment of her husband's "murderers." Students and writers were
seismographs that reflected the feelings of the people.

Riots in Poland influenced developments in Hungary. In the name
of the Soviet Presidium, Anastas T. Mikoyan demanded Rákosi's
resignation at a meeting of the Central Committee of the Hungarian
Communist party. Rákosi resigned and was replaced by his close collaborator, Gerő. The slow liberalization continued. The government
submitted to questioning by parliament. In September, the
Budapest radio announced an amnesty for Catholic priests. At the
end of the month Gerő joined Marshal Tito and Khrushchev at Yalta
reportedly for talks on loosening Soviet control over Eastern Europe.

It is outside the scope of this epilogue to discuss the dramatic
events in October that led to the glorious days of the Hungarian
revolution. Soviet military intervention united the country almost to
a man. Communist-educated youth, indoctrinated workers, and
soldiers—in whose name the regime ruled—organized and fought a
revolution against tyrants and foreigners who exploited them in the
name of the fatherland of the proletariat. The Communist party,
which numbered almost 900,000, disintegrated. Revolutionary and
Workers Councils sprang up all over the country.

Belatedly the Communist leadership tried to take the wind out of
the revolutionary sails. At a stormy meeting in the early hours of
October 25, the Central Committee appointed Imre Nagy prime
minister and selected a new Politburo and Secretariat. Next day
Soviet tanks escorted Mikoyan and Mikhail A. Suslov to headquarters
of the Communist party. Gerő was then removed as first secretary of
the Party, succeeded by János Kádár.

Apart from the state security police and a hard core of party elite,
Moscow had no support in the country. In the first phase of the
revolution the unorganized freedom fighters stalemated the Soviet
army in Budapest. The center of military resistance was the Kilian
Barracks under command of Colonel Pál Maléter, and the revolt
began to spread outside Budapest.

Nagy moved to the parliament building and formed a new government on October 27 that included Communists and non-Commu-

nists. He dissolved the hated security police and abolished the one-party system, promising free elections and the end of collectivization of agriculture. His actions were supported by Kádár, who called for a new Communist party to defend socialism and democracy, "not by slavishly imitating foreign examples, but by taking a road suitable to the economic and historic characteristics of our country." Mikoyan and Suslov again flew to Budapest seeking compromise. On October 30, the Soviet government declared:

> Having in mind that the further presence of Soviet military units in Hungary could serve as an excuse for further aggravation of the situation, the Soviet Government has given its military command instructions to withdraw the Soviet military units from the city of Budapest as soon as this is considered necessary by the Hungarian Government. At the same time the Soviet Government is prepared to enter into the appropriate negotiations with the Government of the Hungarian People's Republic and other members of the Warsaw Treaty on the question of the presence of Soviet troops on the territory of Hungary.

In harmony with this statement the Soviet army withdrew almost completely from Budapest. Nagy reconstituted his government on October 30 and undertook to form a broad coalition based on parties that had existed in 1945. Non-Communist parties began to reorganize. Alarming reports came that Soviet armored divisions were arriving on Hungarian territory. Nagy energetically protested to the Soviet ambassador, Yuri Andropov, on November 1 and 2. When Andropov professed to have no knowledge of these troop movements, Nagy announced Hungary's withdrawal from the Warsaw Pact, declared Hungary's neutrality with unanimous approval of the Council of Ministers, and asked the United Nations to consider the Hungarian situation. He appealed to Dag Hammarskjöld and requested him "promptly to put on the agenda of the forthcoming General Assembly of the United Nations the question of Hungary's neutrality and the defense of this neutrality by the four great Powers."[4]

Nagy again reconstituted his government on November 3, and the Smallholders, Social Democrats, and Communists obtained three ministers each and the Petőfi (Peasant) party two. Minister of Defense Pál Maléter was a non-party man. The same day, negotiations between representatives of the Hungarian government and the Soviet High Command on withdrawal of Soviet troops from Hungary progressed so satisfactorily that general agreement was reached by afternoon. The Soviet High Command invited Maléter and other representatives of the Hungarian army to Soviet army headquarters near Budapest to discuss the settlement of remaining technical details. Hungarian delegates attended a banquet given them by the Soviet High Command—Maléter even telephoned Nagy to report progress in the talks. The delegates never returned. After dinner they were arrested—reportedly by General Ivan Serov, chief of the Soviet security police.

Simultaneously, Soviet armored divisions began to encircle Budapest, attacking the city in the early hours of November 4. Imre Nagy then delivered his last radio address to the Hungarian people:

> Today at daybreak Soviet troops attacked our capital with the obvious intent of overthrowing the legal democratic Hungarian government. Our troops are in combat. The government is at its post. I notify the people of our country and the entire world of this fact.[5]

Ruthless fighting went on in Budapest for three days, and armed resistance continued in the city and in isolated spots throughout the country for a few more days. Joseph Cardinal Mindszenty, freed during the revolt, sought refuge at the United States legation. Nagy and several of his followers were granted asylum at the Yugoslav embassy.

During the last days of Nagy's premiership the turn of events frightened many Communists, who sensed that Moscow would not tolerate return to a multi-party system and Hungary's withdrawal from the Warsaw Pact. Among them was Kádár, who disappeared and returned to Budapest a few days later in the wake of Soviet tanks as the head of the new Soviet-sponsored government. Although he promised to maintain achievements of the revolution, a policy of terror and repression followed for some years. Most of the atrocities reportedly were committed by Soviet authorities, but Kádár had to assume responsibility. In an agreement with the Yugoslav government he gave a pledge of safe conduct to Imre Nagy and his collaborators who had received asylum at the Yugoslav embassy and stated that the Hungarian government did not desire to punish them for past activities. Nonetheless Soviet soldiers arrested Nagy and his associates when they left the Yugoslav embassy, and in June 1958 the condemnation and execution of Imre Nagy, General Pál Maléter, and several others was announced. The Hungarian people were shocked by the treachery that befell persons who believed in Soviet and Communist pledges.

After a period of repression Kádár's rule relaxed, and in the 1960s he made gestures for reconciliation with the Hungarian people. The public began to appreciate the improved living conditions and some freedom, including trips to Western countries. The key to Kádár's success has been a tripartite compromise by his government, by the Kremlin, and by the Hungarian people.

Systematic appraisal of Kádár's rule over the past quarter of a century and more would need a separate volume, and I limit my comments to a few observations. Kádár realized he could not obtain popular support without liberalization and knew from the outset that without the Kremlin's support no major policy changes, let alone reforms, were feasible. Hence, he has established a solid working relationship with Moscow. Nikita Khrushchev put him in power and was his staunch supporter. After Khrushchev's dismissal Kádár succeeded in winning the confidence of Leonid Brezhnev, who praised Kádár's policy publicly on several occasions.

The Hungarian people had defeated the Communists by ballots in 1945 and vainly tried to regain freedom with bullets in 1956, but then they saw in Kádár's policy a better alternative — the other course being repressive Stalinist rule. All the while, Western notes of protest and United Nations resolutions did not affect Soviet abuses in Hungary. Bitter experience made clear to Hungarians that they could not expect effective Western action for alleviation of their fate.

In the course of his reforms Kádár himself visited West European capitals, and foreign dignitaries visited Budapest. This practice, begun in the mid-1960s, had intensified as the years went by. The idea of Danubian cooperation was revived. Hungarian spokesmen emphasized the common destiny of Danubian nations and the necessity of collaboration. They mentioned Austria, Czechoslovakia, Hungary, and Yugoslavia as a nucleus for a Danubian cooperative structure.[6] Soviet occupation of Czechoslovakia in 1968 put an end to such schemes, which Moscow always opposed.

In domestic affairs one of the most daring steps was introduction of the New Economic Mechanism (NEM) in January 1968. Hungarian specialists recognized that the built-in inefficiency of the centrally directed Communist economic system was the major cause of economic stagnation, and they introduced aspects of market economy, allowing operation of the law of supply and demand and including decentralization and increased responsibility of managers. Central planning was retained, but enterprises obtained autonomy in regard to output, marketing, and sales. For managers, performance became all-important. Progress was not continuous because recession in Western countries had adverse effects on the Hungarian economy and hard liners in the Communist party slowed down the efforts of NEM. But in the late 1970s reforms continued for an accelerated adjustment of the economy to the world market on the basis of a more realistic wage and price structure. Since in the orthodox Communist economy there was little correlation between production cost and subsidized market prices, food and other consumer commodity prices were boosted several times. Higher prices of agricultural products tended to reflect the reality of production costs, discourage domestic sales, and facilitate export. But wages and salaries have increased less than food prices, and this has caused hardship for the population. Yet in Hungary both white and blue collar workers may supplement their income in a flourishing private economy. Moonlighting has been widespread for many years, and in January 1982 economic reform legislation allowed formation of private small business companies. Since industry badly needed modern technology, Hungarian enterprises concluded several hundred joint ventures, co-production, and other cooperation agreements with German, Austrian, American, and other Western firms, mainly in machine-building, light industry, and agriculture-related industries.

Contrary to over-industrialization in most Communist countries, resource-poor Hungary decided to invest in all forms of agriculture. Industrial production methods in large collective farms were important to the success of the Hungarian economy. American machinery and production methods were successfully applied. Major American companies, like International Harvester and the Heston Corporation, closely cooperated with Hungarian enterprises like the Rába Works, a heavy machinery factory in Győr. Co-production and licensing agreements were the usual forms of cooperation. The Organization for Economic Cooperation and Development report of December 1981 noted that "In Hungary, a combination of centralized planning with a high degree of individual economic initiative and market orientation has probably contributed to the success of the agro-food sector." The report concluded that Hungary was likely "to improve its food export position in Eastern and Western markets."

Tiny household plots of collective farmers in Hungary are important in agriculture; they provide not merely for the home market but for export to hard-currency countries and the Soviet Union. Managers of state and collective farms run their operations like businesses. After their shifts, workers rush home to till their home plots. At the Party Congress in February 1981, Brezhnev told delegates that the Communist world should learn from Hungary's agricultural policy.

At the present time in Russia's Europe, Hungary probably enjoys the best reputation in Western countries for achievement in economic and financial matters, intensification of cultural relations with Western countries, liberalization of life as much as possible in a Communist country under Soviet occupation, and, not least, skillful handling of foreign dignitaries in Budapest and abroad. But the social fiber of Hungarian society is in critical condition. The national life has ominous features not noticed by casual visitors.

Because ballots in 1945 and bullets in 1956 failed to bring freedom and independence in the Western sense, Hungarians turned to consumerism. *Carpe diem*. Pleasure became the goal of many people not influenced by higher purpose and the nation's future. Abortions, divorces, alcoholism, and suicide rates have been at record highs for many years, and population growth is stagnant because of the low birth rate. This is a danger signal for a small nation in a strategically important crossroad along a highway of invasion. While more than half of Poland's population is under the age of thirty, Hungary has an aging population, with all its problems and forebodings. Admittedly, living conditions are still difficult. Many dwellings were destroyed in Hungary during the war, especially during the siege of Budapest, and later in the Hungarian revolution. Despite efforts to rebuild, housing remains critically short, and this situation has far-reaching social consequences for young couples unable to find decent housing. Privileged people receive housing within a short time, while others have to wait ten years or more for a modest home. As a result of rapid industrialization and introduction of industrial production methods in collective farms, the influx to cities from villages has accelerated and made the housing crisis worse. Government measures have improved the situation of working mothers, giving benefits especially to families with more than two children; but without a change in the moral climate the long-range predicaments of the nation will not change. Children are conspicuously absent even in affluent families. When there is a choice between a child and an automobile, or a trip abroad, the child loses. Churches do not have enough authority and cannot be effective in moral matters as long as their primary obligation is to give all-out support to official policies. Yet individuals and nations do not live by bread alone. There are signs in Hungary in recent years that consumerism no longer satisfies some groups of young people. This trend is perhaps a sign of a better future for the Hungarian nation.

Irrespective of success or failure of domestic policies, Hungary's political predicament remains. Soviet troops in Hungary are not conspicuous; but the government, the army, and security forces at home and intelligence abroad remain under Soviet control. It is paradoxical and symbolic that the sophisticated military fortifications along Hungary's western border have remained, although visa requirements with neutral Austria were dropped. The future is uncertain because of aging leadership in Moscow and Budapest. The Kremlin tolerated reforms in Hungary because Kádár carefully consulted Moscow in advance. Khrushchev, Brezhnev, and Andropov recognized and openly praised Hungary's achievements, especially in agriculture. But Kádár's success has been a unique phenomenon in Eastern Europe, and Hungarians anxiously ask the question; will Kádárism survive Kádár? The Soviet Politbureau and Kádár's successors will determine freedom in politics and economics, in culture and religion. Hungarian authorities are still controlled by Moscow, partly through intergovernmental relations, partly through Communist party channels and the ubiquitous KGB.

In the long haul of history the captive status of the East European countries is bound to change. The USSR is the last multinational imperialistic empire, and in many ways it is a reactionary Great Power. It is not the wave of the future, as people suggested in 1917 and after. Recently Jean-Baptiste Duroselle's seminal book, *tout Empire périra*,[7] reminded that all empires in the past perished and will do so in the future. Yet the declining period of a militarily strong empire could be uncomfortable for subjugated people; disgruntled and frightened rulers are increasingly inclined to use force to prolong their domination. An outright collapse of Russia would create enormous problems, although a dissolution of the Soviet Empire would be in the interest of the world community, and it may take place under unforeseen and unsuspected circumstances. Rapid growth of non-Slavic people in the USSR might lead to internal tension and increasing discrimination. Disregard of elementary needs and interests of large segments of the population combined possibly with competition of antagonistic power groups might cause additional problems. Such developments might expedite change. Although Western diplomacy could cautiously support liberalizing trends and reasonable transformations in the USSR, in reality Western states have seldom used their superior technology and economic power for such purposes. Sharing of Western know-how has helped time and again the growth of Russian industrial and military strength, and Soviet intelligence has carried out many successful operations in this area. Trade and reasonable financial arrangements could be mutually advantageous between Western countries and Eastern Europe. But it should not be a one-way street as it often was during the cozy period of detente and especially in the late 1970s. Transfer of high technology and financial transactions facilitated the gigantic Soviet armament developments both in the conventional and atomic fields and in outer space. At the same time Moscow engaged in expansive and aggressive actions on a global scale.

All the while the external debt of East European states increased rapidly. After 1973, OPEC countries deposited large sums in Western banks, which were eager to lend them in a profitable, safe manner. The credit-worthiness of Communist countries was taken for granted, and Western governments guaranteed many loans. Normal banking procedure would have required examination of the general economy and management of countries soliciting loans, scrutiny of specific projects, and establishment of conditions for loans. Under easy-going banking practices the USSR and other East European countries accumulated approximately $80 billion loans. In most East European states debts to Western banks and governments increased far more than their export potential to Western countries. In this, Hungary has been a notable exception; despite a large foreign debt, it is still considered credit-worthy abroad.

There are other complicating factors in East-West relations. As a result of the Second World War the overlord of the East European countries became a Great Power with largely non-European political and cultural traditions. While most East European nations had participated for ten centuries in West European political and intellectual developments, Russia did not. Greek Orthodox Christianity formed a link with the Eastern Roman Empire, and after the fall of Constantinople the Russians considered Moscow a "Third Rome," that is, the center of true Christianity. In the thirteenth century the Tartar occupation severed Russia's political and cultural relations with the West, and later the Russians lived under the authoritarian rule of the Csars. Even if some of them, like Peter the Great or Catherine the Great, were interested in European industrial development or intellectual currents, such interests did not affect authoritarian rule in Russia. In the twentieth century efforts were made to introduce a parliamentary system, and in 1917 the Kerensky government held nation-wide elections on a multi-party basis. But the Bolsheviks seized power and by military force dissolved the democratically elected parliament in which Communist deputies formed a minority. The basis of their power has become a doctrine, not popular approval. Because of this background, any substantial reorganization of the Soviet Union would be a *pas dans l'inconnue*. Russia did not participate in the major Western intellectual currents, such as the Renaissance, Reformation, Counter-Reformation or the Enlightenment and understood few of the ideas of the American and French revolutions. The Russian people did not have experience with a free government. The authoritarian rule of the Csars was followed by a totalitarian dictatorship. Religious zeal of a "Third Rome" was replaced by a Communist doctrine of global aspirations. The Bolsheviks liquidated the Western-oriented intellectuals and social classes.

Although Lenin and Stalin, like Hitler and Mao, announced clearly what they wanted to accomplish, Western statesmen did not believe what the dictators said — it seemed sheer propaganda. In our time the shortcomings of Communist political and economic systems have become clear in widely separated regions of the world and the attraction of freedom has been nearly ubiquitous, although in some cases blunders of Western diplomacy have annulled the appeals of democratic systems. In the era of radio and other means of mass communication, dictatorships cannot hide the facts of life forever. In the Soviet Union people have little influence on allocation of resources; decisions are made by a handful of persons, usually members of the politburo; production of consumer goods has been neglected, and enormous quantities of armament, both conventional and atomic, have been produced. Moscow has established military bases in far-away regions such as Cuba and countries in Asia and Africa. But people in Communist countries and the Third World cannot eat tanks, missiles, and fighter planes — the major Soviet export items, other than raw materials.

In case of political upheaval in Russia's Europe there would be a general desire for a more humane, cooperative, and productive society in terms of availability of consumer goods and, above all, respect for human rights and fundamental freedom. Under favorable political conditions Eastern Europe could be reorganized in the spirit of the Atlantic Charter and other declarations approved by the principal victorious powers during the Second World War. If the principle of self-determination would be applied, subjugated nations might have several options. One would be a democratic Danubian federation or a larger East European unit. Alternatives have been proposed, but in a fluid situation much would depend on the political acumen and vision of leaders of the East European countries.

The economy of this borderland between East and West needs a massive amount of industrial raw materials and sources of energy from Russia and modern technology from Western states. A neutral East European federation hence could contribute to a cooperative state system, from the Atlantic and the Mediterranean to the Urals and beyond.

Such developments are in the clouds of an uncertain future. Under existing conditions, national character, humanity, stamina, and intelligence will play a role in East European countries. Ability to maneuver will depend on world politics, primarily on the Kremlin's policy and the interaction of three power centers: Washington , Moscow, and the Western European states. In the immediate future, Hungary and the other East European countries will have to muddle through, as best they can, while not losing hope for a better future.

This is a melancholy conclusion because the aspiration of people associated with me since the 1930s was the creation of a democratic federation in Eastern Europe. In this union the centrally located Hungarian people could have cooperated constructively with all neighbors. Such plans were swept away by the Second World War and postwar peacemaking. But it is a consolation and encouragement that the Hungarian nation showed resolve, resistance, and *joie de vivre* amidst apocalyptic events.

Generations of East Europeans fought and refought battles for their freedom. The Hungarian revolutions of 1848–49 and 1956 showed that a small nation cannot prevail against the overwhelming military might of Great Powers. Yet one should not lose faith in the just cause of people living in the borderland between Central Europe and Russia. If leaders of these nations believe in the righteous cause of a cooperative Eastern Europe, some unexpected turn of history might bring opportunity for its realization. People associated with me did not lose faith during difficult years, and I hope that such faith will guide the leaders of East European countries long after I and my contemporaries have passed on.

Notes

Introduction

1. Jean-Baptist Duroselle, *La Décadence: 1932-1939* (Paris: Imprimerie Nationale, 1979) and *L'Abîme: 1939-1945* (Paris: Imprimerie Nationale, 1982).
2. James F. Byrnes, *Speaking Frankly* (New York: Harper and Brothers, 1947), pp. 70-72.
3. *Journal of Central European Affairs* 8 (1948): 317-19.

1. Between Scylla and Charybdis: 1944-1945

1. This conversation took place in Washington on March 14, 1943. Robert E. Sherwood, *Roosevelt and Hopkins* (New York: Harper and Brothers, 1948), p.711.
2. John Pelenyi, "The Secret Plan for a Hungarian Government in the West at the Outbreak of World War II," *Journal of Modern History*, 36 (1964): 170-77.

2. Postwar Hungary

1. *The Christian Science Monitor*, October 9, 1945. Cf. *New York Herald Tribune*, November 6, 1945; *Journal de Genève*, November 9, 1945.
2. Ferenc Nagy, *The Struggle Behind the Iron Curtain* (New York: Macmillan, 1948), p. 154.
3. Cf. Oscar Jaszi, "The Choices in Hungary," *Foreign Affairs* 24 (1946): 462. Jaszi points out the "that Small Landholders' Party is not reactionary, not even conservative; it is a progressive party in favor of social and cultural reforms."
4. H.F.A. Schoenfeld, "Soviet Imperialism in Hungary," *Foreign Affairs* 26 (1947-48): 560
5. Nagy, *Struggle Behind the Iron Curtain*, p. 72.

6. Jaszi, "Choices in Hungary," p. 454.

7. Ibid., pp. 457-58.

8. Joseph Révai, "On the Character of Our People's Democracy." The original article appeared in the *Társadalmi Szemle* (Budapest, March-April 1949). An English translation of the article was published in *Foreign Affairs* 28 (1949): 143-52.

9. The ACC for Italy was established in November 1943 and abolished on January 31, 1947. See *The Department of State Bulletin* (hereafter *Bulletin*) 11 (1944): 137-38, and 16 (1947): 1258.

10. For the debate on the Hungarian reparation at the peace negotiations, see *Foreign Relations of the United States* (hereafter *FRUS*), 1946, 3: 236-37, 626-27, 636-38. *FRUS* 1946, 2: 1294. Cf. *Bulletin*, 15 (1946): 746-48.

11. *Bulletin* 15 (1946): 394-95.

12. For the Soviet-American exchange of notes, see ibid., pp. 229-32, 263-65, 638-39.

13. After consolidation of Communist power these facades were no longer needed. In 1952 Moscow sold sixty-nine Soviet enterprises to Hungary, and in November 1954 even the Soviet Commercial and Industrial Bank and the Soviet share in the joint companies.

14. *Bulletin* 15 (1946): 638, and 16 (1947): 341. Of the total credit authorized for Hungary by the Surplus Property Administration, over 15 million dollars had not been utilized when the U.S. government suspended the execution of the surplus property credit agreement on June 2, 1947, after the Communist coup in Hungary. *Bulletin* 16 (1947): 1166.

15. *Speaking Frankly*, p. 255.

16. *FRUS* 1945, 3: 798-952; 1946, 6: 250-373; 1947: 260-401. Additional material is available in the National Archives. Cf. Louis Mark, Jr. "The View From Hungary," *Witnesses to the Origins of the Cold War*, ed., Thomas T. Hammond (Seattle: University of Washington Press, 1982), pp. 186-209; Hugh De Santis, *The Diplomacy of Silence* (Chicago: The University of Chicago Press, 1980), pp. 141-45, 158-60, 184-85, 194, 208.

17. For the text of the memorandum, see Stephen D. Kertesz, *Diplomacy in a Whirlpool: Hungary between Nazi Germany and Soviet Russia* (Notre Dame, Ind.: University of Notre Dame Press, 1953), pp. 252-59.

18. As the American minister Schoenfeld noted: "Orders had been given by the Soviet Chairman of the Allied Control Commission that communication between the representatives of the Western allies and the Hungarian authorities must be channeled through himself." Schoenfeld, "Soviet Imperialism," 555.

19. *FRUS* 1946, 6: 267-69.

20. Ibid., pp. 289-90.

21. *FRUS* 1946, 6: 297-98, 315-17.

22. See below, p. 201.

23. For Harriman's report See Box 96, R.G. 43, National Archives.

24. I visited Mindszenty at his headquarters in Buda a few times, and in November 1946 his secretary came to my office with the message that the cardinal wanted to see me urgently in the sacristy of the Basilica. I went immediately, and he showed me the rough draft of a telegram to be sent to Cardinal Spellman in New York and Cardinal Griffin in London. The telegram described the plight of Hungarians who had been deported from Slovakia to districts of Sudeten Germans who had been transferred. Mindszenty asked the cardinals to inform their foreign offices of the deportations and do everything in their power to stop these inhuman actions. We discussed the matter, and I took the text with me and gave it to our English translators. Then I made a confidential file of the case and dispatched the cables to the American and English cardinals. Mindszenty gave the text to a news agency. I circulated the file in the Foreign Ministry and criticism was expressed because of my action. I replied that the government must be satisfied this time; it was one of the rare occasions when Mindszenty supported the official policy. See below, pp. 156 ff.

25. *FRUS* 1946, 6: 361.

3. The Great Powers: 1939-1945

1. Sumner Welles, *Seven Decisions That Shaped History* (New York: Harper and Brothers, 1951), p. 216.

2. Omar N. Bradley, *A Soldier's Story* (New York: Henry Holt, 1951), p. 536.

3. Karl von Clausewitz, *War, Politics and Power* (Chicago: Gateway Edition, 1962), pp. 261-62.

4. Charles E. Bohlen, *Witness to History 1929-1969* (New York: W. W. Norton, 1973), p. 175.

5. *Correspondence between Franklin D. Roosevelt and William C. Bullitt*, Orville H. Bullett, ed. Intro. George F. Kennan (Boston: Houghton Mifflin, 1972), p. 599. For Bullitt's several memoranda to Roosevelt see ibid., pp. 571-600.

6. Harley A. Notter, *Postwar Foreign Policy Preparation 1939-1945* (Washington: Department of State, 1949).

7. Senate Committee on Foreign Relations, *Nomination of Charles E. Bohlen to be United States Ambassador to the Union of Soviet Socialist Republics*, 83d Cong., 1st sess., 1953, pp. 2, 7. Later he stated: "We in the State Department felt very strongly about the fact that during the war what I would say the political arm of the United States was not involved to the extent it should be." Ibid., p. 50

8. Winston S. Churchill, *The Grand Alliance* (Boston: Houghton Mifflin, 1950), pp. 644-98. See also Sherwood, *Roosevelt and Hopkins*, pp. 439-78.

9. Churchill, *The Grand Alliance*, pp. 628-31. Cf. *The Memoirs of Cordell Hull*, vol. 2 (New York: Macmillan, 1948), pp. 1165-74.

10. Winston S. Churchill, *The Hinge of Fate* (Boston: Houghton Mifflin, 1950), pp. 326-27.

11. Ibid., pp. 446-48. See also Arthur Bryant, *The Turn of the Tide* (Garden City, N.Y.: Doubleday, 1957), pp. 339-47; Dwight D. Eisenhower, *Crusade in Europe* (Garden City, N.Y.: Doubleday, 1948), pp. 65-73.

12. Churchill, *The Grand Alliance*, pp. 659-61 and *The Hinge of Fate*, pp. 600ff. Cf. Louis Broad, *The War that Churchill Waged* (London: Hutchinson, 1960); Trumbull Higgins, *Winston Churchill and the Second Front* (New York: Oxford Press, 1957). For a comprehensive analysis of Churchill's wartime policy, see Kenneth W. Thompson, *Winston Churchill's Worldview* (Baton Rouge, La.: Louisiana University Press, 1983).

13. Philip E. Mosely, *The Kremlin in World Politics* (New York: Vintage Books, 1960), p. 205.

14. Robert Murphy, *Diplomat among Warriors* (Garden City, N.Y.: Doubleday, 1964), p. 187. Cf. Norman Kogan, *Italy and the Allies* (Cambridge, Mass.: Harvard University Press, 1956); H. Stuart Hughes, *The United States and Italy*, rev. ed. (Cambridge, Mass.: Harvard University Press, 1965).

15. Lack of political preparations, confusion, and antagonism that on some important occasions dominated inter-Allied relations during the Mediterranean campaign are well characterized in the memoirs of General Eisenhower's American and British political advisors, Macmillan and Murphy, who coordinated diplomacy with Allied military operations under most difficult conditions. Harold Macmillan, *The Blast of War, 1939-1945* (New York: Harper and Row, 1968); Murphy, *Diplomat among Warriors*.

16. *Stalin's Correspondence with Roosevelt and Truman 1941-1945* (New York: Capricorn Books, 1965), pp. 84-86.

17. Robert V. Gannon, *The Cardinal Spellman Story* (Garden City, N.Y.: Doubleday, 1962). See Spellman's memorandum of his conversation with Roosevelt on September 2 and 3, 1943, pp. 222-25.

18. In a Russian village, Katyn, in the Smolensk region, the corpses of about 4,400 Polish officers were discovered by German authorities who alleged that the officers were executed by the Soviets in 1940. Without admitting the German accusation, the Polish government asked for an investigation by the Red Cross. Moscow used the Polish request as a pretext to break off diplomatic relations with the Polish government in London. The Soviet guilt in this mass murder was proven without any doubt. See J.K. Zawodny, *Death in the Forest — The Story of the Katyn Forest Massacre* (Notre Dame, Ind.: University of Notre Dame Press, 1962). Cf. Joseph Mackiewics, *The Katyn Wood Murders* (London: Hollis & Carter, 1951); Louis FitzGibbon, *Katyn* (New York: Charles Scribner's Sons, 1971); *Hearings before the Select Committee to conduct an Investigation of the Facts,*

Evidence and Circumstances of the Katyn Forest Massacre, 82d Cong., 1952.

19. For the papers, reports of meetings, protocols, and documents of the Tripartite Conference in Moscow, see *FRUS* 1943, 1: 513-781.

20. Ibid., pp. 638-39, 679-80, 701, 736-37, 762-63.

21. Vojtech Mastny, "The Beneš-Stalin-Molotov Conversations in December 1943: New Documents," *Jahrbücher für Geschichte Osteuropas* (1972): 371. Cf. Stephen Borsody, *The Tragedy of Central Europe* (New York: Colliers Books, 1962), pp. 230-41.

22. Joseph C. Grew, acting secretary of state pointed out in his letter to the secretary of war, Henry L. Stimson, on February 28, 1945, that the EAC had recommended to their governments only three documents: texts of Unconditional Surrender of Germany; protocol between the governments of the United States, the United Kingdom, and the Soviet Union on the zones of Occupation in Germany and the Administration of "Greater Berlin"; agreement between the three governments on Control Machinery in Germany. On July 4, 1945, the EAC approved an agreement between the three governments and the Provisional Government of the French Republic on Control Machinery in Austria. France had been admitted to membership in the EAC in November 1944. See for EAC material, Box 10, SWNCC, National Archives. For EAC activities see Lord Strang, *Home and Abroad* (London: Andre Deutsch, 1956), pp. 199-225; George F. Kennan, "The European Advisory Commission," *Memoirs 1925-1950* (Boston: Little, Brown, 1967), pp. 164-87; A. Roshchin, "Postwar Settlement in Europe," *International Affairs* (1978): 102-14. For the organization and scope of activities of the EAC in 1944, see *FRUS* 1944, 1: 1-483. The conclusive negotiations of surrender terms for Hungary, Rumania, Bulgaria, and Finland were held outside the EAC. It was the position of the United States government that the armistice terms for these countries were proper subjects for consideration by the EAC. But because of Soviet opposition, the EAC discussed only the Bulgarian surrender terms in September and October 1944. Ibid., pp. 39-40. For the work of the EAC in 1945, its final report and dissolution by the Potsdam Conference, see *FRUS* 1945, 3: 1-558.

23. Isaac Deutscher, *Stalin, A Political Biography*, 2d, ed. (New York: Oxford University Press, 1967), p. 512.

24. John R. Deane, *The Strange Alliance* (New York: Viking Press, 1947), p. 89.

25. For details see *From Major Jordan's Diaries* (New York: Harcourt, Brace, 1952).

26. Vojtech Mastny, *Russia's Road to the Cold War* (New York: Columbia University Press, 1979), pp. 73-85; idem, "Stalin and the Prospects of a Separate Peace in World War II," *The American Historical Reveiw* 77 (1972): 1365-88; Alexander Fischer, *Sowjetische Deutschlandpolitik im Zweiten Weltkrieg* (Stuttgart, 1975); William Stevenson, *A Man Called Intrepid* (New York, 1976), p. 381. According to B.A. Liddell Hart, "Ribbentrop proposed as a condition of peace that Russia's frontier should run along

the Dnieper, while Molotov would not consider anything less than the restoration of her original frontier." *History of the Second World War* (New York, 1971), p. 488.

27. Bohlen, *Witness to History*, pp. 140-41. Roosevelt explained later that he succeeded to establish personal relations with Stalin by teasing Churchill "about his Britishness, about John Bull, about his cigars, about his habits." Francis Perkins, *The Roosevelt I Knew* (New York: Viking, 1946), pp. 83-85.

28. Bohlen, *Witness to History*, pp. 136, 138-39.

29. *Tehran, Yalta, Potsdam — The Soviet Protocols*, ed., Robert Beitzell (Academic International, 1970); *Teheran, Jalta, Potsdam — Die sowjetetischen Protokolle von den Kriegskonferenzen der "Grossen Drei,"* ed., Alexander Fischer (Köln: Verlag Wissenschaft und Politik, 1968).

30. Hopkins scribbled a note to Admiral King: "Who is promoting that Adriatic business that the President continually returns to?" To which King replied, "As far as I know it is his own idea. Certainly nothing could be farther from the United States Chiefs of Staff." Sherwood, *Roosevelt and Hopkins*, p. 780.

31. Bohlen, *Witness to History*, pp. 151-52.

32. *FRUS* 1943 "Conferences at Cairo and Tehran": 600-3. For discussion on dismemberment of Germany at Allied negotiations from Yalta to Potsdam, see Mosely, *The Kremlin in World Politics*, pp. 131-54.

33. *Correspondence between Franklin D. Roosevelt and William C. Bullitt*, Bullitt, ed., p. 604.

34. Winston S. Churchill, *Triumph and Tragedy* (Boston: Houghton Mifflin, 1953), p. 59.

35. *Stalin's Correspondence with Churchill and Attlee 1941-1945* (New York: Capricorn Books, 1965), p. 256.

36. Churchill, *Triumph and Tragedy*, pp. 226-27.

37. Albert Resis wrote a comprehensive article on this subject, "The Churchill-Stalin Percentage Agreement on the Balkans," *American Historical Review* (April 1978): 368-87. Cf. Sir Llewellyn Woodward, *British Foreign Policy in the Second World War*, vol. 3 (London, 1971), pp. 149-53; Daniel Yergen, *Shattered Peace* (Boston, 1977, pp. 58-61; Geir Lundestad, *The American Non-Policy Towards Eastern Europe 1943-1947* (New York: Humanities, 1975), pp. 89-92, Joseph M. Siracusa, "The Night Stalin and Churchill Divided Europe, " *The Review of Politics* 43 (July 1981): 381-409.

38. *The Reckoning, the Memoirs of Anthony Eden, Earl of Avon* (Boston: Houghton Mifflin, 1965), p. 560. Cf. Elisabeth Barker, *British Policy in South-East Europe in the Second World War* (New York: Barnes and Noble, 1976), pp. 140-47, 220-22.

39. For correspondence on the attempts of the United States and British governments to furnish assistance to the Polish forces, and their unsuccessful attempts to secure the helpful participation of the Soviet government, see

FRUS 1944, 3: 1372-98. Cf. Stefan Korbonski, *Fighting Warsaw* (London: George Allen and Unwin, 1956); J. K. Zawodny, *Nothing but Honour— The Story of the Warsaw Uprising, 1944* (Stanford, Ca.: Hoover Institution Press, 1978); Jan M. Ciechanowski, *The Warsaw Rising of 1944* (Cambridge: Cambridge University Press, 1974).

40. Churchill, *Triumph and Tragedy*, pp. 278-80.

41. *FRUS* 1945 "Conferences at Malta and Yalta." The decision-making process of the Yalta Conference was scrutinized by Diane S. Clemens, *Yalta* (New York: Oxford University Press, 1970).

42. For reasons of Roosevelt's rejection of the Emergency High Commission, see Notter, *Postwar Foreign Policy Preparation*, p. 394.

43. Churchill, *Triumph and Tragedy*, pp. 507-9. Cf. Mosely, *The Kremlin in World Politics*, 155-88.

44. Churchill, *Triumph and Tragedy*, p. 510.

45. Eden, *The Reckoning*, p. 595.

46. *Roosevelt and Churchill—Their Secret Wartime Correspondence*, ed. Francis L. Loewenheim, Harold D. Langley, and Manfred Jonas (New York: Saturday Review Press, E.P. Dutton, 1975); Joseph P. Lash, *Roosevelt and Churchill 1939-1941* (New York: W.W. Norton, 1976).

47. Elliott Roosevelt, *As He Saw It* (New Yorkk: Duell, Sloan and Pearce, 1946), p. 186.

48. *Off the Record—The Private Papers of Harry S. Truman*, ed. Robert H. Ferrell (New York: Harper and Row, 1980), p. 16.

49. Bohlen, *Witness to History*, p. 222.

50. Marquis Childs, *Witness to Power* (New York: McGraw-Hill, 1975), p. 54.

51. Robert H. Ferrell, *George C. Marshall as Secretary of State, 1947-1949* (New York: Cooper Square Publishers, 1960), pp. 72-73.

52. Raymond J. Sontag, "The Democracies and the Dictators since 1938," *Proceedings of the American Philosophical Society*, vol. 98, no. 5 (October 1954): 313.

53. See for details Jim Bishop, *FDR's Last Year* (New York: William Morrow, 1974); *Churchill Taken from the Diaries of Lord Moran* (Boston: Houghton Mifflin, 1966).

54. According to American military estimates the grand design against Japan would involve about 5,000,000 men, the operations might cost over a million casualties, and fighting would not end until the latter part of 1946, at the earliest. It was thought that battles in Manchuria between the Soviet and Japanese armies would save many American lives. Cf. Henry L. Stimson and McGeorge Bundy, *On Active Service in Peace and War* (New York: Harper and Brothers, 1948), p. 619. Admiral Zacharias commented: "It was an unfortunate and altogether wrong estimate, its authors being deceived by a purely military and quantitative evaluation of the enemy, a treacherous trap into which even the greatest military leaders are likely to fall occassionally." Ellis M. Zacharias, *Behind Closed Doors* (New York: G.

P. Putnam's Sons, 1950), p. 56.

55. John J. McCloy, *The Challenge to American Foreign Policy* (Cambridge, Mass.: Harvard University Press, 1953), p. 44.

4. Challenging the Inevitable

1. For the English translation of Bakach-Bessenyey's report of August 28, 1943, see Miklós Kállay, "Come Over," *The Hungarian Quarterly* (April-July 1962): 7-11.

2. For Hungary's wartime contacts and negotiations with Britain and the United States, see C. A. Macartney, *October Fifteenth, A History of Modern Hungary, 1929-1945*, 2 vols., (Edinburgh: Edinburgh University Press, 1961); Antal Ullein-Revicky, *Guerre Allemande, Paix Russe: le Drame Hongrois* (Neuchâtel, 1947); Nicholas Kallay, *Hungarian Premier* (New York: Columbia University Press, 1954); Kertesz, *Diplomacy in a Whirlpool*; Gyula Juhász, *Magyar-brit titkos tárgyalások 1943-ban* (Hungarian-British Secret Negotiations in 1943) (Budapest: Kossuth könyvkiadó, 1978); Gyula Juhász, *Hungarian Foreign Policy 1919-1945* (Budapest: Akadémiai Kiadó, 1979); Woodward, *British Foreign Policy in the Second World War*, pp. 141-46. For peace-feeler approaches from the Axis nations and the American, British, and Soviet reactions to them, see *FRUS 1943*, 1: 484-512. Cf. *FRUS* 1943, 3: 633-34.

3. Florimond Duke, *Name, Rank and Serial Number* (New York: Meredith Press, 1969).

4. The members of the committee included: Gusztáv Gratz, former foreign minister; Lipót Baranyay and Arthur Kárász, both former presidents of the Hungarian National Bank; Izsó Ferenczi, former secretary of state in the Ministry of Commerce; István Vásárhelyi, secretary of state in the Ministry of Finance; Loránd D. Schweng, special economic adviser, former secretary of state in the Ministry of Finance; and József Judik, head of the research division of the National Bank.

5. See excerpts of this memorandum in Kertesz, *Diplomacy in a Whirlpool*, pp. 266-69.

6. For a short version of these data and argumentation see *La Hongrie et la Conférence de Paris*, vol. 1 (Budapest: Hungarian Ministry of Foreign Affairs, 1947), pp. 63-107.

7. *FRUS* 1946, 6: 275. For a detailed account of United States foreign policy at the time, see Lundestad, *The American Non-Policy Toward Eastern Europe*.

8. *FRUS* 1943, 3: 23. Cf. Mastny, "The Beneš-Stalin-Molotov Conversations in December 1943: New Documents, " pp. 372-73, 382, 401.

9. For its text see, *La Hongrie et la Conférence de Paris*, vol. 1, pp. 1-6.

10. Article 53 of the Hague Convention on the Laws and Customs of War on Land provided that, "An army of occupation can only take posses-

sion of cash, funds, and realizable securities which are strictly the property of the State, depots of arms, means of transport, stores and supplies, and, generally all movable property belonging to the state which may be used for the operation of the war."

11. The armistice division of the Foreign Ministry in May, June, and July, 1945, repeatedly sent notes with similar contents to the ACC. The note of May 25 enumerated 28 factories which were dismantled and removed but were not included in the reparations deliveries. Other notes completed the list and described in detail the various confiscatory actions and other abuses of the Soviet army and asked for restitution and remedies. The ACC refused to negotiate on such matters and Hungary was even made responsible to foreign countries for confiscations and damages caused by the Soviet army. For example, a British note of November 19, 1945, in reply to a memorandum of the Hungarian Foreign Ministry, stated that "all loss or damage to British rights, interests and property in Hungary, *regardless of cause*, is to be reinstated under the terms of Article 13 of the Armistice."

12. *La Hongrie et la Conférence de Paris*, vol. 1, pp. 7-14. For the English text see Kertesz, *Diplomacy in a Whirlpool*, pp. 262-66.

13. Similar commissions were established later between France and the Federal Republic of Germany, and between Poland and the FRG; both commissions produced exemplary results.

14. *La Hongrie et la Conférence de Paris*, vol. 1, pp. 15-20.

15. Ibid., pp. 21-36.

16. The Hungarian representative, foreign minister of the, by then, completely Communist-dominated Hungarian government, did not reply other than by his hundred percent support of the Soviet position, which in fact denied that freedom of navigation for which the Hungarian government had dared to raise its voice three years before. This American statement was made on August 13, 1948. *Bulletin* (1948): 283.

17. For the complete text of the memorandum, see Kertesz, *Diplomacy in a Whirlpool*, pp. 266-69.

18. Cf. Ferenc Nagy, *Struggle Behind the Iron Curtain*, pp. 238-39.

19. *La Hongrie et la Conférence de Paris*, vol. 1, pp. 40-50.

20. Ibid., pp. 51-55.

21. Ibid., pp. 72-107.

22. See, *Népszava*, February 24, March 3, 10, and 17, 1946.

23. The economic adviser was Eugene Rácz who at that time was a nonparty man. Later when he was appointed minister of finance, he entered the Smallholder party.

24. For description of the delegation's Moscow trip and its aftermath, see Nagy, *Struggle Behind the Iron Curtain*, pp. 204-19.

25. Actually Hungarian manpower and Hungarian experts were used for this work performed under the direction of the Red Army. Some of the railroad lines for which Hungary was required to pay were situated *in the neighboring countries*. Cf. Nagy, *Struggle Behind the Iron Curtain*, p. 208.

26. For details see below, pp. 129-33.

5. Territorial and Nationality Problems

1. *FRUS* 1944 "The Second Quebec Conference," p. 215.

2. Ibid., pp. 214-15.

3. Ibid., p. 215.

4. *FRUS* 1945 "The Conference at Malta and Yalta," p. 243.

5. Ibid.

6. Ibid., p. 244.

7. Ibid., p. 245.

8. Ibid., p. 246.

9. Ibid., p. 248.

10. See for details, *Hungary and the Conference of Paris* (Budapest, 1947), vol. 4, p. vii, n. 2.

11. "Policy Toward Liberated States: Czechoslovakia," Notter File Box 143, National Archives, p.7.

12. Ibid.

13. Ibid., p. 8.

14. According to the American proposal compact masses of Magyar populations and towns of Szabadka, Zenta, Topolya, and Magyarkanizsa would have remained in Hungary. Cf. Francis Deak, *Hungary at the Paris Peace Conference* (New York: Columbia University Press, 1942), pp. 28-29 and Map 2 at the end of the volume.

15. Hitler had summoned the Hungarian minister to Germany on the day following the night of the putsch and had offered Hungary "the most enticing pieces of Yugoslav territory." He even dangled Fiume—which incidentally was Italian territory—before the Hungarians. *The Von Hassell Diaries* (Garden City, N.Y.: Doubleday, 1947), p. 183.

16. *Trial of the Major War Criminals Before the International Military Tribunal*, vol. 7 (Nuremberg, 1947), p. 257.

17. Ibid., p. 331.

18. Ibid., pp. 331-33.

19. One of the best English experts on Danubian Europe summed up Teleki's activities in the following way: "Teleki had the terrible task of steering Hungary through the first two years of the Second World War. Although Central Europe was now completely dominated by Germany, and although Hungary had received two pieces of territory from her neighbors as a German present, Teleki fought stubbornly to retain some measure of independence for his country. His efforts compare favorably with those of Roumania in the same period. When resistance was no longer possible and his own Regent and General Staff betrayed him, Teleki took the classical way out." Hugh Seton-Watson, *Eastern Europe Between the Wars 1918-1941* (Cambridge: The University Press, 1945), p. 196.

20. Churchill, *The Grand Alliance*, p. 168. For Teleki's way of thinking during the critical events in 1940 and 1941, see Richard V. Burks, "Two Teleki Letters", *Journal of Central European Affairs*, 7 (1947), 68-73. Cf. Loránt Tilkovszky, *Teleki Pál, Legenda es Valóság* (Legend and Reality) (Budapest, 1969).

21. After the war the American authorities extradited Bárdossy to the new Hungarian regime. He was sentenced to death by the People's Court in Budapest and was executed.

22. Hungarian troops occupied the Bácska, the triangle of Baranya and two small territories along the river Mura. The size of these areas was 11,475 square kilometers, with a mixed population of about one million. More than one third, the largest segment of the population, was Hungarian, and the rest Serbs, Germans, Croats, Rumanians, and other nationalities.

23. See below, pp. 219-20.

6. The Fate of Transylvania

1. Excerpts from Kristóffy's report of July 11, 1940. (113/pol.-1940).

2. *Documents on German Foreign Policy*, July 1940, No. 69, p. 76. For a digest of reports of Hungarian envoys from Moscow see Andor Gellért, "Magyar diplomaták Moszkvában, 1934-1941" (Hungarian Diplomats in Moscow, 1934-1941) *Uj Látóhatár*, 26 (February, 1975): 17-37.

3. *The Ciano Diaries 1939-1943*, ed. Hugh Gibson (Garden City, N.Y.: Doubleday, 1946), December 23, 1939.

4. Ibid., January 6-7, 1940.

5. Csáky requested Ciano to inform the Rumanians of the following: "If Russia attacks Rumania and Rumania resists sword in hand, Hungary will adopt an attitude of benevolent neutrality towards Rumania. On the other hand, Hungary would immediately intervene should one of the three following cases arise: (1) the massacre of the minorities; (2) Bolshevik revolution in Rumania; (3) Cession by Rumania of national territory to Russia and Bulgaria without fighting." Csáky added that even in that case "nothing will be done without previous consultation and agreement with Italy." *Ciano's Diplomatic Papers*, ed. Malcom Muggeridge (London: Odham Press, 1948), p. 331.

6. *The Ciano Diaries*, March 25, 1940.

7. Ibid., March 28, 1940.

8. Ibid., April 8, 1940.

9. Ibid., April 9, 1940.

10. For details see Hóry András, *Még Egy Barázdát Sem*, published by the author. (Vienna, 1967). Hóry was the Hungarian negotiator in Turnu-Severin.

11. Before the occupation of Bessarabia and northern Bucovina, Molotov assured the German government that the Soviet Union "simply wished to pursue its own interests and had no intention of encouraging other states [Hungary, Bulgaria] to make demands on Rumania." *Nazi-Soviet Relations 1939-1941*, Raymond James Sontag and James Stuart Beddie (Washington: U.S. Department of State, 1948), p. 160.

12. According to Hungarian documents, Hitler made statements in this regard to Sztójay on February 1, 1941, and to Bárdossy on March 21, 1941. Hitler told Bárdossy that the Rumanians asked for a quick German interven-

tion because of the preparations of the Red Army to cross the Danube. Cf. Petru Groza, *In Umbra Celulei* (Bucuresti: Editura Cartea Rusa, 1945), p. 276.

13. *The Ciano Diaries*, August 28, 1940.

14. Ibid., August 29, 1940.

15. An area of 43,492 square kilometers with a population of 2,600,000 was reattached to Hungary. According to the Hungarian censuses of 1910 and 1941, the number of Hungarians exceeded the Rumanians in this territory, while the Rumanian census of 1930 indicated a slight Rumanian majority. Following the delivery of the award, Csáky and Ribbentrop signed a treaty assuring special rights to the German minority in Hungary. With the conclusion of this treaty the problem of the German citizens of Hungary ceased to be exclusively within the domestic juridiction of the Hungarian state. For the text of the treaty, see, Matthias Annabring, "Das ungarländische Deutschtum," *Südost-Stimmen* 2 (March 1952), 13-14. For detailed discussion and bibliography, see B. Vágó, "Le Second Diktat de Vienne: Les Preliminaires," *East European Quarterly* no. 4 (1969): 415-37 and "Le Second Diktat de Vienne: Le Partage de la Transylvania," Ibid., 5, no. 1 (1971): 47-73.

16. Molotov considered the Italo-German guarantee to Rumania, with respect to her national territory, as a justification for the supposition that this action was directed against the USSR. For the pertinent exchange of notes, see Sontag and Beddie, *Nazi-Soviet Relations 1939-1941*, pp. 178-94.

17. It is a curious historical parallel that Article 22 of the peace treaty of February 10, 1947, authorized the Soviet Union "to keep on Hungarian territory such armed forces as it may need for the maintenance of the lines of communication of the Soviet Army with the Soviet zone of occupation in Austria." However, the difference was that the German military personal was restricted to a few railroad stations, while the peace treaty permitted keeping an unlimited number of Soviet troops in Hungary.

18. The government was violently attacked by the opposition in both houses of parliament because of this step. Count István Bethlen and Tibor Eckhart, leader of the Smallholder party, strongly criticized this move. The Hungarian minister to Washington, John Pelényi, resigned in protest.

19. Cf. Ullein-Reviczky, *Guerre Allemande Paix Russe: le Drame Hongrois*, pp. 71-73.

20. According to a German diplomat, Erich Kordt, the German General Staff arranged the bombing. See *Wahn und Wirklichkeit* (Stuttgart, 1948), p. 308. At the Nuremberg trials General István Ujszászy, that time in Russian custody, stated that he was convinced "that the bombarding was carried out by German planes with Russian markings." The Kassa incident is still a much debated question. See for the intricacies involved: N.f. Dreisziger, "New Twist to an Old Riddle: The Bombing of Kassa (Košice), June 26, 1941," *Journal of Modern History* 44 (1972): 232-42; idem, "Contradictory Evidence Concerning Hungary's Declaration of War on the USSR in June

1941," *Canadian Slavonic Papers* 19, no. 4 (December 1977): 81-88. Regarding the political influence of military leaders in these crucial years, see Dreisziger, "The Hungarian General Staff and Diplomacy, 1939-1941," *Canadian-American Review of Hungarian Studies* 7, no. 1 (Spring 1980): 5-26.

21. *Trial of the Major War Criminals*, vol. 7, p. 335.

22. The British note was handed to Bárdossy on November 29, 1941, by the American minister to Hungary. It read as follows: "The Hungarian Government has for many months been pursuing aggressive military operations on the territory of the Union of Soviet Socialist Republics, ally of Great Britain, in closest collaboration with Germany, thus participating in the general European war and making substantial contribution to the German war effort. In these circumstances His Majesty's Government in the United Kingdom finds it necessary to inform the Hungarian Government that unless by December 5 the Hungarian Government has ceased military operations and has withdrawn from all active participation in hostilities, His Majesty's Government will have no choice but to declare the existance of a state of war between the two countries."

23. The British ultimatum was delivered to Finland, Hungary, and Rumania as a result of Stalin's repeated and pressing appeal. Prime Minister Churchill tried in vain to convince Stalin that the declaration of war against these countries would not be beneficial to the Allied cause. Churchill explained to Stalin in his telegram of November 4, 1941, that these countries "have been overpowered by Hitler and used as a cat's-paw, but if fortune turns against that ruffian they might easily come back to our side. A British declaration of war would only freeze them all and make it look as if Hitler were the head of a grand European alliance solid against us." Churchill, *The Grand Alliance*, p. 528. Bárdossy's record of his conversation will Pell and Travers is in the files of the Hungarian Foreign Ministry.

24. Bárdossy's instructions sent to the Hungarian ministers in Berlin and Rome on December 11 and 12, show how he tried to avoid involvement in war with the United States. For the text of the instructions see, *Diplomacy In a Whirlpool*, pp. 234-36.

25. *The Memoirs of Cordell Hull* (New York: Macmillan, 1948), vol. 2, pp. 1114, 1175-76. Cf. *Documents on American Foreign Relations*, vol. 4 (1942), pp. 123-24. Senator Vandenberg suggested that the declaration of war on Hitler's Danubian satellites was done in response to Russian demand. See also *The Private Papers of Senator Vandenberg*, Arthur H. Vandenberg, Jr. (Boston: Houghton Mifflin, 1952), pp. 31-33.

26. Filippo Anfuso, *Du Palais de Venise au Lac de Garde* (Paris, 1949), p. 221.

27. Hungary's military participation on the war against the Soviet Union was limited. The number of combatant Hungarian divisions in Russia was five in 1941, ten in 1942, none in 1943, and fourteen in 1944. During the same period, the number of divisions for occupation duties varied between

two and six divisions. The number of combatant Rumanian divisions was twelve in 1941, thirty-one in 1942, twenty-five in 1943 and 1944. There were only three Rumanian divisions for occupation duties in 1942 and 1943. For details see *La Hongrie et la Conférence de Paris*, vol 1, pp. 86-90. It should be noted that during this period, the population of both Hungary and Rumania was around fourteen million.

28. About my assignment, see Csatári Dániel, *Forgószélben: Magyar-román viszony 1940-1945* (Budapest: Akadémiai Kiadó, 1968), p. 123.

29. Memorandum of the conversation between the Fuehrer and the Duce, with Ribbentrop and Ciano also present, at Klessheim near Salzburg, April 29, 1942. *Bulletin* 15 (1946): 59.

30. For the activities and report of this commission, see Csatári, *Forgószélben*, pp. 124-32. This book with some abbreviations was published in French under the title: *Dans la Tourmante: Les relations Hungaro-Roumaines de 1940 à 1945* (Budapest: Akadémiai Kiadó, 1974). For the Italo-German Commission see pp. 111-18.

31. The Hungarian government inquired and found out that the German and Italian governments did not know of this Rumanian allegation.

32. For details see Csatári, *Forgószélben*, pp. 229-51 and *Dans la Tourmante*, pp. 209-24. Cf. Elemér Illyés, *Erdély Változása* (Change in Transylvania) (München: Auróra Könyvek, 1976).

33. He indicated his feelings frankly to the Rumanian foreign minister, Gafencu, on April 19, 1939. "They say that I want to restore the grandeur of Hungary. Why should I be so ill advised? A greater Hungary might be embarrassing for the Reich. Besides, the Hungarians have always shown us utter ingratitude. They have no regard or sympathy for the German minorities. As for me, I am only interested in my Germans. I said so frankly to Count Csaky. . . And I have said so without equivocation to the Regent Horthy and to Imredy: the German minorities in Rumania and Yugoslavia do not want to return to Hungary; they are better treated in their new fatherland. And what the German minorities do not want, the Reich does not want either."Grigore Gafencu, *Last Days of Europe, A Diplomatic Journey in 1939* (New Haven: Yale University Press, 1948), pp. 68-69.

34. Paul Schmidt, *Hitler's Interpreter* (New York: Macmillan, 1951), pp. 205-6.

35. Ibid., p. 244. As to Hitler's encouragements given to Antonescu concerning the ultimate fate of Transylvania, see *Trial of the Major War Criminals*, vol. 7, p. 322. Hitler and his underlings juggled with promises and threats to keep Hungary and Rumania in line. This was especially the case when political leaders of these countries visited Hitler. Ibid., pp. 320-23.

36. *The Ciano Diaries*, August 25-27, 29, 1942. Mussolini considered the Hungarian plan as part of an anti-German conspiracy which would have caused a crisis in Italo-German relations. For the details of the affair, see Anfuso, *Du Palais de Venise*, pp. 230-31.

37. *The Ciano Diaries*, November 5, 1942.

38. Kállay, *Hungarian Premier*, p. 147.

39. For the entire exchange of views, see ibid., pp. 145-61.

40. Bova Scoppa, *Colloqui con Due Dittatori* (Roma: Ruffolo Editore, 1949).

41. Ibid., pp. 102-8.

42. Ibid., p. 109.

43. Ibid., pp. 112-14.

44. See for details, Gustav Hennyey, *Ungarns Schicksal zwischen Ost und West* (Mainz: Von Hase und Koehler Verlag, 1975), pp. 59-61.

45. These excerpts are parts of the notes Foreign Minister Gyöngyösi took at the Moscow negotiations. Box 100, R.G. 43, National Archives

46. Stalin was not secretive about his aims during the war. When the British foreign secretary, Anthony Eden, visited him in December 1941, Stalin explained his ideas concerning the postwar territorial and political settlement. He stated that "Rumania should give special facilities for bases, etc. to the Soviet Union, receiving compensation from territory now occupied by Hungary." Churchill, *The Grand Alliance*, p. 629.

47. *La Hongrie et la Conférence de Paris*, vol. 1, pp. 108-11.

7. Conflict With Czechoslovakia

1. In 1938, Hungary was the only neighbor of Czechoslovakia which attempted to regain the territories inhabited overwhelmingly by Hungarians not by threat of force, but by direct negotiations as it was suggested by one of the annexes to the Munich Protocol of September 29, 1938. After protracted negotiations and exchange of notes, the Hungarian government in a note of October 24, suggested a plebiscite in the disputed areas or international arbitration. The government of Prague chose the arbitration of the Axis, and on November 2, 1938, Ciano and Ribbentrop arbitrated the Hungarian claims in Vienna. The award based mainly on ethnographic factors, restored to Hungary 12,103 square kilometers (4,605 sq. miles) and over one million population. The overwhelming majority of the people living in the territories reattached to Hungary were Magyars. For the Hungaro-Czechoslovak exchange of notes and other connected documents see, *La Documentation Internationale Politique, Juridique et Economic* (Paris, 1939). Cf. Edward Cháopszár, *Decision in Vienna* (Astor, Florida: Danubian Press, Inc., 1978); Charles Wojatsek, *From Trianon to the First Vienna Arbitral Award* (Montreal: Institute of Comparative Civilizations, 1981).

2. Vladimir Clementis, "The Czechoslovak-Magyar Relationship, *The Central European Observer* (1943): 69.

3. "I fought desperately against everything. I had an internal front, the so-called Sudeten-German front, then the Slovak front, and the French and English front and besides there was Hitler." Dr. Eduard Beneš, *Sest Let*

Exilŭ A Drŭhe Světove Války (Praha: Orbis, 1946), p. 16. In his enumeration President Beneš did not mention the Hungarians, who probably did not cause him any uneasiness. For detailed material see the two memoranda submitted by the Hungarian delegation to the Conference of Paris on September 19, 1946: 1. "Czechoslovak declarations concerning the loyal and democratic attitude of the Hungarians in Slovakia" and 2. "The Slovaks and the disintegration of the Czechoslovak Republic." *Hungary and the Conference of Paris*, vol. 4, pp. 48-59, 79-81.

4. Sir John Wheeler-Bennett, *Munich: Prologue to Tragedy* (London: Macmillan, 1948). For subsequent developments in Czechoslovakia see George F. Kennan, *From Prague After Munich — Diplomatic Papers 1938-1940* (Princeton, N.J.: Princeton University Press, 1968); Wenzel Jaksch, *Europe's Road to Potsdam* (New York: Praeger, 1963), pp. 328-48.

5. Jaksch, *Europe's Road to Potsdam*, pp. 351-458.

6. *FRUS* 1944, 3: 967.

7. Serie Y, Carton 45, Dossier 6, Archives du ministère des Affaires étrangères (hereafter MAE).

8. Mastny, *Russia's Road to the Cold War*, p. 227. Beneš stated in early 1944: "For twenty years we have settled the Ruthenian question temporarily, but the final settlement can only be union with the Soviets." Compton Mackenzie, *Dr. Beneš* (London: George G. Harrap, 1946), p. 290.

9. Mastny, "The Beneš-Stalin-Molotov Conversations in December 1943: New Documents, pp. 367-402.

10. *Příspěvky k historické demográfii Slovenska* (Praha, 1928), pp. 306, 311.

11. See for the pertinent facts and bibliographical references, the memorandum submitted to the Conference of Paris by the Hungarian delegation on September 14, 1946, under the title "The Hungarian Population of South Slovakia." *Hungary and the Conference of Paris*, vol. 4, pp. 128-75.

12. For the list of discriminatory laws and decrees see, *Hungary and the Conference of Paris*, vol. 2, pp. 150-52; and vol. 4 pp. 176-86.

13. Ibid., vol. 2, pp. 1-3

14. Ibid., pp. 10-12.

15. For the list of the protests, see Ibid., pp., pp. 155-63.

16. Ibid., pp. 13-14.

17. Ibid., pp. 15-29.

18. Ibid., pp. 53-54.

19. Ibid., pp. 54-55. The latter part of the British refusal referred to certain Hungarian proposals put forward at the negotiations in Prague in December, 1945 by the Hungarian delegation and communicated to the three powers by the note of December 11, 1945. Ibid., pp. 50-53.

20. Ibid., pp. 4-5.

21. Ibid., p. 5.

22. Ibid., pp. 5-7.

23. *Népszava*, October 25 and 27, 1945.

24. *Hungary and the Conference of Paris*, vol. 2, pp. 30-34.

25. Ibid., pp. 35-38.

26. Ibid., vol. 4, p. 29.

27. *Statistický Zpravodaj*, Official Bulletin of the Czechoslovak Statistical Office, 1945, no. 6, p. 114.

28. "The number of Slovaks in Hungary was uncertain. In the twenties it had been about 150,000, but it had decreased. Fantastic figures were current in Slovakia. The Slovak Communists showed themselves wilder chauvinists than the Slovak nationalists, even more than the Fascists of Tiso. Husak, the communnist chairman of the Board of Commissioners, claimed that there were 400,000 Slovaks in Hungary, and that 400,000 Hungarians could therefore be expelled." Hugh Seton-Watson, *The East European Revolution* (New York, 1951), p. 344. Seton-Watson remarked that he personally heard these fantastic figures from the mouth of Husak, in April 1947. Clementis repeatedly alleged at the Prague negotiations and in September 1946, at the Conference of Paris, that there were 450,000 Slovaks in Hungary. *Hungary and the Conference of Paris*, vol. 4 pp. 28, 62.

29. *Hungary and the Conference of Paris*, vol 2. pp. 42-43.

30. Ibid., pp. 44.-47.

31. Ibid., pp. 48-49.

32. My report of this conversation was deposited in the Hungarian Foreign Ministry (76/Be - 1946).

33. *Hungary and the Conference of Paris*, vol. 2, pp. 50-53.

34. Ibid., pp. 61-64.

35. Before we left for Prague, a Transylvanian politician, Béla Demeter, informed me at the railroad station that Marshal Voroshilov recently told the president of the republic, Zoltán Tildy, that the problem of Transylvania would be solved to our satisfaction if we took a more conciliatory attitude toward Czechoslovakia and, as a first step of a reasonable policy, would conclude the population exchange agreement with Prague.

36. For the text of the Czechoslovak reply and my note of the conversation with Krno see *Hungary and the Conference of Paris*, vol. 2, pp. 65-66.

37. Ibid., pp. 78-79.

38. For the text of the agreement concerning the exchange of populations, with Annex, Protocol, and the letters exchanged, see *Hungary and the Conference of Paris*, vol 2, pp. 69-87. The subsequent narrative in this chapter is based on published documents and other texts included in the *Confidential Gazette* prepared by the political division of the Hungarian Foreign Ministry in 1947-48, for the information of Hungary's diplomatic representatives abroad. Francis Wagner, Hungarian consul in Bratislava until November 1948, gave me valuable information concerning the execution of the population exchange and related happenings.

39. For the text of the debates, see *Nemzetgyülési Értesítő*, (Official Gazette of the National Assembly) sessions 31, 32, 33, pp. 7-19, 37-115.

40. *Hungary and the Conference of Paris*, vol.2, pp. 88-90.

41. Ibid., pp. 91
42. Ibid., pp. 131-138.
43. Ibid.., p. 137.
44. Ibid., p. 119.
45. For the full text of the two notes, see ibid., pp. 92-130.
46. Ibid., vol. 4, pp. 41-42.
47. Ibid., p. 67.
48. Ibid., pp. 82-83.
49. The commission was formed according to the provisions of the population exchange agreement and began its sessions in Bratislava on June 3, 1946.
50. See for the full text of the Clementis-Gyöngyösi exchange of letters, *Hungary and the Conference of Paris*, vol. 4, pp. 120-24.
51. *Pravda*, Bratislava, November 1, 1946.
52. *Narodna Obroda*, November 13, 1946.
53. *Pravda*, Bratislava, November 16, 1946.
54. For a detailed description of concrete cases, see *The Deportation of the Hungarians of Slovakia* (Budapest: Hungarian Society for Foreign Affairs, 1947).
55. Prime Minister Zdenek Fierlinger stated on January 30, 1947, that 30,000 Hungarian workers (with their families, 90,000 persons) were removed from Sovakia.
56. The Hungarian representatives complained because of the persistent expulsion and deportations of Hungarians. Moreover, the promised social assistance was not given to Hungarians who have been deprived of their employment or pensions. The confiscation of properties of Hungarian individuals and churches were continued.
57. The text of the agreement was published in the March-April 1947 issue of the *Confidential Gazette* of the Hungarian Foreign Ministry, pp. 18-24.
58. György Lázár, "A népek barátságáért,a reakció és a sovinizmus ellen" (For the friendship of peoples, against reaction and chauvinism), *Tiszatáj* (1981): 24-30.
59. These data were included in a report by the East European Research Institute in Budapest. Cf. Francis S. Wagner, *Hungarians in Czechoslovakia* (New York: Research Institute for Minority Studies, 1959), pp. 11-37; idem, "The Nationality Problem in Czechoslovakia After World War II," *Studies for a New Central Europe*, series 2, no. 2 (1968-69): 73-82.
60. Yuraj Zvara, *A magyar nemzetiségi kérdés megoldása Szlovákiában*. (The Solution of the Hungarian Nationality Question in Slovakia) (Bratislava, 1965), p. 36. See also Kalman Janics, *Czechoslovak Policy and the Hungarian Minority 1945-1948* (New York: Social Science Monographs, distributed by Columbia University Press, 1982.) The author is a Czechoslovak citizen who described the experiences of the Hungarian minority in Slovakia during the era of persecution. This volume was published in Hun-

garian in Munich in 1977, under the title, *A hontalanság évei* (The Homeless Years). The translator, Stephen Borsody, wrote a preface and Gyula Illyés, the Introduction.

61. The number of the actually expelled "war criminals" outnumbered several times this figure.

8. The Framework of Peace

1. Eden, *The Reckoning*, pp. 632-34.

2. W. Averell Harriman, *America and Russia in a Changing World*, (London: George & Unwin, 1971), p. 44.

3. *FRUS* 1943 "Teheran Conference," pp. 566-67.

4. Ferrell, *Off the Record*, p. 53.

5. Harry S. Truman, *Year of Decisions* (Garden City, N.J.: Doubleday, 1955), p. 350.

6. Pierson Dixon, *Double Diploma* (Hutchinson of London, 1968), pp. 175-77.

7. Ibid., p. 176.

8. Ibid.

9. Ibid., p. 177.

10. See for the pertinent exchange of notes, *FRUS* 1945, 2 "Conference of Berlin," pp. 1543-56.

11. Ibid., p. 1553.

12. A British witness, Sir Pierson Dixon, described the emotional debates of the Big Three concerning the interpretation of the Potsdam formula for peace negotiations. Dixon, *Double Diploma*, pp. 183-94. Prime Minister Attlee addressed a long telegram to Stalin on September 23 in which he summarized the Western interpretation of the Berlin Protocol and asked Stalin to authorize the Soviet delegation to adhere to the decision taken on September 11. Francis Williams, *A Prime Minister Remembers* (London: Heinemann, 1961), pp. 151-53.

13. I received this information from a member of the American delegation, Philip E. Mosely. Molotov's question was facetious. He had recognized the Hungarian aspiration for Transylvanian territory when he proposed in 1940 that Hungary cooperate with the Soviet Union against Rumania. He considered the Hungarian claim justified and promised support.

14. Byrnes, *Speaking Frankly*, pp. 104-5.

15. *Bulletin* 13 (1945): 710.

16. For the text of these documents, see *FRUS* 1945, 5: 633-41. Cf. Mark Ethridge and C.E. Black, "Negotiating on the Balkans, 1945-1947," in *Negotiating with the Russians*, ed. Raymond Dennett and Joseph E. Johnson (Boston: World Peace Foundation, 1951), pp. 171-206; Cyril E. Black, "The Start of the Cold War in Bulgaria: A Personal View." *The Review of Politics* 41 (1979): 163-202.

17. Harriman, *Special Envoy*, pp. 511-22; James F. Byrnes, *All In One Lifetime* (New York: Harper & Brothers, 1958), idem, p. 319; *Speaking Frankly*, p. 108. Harriman informed the French ambassdor to the USSR General Georges Catroux of his negotiations with Stalin and Molotov, and Catroux had sent reports to Paris although he did not receive satisfactory explanations why France was left out from the forthcoming meeting of foreign ministers. MAE, Serie Y, Carton 45, Dossier 7, 1945, Conférence de Moscou.

18. Harriman, Ibid., p. 523. Byrnes, *Speaking Frankly*, p. 109; idem, *All in One Lifetime*, pp. 326-27.

19. See Bonnet's report of December 8 to Paris. MAE Serie Y, Carton 45, Dossier 7, 1945, Conférence de Moscou.

20. For the United States record of the Moscow Conference, see *FRUS* 1945, 2: 560-826. Byrnes reported on the Moscow meeting of foreign ministers in a radio address on December 30, 1945, see *Bulletin* 13 (1945): 1033-36, 1047.

21. Byrnes, *Speaking Frankly*, p. 255. For President Truman's criticism concerning Byrnes' actions and behavior in Moscow, see Truman, *Year of Decisions*, pp. 546-53.

22. Sumner Welles, *Where Are We Heading?* (New York: Harper & Brothers, 1946), pp. 60-72

23. See Chauvel's memorandum of the conversation, December 31, 1945. MAE Serie Y, Carton 45, Dossier 7.

24. There is no evidence that Molotov neglected Bevin on social occasions. Cf. Dixon, *Double Diploma*, pp. 199-206.

25. Dejean's telegram of January 3, 1945. MAE Serie Y, Carton 45, Dossier 7. After a victorious battle in June 1807, Napoleon met Alexander I and Frederick William III on a raft in the Niemen River and concluded with Russia and Prussia the treaties of Tilsit of short duration.

26. Ibid.

27. See Ibid., Bonnet's report of December 31, 1945.

28. For the full text see the press release issued simultaneously in London, Paris, and Washington on January 15,1946. *Bulletin*, January 27, 1946: 112. For Ambassador Caffery's reports see *FRUS* 1946, 2 : 1-6

29. Truman, *Year of Decisions*, pp. 547-52. The letter was first published in 1952 in William Hillman's *Mr. President*, and Byrnes denied immediately that Truman ever had read it to him; in his memoirs, *All in One Lifetime*, he characterized their meeting aboard the *Williamsburg* as "cordial" (p. 343) and quoted Truman's press conference of January 8, 1946, when he "repeated the commendation of my course at Moscow which he wholeheartedly gave me on the *Williamsburg* after my return." (p. 347) About the letter controversy see, Ibid., pp. 400-403. Cf. Ferrell, *Off the Record*, pp. 78-80. George Curry, *James Francis Byrnes*, vol. 14 in *The American Secretaries of State and Their Diplomacy* (New York: Cooper Square Publishers, 1965), pp. 183-90, 313-14.

30. For the conference of Deputies see John C. Campbell, *The United States in World Affairs, 1945-1947* (New York: Harper & Brothers, 1947), pp. 111-18. Cf. *FRUS* 1946, 2 : 10-87.

31. Bohlen, *Witness to History*, p. 255.

32. *FRUS*, 1946, 2 "Council of Foreign Ministers," pp. 124-26.

33. Ibid., pp. 146-48

34. *FRUS* 1946, 2: 277-78, 309.

35. For the second session of the Council of Foreign Ministers see *FRUS* 1946, 2: 88-940. Cf. Byrnes, *Speaking Frankly*, pp. 124-37; idem, *All in One Lifetime*, pp. 357-80; *The Private Papers of Senator Vandenberg* ed. Arthur H. Vandenberg, Jr. (Boston: Houghton Mifflin, 1952), pp. 262-303; *My Name is Tom Connally*, Senator Tom Connally as told to Alfred Steinberg (New York: Thomas Y. Crowell, 1954), pp. 297-303; Curry, *James Francis Byrnes*, pp. 210-83; Campbell, *United States in World Affairs*, pp. 118-45.

36. *FRUS* 1946, 2: 852-54. Article VII provided that "The Conference may decide to amend or suspend the provisions of the rules of procedure after their adopting."

37. Byrnes, *Speaking Frankly*, pp. 187-94; idem, *All in One Lifetime*, pp. 367-70.

38. *FRUS* 1946, 4: 875, footnote 71. Byrnes, *Speaking Frankly*, pp. 239-48; idem, *All in One Lifetime*, pp. 371-76. Truman, *Year of Decisions*, pp. 355-60.

39. Philip F. Mosely, "Peace-Making, 1946," *International Organization* 1 (1946): 31.

40. *FRUS* 1946, 3: 645-48.

41. Harold Nicolson, "Peacemaking at Paris: Success, Failure or Farce?" *Foreign Affairs* 25 (1946-1947): 190. He mentioned in the article that an unofficial poll was taken among the journalists of 27 countries who had followed the proceedings. They were asked whether they regarded the conference as having been (a) a success; (b) a failure; (c) a farce? "Of these journalists, 31 replied that it had been a success, 56 that it had been a failure, and 33 that it had been a farce." Ibid.

42. Bohlen, *Witness to History*, pp. 255-56. Cf. Byrnes, *Speaking Frankly*, pp. 152-54; idem, *All in One Lifetime*, pp. 382-83.

43. For the record of the New York session see, *FRUS* 1946, 2: 965-1563.

44. Milovan Djilas, *Conversations with Stalin* (New York: Harcourt, Brace & World, 1962), p. 114.

45. Secretary Brynes defended vigorously the Potsdam arrangement for peacemaking in *Speaking Frankly*, p. 159.

46. Article 22 of the Hungarian treaty provided: "Upon the coming into force of the present Treaty, all Allied forces shall, within a period of 90 days, be withdrawn from Hungary, subject to the right of the Soviet Union to keep on Hungarian territory such armed forces as it may need for the maintenance of the lines of communication of the Soviet Army with the

Soviet zone of occupation in Austria." (The same text is Article 22 in the Rumanian Peace Treaty.)

47. Philip E. Mosely, "Hopes and Failures: American Policy Toward East Central Europe: 1941-1947" in *The Fate of East Central Europe*, ed. Stephen D. Kertesz (Notre Dame, Ind.: University of Notre Dame Press, 1956), p. 74.

9. The Paris Conference: Part One

1. *La Hongrie et la Conférence de Paris*, vol. 1, pp. 178-81.
2. *FRUS* 1946, 3: 84.
3. *Memoirs of Michael Karolyi* (New York: E. P. Dutton, 1957), p. 333. During the war Karolyi supported the idea of a federal Europe in which the Danubian federation would have formed a part. Ibid., p. 303.
4. Iván Boldizsár published his notes and comments on the Paris Conference in a Hungarian periodical, *Kortárs*, March and April, 1982.
5. For complexity of Bulgarian developments in 1944-1947, see Cyril E. Black, "The View from Bulgaria," in *Witnesses to the Origins of the Cold War*, ed. Thomas T. Hammond (Seattle: University of Washington Press, 1982), pp. 60-97.
6. Max Jakobson, *Finnish Neutrality* (New York: Praeger, 1969), pp. 22-23.
7. *FRUS* 1946, 3: 239.
8. Ibid., p. 242.
9. *Refuge en Hongrie 1941-1945* (Paris: 1946), published by the escaped French war prisoners.
10. For the Draft Peace Treaty with Hungary, prepared by the Council of Foreign Ministers, see *FRUS* 1946, 4: 102-9; for Observations on the Draft Peace Treaty with Hungary by the Hungarian Government, ibid., pp. 249-82; for the Report of the Political and Territorial Commission for Hungary on the Draft Peace Treaty with Hungary, ibid., pp. 526-68; for the Record of Recommendations by the Conference on the Draft Peace Treaty with Hungary, ibid., pp. 937-49.
11. *FRUS* 1946, 3: 258.
12. Foreign Minister Masaryk complained about this incident. The comments appearing in *Newsweek* (August 26, 1946, p. 36) on Gyöngyösi's speech reflected the atmosphere in Paris:

The Hungarian spokesman, Foreign Minister János Gyöngyössy, turned out to be a mild but tough man of peasant stock with a lined face and silver hair, who stayed up nearly all night to write his speech and then delivered it clearly in French. When he finished the Luxembourg corridors echoed with: "What cheek . . . what a nerve . . . quel toupet." For Gyöngyössy had chosen two of Russia's friends as targets. He asked for an investigation of the status of Hungarian minorities in Rumania and Czechoslovakia. The next day Jan Masaryk asked: "Who won this war — the United Nations or Hungary?"

The Russians gave the Hungarians no support in this question, but Vyshinsky seized the occasion to insist that Russia "wished to aid in the restoration of Hungarian economy. . . . The real sources of economic disorder in Hungary . . . reside equally in the fact that a great quantity of Hungarian wealth was taken away . . . and that most of this wealth is located at the present time in the American zone." He omitted to mention that the Hungarian gold reserve had just been returned from Germany by the Americans.

13. *La Hongrie et la Conférence de Paris*, vol. 1, pp. 79-90.

14. *FRUS* 1945, 4: 823-24.

15. For questions involved in the transfer of archival materials, see the notes of September 24 and October 3, 1946, addressed to Siniša Stanković, chairman of the Hungarian Commission. Article 11 of the peace treaty with Hungary was a compromise solution.

16. John C. Campbell, "The European Territorial Settlement," *Foreign Affairs* 26 (1947-48): 214.

17. *La Hongrie et la Conférence de Paris*, vol. 1, pp. 182-83.

18. *La Hongrie et La Conférence de Paris*, vol. 1, pp. 135-71.

19. Notter File Box 144, RG 59, National Archives.

20. John C. Campbell, "Diplomacy and Great Power Politics," published in *Diplomacy and Values: The Life and Works of Stephen Kertesz in Europe and America*, ed. Kenneth Thompson (Lanham, MD: University Press of America, 1983), pp. 51-52.

21. Murphy, *Diplomat Among Warriors*, p. 207.

22. Telegram to the War Department on September 20, 1946, by Colonel Charles H. Bonesteel, Adviser, United States Delegation. *FRUS* 1946, 4: 874-75.

23. Regarding the visit see, *Bulletin* (June 23, 1946): 1091, and the prime minister's account, Nagy, *Struggle Behind the Iron Curtain*, pp. 225-34.

24. For the Summary of the Memorandum and the conversations in the State Deparment, See *FRUS* 1946, 3: 306-17.

25. Nagy, *Struggle Behind the Iron Curtain*, pp. 234-35.

26. Ibid., p. 235.

27. The source of the conversation with Foreign Secretary Bevin is a record prepared by János Erős, counselor to the Hungarian legation in Paris

28. Nagy, *Struggle Behind the Iron Curtain*, pp. 236-37.

29. See *FRUS* 1946, 6: 318-41.

30. *FRUS* 1946, 3: 370.

31. Ibid., pp. 371-72.

32. Ambassador Caffery's report of September 7 to the Acting Secretary of State *FRUS* 1946, 6: 332-33.

33. Nagy, *Struggle Behind the Iron Curtain*, pp. 272-73.

10. The Paris Conference: Part Two

1. *Le Problème Hongrois par rapport á la Roumanie* (Budapest: Hungarian Ministry of Foreign Affairs, 1946). For the grievances of the Hungarian minority in Transylvania, see notes of May 20, 1946, and of July 15, 1946, addressed to the great Powers and sent to all countries participating in the Paris Conference.

2. *FRUS* 1946, 2: 259-60, 309-10.

3. *FRUS* 1946, 2: 441-42.

4. Territorial Problems: Transylvania, Box 99. H-43a, RS 43, April 20, 1944, National Archives.

5. The following delegations supported the Australian motion: Australia, Canada, France, Great Britain, Greece, New Zealand, Union of South Africa, USA. The following delegations voted against it: Byelorussia, Czechoslovakia, Ukraine, USSR. See for details, *FRUS* 1946, 3: 311-12.

6. Ibid., pp. 330-31.

7. Ibid., p. 339.

8. Ibid., pp. 375-76.

9. Ibid., pp. 376-77.

10. Ibid., p. 528.

11. *FRUS* 1946, 4: 851-53. John C. Campbell, *United States in World Affairs*, pp. 67, 115, 117, 123, 142 and "The European Territorial Settlement" *Foreign Affairs* 26 (1947): 211-213. Philip E. Mosely, "Soviet Exploitation of National Conflicts in Eastern Europe, " in *The Soviet Union*, ed. Waldemar Gurian (Notre Dame, Ind.: University of Notre Dame Press, 1951), p. 75.

12. *FRUS* 1946, 3: 761.

13. *FRUS* 1946, 2: 1074-75.

14. *FRUS* 1946, 3: 217.

15. The truth of the matter was that the Hungarian delegation had a short deadline for the drafting of the foreign minister's address and so the usual distribution several hours in advance was impossible.

16. *FRUS* 1946, 3: 222.

17. Ibid., pp. 226-28, 236.

18. Ibid., pp. 381-82.

19. Ibid., pp. 410-12.

20. Ibid., pp. 481-82. For the full text see *Hungary and the Conference of Paris*, vol 4, pp. 35-47. See in the same volume the speeches supporting the Czechoslovak amendment concerning the transfer of 200,000 Hungarians from Czechoslovakia to Hungary, delivered by Masaryk, Clementis, Kiselev, and Vyshinsky.

21. *FRUS* 1946, 3: 498-500.

22. Ibid., pp. 525-27.

23. According to census figures of 1941 the number of German vernacular in Hungary amounted to 477,057, while those of German nationality to 303,419.

24. The source of this information was Philip E. Mosely who was a member of the American delegation.

25. A press release of the State Department published the decision of the Allied Control Council on December 7, 1945.

26. See for details, Stephen Kertesz, "The Expulsion of the Germans from Hungary; A Study in Postwar Diplomacy," *The Review of Politics* 15 (1953): 179-208.

27. *FRUS* 1946, 3: 122-23. A United States delegation memorandum of August 18, 1946, noted Masaryk's inclination for territorial cession and added that "part of his delegation, particularly Clementis (Foreign Ministry Under Secretary, who is a Slovak) opposes and this group is desirous of carrying out the full deportation of the Hungarian minority without delay." *FRUS* 1946, 4: 836.

28. See for the discussion of the Czechoslovak and Hungarian delegations on September 29, 1946, *Hungary and the Conférence of Paris*, Vol. 4, pp. 89-94.

29. Ibid., pp. 95-100.

30. A report of my conversation with General Pope was deposited in the archives of the Hungarian Peace Delegation (859. Konf. 1946).

31. My report of the conversation was deposited in the archives of the Hungarian Peace Delegation (860. Konf. 1946).

32. The Hungarian Commission made the final decision on the Czechoslovak amendment on October 3, 1946. *FRUS* 1946, 3: 642-45.

33. For Ambassador Steinhardt's full report, see RG 43, Box 96, National Archives. Clementis took it for granted in early 1945 that the expulsion of Hungarians could be done on the basis of an agreement between the USSR and Czechoslovakia.

34. *FRUS* 1946, 4: 275. The Hungarian Observations brought up some important hydraulic and hydrographic questions which required multilateral settlement in the Carpathian Basin.

35. *Szigorúan Bizalmas Értesítő*, kiadja a Magyar Külügyminisztérium politikai osztálya (Budapest, February 1, 1947): 23. (*Strictly Confidential Bulletin* published by the political division of the Hungarian Foreign Minister).

36. Ibid., p. 24.

37. *La Hongrie et la Conférence de Paris*, vol. 1, pp. 21-36.

38. Art. 2, par. 1, Hungarian Treaty. The same provisions are embodied in Art. 2, Bulgarian treaty; Art. 6, Finish treaty; Art. 15, Italian treaty; Art. 3, par. 1, Rumanian treaty. These provisions are due to American initiative and were considered a better alternative to the minority protection system adopted at the peace settlement after the first World War. Cf. Stephen Kertesz, "Human Rights in the Peace Treaties," *Law and Contemporary Problems* 14 (1949): 627-47. In a memorandum addressed to the Council of Foreign Ministers, the Hungarian government pointed out the importance of reviving and strengthening provisions for the international protection of minority rights. Later the Hungarian peace delegation submitted an

elaborate draft treaty for the protection of minority rights, with the system of mixed commissions and tribunals to enforce them under the supervision of the United Nations. Cf. *La Hongrie et La Conférence de Paris*, vol. 1, pp. 135-71.

39. The Australian proposal intended that "a new Part should be included in the Treaty providing for the establishment of a European Court of Human Rights with jurisdiction to hear and determine all disputes concerning the rights of citizenship and enjoyment of human rights and fundamental freedoms provided for in the treaty. The Australian case for this proposal rested on the belief that the general declarations contained in the treaty in support of human rights and fundamental freedoms were not sufficient, standing alone, to guarantee the inalienable rights of the individual and that behind them it was essential that some sufficient sanction and means of enforcement should be established. It was proposed that the Court of Human Rights should have the status parallel to that of the International Court of Justice and that the Court would have the additional obligation of making reports to the Economic and Social Council of the United Nations on its working in relation to the rights within its jurisdiction. It was contemplated that the jurisdiction of the proposed tribunal should be voluntarily accepted by States as an essential means of international supervision of the rights of individuals and as necessary method of U.S. Department of State, *Paris Peace Conference, 1946, Selected Documents* (hereafter, *Selected Documents*), pp. 444-45.

40. *Selected Documents*, p. 608.

41. Cf. Martin Domke, "Settlement-of-Disputes Provisions in Axis Satellite Peace Treaties," *American Journal of International Law* 41 (1947): 911-20.

42. Cf. Yuen-Li liang, "Observance in Bulgaria, Hungary and Rumania of Human Rights and Fundamental Freedoms: Request for an Advisory Opinion on Certain Questions," *American Journal of International Law* 44 (1950): 110-117; Kenneth S. Carlston, "Interpretation of Peace Treaties with Bulgaria, and Rumania, Advisory Opinions of the International Court of Justice," *American Journal of International Law* 44 (1950): 728-37.

43. Byrnes, *Speaking Frankly*, p. 130.

44. *FRUS* 1946, 2: 261-64.

45. Ibid., p. 613.

46. Ibid., p. 629.

47. Ibid., pp. 630-33, 640, 683.

48. *FRUS* 1946, 4: 547-48.

49. *FRUS* 1946, 3: 833-34 Cf. *FRUS* 1946, 4: 923.

50. *FRUS* 1946, 2: 1067-68, 1090, 1312-13, 1334-37, 1339-40, 1427-28, 1436.

51. Ibid., p. 1446.

52. For details see, John C. Campbell, "Diplomacy on the Danube," *Foreign Affairs* (January 1949): 315-27.

11. The Aftermath

1. Balogh Sándor, *A népi demokratikus Magyarország külpolitikája, 1945-1947* (Foreign policy of the people's democracy of Hungary, 1945-1947) (Budapest: Kossuth Könyvkiadó, 1982). This well-researched book has 1166 footnotes and several chapters on peace preparation in Hungary and the Paris Peace Conference, but the author did not use pertinent documents of the Hungarian Foreign Ministry, and the three volumes published by the Foreign Ministry in 1947, *Hungary and the Conference of Paris*. For this reason the narrative is incomplete.

2. Byrnes, *Speaking Frankly*, p. 166.

3. Nagy, *Struggle Behind the Iron Curtain*, pp. 345, 365. Cf. *FRUS* 1947, 4: 294, 298.

4. The chief of the United States representation on the ACC for Hungary, Brigadier General George H. Weems, submitted a report on December 31, 1946, to the War Department on the arrests and conspiracy accusations. *FRUS* 1946, 6: 357-59.

5. *FRUS* 1947, 4: 273-75.

6. Ibid., pp. 277-78.

7. Ibid., pp. 280-81, 285-86.

8. See for details, Nagy, *Struggle Behind the Iron Curtain*, pp. 311-400; *FRUS* 1947, 4: 260-91. Emilio Vasari, *Die ungarische Revolution 1956*, (Stuttgart: Seewald Verlag, 1981). pp. 72-96. Imre Kovács, *Magyarország Megszállása* (The Occupation of Hungary) (Toronto: Vörösváry Publishing Co., 1979), pp. 348-460.

9. Because of such articles and the announcement in Budapest, I received scores of congratulatory telegrams, and several serious publications included my name as foreign minister of Hungary in 1947. *The Americana Annual* 1948 relates these events with the remark that "on May 31 Foreign Minister János Gyöngyösi was replaced by István Kertész" (p. 319). It is interesting that a book published in Budapest in 1970, mentioned my name as foreign minister from May 31 till September 4, 1947. See Isván Kende, *Forró Béke – Hideg Háboru, A Diplomaciai Kapcsolatok története* (Hot Peace – Cold War, A History of Diplomatic Relations) 1945-1956, p. 324. Such errors are understandable, but I was surprised to find my name listed as foreign minister of Hungary in *Regenten und Regierungen der Welt* (Sovereigns and Governments of the World), famous for accuracy, and edited originally by Minister-Ploetz (Würzburg: A.G. Ploetz Verlag, 1964). I asked for correction of this error, and the editor promised to do so in the next edition.

10. *Public Papers of the Presidents of the United States: Harry S. Truman, 1947* (Washington: U.S. Government Printing Office, 1963), pp. 262-266.

11. *FRUS* 1947, 4: 312. Cf. ibid., pp. 314-15.

12. I did not know at that time that the State Department and the

British Foreign Office considered taking the Hungarian case to the United Nations but eventually rejected this course of action. Ibid., pp. 311, 313-14, 332, 349.

13. *New York Times*, July 8, 1947.

14. Ibid.

15. Ibid., July 9, 1947.

16. See for an explanation of the events, *New York Times*, July 11, 1947; Ivo Duchacek, "The February Coup in Czecho-slovakia," *World Politics* 2 (1950): 516-17; and Hubert Ripka, *Le Coup de Prague* (Paris, 1949), pp. 48-65.

Epilogue

1. József Cardinal Mindszenty, *Memoirs* (New York: Macmillan, 1974).

2. The name of the party was changed after the revolution of 1956 to Hungarian Socialist Workers Party. This chapter will continue to call it Communist party, since this corresponds more to reality.

3. Imre Nagy, *On Communism* (New York, 1952), p. 252.

4. United Nations, General Assembly, *Official Records, Second Emergency Special Session, 4-10 November 1956, Plenary Meeting and Annex* (Doc. A/3251), Annex, p. 1.

5. Free Europe Committee, *The Revolt in Hungary: A Documentary Chronology of Events* (New York, 1956), p. 82.

6. János Péter, "Hungary and Europe," *The New Hungarian Quarterly* 7 (1967); Tibor Pethő, "Modern Forms of Cooperation in the Danube Valley," *Hungarian Quarterly* 8 (1967): 10-16; Charles András, "The Slow Drift to Danubian Cooperation," *East Europe* 17 (December 1968): 19-25.

7. J.-B. Duroselle, *tout Empire périra* (Paris: Publication de la Sorbonne, 1981).

Notes on Documents

Documents pertaining to the topics discussed in this volume will be included in the forthcoming book by Stephen D. Kertesz, *The Last European Peace Conference—Paris 1946: Values in Conflict*, co-published by the White Burkett Miller Center of Public Affairs at the University of Virginia and the University Press of America (Lanham, Maryland) in the Exxon Education Foundation series.

The notes in Transylvanian affairs addressed by the Hungarian government to the victorious Great Powers, and subsequently to the Council of Foreign Ministers and the Paris Conference; and envoy Paul Auer's address delivered in the joint session of the Hungarian and Rumanian Commissions at the Paris Conference on August 31, 1946, were published in a book, *Transylvania*, edited by John F. Cadzow, Andrew Ludanyi, and Louis J. Elteto, Kent University Press, 1984.

Index

Budapest 1945